D1108482

THE REPORTER'S TRADE

JOSEPH *and* STEWART

A L S O P

THE

REPORTER'S

TRADE

REYNAL & COMPANY, NEW YORK

Library of Congress catalog card number: 58-12943

Printed in the U.S.A.

Contents

Foreword

There is one item of information which the reader perhaps needs before beginning this book. During our years of work together, all sorts of things—generally remarkably silly things—were said about our political affiliations. Since the question is now to be raised again, it had better be answered at once.

We are Republicans by inheritance and registration, and we are conservatives by political conviction. When we say that we are conservatives, we mean, for instance, that we both have a strong distaste for governess-government, that we think economic freedom is a necessary ingredient of political freedom, and that we particularly fear extremists of all kinds, whose rule-or-ruin policies are always destructive. But above all we mean that we believe in conserving the basic values of our free society, at all costs.

During most of our working lives, the chief threat to the basic values of the free societies has been, not from within, but from without. The world struggle between the free and the unfree has been the central drama. Hence we have judged the successive American administrations—the necessary leaders of the cause of freedom—primarily by their foreign and defense policies. For a government which is ideally conservative at home is still not a conservative government in any serious sense of the word, if it fails to make the efforts and take the risks to defend our basic values against attack from abroad.

I

Some Trade Secrets

W E HAD AN UNCLE, a most agreeable man, who drank rather more than was good for him. This book has to start with our uncle because it is a book about the reporter's trade; and if you get right down to it, our uncle was the real reason why both of us became reporters. He haunted our youths. As each of us went off to college, where the uncle had chosen the primrose path, all our vast tribe would fix its powerful collective eye upon the new-fledged freshman, to see whether he too would choose the primrose path. In each case, the same sad pleasure-loving signs that had been observed thirty years before, were once again observed with apprehensive horror. In each case, the tribe concluded that it probably had another alcoholic on its hands.

This was the tribal consensus when the elder of these reporters was finishing Harvard college and peacefully looking forward to going to the law school, with a tranquil, well-upholstered career in a New York law office to follow. At this point the elders of the tribe convened their council. They decided that another three years in the notoriously bibulous Harvard neighborhood would be "too dangerous for Joe."

1

They further decided that his incapacity to add a simple column of figures unfitted him for business. They noted with relief that he could at least read and write. They also noted that Mr. and Mrs. Ogden Reid, the publishers of the "New York Herald Tribune," were very old tribal friends. The Reids were approached, and were responsive. Another tribal friend, Ambassador Henry Cabot Lodge, who had then just finished a stint as a "Tribune" reporter, put in a good word with the "Tribune's" managing editor, wise Grafton Wilcox.

The unknowing subject of these negotiations finally learned about his future life's work in a letter from his grandmother, who announced that it was "all arranged," and added the happy forecast that "it would all be for the best." A little later, Grafton Wilcox and the "Tribune's" great city editor, Stanley Walker, were confronted with a very fat, very rumpled, very nervous youth with a high, peculiar Harvard accent. The spectacle so appalled them that they staged a brief rebellion. They would not, they said, they really could not hire this Alsop. But the Reids were adamant, and on July 5, 1932, the "Tribune" acquired a new city-room reporter at the wage of $18 a week.

As for the younger member of our partnership, he was recruited by the senior when the war was over and both of us were just getting out of uniform. His preparation was considerably better than his brother's. He had already written more than a college essay; he was not fat; his accent was not peculiar; and he had already used a typewriter. But he had never entered a newspaper office in all his working life. A high-minded high school senior subsequently wrote him, to ask "what was the best way to become a newspaper columnist, since I have a lot of thoughts I'd like to give the world." He probably disconcerted the high-minded senior a little by replying that "the best way to become a columnist is to have a brother who is one already."

Such were the odd beginnings of careers which both of us have enjoyed vastly and worked at, as we like to think, very hard indeed. They were perhaps a little discreditable—after all, the fear of alcoholism gave the push that got the first Alsop into the newspaper business; and family friendship in a most literal sense gave the pull. Certainly no beginnings could have been more outrageously contrary to the scientific principles of modern personnel-placement.

In one way, it must be added, these beginnings of ours are not wholly relevant to the purpose of our book. For this is first of all a retrospect of the twelve years in which we worked together as partners.

In the first dozen pieces we wrote together—in the first three weeks of 1946—there are two about the Azerbaijan crisis, which drew the lines of the cold war. And there is also a column suggesting that "no one has yet grasped the fullness of the change in world power relationships wrought by the scientists of World War II." The long, grim struggle of the cold war; the insidious but enormous transformation of all our world by the new weapons remorselessly produced by the new technology—these two themes that we stated at the outset have continuously dominated the history of the last twelve years. And these same two themes have also dominated our own writing, although we have always tried to cover the national-international waterfront and our own domestic politics as well.

When circumstances dissolved our partnership, we glanced back over the work we had done together. It seemed to us that a selection of our pieces, unaltered and untrimmed so that they would retain the contemporary flavor, might make a sort of "Only Yesterday." It seemed to us, too, that it was worth taking a backward glance at the twelve most remarkable, most testing years America has ever lived through, excepting only the years of Civil War. So this book is a retrospect in the most obvious sense. It shows, by our own contemporary evidence, how much has changed and how much has remained the same in this decisive period of the history of our country and the world.

But we have another purpose too. With due humility, we want to try to set down what we have learned from our own experience as reasonably hard-working reporters. In particular we want to try to set down what we have learned about our own line of work, its character, its oddities, its high moments, its limitations and above all its public function. There are several reasons why it is useful to begin this other, more specialized retrospect with the stories of our own singular debuts as newspapermen.

It is useful above all, because it is necessary to emphasize at the outset that newspaper reporting is not a profession, despite the complacent contrary belief of a good many reporters who have achieved the upper-brackets. You may go to journalism school before you become a reporter. You may save valuable time there, learning things in school that you would otherwise have to learn on the job. But you can still achieve a fair measure of success as a reporter without any of the long, specialized prior training that is the mark of a professional man. So the fact has got to be faced: newspaper reporting is a craft or trade, like undertaking, which it sometimes resembles.

It is a trade, of course, that has its own well-defined requirements. All reporters need sturdy constitutions, good feet, and some feeling for the English language. For men in our branch of the trade, which is political reporting, a knowledge of history and an interest in political processes are also highly desirable. These traits help political reporters as interest in sports helps sports reporters. You must never be bored by the subjects you are trying to learn about and write about. Otherwise you will learn very little and what you write will surely bore your readers into fits.

This, then (plus a job in Washington), is the limited equipment that an aspiring young man or woman really needs to embark on a reportorial career in Washington. It is also a good idea for the aspirant to realize, at the very outset, that the common notions about the life and work of a Washington correspondent are very nearly as silly as the common notions about newspaper life in general that have been engendered by "The Front Page" and kindred dramas.

A Washington correspondent does not get his news from a series of delightfully convenient pipelines. We have published our fair share of major exclusive news, but we have never had a pipeline. We both wish we could have had one; it would have made our work a lot easier; but pipelines to really major news simply do not exist, in our experience. Again, you do not get your news from leaks at cocktail parties, where Washington's highest officials, gorged with canapés and loose-tongued from fine wines and costly liquors, spill out all they know to eager audiences. Cocktail parties are a melancholy and familiar feature of life in Washington, undoubtedly. But they are principally attended by Washington's bizarre sub-species of the human race, the hat-bearing females. The conversation most often concerns real estate, which is the popular substitute for sex among the kind of Washingtonians who regularly go to cocktail parties. High officials only appear at cocktail parties when they are forced to do so, as when a foreign embassy is putting on a show for a visiting potentate; and even then, they usually hurry in and out like the White Rabbit, murmuring apologies instead of spilling secrets. We have never heard of any case of a leak at a cocktail party, possibly because we almost never go to cocktail parties ourselves.

Finally, just to finish off the last tattered remnant of the Washington-correspondent-legend, the nation's capital is not full of persons who make a practice of supplying reporters with bundles of classified documents. We have never encountered even one person of this sort. In fact, neither of us has ever read a classified document since the year 1947, when James V. Forrestal and Robert Patterson, in their capacities as Secretary of the Navy and Secretary of War, gave us a modified clearance to do the first authoritative article on guided missiles that was ever offered to the general public. Furthermore, if anyone now made us a present of a classified document, we should reject it as firmly as we should reject a pot of poison. Without such clearance as Forrestal and Patterson honored us with long ago, any reporter is a fool to touch a finger to documents of this kind. Nowadays particularly, and particularly if he intends to publish what the government does not want published, a reporter needs to be able to assert, with perfect truth, that he has used no information coming to him from any classified source.

So much for the legend. What then is it like to be a Washington correspondent? Basically, it is very much like being a reporter anywhere else. You work with a different sort of raw material, politics, and with a different sort of people, politicians and officials. You also inhabit a different sort of city, with its own peculiar charm and its own peculiar dullness. (Social conversation in Washington is almost invariably composed, in equal parts, of personal gossip, political dispute and the eternal news of real estate, which fascinates Washingtonians because so many of the city's politicians and officials are only birds of passage, and are therefore always changing nests. Only the rare eccentrics, like Alice Roosevelt Longworth, can ever be induced to talk about books; and the arts, history, philosophy and such-like subjects are best avoided, unless you want the reputation of an infernal bore.) But although the Washington correspondent's raw material and range of acquaintance and place of habitation are all localized in this manner, the rules of his craft remain the eternal rules of the whole reporting craft.

His feet, to cite the first rule, are a much more important part of a reporter's body than his head. Rarely—very rarely—the newspaper business produces a news analyst who can spot the essential outline of a situation from the vantage-point of his own desk, with no more help than the morning newspapers may give him. Raymond Aron of "Le Figaro" is one of these rare creatures. Another is Walter Lippmann, who can go on making perfectly good sense about current news when he is taking a long semi-vacation in Maine. But both Aron and Lippmann take great pains to refresh their analytical powers by frequent, direct contact with people and events. Not even the most astute analyst can possibly know what the news means by sheer mental telepathy.

We too were columnists as Lippmann and Aron are; and one of us is still a columnist. But as columnists, we always regarded ourselves as reporters first and foremost, no different from any other reporters except in having a somewhat wider liberty of judgment and expression. We tried, and the surviving columnist still tries, never to print a column lacking at least one previously unpublished and significant item of factual information. So the rule of the reporter's feet applied and still applies to us, just as much as it applies to anyone else. In Washington terms, the rule of the feet means that a reporter should try to see—not telephone—at least four officials or politicians every working day. This works out to about twenty-four major interviews a week, which should be further supplemented by casual contacts. The telephone, of course, is an essential instrument in the newspaper business. All reporters, no matter how successful, spend an inordinate amount of time telephoning other people to ask for appointments and waiting for appointments in other people's ante-rooms—and the more important the other people are, the more troublesome the telephoning and the longer the wait in the ante-room. But the telephone is in the same category as public relations men. It, or they, may be employed to make arrangements for getting information; but neither it, nor they, should be used as a direct channel of information. This sub-clause of the rule of the feet tends to pain public relations men, who always wish to speak for their masters. Fortunately it gives no pain to the telephone company.

The essential point of the rule of the feet is simple enough. If you get out, and see what is going on yourself, and talk to a great many people who are responsibly involved in what is going on, you can hardly help doing a good job of reporting. One way or another, significant developments come to your notice in the early stages; and so you always find something to say that is worth saying, or you observe something that is worth describing. For ourselves, since we also practice as reporters overseas and even as combat-reporters when the occasion arises, we carry the rule of the feet a degree further than is perhaps usual in Washington. Having reached the dreary stage in middle life when one tends to come apart at the seams, we do the dreary exercises that are needful to keep the seams reasonably well-caulked. Otherwise, we could not have clambered down a net into a landing-craft off Inchon, or gone on a patrol in the Malayan jungle, or followed a French battalion on operations in the Algerian hills—which are all things one or the other of us has had to do in our years of work together.

That patrol in Malaya was far the worst; for the jungle there is like a mountainous swamp, if you can imagine such a thing. The swamp also nourishes a thick, rank vegetation that always fills your hand with spines if you grasp a branch to pull yourself upwards in the slime or to slow your slime-speeded descent. The patrol was composed of hardened British youngsters with the good wind of nineteen-year-olds. It was led by a Borneo tracker, a little Dyak with hair as long as the famous locks of the Seven Sutherland sisters and pointed gold teeth alternately enamelled red and green. This ex-head-hunter seemed frail and even rather girlish until the plunge into the jungle, after which he never departed from a steady, light trot. Keeping up with him was essential, because the next man ahead in a jungle patrol merges into the jungle scene at any distance beyond 25 feet; and if you lose sight of his always disappearing rear, you lose the patrol. Keeping up very nearly killed the reporter. But at any rate he did keep up, unlike the athletic escort officer whom Sir Gerald Templer hopefully sent along to watch the ignominious collapse of an aging American journalist. This was a consolation for the reporter, 'though a disappointment for General Templer, who enjoys practical jokes. The other consolation was seeing what the jungle war was like. For a reporter, there is no substitute at all for seeing what it is like at first hand.

Yet we do not wish to suggest that keeping moving is the be-all and the end-all of the reporting trade; for there is a second rule almost as important as the rule of feet. Besides getting out and seeing the thing at first hand and asking the question yourself, you must also have some general idea of the right questions to ask. Events you can observe, but problems you have to ask about. Your feet only carry you to the politicians and officials who are the sources of your information about problems. It is asking the right questions that makes politicians and officials into sources of news.

This word source is as commonly abused, in talk about the newspaper business, as that other word, pipeline, which we have already warned against. People speak of a newspaperman's sources as though these sources were so many freely bubbling, always gushing springs. Yet the voluntary source is almost as rare as hen's teeth. In our combined experience, indeed, there has only been one instance when one of us was spontaneously offered a really big news story, complete in all its details. It was in the darkest moment of the last war, after the fall of France and before the battle of Britain. The senior of these reporters was then almost more engaged than a reporter ought to be in the great controversy over the American role in the struggle against the dictators. One evening—surely it can now be told—he received an unexpected visit from the astute and unconventional John Foster. Foster is now an eminent Queen's Counsel and member of parliament, but in those days he was an attaché at the British Embassy in Washington. Throughout the previous week, Foster had watched with agonized apprehension an exchange of telegrams between Sir Winston Churchill and President Roosevelt about Britain's desperate need for destroyers. Churchill had gravely warned that the destroyer-shortage might permit a German landing in Britain. He had begged for a few of the scores of over-age destroyers in the American Navy's mothball fleet. Roosevelt had replied non-committally but very discouragingly. Foster, who had an uncanny understanding of the tides of American opinion, had then decided to do a very bold thing. Without authorization from his superiors in the embassy, he had decided to tell the reporter about this super-secret exchange between Churchill and Roosevelt, and about the value to Britain of the destroyers America did not need. The resulting quiet conversation in a Georgetown garden led on to the powerful agitation for transfer to Britain of the over-age destroyers (but not before the reporter had asked Secretary of the Navy Frank Knox whether this transfer would serve American interests). Many others joined the effort. Big guns were made to bark in favor of the destroyer transfer—the reporter and Walter Lippmann worked together on the radio speech that General Pershing delivered; and if memory serves, Archie McLeish was one of the authors of the companion-speech by Admiral Standley. All sorts of persons with influence on Roosevelt were persuaded to go to the White House to make similar but more private speeches. In these ways a climate was created that helped to make possible the famous destroyer deal of that summer.

But to return to our subject, a reporter may go through life without ever having important information volunteered to him as John Foster volunteered the destroyer story on that long-ago evening. How then can one develop these famous sources, that all fairly successful reporters undoubtedly need to have? The answer is really rather simple. The vast majority of politicians and officials are passionately interested in the problems they have to deal with. They enjoy talking about those problems with anyone who can discuss the problems fairly intelligently. Other things being equal, they like their own pet problems to be sensibly presented to the general public. So if you have a fair understanding of the nature of a problem, the responsible official will usually be glad to talk to you about the problem with considerable frankness. The rub is that an immense amount of homework may be needed before the reporter has the necessary general grasp of the problem he wants the official or politician to talk about. In these grimly complicated times, technology in all its most awe-inspiring branches, and the higher forms of economics, and political-strategic geography, and many other arcane subjects have merged into politics. So you need at least a nodding acquaintance with all these subjects, if you wish to do your job the right way, always covering the really big, truly significant stories. We shall have more to say later about the far-reaching implications of this new trend, which began during the last war. For now, it is enough to say that a reporter can have no more satisfying moment than the moment when a man in high position says, "I don't mind talking to *you,* because you know what I'm talking about." That really happened to one of us, once, and the speaker was a man of extreme brilliance, carrying a staggering load of national responsibility, with a ferocious reputation for hostility to newspapermen.

At this point, the reader may perhaps be wondering why it is worth devoting so much legwork and so much headwork to a trade that is not notably highly paid, and sometimes resembles the trade of undertaking. The answer is, obviously, that undertaking is a necessary public function, and so is reporting. Undertaking, beyond question, generally offers larger material rewards. Reporting, in compensation, offers larger intangible rewards. Above all reporting offers the sense of being *engagé* in the political process of one's own time. The reporter who is not consciously *engagé* is in fact likely to be a very bad and unsuccessful reporter. Of course no reporter should indulge in excessive political partisanship. Of course, all reporters must also be sternly loyal to the facts, whether the facts help or harm friend or foe. But even if a

reporter meets both these tests, he must still be *engagé,* if only because he himself is a most necessary part of the political process.

In a democratic society, although the politicians and officials rather
often forget it, the master is the people. The reporter who covers national affairs is, in effect, the people's eyes and ears. He has the task of
making the people's government the people's business. He is the instrument that creates an informed public opinion. The very greatest
political leaders may mold public opinion by their own, individual
utterances. But in the first place, Churchill, Roosevelt and, in a lesser
measure, Charles de Gaulle and Konrad Adenauer are the only democratic leaders who have had this personal, direct opinion-molding
power in our own time. And in the second place, even the greatest
democratic leader cannot *make* public opinion; he can only persuade
the people to see the facts already known to them in a new and different light. In the democracies opinion is mainly made, in truth, by
the daily publication of an infinite variety of facts, sometimes trivial,
sometimes profoundly important, sometimes commonplace, sometimes
desperately remote from normal human experience, but all somehow
bearing on the national situation. No one has ever explained how this
daily factual bombardment is transmuted into public opinion. One
city with a poor newspaper will get far fewer facts than another city
with a good newspaper. One sober, industrious citizen will read only
his newspaper's sports and comic pages, while another, living in an
identical ranch-house next door, will follow the national and foreign
news with minute attention. Apparently the process works by the law
of averages, like the processes involving sub-atomic particles, simply
because so many people are daily exposed to so many facts. At any
rate, the process does work quite remarkably well, when the facts are
fully and convincingly published.

Tell the people the truth about their situation, and people will respond to any challenge that the truth offers. That is the fundamental
rule of democratic society. If you do not believe it, you do not believe
in democracy. And it is the reporter's job to see that the truth is told.

In the American democracy, moreover, the reporter has a very
much more important role than in the other western democracies. No
government in history, alas, has ever voluntarily told the whole truth,
or anything like the whole truth, in its official statements, its approved discourses and its organized press conferences. The whole
truth is only revealed or approximated by long public debate; the

realistic estimate is only reached after viewpoint has been tested against viewpoint, and all the facts, pro and con, have been weighed against each other. And in the United States, the debate about the nation's situation and the nation's policy is mainly carried on in the press (and of course in the other media of communication which still almost entirely reflect the press).

This is the most important point of difference, we sometimes suspect, between the American system and the British system. Under the British system, both executive and legislative responsibility are centered in the House of Commons. In Britain the men on the opposition front benches do not have executive responsibility now, but they at least had executive responsibility in the quite recent past. They too, therefore, have had to bear the burden of making great national decisions. They too have seen and weighed most of the relevant data that their successors now have before them. They too, in sum, know where the bodies are buried. So in Britain, for just these reasons, the national debate can be and actually is quite largely carried on in the House of Commons itself. The British press therefore has far less national responsibility than the American press. This difference perhaps explains why British popular newspapers make our most crime-filled tabloids seem serious and responsible, and why British serious newspapers are too often pretentious shams, with very little behind their fine, impressive, literate façades. (After watching the great "Times" cover the Korean war from New York, from the moment poor Ian Morison was killed until the end, it has always been difficult for us to hold the "Times" in awe, especially since we have also observed the "Times" covering the worst of the Formosa crises from Singapore and the Indo-Chinese war from Paris. There are only two of us, but as we do not have the peculiar knack of super-telescopic vision, one of us was *there* when we published our accounts of these great events.)

In the United States, in contrast, the national debate cannot be and is not carried on within the government. The American Congress is constitutionally deprived of executive responsibility. No member of Congress, by virtue of his office, sees and weighs any large part of the data on which national decisions must be based. Almost no Senators or Representatives have the time left over from all their other duties to find out where the more important bodies are buried. Hence there has been only one real Congressional debate, absorbing the country's attention and fully ventilating a great national issue, in the whole quarter-century of the senior of these reporters' working life. That was the debate on Franklin Roosevelt's court bill. This issue, involving the actual balance of the governing branches, briefly transformed the Senate into a new constitutional convention. But nothing like this has happened since, and we shall probably go to our graves before Congress stages another true debate about a great issue.

There is also less and less open debate between the chief officials of the executive branch, who used to argue out their differences in public, but now do so no longer. (This we think an unhealthy trend for reasons we shall also set out later on.) Hence sheer force of circumstance has made the American press almost the only forum in which our national debate is carried on. The fact itself is little understood. The mode of the debate in the press is equally little understood. For it is not carried on by fusillades of opinion fired by editorial writers and columnists. It is mainly carried on in the news columns (or, as we hope, by columnists dealing in facts), by the publication and counter-publication of barrages of information on all sides of every major issue. The process is inchoate, formless and undirected. But it is still the reporter's share in this process, his vital role in the national debate, that makes the reporter's trade more rewarding and exciting than the undertaker's.

It means that the reporter, while always remembering that he is only an honest tradesman, must also remember that he has a high and necessary public function to perform. He performs his function if the information the people need is transmitted to the people, as a sewage commissioner or a water commissioner performs his function if the flow through the pipes is maintained. (And what public functionaries have greater reasons for pride, unalloyed by doubt, than efficient water and sewage commissioners?) Furthermore, the reporter has just as much right to be indignant if he is prevented from performing his function of transmitting information as a sewer or water commissioner has a right to be indignant if his precious pipes are tampered with.

This in turn determines the relationship between the reporter and the politician and/or official. We have acquired a reputation, in our opinion unjustified, for bringing a touch of arrogance to this relationship. A story is told about a meeting between the older member of our partnership and Admiral Lewis Strauss, just before the ineffable Admiral's appointment as chairman of the Atomic Energy Commission. The meeting ended when the reporter rose and remarked coldly, "Admiral, you have wasted half an hour of my time."

The story, as it happens, is quite true. The Admiral, not the reporter, had proposed the meeting. His only intention was to conciliate a newspaperman who might perhaps make trouble later on, by shedding the beams of his peculiar personality upon this potentially dangerous fellow. His notion, apparently, was that one ought to go away happy after such a pleasurable experience. As a flatterer, Strauss is an exceptional performer. But the reporter came to the meeting, not to be told he was a dear good fellow, but to discuss the profoundly significant public matters for which Strauss would soon have the highest responsibility. The reporter gradually discovered that Strauss had no intention whatever of discussing these matters. When the reporter discovered that Strauss did not wish to talk about serious matters, he considered that his time had been wasted, as indeed it had. He also considered, and still considers, that as a responsible newspaperman he had both a right and a duty to ask about key facts of the national situation. He further considered that he had been taken for a fool, as he had been. So he made the remark above-quoted, and departed forthwith.

If a reporter errs at all, it is better to err on the side of arrogance (or decent self-respect, as we should prefer to say) than to err on the side of meeching. It is mighty tempting for any reporter—a mere practitioner of a useful trade—to be pleased when he is figuratively patted on the head by public men in posts of great power and responsibility. It is even more tempting when the public man occasionally tosses a tit-bit of information between the head-pats, as you might give a spaniel an occasional biscuit. But reporters who allow themselves to fall into this spaniel-like relationship to public men automatically cease to perform their own public function. So the temptation must be resisted at all costs.

The truth is that any good reporter must be prepared to lose a friend, at least for a while, if the friend is promoted to one of the principal public offices. When a man reaches the real heights—when he becomes Secretary of State, say, or Secretary of Defense, or Secretary of the Treasury—he becomes a chief actor in the public drama, always on the stage, always joining in the dialogue. Comment on his performance in turn becomes continuously necessary; and if the reporter's comment is honest, the public man will not always like it. All actors think the drama critics under-rate them, and sooner or later, all public men whose actions are continuously reported begin to think reporters misunderstand them. Sometimes the public man will have a good case because, in the nature of things, the reporter sometimes has to call the turn without all the essential facts in his possession. But if the reporter has done his utmost to find out all the facts, he must then call the turn as he sees it, without considering the consequences. Otherwise, he will be a bad reporter.

Within the limits of human fallibility, which are very wide indeed, we have tried to call the turn as we saw it, and we have lost eminent friends by doing so. Dean G. Acheson, for example, was another old tribal friend, born in the same town that our family comes from; and now that he is Secretary of State no longer, we like to think he has become our friend again. But he was not pleased by our reporting of his performance as a chief actor on the public stage, perhaps quite justifiably. So he was not our friend when he was Secretary of State.

By the same token, we were on friendly terms with Louis A. Johnson when he became Secretary of Defense—to the extent, at least, one can be on friendly terms with a man one neither likes nor trusts. (This peculiar form of friendship, which we call business friendship, is widespread in Washington.) Johnson's performance as Under Secretary of War in Roosevelt's time had not been calculated to arouse admiration for his character. Yet he had at least fought against his Secretary, Harry Woodring, for a greater national defense effort when such an effort was desperately needed. A certain intimacy had grown up in this long past struggle. Johnson even gave us his private telephone number when he became Defense Secretary, which his predecessor, Jim Forrestal, had never given us. Johnson was also an accomplished practitioner of the trick some high officials have—the trick of keeping newspapermen sweet by giving them highly confidential and often damaging information about other high officials and departments other than their own—and we were among the first he tried the trick on. But we did not stay friends with Louis Johnson. No honest reporter could possibly stay friends with Johnson, since the price of staying friends with him was failing to report what Johnson was really doing to the defense of the United States. We could cite other cases of old friends lost or enemies newly made in similar circumstances. In some of these cases, we are still sure we were right and we are proud of what we did. In other cases, we are not so sure, and the opposite of proud. And to balance all these cases, we can name only two officials on the very highest level with whom our friendship grew continuously warmer and more intimate while they were in office.

The first was James F. Byrnes, whose great services as President Truman's Secretary of State are now too often forgotten. In those immediately post-war days when Byrnes was Secretary, the governmental mania for secrecy had not reached the psychotic stage. There was also a great need to correct the American public's wartime delusions about the character and purposes of their former Russian ally; and it had to be done just as rapidly as possible. So the reporters who rode the post-war conference circuit, and the officials on the second level like Charles E. Bohlen and George F. Kennan and Benjamin V. Cohen, and Senator Arthur H. Vandenberg and Senator Tom Connally and Secretary Byrnes himself, all travelled together and worked together and lived together, forming the kind of cosy family that must be formed by a small, well-run, itinerant circus. The result was a swiftly altered, newly realistic American public opinion concerning Soviet purposes. The whole experience rather finely proved how wise officials, working with responsible newspapermen with the common aim of informing the public, can achieve this vital aim with great rapidity and against rather heavy odds.

As for the other high official with whom our intimacy grew in office, he was Jim Forrestal. He too had been a family friend before he entered public life—we have been unusually lucky in that way. Probably our intimacy with him grew during his long years of service in Washington because he was almost the only public man whom we have thought invariably right. To us, Forrestal seems the tragic hero of the post-war years. He was whipped onwards by the fierce whip of an intense patriotism. He carried a burden of foresight, a vision of the dangers of the future, that gave him no rest by night or day. He was killed by his own foreknowledge, and by his unrelenting struggle to prevent what he foresaw from becoming the future's terrible reality. America, today, is just beginning to live with the consequence of Forrestal's defeat by littler men. And Americans will do well to pray that when all the returns are in, those consequences will be less evil and inhuman than now seems entirely possible.

It must be added that this matter of friendship with men in government is always a prickly problem for the Washington correspondent, even when you go down to the second and third and fourth level of official. These Indians, as they now call them, do not make the final decisions. They rarely see their names in print, so they are not personally offended by what reporters write about them. They constitute the vast majority of the citizens of political Washington. They also form the vast majority of every Washington correspondent's personal friends.

To be sure, there are other Washingtons besides political Washington. There is business-Washington, a city we do not know at all, which probably resembles Cincinnati, Ohio. There is lobbyists'-Washington, a richly furnished vipers' nest. There is diplomats'-Washington, a ghastly community from which all able and sensible diplomats seek to escape into political Washington. But a Washington correspondent does not live in these other Washingtons. He lives in political Washington, which is a one-industry town. If he has any friends at all, most of them are bound to be men in government. And since life without friends is a pretty bleak business, the reporter must go to considerable pains to maintain a correct relation between his trade and his personal life.

Obviously, a reporter cannot make a practice of reporting after working hours. If he does so, he will soon achieve the approximate popularity of an insurance agent who takes along a bundle of contracts to every party he goes to. Equally obviously, since men who are his friends are also men in government, the reporter must sometimes ask his friends for information or guidance. The rule is, however, that such questions are only put in a man's office or at the luncheon table— the luncheon table being barbarously considered in Washington as a mere extension of the office. And sometimes even this rule is not strict enough to solve the problem. Our two best friends in Washington happen to be men in rather sensitive positions, who could no doubt tell us many things of extreme interest. But we long ago decided that the price of retaining these particular friends was never trying to discuss with them any matters within the area of their official responsibility, in office hours or out of office hours; and we have never done so. Fortunately, our two friends have other topics besides the familiar Washington triad, gossip, politics and real estate; so the conversation rarely lags despite the impossibility of talking about our friends' work.

In the Washington correspondent's life, hospitality is another problem that perhaps needs touching on. We come from a tribe that has an almost pathological fondness for giving parties, and we both enjoy being hospitable ourselves. In political Washington, moreover, you cannot just ask your close personal friends to your table. There is a strong touch of the zoo in Washington life, and everyone in Washington likes to see the lions, who also like to be seen. Washington dinner-giving is not quite so formula-ridden as it was in the old days before the war, when a prospective host or hostess would begin by asking, "Who shall I have for the Ambassador, who for the Supreme Court Justice, who for the Senator?" because one-of-each was a necessary ingredient in the recipe for a successful dinner. But even today, your dinner will please everyone more if there is a lion or two to roar away at the head of the table. Even your closest friends will be a little disappointed without lions. And it is also useful to a reporter to feed the lions, if they will consent to be fed.

On the other hand, the purpose of feeding the lions is not the purpose that is widely suspected. One of us well remembers asking to dinner a man who now holds a key ambassadorial post, and stands very high on the list of John Foster Dulles' bad jokes on the American people. He refused dinner but asked if he could come in afterwards. In due course he appeared; but he drank only soda water, hardly said more than "good evening" and "good-bye," and from time to time was visibly shaken by an inner paroxysm of unexplained alarm. The reporter learned later that his guest, who is a very fearful man, had feared that evening being overloaded with wines and liquors, and then persuaded to say much he should not have said. But you do not ask lions to feed with you in order to ply them with intoxicants and then with questions. Aside from wanting to make up the kind of Washington party that gives pleasure, you ask lions as well as closer friends because you want to know what sort of men the lions are, which is best discovered out of office hours, and because you want them to know you too. If they know you, and have decided that you are reasonably well-motivated, it will be easier to discuss public matters with them when you have to ask for a business appointment.

But this examination of the big and little personal problems and the working methods and the public function of a reporter in Washington has run on long enough. At bottom it is intended as an answer to another man we are proud to count as friend, the leading American expert on the Soviet Union who is now, when his *expertise* is so badly needed, rather oddly assigned to the American Embassy in Manila.

Charles E. Bohlen, who wisely guided many newspapermen when he was charged with this duty by the State Department, none the less has always contended that "officials and reporters are natural enemies, because the reporter always wants just what the official should not give him."

We think, on the contrary, that the reporter and the man in government are natural allies; since it is the reporter's business to portray the national situation to the American people, and since the man in government cannot do what needs doing unless the American people understand the national situation. It is not always an easy alliance, for obvious reasons. But in our experience, the alliance has always existed and has always functioned well, whenever the American government has been strong and clear of purpose. When the government wishes to respond to the hard challenges of these difficult times, and when the government knows its own mind about the appropriate responses, then the government is only too eager to tell the people just how matters stand for America. It is necessary to do so, or public opinion will not support the efforts and the risks required to meet the challenges. In these periods of strong, clear-purposed government, the responsible reporter's life in Washington is immensely exciting and immensely satisfying. It becomes less pleasant when a weak government does not know what to do, and so wishes to conceal from the nation the need to do anything. Then the government's aim is to hide the challenges, so that there will be no call for any response; the government's hope is to paint the national situation in false colors, so that there will be no disquiet about it. In such times as these, the reporter must fight hard to perform his public function, and in such times as these there may indeed be real enmity between many time-serving officials and reporters who will not agree to print the prevailing official falsehoods. But although this recurring situation is neither easy nor agreeable, the reporter at least has one compensation. When the government is not telling the truth to the people, the reporter's truth-telling becomes immeasurably more important.

Both reportorial situations—truth-telling with strong government and truth-telling despite weak government—are represented in the collection of our pieces in this book. The reader may be interested in seeing the results, as well as enjoying, as we hope, those pleasures of recognition and recollection which go with a look backwards to the time that was only yesterday, and still shapes events today.

II

Political Reporting

Up TO 1948, THE YEAR of the Marshall Plan, most Americans thought and all Americans hoped that our national life would again resume the ancient, easy, inward-looking, course that everyone who was of age when the war began regarded as normal and proper. It was acknowledged, of course, that we had a duty to help in tidying up the ugly debris that the war had left in almost every nation it had touched. It was further agreed that we must not again make the mistake of 1920 —that we must not retreat into total, irresponsible isolation. But even after allowing for these new national duties, it really seemed possible for a while that everything, one day, would be almost the same as it always had been. Then, in 1948, it became apparent that nothing would ever be the same again; and this passage of a great unseen divide, affecting every aspect of the American political process, has most particularly affected the primary branch of our trade, political reporting.

It has to be admitted that reporting American politics, nowadays, is decidedly less enjoyable than it was when the elder of these reporters set up in business as a columnist at the green age of 27. In the year 1937, the city of Washington was still a village, and the American political scene still had something of the parish-pump character, something of the intimacy and unashamed idiosyncrasy of the nineteenth century.

There were real bosses still—old Crump in Memphis, and Frank Hague, who looked so like a lace-curtain-Irish snapping turtle, and Ed Kelly of Chicago, and the agreeable and intelligent Ed Flynn of the Bronx. There were still figures, too, who genuinely deserved that dreadfully over-used adjective colorful. The most lurid were the old-fashioned, neo-populist Southern demagogues like Bob Reynolds of North Carolina and the Man Bilbo of Mississippi. These continuators of the tradition of Sockless Jerry Simpson were civically deplorable in the last degree; yet they were seldom deplorable in the McCarthy manner; and one regrets them just a little because they were so wonderfully productive of good stories.

It is not altogether relevant, but one cannot really resist telling the best of the Bilbo stories, even at this late date, if only because it could never be adapted to a family newspaper and so has never seen print before. It concerns the interlude between Bilbo's disgraceful governorship of Mississippi and his even more disgraceful service in the Senate, when he was seriously thinking of running for the Senate seat held by that very different Mississippian, Pat Harrison. Harrison belonged to the other main Southern tradition, the tradition of the Southern Senatorial grandees—of the powerful old tyrant, Joe Robinson of Arkansas, with whom Harrison ran the Senate in tandem for years; of James F. Byrnes of South Carolina, who was one of the most effective Senators of the XXth century; and of Lyndon Johnson of Texas and Dick Russell of Georgia in our own time. Pat Harrison was witty, cynical, wise and hard working. He was a first-rate Senator, too—as Charley McNary of Oregon used to say, "he always gave the country an even break when he could possibly afford to." But at all times he was a practical politician.

Being a practical politician, he wanted to get Bilbo a soft place on the Federal payroll in order to keep him out of the Senate race. For this purpose Harrison applied to his friend George Peek, the first head of the forgotten Agricultural Adjustment Administration. Harrison gave Bilbo a big build-up as an able, patriotic fellow, while delicately insisting that the job he was asking Peek to provide for Bilbo would have to carry a substantial salary. Peek, who understood practical politics very well, immediately granted Harrison's request. Harrison thanked him profusely and said good-bye. Then, as he was about to leave Peek's office, he turned and began again:

"Now George, I don't want you to get me wrong. This man Bilbo will do a great job for you and the government, I've no doubt about that. But he comes from our piney woods districts, where people are still pretty wild, so I just don't believe I'd put him in any job where he'd have to do any speaking for you. Maybe he'd embarrass you."

Peek thanked Harrison for the tip. Harrison again thanked Peek profusely, said good-bye, and this time got halfway through the door. Then he turned and began a second time.

"Now George, don't get me wrong. As I've said, this man Bilbo will do a great job for you and the government. But in our piney woods districts where he was raised, the people just aren't used to handling big sums of money, and if you haven't got the habit of resisting it, money temptation can be an awful thing. So I guess you'd better not put money temptation in his way either."

Once more Peek thanked Harrison for the tip. Harrison thanked Peek for the favor, said goodbye, and departed, this time actually closing the office door behind him. But then he opened it slightly, and, speaking as though he had just one more after-thought, he began yet again:

"Now George, please don't misunderstand me. I promise you this man Bilbo will do a great job for you and the government. But in our piney woods country people are mighty free and easy, sometimes maybe even a mite rough in their ways with women. So I believe I'd choose girls for Bilbo's office staff who are—uh—kind of on the older side."

"OK Pat," said Peek, with a roar of laughter. "I see just what you mean. Your man Bilbo is going to make a great public servant if I just gag him, bind him and geld him. He's hired on that basis."

He was hired, too, at $6,000 a year, and he spent a long time in a cubby hole in the AAA, gloomily cutting out newspaper clippings with the help of a secretary who looked as though she had entered government service in the administration of Millard Fillmore.

In the older America of little government, bargains and maneuvers and personalities and patronage often had more day-to-day political importance than issues; and the politics of bargain and maneuver, personality and patronage had its own folklore, of which the Bilbo-

Harrison-Peek story is a fair sample. It even had its own proverbial wisdom, and the proverbs were always attributed to famous figures, in the manner of the "Wisdom of Solomon." Claude Swanson, the ancient Virginian whom Roosevelt made his first Secretary of the Navy, was the author of "the first law of politics—when the water reaches the upper deck, follow the rats!" McNary, the astute and generous-hearted Republican Senate leader who loved Franklin Roosevelt and detested all stuffed shirts, invariably offered this advice to his novice colleagues: "Remember, everybody hates a man who demagogues when the doors are closed." Frank Kent, a great reporter, first proclaimed the rule that all reporters should always remember: "For an honest newspaperman, there's only one way to look at 98½ per cent of public men—down!" After examining the elaborate *treillage* that covered Arthur Vandenberg's bald spot, Alice Longworth proposed still another rule that is somewhat more fanciful but far from worthless: "Never trust a man who starts parting his hair under his left armpit!"

This rambling on is no mere exercise in nostalgia. It is meant to suggest something of the cosy, perhaps all-too-human atmosphere of the older America of little government, which was a paradise for political reporters. Even in the late '30s, the atmosphere of this older America still survived in Congress; and the senior generation of political reporters, survivors from the Wilson-Harding-Coolidge-Hoover era into the new era of Franklin Roosevelt, rather desperately took refuge on Capitol Hill. These older reporters still clung to such men as Robinson and Harrison, McNary, Vandenberg and, in the executive branch, to Cordell Hull and the few others like him, because such men were American political types easily identifiable by past experience. By the same token, most senior political reporters of those days regarded the New Dealers as eery, strange and un-conversible. This gave a considerable competitive advantage to younger newspapermen who saw nothing particularly alarming in the presence in government of men like Tom Corcoran, and William O. Douglas, and Robert H. Jackson, and the most selfless, most brilliant and most nearly eery of the lot, Ben Cohen, whose inconspicuous signature is to be found on an actual majority of the truly fruitful great measures of the Roosevelt years.

By the late '30s of course, Roosevelt and his New Dealers had already carried the country through the transition from little government to big government; but this transition had by no means produced its full and inevitable final effects. As has been remarked, Washington was still a village. A hard-working newspaperman could quite easily know and keep in touch with the professional politicians on the Hill, and the territorial grandees in their strongholds across the country, and the New Dealers grouped around the White House, and the more important permanent officials of the Federal Departments and agencies. Then too there was hardly such a thing, as yet, as a classification stamp in all of Washington. (Read the "pumpkin papers" that Alger Hiss stole for Whittaker Chambers, and you will see how pitifully insignificant and un-secret the government's supposed secrets then were.) Most important of all, no one at all then doubted that the people's government was the people's business. A reporter, being charged with the task of describing the government to the people, had an unqualified right to ask about any aspect of the people's business which he thought interesting or significant.

For all these reasons, political reporting in that earlier time was not only more enjoyable; it was also far more comprehensive. Precisely because the political process was vastly more open and more easy to report in human terms, vastly more of the process was customarily reported to the general public.

The big stories were often of a sort that would now be briefly covered in specialized sections of the newspapers—stories about the policies of the Securities and Exchange Commission, for instance. Just about the biggest story, each year, was the titanic struggle that annually occurred between the Keynesians and the budget-balancers. Secretary of the Treasury Henry Morgenthau was a stout budget-balancer. Roosevelt, who thought the Keynesian theory rather silly if he thought about it at all, was always inclined to back Morgenthau and sound money. But Tom Corcoran, the Keynesian, was an amazing political general who had planted his men in every government office, including Morgenthau's Treasury. He would mobilize his New Dealers for a long and bloody war, full of ambushes, flank attacks, night marches and sanguinary open combats. In the end, Morgenthau would always be defeated, and so there would be another New Deal budget, with a deficit that seems ludicrously small by current standards, but was quite big enough then to cause all conservative persons to predict the immediate end of the world.

All of this, one hopes, will at least have begun to suggest the essential point—the point that in the period covered by the pieces in this volume, the people's government has come to be less and less the people's business. There are several different reasons why American political reporting today is less informative and vivid and above all less complete than it used to be. One reason is simply the proliferation of classification stamps in this Washington of ours in which such a thing hardly existed only two decades ago. Today, as someone remarked, all papers in all government departments are classified, except for one kind only—the toilet paper. In the Pentagon, there are probably "Confidential" Men's Rooms. But this is a most complex subject, with the very gravest implications for the future of democracy, which we shall try to discuss in detail later on.

Besides the omnipresence of classification stamps, there is the increasing hankering for respectability, the progressive *embourgeoise-ment,* the growing desire to put up a good front, by which our government has been oddly overtaken. In the Roosevelt and even in the early Truman years, no one was particularly shocked if the most blazing rows, the most venomous vendettas, the most furious disputes inside the administration, were carried on in full view of the general public. It gave our government a rather disorderly appearance, even an alarmingly disorganized and bohemian appearance, in foreign eyes. But in fact it was not at all a bad thing to have the whole country know about the annual struggle over the budget between the Morgenthau and Corcoran forces, or about the even more extraordinary though more brief vendetta between Henry A. Wallace and James F. Byrnes, which Truman ended by firing Wallace. These great intra-administration disputes concerned great issues of principle. The country was helped to understand the issues by the very openness of the disputes. It was even helpful that the disputes could be reported as human and personal contests—for issues are always more easily apprehended if they can be conveyed in human, even all-too-human terms. The rows gave savor and interest to the debate by which democracy lives and has its being. By the same token, the big, basic issues are far more difficult to report and ventilate when debate is muffled, and the governmental rule is a prim pretense of happy unanimity.

In this respect, by far the worst period was the first Eisenhower administration—the years of the "team," as the members of the administration always complacently called themselves. In truth, they were not really like a team. They were like the executive hierarchy of a self-satisfied (because monopolistic) industrial corporation in a one-company town. The corporation's chairman of the board, revered but remarkably remote, was President Eisenhower. The active, ever-present, all-managing and much feared president of the company was former Secretary of the Treasury George M. Humphrey. Even the administration wives fell into the pattern, treating Pam Humphrey, a charming woman with a whim of iron, much as the wives of lesser industrial executives treat the wife of their company president. Not only was Eisenhower's first administration organized in this peculiar manner. In addition, most of its key members were big businessmen, with no previous experience of dealing with an independent and inquiring press. Thus ventilation of the issues was reduced to an absolute minimum between 1953 and 1957. The greatest efforts were made to conceal such differences as there were—and there were not many, since George Humphrey almost always got his way at the outset. The arguments for and against any given course of action did not naturally emerge. It took the hardest sort of work to learn about any arguments at all, except those that were included in the official press releases. Journalistic curiosity which went beyond the press releases was even thought to be a mark of subversive tendencies; for the team also held the view that the country "only needed to have faith in Eisenhower," presumably because it was well known that he walked on the water-hole at the Burning Tree golf course.

In the second Eisenhower administration, Eisenhower's luck has run out; so the responsible officials in government talk much more freely. Officials who are frightened always talk more freely. But even this relatively greater governmental openness—even indeed the intimacy of a family circle that prevailed between the reporters who rode the postwar international conference circuit and Jimmy Byrnes and the other officials who attended those conferences—cannot overcome the effect of another development of the past two decades. The people's government is nowadays less and less the people's business, for the purely physical reason that the people's government has grown too big.

In the days when the policies of the SEC made front-page news, the subjects that now preoccupy the nation "were not subjects," as Oxford dons say of topics unworthy of discussion. Consider, for instance, the state of the War Department in 1938, which in some sense indicated the state of national defense as a subject. The G-2, the intelligence of the U. S. Army, was in those days entirely controlled by a group of formidable, elderly females—ladies with very large busts covered by old-fashioned silk shirtwaists, from which depended those intimidating fleur-de-lys pseudo-broaches that swallow or disgorge thin chains for pinces-nez. The ladies had gone to work in G-2 in the first world war. They had stayed there ever since. They alone knew where all the files were and what all the procedures were. The colonels —for the chief of intelligence of the U. S. Army *was* only a colonel in 1938—might come and go. The ladies went on forever; and by their very permanence they came to have great influence, not only on appointments of officers to intelligence posts, but even sometimes on War Department intelligence estimates.

In this innocent and primeval War Department, there was hardly any news at all, except for the news of the quarrels between the Department's two civilian chiefs, the silly little Secretary of War, Harry Woodring, and the Under Secretary, Louis M. Johnson. When the Second World War broke out, these two men who had primary responsibility for the good condition of the American army were really not on speaking terms; and one could go to either of them, any day, and hear the faults of the other described at length, with extreme frankness and accuracy. Similarly, the only real news in the State Department was being made by the feud between Cordell Hull and Sumner Welles, except of course for the news of Hull's eternal trade agreements, which interested no one but the "New York Herald Tribune," the "New York Times" and the trade papers of the protected industries. By Munich-time, the senior of these reporters had a pleasantly successful column, syndicated in about a hundred newspapers, yet he had never felt compelled to write about America's national defense or America's foreign relations. It was Munich that woke him up, and began to wake up the country, to the existence and the menace of the rest of the world.

This awakening to the existence and the menace of the rest of the world has altogether revolutionized the political reporter's task. In the '30s, the front pages of the American newspapers were wholly dominated by the great social and economic new departures of Roosevelt's New Deal. Since the second world war ended, however, the front pages have been continuously dominated by the great struggle between the war-created Soviet empire and the rest of the world. This whole period, in fact, produced only two purely domestic, purely social and economic issues big enough and grave enough to have far-reaching national consequences. One was the labor issue, which put the Taft-Hartley act on the statute books. The other was the civil rights issue. And although a civil rights act was passed in 1957, none of the really basic decisions about civil rights have been made by the executive or legislative branches of the government. They have been made, instead, by the Supreme Court.

Besides these two issues, many others from the OPA onwards have of course caused much clamor. But they either came to nothing, like the Dixon-Yates contract, or they were outright frauds to begin with, like President Truman's celebrated and wonderfully entertaining Fair Deal. The Fair Deal boiled down in essence to two proposals—the Brannan farm plan and the Ewing health plan. Neither was ever a real issue in the sense that there was ever a ghost of a chance of its becoming the law of the land. The whole Fair Deal was, in fact, simply a handy, invented stick which Harry Truman used to beat the Congress over the head. One suspects that Truman would have been almost as horrified as Robert A. Taft if the Ewing health plan had actually passed the Congress.

As for the Eisenhower Administration, aside from its belated and largely unsuccessful attempt to use civil rights to win back the Negro vote to the Republican Party, it has introduced no domestic legislation of real national significance. It has merely accepted (and denounced) the basic postulates of the New Deal, while consistently favoring business-conservative interests in the administration of the law. In this sense it has performed—and performed very well—the proper domestic function of a conservative régime following on a long period of experiment and change.

But, the reader may say, surely McCarthyism was also a big domestic issue. The answer is simple. No purely political issue seemed to us bigger or more burning in the whole period of our work together. But to call it a domestic issue is to misconstrue the real nature of McCarthyism. Like almost all the other greatest political excitements of the postwar years—the Alger Hiss trials, the flaming B-36 row, the brief but savage rumpus over the firing of General MacArthur—McCarthyism was a by-product of the cold war.

More specifically, McCarthy was a by-product of the time when the cold war became hot—the time of the fighting in Korea. Before the summer of 1950, McCarthy was essentially a fringe politician. Mc-

Carthyism was an ugly phenomenon of which the political reporter had to take account, but no more than that. It was only after the Korean war began that McCarthy became the decisive, dominating political force which he remained for four sordid, shameful years.

It was McCarthy's great service to the Kremlin, of course, that he was able to direct so great a share of the nation's attention and emotional drive away from the danger to national survival inherent in the Kremlin's rapidly growing power. To a great many American citizens, riding about in their newly acquired Cadillacs during the Korea-stimulated boom, McCarthy provided a comforting and guilt-dissipating escape. By loudly supporting McCarthy's persecutions of minor government servants, they could achieve a reassuring sense of being as staunch and courageous anti-Communists as the handful of American soldiers in Korea. (Why, incidentally, do all politicians and many writers nowadays refer to American soldiers as "boys"? Surely the word soldier is a good and honorable word.)

There was a time, to be sure, when the danger of internal Communist subversion was a quite genuine danger, although it was always wholly subsidiary to the far greater external threat. In the years immediately after the war, the Communists, although they boasted hardly more conscious adherents than the Holy Rollers, very nearly captured one of the two great labor groupings—the CIO. Indeed, they would have taken over the CIO if they had captured Walter Reuther's UAW, as they came close to doing. Before the 1948 election, it also seemed just possible that the Communist-run Progressive Party, with Henry Wallace as its pathetic figurehead, might actually achieve the balance-of-power position between the two major parties which the Communists had planned for it.

Long before McCarthy became the Great Inquisitor, however, the Communist party in America had gone into ignominious decline. The decline began after the failure to capture the two central Communist objectives. We like to think we contributed to that failure by writing piece after piece exposing the Communist threat in the CIO and the Communist hold on the Wallace movement. Somewhat ironically, it was largely because of Henry Wallace, whom we had so often attacked, that we were also enabled to expose another by-product of the cold war—the cult of the professional ex-Communist informer. The exposure of the professional informers was our only old-fashioned journalistic crusade.

It began in 1954, when Louis Budenz, a former editor of the "Daily Worker," testified before the Senate Judiciary Committee of McCarthy's great ally, the late, unlamented Pat McCarran. Budenz swore that Wallace, during his mission to China as Vice President in 1944, had been "under Communist guidance." From intimate personal experience, the elder of these reporters knew that Budenz's sworn testimony was totally and proveably false.

The reporter had been in China during Wallace's visit, and he had actually drafted Wallace's report to the President, which was the only significant outcome of the Wallace mission. Wallace strongly recommended in his report that General Joseph Stilwell should be replaced as the American commanding General in China. Stilwell, a brave but remarkably foolish man, was the bitter enemy of Chiang Kai-shek and his Nationalists; and he further represented the Chinese Communists' great hope for supplies of American arms in wartime. General Albert C. Wedemeyer, whom Wallace recommended to replace Stilwell, held precisely opposite views. He was stoutly anti-Communist; and he believed that with American help, the Nationalist Government could be reformed effectively from within, and that it would then be able to defeat the Communists and hold China.

Wallace's only recommendation from China was thus, by its very nature, a profoundly anti-Communist act. The reporter who had firsthand experience of this fact so wrote, in effect accusing Budenz of perjury. He was thereupon called to testify before the McCarran Committee. The testimony had little direct effect, since McCarran's mind was already, of course, firmly closed, while in the atmosphere of those years the other members of the committee were politically in a catatonic state. But the experience led us to inquire further into the phenomenon of the professional ex-Communists, and what we discovered was credible only in the context of those times.

What we discovered was, quite simply, that the United States government had in its employ a considerable number of demonstrable perjurers, whose function it was to invent evidence against American citizens, whenever the government happened to lack the needed evidence for a conviction in court or an adverse decision in an immigration proceeding. Most of the citizens thus handled by the government and its perjurers were thoroughly bad lots; but it seemed to us that they still had the rights of citizens. Our columns on the subject gave names and details. Here it is enough to say that, although we were repeatedly threatened with suit by the ex-Communist informers we exposed, no suit was ever brought to court; and that, in the end, as a rather direct consequence of the pieces we wrote, the perjured informers were dropped from the government payrolls.

The era of the perjured informers reached its height during the first years of the Eisenhower Administration. So did the "numbers game," one of the sleaziest political tricks of our times, and the shameful book-burning in the USIA libraries abroad, both of which we first exposed. It was in those years too that Robert E. Oppenheimer was offered up as a burnt offering by Lewis Strauss. As some of the columns which follow will suggest, we were repeatedly infuriated or made ashamed by the Administration's appeasement of McCarthy, and by its imitation of McCarthyism in the person of such figures as the State Department's Little Inquisitor, Scott McLeod.

Yet in fairness one thing must be said. McCarthyism, like McCarthy himself, died before the first Eisenhower Administration ended. It seems only fair to give some of the credit, at least, for the lancing of the McCarthy boil to Dwight D. Eisenhower. As we wrote (perhaps a bit emotionally) at the time of the President's heart attack, Eisenhower helped to bring the country back "to a sense of the true American style." Whatever his faults and weaknesses as a President may be, Eisenhower is not the sort of President under whom a blind and ugly extremism could flourish indefinitely.

Yet, although McCarthyism may be dead, another by-product of the cold war, which may prove more dangerous in the end, is still very much with us. Year by year, the picture of the American government transmitted to the American people, who are supposed to be the real masters of the government, becomes more dim, unreal, and incomplete.

The essential reason for this progressive loss of contact between the government and the people is simple enough. The problems of defense and foreign policy have not merely become "subjects," in the sense given to that word a little earlier; they have become predominant, all-affecting, over-mastering subjects. Vast, infinitely complex new governmental organisms have come into being, charged with dealing with these problems. A whole elaborate system of secrecy has been developed, charged with limiting the people's knowledge in these areas. And the habit of secrecy has now spread, by a sort of noxious contagion, to other government agencies and departments that have no shadow of an excuse for secretiveness.

Thus you quite innocently ask who were the members of the inter-departmental committees responsible for the Eisenhower administration's policy (or rather lack of policy) towards the crisis in the railroad industry. The normally sensible Commerce department official to whom the question is addressed turns dough-faced with alarm, and reprovingly replies: "That's a question you'll have to ask the Secretary." Of course you do not ask men of Cabinet rank to answer such a routine question. Of course you can get the answer somewhere else, by enough hard work. But since it is often necessary to fight, now-adays, to get answers to questions of the most routine sort, a novel additional handicap is imposed on every political reporter. This handicap automatically reduces, at least by a little, the amount the people learn about the people's business from the men and women who hold a watching brief.

On the other hand—and much more important—the staggering growth of the governmental organisms with defense and foreign policy responsibilities is only one part of a larger process of general growth. It has been partly necessary, partly inflationary, and it seems to be wholly irreversible. But this growth of government has not been paralleled by any comparable growth of reportorial range. On the contrary, the domestic political range of the average reporter has been progressively restricted, mainly because of the need to spend a great deal of time on foreign policy and defense questions. If he tries to keep abreast of defense and foreign policy and the main doings of the Congress, any reporter is bound to have only a limited amount of time left over for the domestic politics and policies of the executive branch. It does not greatly matter, either, that some newspapers and all the press associations maintain large Washington bureaus, with a multiplicity of reporters. The newspapers themselves suffer from much the same limitation that a single reporter suffers from. Their front pages, like his head, can only carry a restricted number of subjects; and their readers can only be induced to take an interest in a restricted number of subjects. So the multiplication of specialists in the great news bureaus does not proportionally increase the range of information that reaches the general public. The big stories about the executive branch are nowadays pretty well limited to news of the White House, plus news of any matter of special current interest, such as the government's response to the recession or the more recent case of Sherman Adams and his vicuna coat.

Long before the war, to be sure, ordinary Washington reporters had ceased to pass the moss-grown portals of the Interstate Commerce Commission, or to try to understand the antique, moss-grown tangle of ICC rules and regulations. Coverage of the ICC had been virtually abandoned before Hoover's time, except by the trade papers of the transportation industry. There were other such agencies, too. Today, however, all the great regulatory agencies and even a majority of the Cabinet Departments have almost sunk to the status of the ICC. There is no part of the American government, of course, that is not closely watched by some journal or other. But these journals are customarily supported by and written for the special interests immediately affected by the agencies they watch. So they hardly give the agencies they watch the sense of constant and alarming surveillance by the stern, collective eye of the American people.

In our opinion, this is an acutely dangerous development. In a democratic society especially, unwatched politicians are always untrustworthy politicians. Many politicians and officials who are now un-watched carry responsibilities of the most profound importance to the national future, such as the responsibility for national resources policy. The politicians' appointments have often been pay-offs for campaign contributions from the special interests that stand to lose or gain vast sums of money by their decisions on policy. In any case, the politicians are always subject to the most massive and continuous pressures from these special interests; and their responses to these pressures are seldom generally observed. Grave damage to the national interest is bound to result from this situation. The damage will not be averted, either, by an occasional Harris investigation, that explodes the unearthly self-righteousness of a Sherman Adams and then comes to a satisfied end. As we have remarked, the problem cannot be solved by extending the range of newspaper coverage to its former limits. Newspapers must give priority to the subjects of most pressing import; and H-bombs, unhappily, are more pressingly important than the management of the nation's grazing lands. So ways will have to be found to make it safer not to watch these huge governmental areas in which, nowadays, special interests and political appointees play a perpetual private game together. One obvious remedy is a thorough reform of the American civil service, to provide really qualified administrative and expert branches. After that, the civil service system can be extended to the commissionerships that are now so often passed out as pay-offs for campaign contributions from the very interests the commissions are intended to regulate.

If not this way, then some other way over the difficulty will surely be found in the end. One can be sure of that, because the marvellous adaptability of the American political system is the greatest single lesson one learns from any long experience as a political reporter. Even nowadays, when the American government is so much more prim, the appearance it presents is not always re-assuring. In the bohemian-Rooseveltian past, the appearance was so appalling that some people could never look beyond the surface; *that* alone blinded them with horror. There was a British Minister once, a Christian Scientist and a remarkably fat-headed man, of whom it was told that he only got through his day's dealings with the American government by giving himself a Coué course while he shaved. "It isn't there, it isn't there, it isn't there, it really can't be so!" he was reputed to mutter to himself encouragingly. And so he would go out to confront the horror of the U. S. Government anew, with renewed hope that it might not be so horrible; and by the day's end he would come home again in a state of total collapse, hardly able to raise a reviving glass to his pale lips.

But anyone who wants to understand government in America, and above all any serious political reporter, must always try to look beneath the surface disorder and see the strange but relatively orderly process that goes on beneath the surface. This is not easy to do, either, because the divergence between theory and practice is greater in the American government than in any other known to these reporters.

Beginning at the very beginning, consider our proud boast that we are the most ancient of the world's political societies operating under a written constitution. It sounds very fine, but it is a phony boast, for the quite simple reason that since the Bill of Rights, an actual majority of the most significant amendments of our constitution have been unwritten. The Justices of the Supreme Court cannot cite Andrew Jackson in their opinions, yet he was, in his own person, an un-written amendment. The revered founders thought that political parties (which they called "factions") were sinister and undesirable. The clearest safeguards against this "curse of faction"—most notably the clauses setting up the curious machinery of the electoral college—were included in the constitution. But a party system had begun to exist in embryo by the time Thomas Jefferson took office. Andrew Jackson, who blithely threw all the Federalist hold-overs out of the government departments, brought to birth the American party system as it has existed ever since his time.

The civil war was another un-written amendment. It settled for good and all the relationship between the states and the federal government; and the settlement was quite different from the careful equilibrium certainly intended by most of the founders. The 14th and other post-civil war amendments do not so much as mention this settlement. Yet after Appomattox any further talk about state's rights has always been mere empty theorizing. It was then established that the federal government would always prevail over the state governments whenever any conflict arose between the states and the center; and this result will not be altered by all the pompous prating of businessmen whose lobbyists control our often remarkably corrupt state legislatures.

Still another un-written amendment, and the most curious of all, was Franklin Roosevelt's court bill. The bill did not even pass; but it none the less radically altered the relationship between the three coordinate governing branches. Never again, one can be pretty confident, will the judicial branch claim real equality with the executive and legislative branches, except in its own wisely reserved field of safeguarding the personal rights and freedoms guaranteed by the Bill of Rights and unchallengeable by either President or Congress. As these words are written, moreover, a fourth un-written amendment is gradually crystallizing out of past precedents and current practices. It deserves to be called the Vandenberg amendment, for it was Arthur Vandenberg, that flawed great man, with his vanity, his great kindness and his genuine largeness of heart and view, who first made possible the so-called bi-partisan foreign policy. "By-partisanship" is a misnomer for the vital constitutional innovation that had its origin in the partnership of Arthur Vandenberg and James F. Byrnes. The change that began in those days was no mere suspension of partisan contest on questions of foreign and defense policy. There was no such suspension. The more extreme partisans, like Robert A. Taft and William F. Knowland, always carried on the partisan contest, and they always will. The real innovation was the general acceptance of a quite new convention, that the Congress and the executive must try very hard to forget their natural differences, and must make very great efforts to work together, in close, continuous, national-minded collaboration, on all matters touching our defense and foreign relations. In fact "Bi-partisanship" was and is really another change in the relations between the governing branches. This further alteration of the coordinate branches' relationship seemed fragile at first, but it is being proved surprisingly durable by the test of time. It is a most significant phenomenon, a most far-reaching change, and we have not seen the end of it.

"Things are not what they seem," is the great law of American politics, as the never-noticed story of the un-written amendments of our written constitution rather plainly proves. The law applies, moreover, to every department of our political process. The National Security Council, for instance, is supposed to be the highest policy-making organ of the executive branch; but under the Eisenhower administration particularly, the NSC has clearly become the most important non-policy-making organ in the modern world. It not only fails to make policy itself; it also impedes policy-making by those officers of the government who really might do their jobs if they were given half a chance.

The reason for this is simple. The NSC machinery, expanded by Eisenhower to Rube Goldberg dimensions, makes a loud, awe-inspiring, clanking noise. In profound secrecy, but with infinite effort, the NSC papers are ground out. The immense numbers of man-hours spent in committee meetings of every sort, the long battles that take place over the language of the draft documents, the august rank of the personalities who finally gather at the council table—all these combine to give everyone concerned the happy illusion that decisions of inestimable national importance are being taken by the NSC. We have never seen an NSC paper. But the record plainly proves that the average NSC paper is now a decision not to decide, containing two beautiful, mutually cancelling clauses—"No. I, On this subject, as always, the United States must have its cake," and "No. II, On this subject, as always, the United States must eat its cake." Thus the really major policy decisions are in fact made, higgledy piggledy and hugger-mugger, under the sudden, ruthless pressure of events. Or they are made without any special regard to national interest, because of the personal outlook of the chief men in government, like the Eisenhower administration's central and desperately dangerous decision to abandon the hard struggle to maintain the world balance of power for the sake of lower taxes and an intermittently balanced budget.

If things are not what they seem in the executive branch, they are even less what they seem in the Congress, which most people fondly or unfondly regard as a legislative body. Legislating, in the normal sense of the word, is the act of devising legislation; and this is just what our Congress does not and cannot do. In the simpler past, Congress did indeed legislate. As late as the first Roosevelt's term, the great enactments customarily originated on Capitol Hill; and Theodore Roosevelt's close friend, the first Senator Lodge, once read the White House a sharp lecture for daring to send a ready-written bill up to the Hill. But all that ended, for good or ill, in the term of the second Roosevelt. At the beginning of his 100 days, his first banking act was introduced and passed in the House of Representatives in the form of a roll of newspaper, because the draft of the law prepared by the White House had not yet been properly engrossed.

In the years since then, the Taft-Hartley law has been just about the only truly major statute, importantly affecting the design of American life, that has wholly originated in the Congress, without any guiding or stimulating impulse from the executive branch. Congress has in fact become an organ that is in some way comparable to the French *parlements* in the time of the monarchy—or comparable, rather, to what the *parlements* were in theory but never were in practice. On almost all major questions, the role of Congress is to receive legislation from the executive; to make representations concerning the proposed legislation, in conformity with public opinion; to amend the proposed legislation as the trend of opinion requires; and finally to register or reject the proposed legislation as the majority may desire.

Congress, in other words, does not initiate policy, as the House of Commons may be said to initiate policy through the leaders of its majority. Congress adapts, adopts or rejects the policies initiated by the executive. Its role is female; the executive has the male role. You may like this situation or you may be horrified by it, but you cannot alter it, because the changed role of Congress is another natural result of the dubious process that we strangely call progress. Even in the days of the first Senator Lodge, the problems confronting the nation were not too complex for the average man—which means for the ordinary Senator or Representative. With its battalions of lawyers to do the drafting, the Congress in those days could and did propose its own solutions for those problems. But now the problems have grown infinitely too complex, because our society has grown too complex. So the Congress today must let the executive branch study the problems and propose the solutions; and after the executive has proposed, the Congress duly adapts, adopts or rejects the proposal. Thus we have come to have what may be called a fully Presidential system of government. With a strong President it is an excellent system; but it can hardly be said to work at all, in the difficult conditions of this gloomy age of ours, when the man in the White House is weak of will or mind or even weak of body.

There, in our opinion, is the potential Achilles heel of the American democracy. If you have attended many Presidential conventions (and we cannot forget about them in this essay on political reporting), you may wonder why its Achilles heel has not brought the system down already. Nothing on earth is quite so exhilarating, quite so stirring as one of these strange quadrennial festivals of ours. You cannot understand them at all unless you remember the "Golden Bough"—the Year-King waiting at the stone of sacrifice; the first glimmer of the mid-summer sun; the quick plunge of the mistletoe knife and the sudden gush of the Year-King's blood that guarantees the richness of the land; the wild orgy in the fields to encourage nature's fruitfulness by the magic of example; and the choice of the new Year-King to carry the burden for another twelvemonth. It was Alice Longworth, once again, who offered this comparison to explain the peculiar atmosphere of fervency, excitement and abandon that pervades every Presidential convention. In a way, we do indeed treat our Presidents as the men of the past treated their Sacred Kings, holding them magically responsible for the prosperity of the land. And our system of choosing them, with all its excitement and fascination, is not much more logical than the "Golden Bough" system—choosing the winner of a foot-race of red-headed youths as the doomed but glorious King-of-the-Year-to-Come.

Precisely because of the fervency and abandon of these astonishing occasions, reporting Presidential conventions is at least immensely entertaining. Formerly, however, we felt very differently about reporting Presidential campaigns. In the first place, there is no pleasure in the traditional method, which is to traipse from state to state, gloomily interviewing professionally mendacious local politicians, and then trying to forecast the state-by-state results by guessing the right discount for each man's mendacity. In the second place, we have learned by harsh experience that the behavior of American voters at any given moment is a great deal harder to predict than the behavior of the tides of history. We have made many mistakes—all newspapermen do, if only because they have such innumerable opportunities for error. But the two worst mistakes we have ever made were predictions of voting behavior. The first was in 1948, when the older member of our partnership insisted on assuming that Thomas E. Dewey would surely be elected. The second was four years later, when Senator Estes Kefauver ran against President Truman in the New Hampshire primary; and the younger partner wrote off Kefauver as a hopelessly lost cause just before Kefauver scored a signal triumph.

After that, we stopped making positive and unqualified election predictions, at any time, anywhere. But the least a reporter can do is to try to find out the trend, in elections as in other matters. So we invented a novel system, that gives interesting indications of voting trends yet permits the reporter to deal only in hard facts, collected by the expenditure of energy and shoe-leather. The system, which the younger member of our partnership first thought of, is simply to imitate the professional pollsters, and sometimes even to join pollster friends on their rounds. This direct sampling of large and (one hopes) representative slices of the voting mass has its own peculiar rules. You must always, for instance, carry an official looking questionnaire, as a sign of your *bona fides;* and you must never try to pass the screen door unless you are invited to enter the house. (This is the proof you are not selling anything.) If you do it rightly, an extraordinarily high percentage of the citizens you talk to are quite ready to talk frankly to you. Depending on your choice of samples, your results may or may not foretell the election's outcome. But at least your results have their own immediacy, their own richly human character derived from direct contact with great numbers of people. And when you report your results, you at least speak whereof you know.

These doorbell-ringing forays have left us more than ever mystified by the strange process that produces majority opinions in democracies like our own. On the one hand, the citizens whose doorbells you ring are so often ill-informed about the most ordinary facts, even garbling the names of the public men they must vote for at the polls. On the other hand, even the most ignorant are so often strangely and instinctively shrewd, magically and correctly picking the weak or strong spots in the characters of the very same public men whose names they get wrong. At any rate, the process generally seems to work, after a fashion. As political reporters, we must confess to what is perhaps a fault of judgment on this point. Possibly because we have always had too high a view of the role and the desserts of the United States, we began by thinking Franklin Roosevelt not altogether worthy of the country he led. Then, after Roosevelt, we found Truman unworthy by comparison with Roosevelt. And then, after Truman, we have found Eisenhower unworthy by comparison with Truman. All the same, with all the errors and all the faults and all the weaknesses that have had to be noted, we have seen the American system achieve things beyond the reach and measure and imagination of any other democracy. And it is just this that still makes political reporting a fascinating pursuit in the age of the H-bomb and the ICBM.

Perhaps the right way to sum up is with the old story of one of Mrs. Borden Harriman's famous political Sunday suppers. This particular Sunday supper took place at the envenomed peak of the Roosevelt court fight; and Mrs. Harriman had brightened the occasion by seating at the same table a very hot-tempered Justice of the court's rightwing, and a rather leftwing newspaperman who had published fairly sharp personal aspersions on the Justice. Not very long after the coffee cups were removed and the discussion began, the Justice and the newspaperman utterly and simultaneously lost their tempers. For a moment, it really appeared as though they would come to blows. But Mrs. Harriman (a genuine specimen of that rarest of creatures, "a Washington hostess") swiftly rose, casting her charming smile over the room as one might cast water upon flames. "Well," she said, beaming, "isn't it all great fun!" On this note, the drama ended.

The reader of our political columns may perhaps suspect that it has not always been great fun for us. But it has. The truth is, thank God, we like a fight.

III

Foreign Reporting

Nowadays, IF YOU ARE A REPORTER writing about national affairs, you can hardly avoid writing about foreign affairs too. The foreign relations of the United States now influence just about every internal relationship. They dominate the budget. They make or break the reputations of the most conspicuous men in government. They are the subject of tense, continuous negotiations between the White House and the Congress. From time to time, they even intimately affect the pattern of our purely domestic politics. Dwight D. Eisenhower was of course quite right, for instance, when he rather vaguely remarked that he "guessed he had become a candidate" because Robert A. Taft was an isolationist. And if Taft had not been an isolationist, he would surely have been the Republican Presidential nominee in 1952.

In these circumstances—in themselves the mark of a revolutionary change in our national situation—any Washington correspondent who tries to do a comprehensive job is really compelled to write about our foreign policy and its problems. A good many Washington correspondents still do this the painless way, by reporting official Washington's information and opinion about developments abroad and their meaning to the United States. But we have never done it the painless way, for the best of causes. The senior member of our partnership tested the system extensively, and finally discovered its total unreliability, in the period between Munich and his wartime service overseas. It just did not work, yet he had many advantages when he tested it.

In that time of American innocence, a bold reporter could quite easily play a certain role in major national policy decisions. Being bold, or perhaps one should say presumptuous, he played such a role in more than one fairly significant decision, like the decision to make the first big loan to the Chinese National Government. Hence he became an insider as well as a reporter. He was accepted as an advisor by Dr. T. V. Soong.* He was in frequent touch with all the American governmental experts on China. He was involved, in one way or another, in most of the arguments and intrigues from which our wartime China policy (or pseudo-policy) rather haphazardly evolved. In addition, he dutifully read all the available literature on China's current problems. So he wrote about these problems, and about America's proper approach to them, with lordly self-confidence throughout 1940 and the first months of 1941.

To this day, for that very reason, he cannot recall his arrival on the actual Chinese scene without a prickle of mingled excitement and intense shame. The time was the late spring before Pearl Harbor. The Japanese already held a wide strip of territory between Hong Kong and Chiang Kai-shek's wartime capital in the far interior. So the plane to Chungking flew out of Hong Kong in darkness, in order to avoid the Japanese ack-ack; it droned on for hours through the night; and then, at first light, the deep gorge of the Yangtsze river was revealed, far below, through a tear in the mist that veiled the land. The plane plunged through the tear in the mist, and side-slipped into the gorge itself. It flew breathlessly onward between the high cliffs above the turbid river, and it finally landed on a tiny, stone-paved island in midstream. Some years later, when he made the same landing, the great General H. H. Arnold emerged from his aircraft shouting indignant orders that the island-airfield must be instantly condemned as "unfit for any landing at any time." Yet thousands of safe landings were made there by the buccaneering American and Chinese pilots of Chiang Kai-shek's civilian airline.

* Then the Generalissimo's personal representative in Washington, later Foreign Minister of China.

If the arrival was a sharp surprise to the self-appointed China expert, everything that followed the ascent into the dirty, bomb-scarred, ant-hill city was even more surprising. The surprises culminated the same evening, at dinner with that brave, complex, strange man (born out of his time, for he should have been one of the court-and-cabinet diplomats of the eighteenth century) the British Ambassador to China, Sir Archibald Clark-Kerr.* The whole picture of the long-ago evening remains sharp in the mind's eye in all details—the table under the stars, with the fireflies hovering above the lamps; the white-gowned servants, ghostly in the heavy scented night-time garden; the strained look on the face of a tired guest who correctly forecast "a bad bombing day tomorrow"; and the puckish answering grin of Archie Clark-Kerr who was one of those rare men with a positive liking for danger. But far more vivid still is the remembered sense of humiliation, the sense of having been a pompous, presumptuous ass. This shame began, and gained power, and grew utterly overwhelming, as the chance remarks at the dinner table progressively showed up as purest drivel everything that had been written about China with such lordly self-confidence.

At that very instant, in that garden on the hill above Chungking, the first rule of our postwar partnership originated. It has taken both of us around the world more times than we have counted. It has led us into the Indochinese *brousse,* and a sampan on the River Mekong, and a hotel in mid-winter Siberia where the massive, felt-booted maid-servants used hatchets to clean the outdoor plumbing, and a lot of other unconventional places, as well as all the usual ports of call. "Go see for yourself" was this rule that we adopted at the outset. We followed it to the end of our partnership; and even now, when we are going our separate ways, we like to think that we still follow it.

It may seem odd, it may perhaps seem almost as presumptuous as writing about China without going there, for Washington correspondents to try to function as foreign correspondents too. But at least going there is always immeasurably better than not going there. In order to go there more continuously, one of us became a permanent foreign correspondent for a while, after Suez insured a sort of chain-reaction of crises overseas. And even when we were both just ducking in and out—spending three weeks in London, and a week in Bangkok, and ten days in Djakarta, and a fortnight in Teheran, and another fortnight

* Later Lord Inverchapel, and successively ambassador to Moscow and Washington.

in Bonn—it was neither an odd thing to do, nor a presumptuous thing to do.

In the first place, there is the curious phenomenon of the weather in the streets, as we like to call it. It is not easy to explain, but it is a wholly real phenomenon. Go smell the weather in the streets. Go spend no more than a few hours in the midst of a foreign situation you have minutely studied at long range. Suddenly, even before you can consult the local experts, or call on the ambassador, or interview the prime minister, the whole outline of the situation begins to change in your own mind, simply because the weather in the streets has an altogether unexpected smell. Perhaps this happens to us because we have overly concrete minds. We are both sadly incapable of dealing with large abstractions, or imagining landscapes and people we have not seen ourselves. Yet we privately suspect that all really unfamiliar situations overseas come under the heading of the famous joke that Charles E. Bohlen once aimed at the Russian-experts-by-remote-control: "The Soviet Union is like the act of love. You can read and memorize every page of all the literature about it. But you can't possibly tell what it's really like, until you've experienced it yourself."

We do not mean, for one moment, that just smelling the weather in the streets of a city halfway round the world permits a reporter to write intelligently about what is happening in that city. Reporting abroad in fact demands very much harder work than reporting in Washington. Just getting there is bad enough. The most agreeable form of transportation that either of us has ever experienced was the sedan chair, with eight bearers, in which one of us once did a rural jaunt in the Szechuan hills—a jaunt that was like a marvellous journey through a Chinese landscape painting, with endless, richly human incident to set off the landscape. By the same token, the least agreeable form of transportation is quite certainly the airplane, which reporters in a hurry always have to take.

The trouble with airplanes is not that they are dangerous—although the younger member of our partnership still rather queasily remembers a certain moment in small and antiquated aircraft flying above thick cloud over the terrible mountains on the way to Teheran. At this too-well remembered moment, the mustachioed ex-RAF pilot cheerily announced to his passengers, "I say you chaps, I'm afraid I don't see how we can get down through this soup; we'll just have to risk hitting a mountain, you know." The eyes of the passengers, behind their oxygen masks, looked like the eyes of terrified owls as the plane plunged blindly into the rock-filled soup. Anyone who flies a great deal and often visits rather out-of-the-way places, is bound to have such owl-eyed, goose-pimply moments. Yet these moments are rare; and the real trouble with airplanes is simply that travelling in them is infinitely boring, inexplicably exhausting and somehow both physically and spiritually rumpling. Possibly this is because air travel begins and ends at airports. Both of us are convinced that when we go to our eternal punishments, we shall find ourselves eternally wait-listed in one airport or another. One of us foresees his condemnation to the airport at Ryadh, in Saudi Arabia; the other thinks that *his* particular, private Hell will be a certain airport in Greece. The daily, extra turn of the screw that makes the sinner really scream will be the long-prayed for announcement that the flight is ready, followed by that other so-often-heard announcement, after the passengers are all in their seats, that "there will be a slight delay owing to mechanical causes."

But reporters share this always boring, always rumpling experience of endlessly getting there by air, only to depart again, with members of other trades such as commercial travellers. The real reportorial work begins when you have got there, and have smelled the weather in the streets, and must decide how you are going to tackle the new situation that lies before you. In the jargon of our partnership, the two possible approaches are called the worm's-eye view approach, and the synthesizing approach. The worm's-eye view approach is mainly useful for events of an essentially dramatic character, such as wars, civil conflicts, and the like. It consists, quite simply, of going out, getting yourself involved in the event, and then describing what you have seen.

For middle-aged persons, this can be rather taxing, as suggested in the already-related story of a jungle patrol in Malaya. But most often it is also strangely and wonderfully exhilarating. It is exhilarating because you escape into intense experience from the petty political round, the only half-human life of capital cities that are the normal news centers. We have both felt the same exhilaration (often mixed with the most lively apprehension), whether at the front in Korea, or in a canal-boat sluggishly traversing a Communist-controlled province of Indo-China, or even among the wolfish horrors of the guerilla war that freed Morocco. What you see is not always pretty. Some experiences, in honest truth, are so horrible that they cause a deep depression, like the massacre at Oued Zem. It was not easy to forget the burned and mutilated corpses, lying twisted in strange attitudes along the squalid blood-stained streets, which seemed to mean nothing but another dull, unnecessary proof of man's essential inhumanity to man. But unless the horrors are very horrible indeed, or you are very frightened indeed, any escape into intense experience will somehow make all life's colors, light and dark, seem richer, stronger and more magnificent. It will make your companions of the moment, whether good men or bad, take on an extra, almost always endearing, human dimension. And it will usually leave you something you like to remember—often something odd, unexpected and tinged with irony, but still well worth remembering.

Irony, we both fear, is memory's best fixative. Why else should the single most vivid memory of the Korean fighting be the long, leisurely and deeply moving conversation with a young marine officer, all about life's meaning and which first things to put first, during the long, lumbering journey in an Amtrac to the crossing of the River Han? (We were so serious, because we thought the river-crossing on the way to Seoul would be a very nasty business, which it was not. The conversation ended, as the Amtrac wallowed into the Han, with a pressing invitation to the officer to bring his family to stay in Washington, "when all this is over, if we both last that long." So the eventual sequel was three days of unaccustomed but surprisingly pleasant baby-sitting by an amateur uncle.) And again, if irony is not the strongest fixative, why should the most vivid memory of the Indo-Chinese canal trip be the other passengers' roars of delighted laughter, because of the not abnormally thick hair on a Westerner's bare legs? (The joke was bawdy. The smooth-skinned Vietnamese think hairy legs are a sign of tigerish passions. But the shared joke made us all friends; and this was just as well. The friendly public opinion on the canal boat later persuaded the Communist police to accept a Viet-minh *laissez-passer* which the reporter had just learned was a gross forgery.)

Yet every newspaperman who has often taken the worms'-eye view approach to great events has quite enough memories, both stirring and ironical, to make him the prize bore of any club on earth. We must resist the temptations of recollection. We must try to describe the other approach, which a reporter more often has to choose when he arrives in a strange but news-filled place. We call it the synthesizing approach because it is just that.

Except for a few who spend years on end in their chosen countries, reporters abroad cannot know of their own knowledge, or understand with their own understanding. They can describe what they see with their own eyes, whether it is a street fight or a coronation. But they cannot themselves instinctively trace the complex interplay of forces in a foreign land that may produce the street fight, or cause one ruler to abdicate and another to be crowned. Hence any serious foreign correspondent has to synthesize the best on-the-spot opinion he can get. This means, in effect, talking to all your own country's experts on the scene, in the embassy particularly, and among other foreign correspondents if you are a ducker-in-and-out. It means talking to other foreign experts, among whom the most rewarding are most often found in the British embassy. It means, above all, talking to as many of the local political leaders of all parties, and local journalists of all viewpoints, and other influential and representative people, as you can induce to talk to you.

It is this last requirement that makes reporting abroad such re-morselessly hard work, especially for a ducker-in-and-out struggling to see everyone who counts in a week or ten days—which is all the time you may have in a small country. Talking with the men who count is by no means easy. It is surprisingly depleting, both intel-lectually and even physically, to try to make some sort of human contact, to try for some sort of shock of mind against mind, with four or five or six total strangers a day for many days on end. But this part of the process offers the immense compensating excitement that good detectives must also feel. What is really tiring is simply making appointments to see the men who count. The reporter's trade would be pretty nearly ideal, as trades go, if it were just possible to have all necessary appointments supernaturally arranged in advance, and if one could only get from place to place by magic carpet. But one can-not do this, so one hangs on the wretched telephone, and writes polite little notes, and smiles to *chefs de cabinet;* and finally the Prime Minister, the Finance Minister and the Foreign Minister all grant interviews at the same hour on the same day, which happens to be just one day after the best plane leaves for the next reportorial port of call. (This is almost invariable in small countries; the larger and more important the country, the easier it is to arrange appointments in an orderly manner, possibly because politicians and officials of large important nations do not feel the same need to underline their own importance.)

In the later years of our partnership, particularly, we were better off than most other reporters in this matter of getting to see the men who count. For one thing, most foreign correspondents in Washington have a habit of quoting American newspaper opinion at length; and as our column was rather often quoted, our names became known abroad. For another thing, we have always been given a most flattering build-up by the Kremlin, being attacked by name by the Soviet representatives at the United Nations, repeatedly denounced as leading Fascist beasts by the Soviet press and radio, and so on and on. Even behind the iron curtain, this was a big help; for there we had the curiosity value of itinerant monsters, and supposedly influential monsters at that.

Oddly enough, the very fact that we *were* duckers-in-and-out was often advantageous to us, too. More permanently stationed foreign correspondents cannot use the argument that they must leave next Tuesday, in order to achieve a complete spectrum of appointments and thus gather a complete spectrum of opinion, within the space of a week or two. We could do just that. Furthermore, if we were lucky in our timing, we might therefore find ourselves talking with the men who counted at a moment of crisis, and so we might be the first to spot a major turning point. In just this manner, the junior member of our partnership ducked briefly into Athens in 1947. He came out with the information that the British were transferring to the United States the whole burden of supporting the cause of freedom in Greece and Turkey—the information that forecast the Greek-Turkish aid bill and the entire subsequent development of a new system of American foreign relations.

That was very important information indeed. But it was information of a perfectly hard, factual character, which could be reported without a qualm of doubt. Getting that kind of information is a matter of luck, plus perseverance in questioning, plus the shrewdness that is needed to go where the news may be. In some ways, it is rather more difficult to get the other kind of news that the reporter overseas must also look for —the broad, non-factual estimate of a situation that may, in itself, foretell developments just as important as the hard fact of the British decision about Greece and Turkey. Estimating any situations—particularly foreign situations—with complete accuracy is of course impossible. But in our experience, if you work like a nailer to see everyone imaginable who may have something significant to say, and if you make an intelligent synthesis of all that is said, you can generally make a situation-estimate that will be accurate for about four months. If you come back to the same country six months later, the situation will quite surely have changed, sometimes subtly, sometimes very radically, and always unforeseeably. After six months, you must expect to be surprised and quite possibly astonished. But you can venture to call the turn at three or four months' range with a fair measure of confidence—always presuming you have done your legwork first.

Calling the turn in this manner of course requires the exercise of independent judgment. This is all the more true nowadays, since the Eisenhower administration has either driven out, or silenced, or exiled the great majority of the more tough-minded members of the American foreign service. Nowadays, in most American embassies, the best you can hope for is a briefing on the routine facts of the local problems, which is useful of course. But you must also expect the average Eisenhower-Dulles ambassador and all his staff to be hoping for the best without preparing for the worst, in flattering imitation of their masters in Washington. There are times, moreover, when you have to go beyond making allowances for the shocking effects of our foreign service of John Foster Dulles' blackmail-payments to the late Joseph R. McCarthy. Sometimes, indeed, you have to call the turn in defiance of the judgment of men on the spot whom you know well and would normally trust. This happened to the older member of our partnership when he reached Paris at Christmas time in the sad winter of Dienbienphu.

To be sure, he had seen what his friends among the American correspondents and the U. S. embassy officials in Paris had not seen. He had just passed a month in Saigon and at the front in Indo-China, and he had seen that the unending French effort against the Vietnamese Communists was nearing the exhaustion-point. He was privately convinced that the exhaustion-point would occur rather soon, unless the United States came to France's aid with men and ships and planes, as well as the money and material that were already being provided. No French politician in power had as yet even hinted at such a possibility, and all American observers in Paris believed that the French would stumble on indefinitely, without thought of giving up. There was a further complication, too. The State Department had virtually commanded our embassy in Saigon to emphasize the positive in all its reports. Hence the normally capable staff of the Paris embassy had been grossly misled about the gravity of the situation by reports from Saigon that were much too optimistic; and the embassy staff had in turn misled the resident American correspondents.

In these tangled and obfuscating circumstances, the then-Foreign Minister, Georges Bidault, sent for the reporter. Bidault spontaneously admitted, with great emphasis, that France would indeed have to abandon the Indo-Chinese struggle within a few months, unless the United States proved willing to intervene on the ground. When published, the interview with Bidault caused consternation in Washington. The Eisenhower administration had been complacently relying on the French to protect Southeast Asia against the inevitable consequences of our own acceptance of concealed defeat in Korea. Telegrams flew back and forth between Washington and Paris. Bidault had in fact used the reporter to tell the American government unofficially what he dared not say officially, because he was not ready to face the domestic political repercussions of an official communication. He now blandly explained that the whole trouble had arisen because of the reporter's bad French—which may not be very good, but was quite good enough to understand Bidault making the same flat, unadorned statement four times over. This explanation was primarily intended to protect Bidault from political attack at home. Meanwhile, Bidault of course expected the American authorities to question the reporter closely about what had passed during the interview, and to draw the necessary conclusions. No such inquiry was ever made. The Embassy in Paris accepted Bidault's explanation with happy relief.

Even the best resident American correspondents in Paris joined the embassy in knocking down the story—because reporters do not like being beaten. The State Department also swallowed the Bidault explanation with open cries of joy—entirely because the State Department was desperately anxious to avoid hard fact-facing concerning Indo-China. When the reporter got back to Washington, he encountered many a smug, patronizing smile and many a joke about his linguistic failings, which was more than a little irritating. It was no consolation, either, when the forecast of the Bidault interview was substantiated, in all its unhappy details, within the short, predicted space of three months.

That incident left some personal scars that have not healed to this day. But if you are very lucky indeed, you may sometimes make friends because you have called the turn correctly. That happened to one of us in the spring before the Korean attack. At that time, we were both passionately convinced that the Soviets would be tempted into some sort of aggression by the feckless disarmament of the West, for which President Truman and Secretary of Defense Louis A. Johnson must bear the chief responsibility. The reporter therefore turned up in London in a state of near-obsession with the problems of Western defense. In London, as in Washington, almost no one was then interested in those problems. Most of the scores of British leaders and officials whom the reporter saw were either bored, or amazed, or downright amused by his ingeminations. There were just three wonderfully contrasting exceptions.

The first and most astonishing was the Prime Minister. Of all the trying reportorial experiences either of us has ever had, an average interview with Clement Attlee must surely lead the list, not because he is inhuman or un-cordial or arrogant, but simply because he is the one politician either of us has ever met who really seems to dislike the sound of the human voice when uttered by himself. Of course you do not go to see the Prime Minister of England in the expectation of a jolly chat. It is fairly intimidating to be received in the long Cabinet Room at No. 10 Downing, with half of the most majestic ghosts in the history of the English-speaking peoples seeming to gibber in the corners, and the portrait of Sir Robert Walpole above the fireplace, in his place of honor behind his successor's special chair. Moreover, Prime Ministers tend to be rather busy men, so you go to your appointment with not more than four carefully prepared questions which you regard as especially important. On two previous occasions, the result of this approach to Attlee had been really comically extraordinary. He would receive his caller with extreme pleasantness. He would sit back in his chair, as though to indicate that he was ready for questions, meanwhile smoking his pipe so fiercely that loud, guggling, noises were emitted from time to time. The first question would be asked. The pipe would be removed from the clenched jaws just long enough to permit some non-committal monosyllable, such as "Quite," to pass the Prime Minister's lips. Then the jaws would clench again, the guggling would continue through the next, more nervously stated question, and the whole frustrating performance would be repeated. After four repetitions of this surrealist dialogue of "Question— Guggle, Guggle—Quite," the caller would thank the Prime Minister, who would say a most cordial farewell, always asking for another visit; and so the interview would end.

On that bright spring morning not very long before the attack in Korea, just the same dialogue was again repeated three times over. But the fourth time, the reporter merely used the phrase "Western defense," and the result was like bursting the bung of a barrel. Out came the pipe for good and all; and the Prime Minister launched into an eloquent, closely informed discussion of Western defense and its weaknesses, the risks that these created, the remedies that should be applied, and the need for America "to give a lead," because Britain, with her strained finances, could not give "the lead I'd like to give." Before the end, private secretaries were popping into the room to see what on earth had happened, only to be waved away again by a Prime Minister too absorbed in his subject to worry about his next appointment.

One could not, after that, claim the Prime Minister as a friend; but one could at least appreciate the stoutness of spirit, the sturdy good sense, the tough-minded willingness to face up to unpleasant facts, that make Lord Attlee a big man; and after that the other Attlee interviews were at least a little easier. And in the same fashion, on that same spring visit to London, three true and valued friendships happily originated.

The first rather oddly began in the cavernous recesses of the Reform Club. In those chill halls a sort of spontaneous two-man rally in favor of Western defense, not completed until the end of an entire bottle of port, was held by the reporter and Sir Robert Hall, a rare Treasury official who can look beyond the Treasury's narrow, penny-pinching interests. The second friendship began at Hatfield, that great house of a great man where both of us have known much kindness. At Hatfield, during a long weekend, the reporter was first allowed to glimpse the singularly powerful and original mind that Antony Head* usually hides from the world behind his mask of easy charm. Once again, a common interest in Western defense was the cause of this unmasking. As for the third of these friendships born of happy chance and gloomy foresight, it started in the grandiose office of the Chancellor of the Exchequer, when Hugh Gaitskell all but laughed the reporter out of the room for his nightmarish pre-occupations. Later on,

* Later Secretary of State for War; later still, Defense Minister; now, alas, out of office.

when the Korean attack was launched, and Gaitskell had risen to the challenge with admirable courage, he concluded, quite wrongly, that he had perhaps been rude. The Chancellor therefore wrote the reporter a most generous letter that would have made any man his friend.

In truth, sheer luck plays a great role in a reporter's meetings with the movers and shakers of this world, and sometimes you must be very patient while you wait for the luck to turn. The younger member of our partnership too well remembers an interview with Jawaharlal Nehru, which turned out like the Attlee interview above-described, but was much more disconcerting at the outset. It was just before the monsoons, when Delhi's horrible heat is at its worst. Nehru does not possess Attlee's unfailing politeness. He simply lay back on a sofa in an exhausted attitude, smoking a cigarette in a holder, and answering question after carefully prepared question with an openly, even arrogantly bored "Yes" or "No," and once with "Does it really matter?" But finally the reporter asked Nehru about the conflict between Communism and Asian nationalism. That opened the flood-gates for fair. Nehru forgot the heat, sat straight up, and talked passionately for almost an hour, with a profound perceptiveness that his subsequent public statements have not always shown.

Looking backwards, it is hard to know which kind of luck to value more—the occasional and special luck of *getting through* to a remarkable mind like Nehru's, or the continuous and general luck of seeing our own country respond to the challenge of world leadership, and being, in our own small way, involved in this great process of America's response. We were arguing about it, just before these words were written, and at first we were inclined to think that our most singular good fortune was to have seen at close hand just about all the greatest leaders, good and evil, wise and lunatic, of just about the whole postwar world except Communist China. Their images are still vivid in our minds:

Nikita Khrushchev, with his small shrewd eyes and his three prominent wens, acting the jovial clown at a party, and then during a long two-hour interview, always serious, impressively intelligent, obviously tough, obviously a gambler, and frighteningly limited in his view of the outside world. Adenauer, "der Alte," with his almost saurian face and his wisely precise answers. Charles De Gaulle, out of power, a seeming has-been, glumly but eloquently predicting the course of events in France almost precisely as they have since transpired. General MacArthur, striding up and down in his tacky office, corn cob pipe in hand, orating to the embarrassed reporter as to an audience of millions—and then, with a thrust of his pipe and a "You get me?" settling down in a chair and talking with the simple shrewdness of a country lawyer. Old Mossadeq, seeking to play the role of Sampson in the Iranian temple, lying in an unmade bed in rather dirty striped pajamas, alternately giggling at the dangers he invited and weeping to think how the wicked world misunderstood him. Marshal Tito, shrewd, courageous, and quite exceptionally impressive despite his irrepressible fondness for rich personal upholstery. But the list of great and famous faces we have seen could be prolonged indefinitely; and our argument about the best part of our luck ended differently anyway. We concluded that all our glimpses of the great were worth less to us than the absorbing spectacle of our own country's performance, in circumstances wholly novel to every American who came to maturity before or even during the second world war.

God knows, it has not been a perfect performance by any means. It could not have been. The second world war left America with an awe-inspiring world responsibility; and aside from the geography lessons learned in the war, America did not even know where the rest of the world was. In 1945, Tarawa, for most Americans, was infinitely easier to place on their mental maps than the crucial Korean peninsula, concerning which decisions of the most far-reaching consequence then had to be made at once. China, concerning which even greater decisions had to be taken with almost equal rapidity, was less well known on the very highest levels of the government than it had been known by the older of these reporters six months before Pearl Harbor. Great errors were inevitable, and great errors were made.

What else could one expect? Consider, for instance, the grave telegrams sent by General Albert C. Wedemeyer at the end of the year 1945. In these telegrams, the American commander in China warned that the U. S. government must almost certainly choose between all-out support for the Nationalist government or an eventual Chinese Communist victory. General Wedemeyer has subsequently said that he was surprised by the eventual response to these telegrams, which was the mission to China led by General George C. Marshall.

Yet Wedemeyer really should not have been surprised. The Secretaries of War and the Navy, Robert Patterson and James Forrestal, favored responding with a decision to give the Nationalists all-out support, while making a simultaneous all-out effort to clean up their messy government. But the Wedemeyer telegrams certainly did not invite this response. As military men will, when they think higher headquarters ought to take the ultimate responsibility, General Wedemeyer had heavily underlined the risks of the bolder of the two choices. He had said that supporting Chiang would mean involvement in a "fratricidal conflict." He had even suggested that this kind of involvement might lead to war with the Soviets in Manchuria—which was more than far-fetched, for if we had shown a bold front at that time, the Soviets would almost surely have kept their Yalta promise to support and work with the government of Chiang Kai-shek. Then too, these fairly horrifying warnings of Wedemeyer's were balanced by the recent promises of the American ambassador to China, Patrick C. Hurley, that it would be quite easy to bring the Communists and Nationalists together in peace and harmony. In addition, under violent pressure from every Representative and Senator, with Robert A. Taft in the lead, our armed forces were already beginning their pell-mell demobilization.

So James Byrnes, who can hardly be suspected of softness towards Communism, made the final decision to reject the advice of Patterson and Forrestal. It was Byrnes' decision to "get someone out (to China) to get the two sides together."* Hurley actually accepted Byrnes's commission to go back to China and bring the two sides together; but then he strangely and publicly attacked the State Department as a nest of Communists only a few hours later. The news of Hurley's attack reached Byrnes at a Cabinet meeting. The Secretary of Agriculture, Clinton Anderson, was the man who suggested that only General Marshall had the prestige now needed for the job in China. Thus Marshall was sent to China on Anderson's nomination, and with a directive faithfully reflecting the original decision of Byrnes.

From the outset, we were intensely concerned about the outcome of the Marshall mission, because one of us had spent the war in China and knew the situation there. But the Chinese situation was then about the only one that either of us knew at first hand (for you did not learn much about French politics by parachuting into France to join the *maquis*); and our own education paralleled the education of the whole American people. About Soviet purposes, we learned first from the brilliant experts the Eisenhower administration has now brushed

* The quotation is from the Forrestal diaries.

aside, Bohlen and George F. Kennan; and these men, with others like Forrestal and Averell Harriman, were also the country's first source of the truth about the Kremlin. What else we learned thereafter, we also learned as the country did. For we would always make our trips to places where a crisis threatened, and those were just the places that also focussed the national attention.

Having been intimately involved in this vast process of America getting acquainted with and beginning to respond to the rest of the world, we have a theory about the way it has worked and is still working. In brief, we think the American people begin by learning where another country is, or perhaps where other countries are. This geography lesson starts when the headlines give their opening hints of trouble ahead in a given region of our planet. Then as the trouble unfolds, our public opinion gradually sorts out the issues and the personalities. Finally—sometimes too late, as in the case of China—public opinion crystallizes with great firmness, deciding who is our friend and who is our enemy and which side of the issues we ought to be on. After that, we have a firm national policy concerning another situation that no one in America had even bothered to think about for a moment only a year or so earlier. Sometimes, moreover—again the case of the Far East comes to mind—the crystallization of opinion is almost too rigid, leaving the government insufficient room for policy maneuvers.

However the process may work, at any rate, America has often responded with magnificent boldness to the challenge of its new responsibility as leader of the cause of freedom in the world. There are many "crimes, follies and misfortunes" (Gibbon's phrase to sum up history) in the postwar American record of foreign policy-making. But we ourselves still feel about this record in a way that can best be conveyed by describing the greatest single privilege either of us has ever enjoyed. It was Sir Winston Churchill, in fact, who finely expressed our own feeling about the American performance overseas. And this highest privilege above-noted was a luncheon with the greatest leader of the West in the last half century. It was a private luncheon, but surely, after so many years, the story can now be told.

It was just after the first great American foreign policy measures— the Greek-Turkish aid bill, the Marshall plan, and the rest—had been successfully launched. Churchill was still the leader of His Majesty's opposition. The younger member of our partnership and Sir Winston's only son, Randolph Churchill, had struck up a friendship while wan-

dering about the continent together, and an invitation to lunch at
Chartwell, the Churchill country place, resulted. The luncheon turned
out to consist only of the great man, Randolph, and the reporter, and
at the beginning it was a decidedly sticky affair. Churchill was in
his siren suit, looking like an ancient, angry baby, and he was clearly
not pleased to find that an American journalist he had never seen
before had been asked to lunch with him by his son. Randolph was on
the wagon, which made him nervous. The reporter was all but struck
dumb with genuine, deep felt awe.

Before the meal, and during the entire first course, the old man said
not a word, confining his conversational efforts to an occasional eloquent grunt—which meant that the reporter, being trained in American politeness, had to force himself to make semi-hysterical conversation to fill the terrifying silence. It was a desperate business, but as
the champagne was passed, and as it appeared that the visitor was at
least harmless, the old man began to enjoy himself. He was wise, witty,
and—it must be added—malicious, by turns. Asked how he managed
to get so much literary work done and still lead the opposition, he
grinned happily. "Of course when there is a really important debate,"
he said, "I must be in my accustomed place in Commons. But when
the issue concerns a new sewer system for Little Hard-scratch, or
something of that sort, I ring up Anthony, and I say, 'Anthony, here
is a great chance to prove yourself, my boy—you can lead this important debate.' "

Over the brandy, perhaps recalling that his dim guest was an American, he began to talk about his experiences in the United States, and
especially his friendship with Franklin Roosevelt. "America," he said,
musingly, "a great and noble country, like some powerful horse pulling the rest of the world behind it, out of the slough of despond,
towards peace, and prosperity."

Then suddenly he fixed the reporter with his amazingly penetrating
old eyes.

"But will America stay the course?" he asked.

Sir Winston (he was Mr. Churchill then) asked that unanswerable
question a good many years ago now, shortly before the greatest and
noblest American postwar act, the response to the Korean aggression.
In those days, the reporter had no hesitation about answering in the
affirmative, and not without a ridiculously choky feeling induced by
the Churchillian praise for his country that preceded the Churchillian

question. Nowadays, what would the answer be? We cannot be so certain; for in the Eisenhower years, America has been like a powerful horse slacking back from the collar, not pulling its weight, seeking its own ease and comfort; and yet the hill has grown far steeper and the slough that threatens the free world has grown much deeper. Yet we are certain, after all. Give us a Churchill, give us even half a Churchill or quarter of a Churchill, and America will pull the cart over the hill at last, to the grand goals all Americans wish to reach.

IV

Defense Reporting

THE NEWEST and most difficult branch of the reporter's trade—only added since the second world war and growing more difficult year by year—is what we call defense reporting. Defense reporting is altogether different from war reporting, which has not greatly altered since the first war reporters took the field at Sebastopol and Bull Run. The defense reporter follows scientific publications instead of troops. He studies budgets instead of tactics. He struggles against the fatigue of official secrecy rather than the fatigue of life in the line. Thus he tries to report currently on the enormous changes in the national strategic situation that are continuously taking place in this era of runaway technology.

This extreme fluidity of every nation's strategic situation, even the situations of the giant powers, is an altogether new thing in the world. The tactics, training and equipment of the Spartiates remained very much the same from the dim period when the Spartan constitution evolved, until Epaminondas and his sacred band at last broke the Spartan phalanx and Sparta too. In all those centuries, Sparta's situation was maintained by the Spartan hoplites, who were always the best infantry of the ancient world from Greece's dawn-time until bloody Mantinea. In Nelson's line at Trafalgar, there were ships that had seen service before great Chatham's wars (when Horace Walpole wrote "that we are forced to ask every morning what victory there is, for fear of missing one.") The British line of battle, with its ships that were as much as a century old, none the less ruled the seas against Napoleon, and so more than maintained Britain's historic situation. Even a century and a quarter later, at the outset of the second world war, weapons left over from the previous conflict still could be put to valuable use. Run-away technology has now changed all that, however. Furthermore, the unseen changes wrought by the ghastly and implacable progress of weaponry have almost the same practical effects as great changes of geography. Everyone would realize instantly that the national situation of the United States had been radically altered, if broad land bridges were suddenly heaved up from the depths of the Atlantic and Pacific Oceans. But these surrounding oceans, which once so surely protected our comfortable, easy isolation, today afford no more protection than half-dry irrigation ditches against some of the new weapons. Still other new weapons—submarine-launched missiles, particularly—have transformed our once-protecting oceans into broad highways of attack.

In our opinion, despite all the gee-whiz stories that are printed about defense developments, the American press as a whole still pays far too little attention to the vast and novel national problems that now center in the Pentagon. For instance, every newspaper in the country would have picked up our story, if we had been the first to publish an official report showing that the White House secretariat had been accepting mink or vicuna coats, or Persian rugs, in exchange for petty favors done for businessmen. Petty malfeasance in the White House staff is not life-and-death stuff, exactly; but everyone understands it; everyone gets excited about it; and when it occurs, the resulting uproar is deafening and nationwide. In contrast, almost total silence reigned when we broke the story of the Lincoln Report, which really was life-and-death stuff. This report, compiled in 1951-52 by an imposing array of scientists for the U. S. Air Force, contained the first factually buttressed official warning that the United States had become nakedly vulnerable to Soviet air attack with atomic weapons. The chief feature of our former national situation was our virtually complete invulnerability to any form of foreign attack. Thus this report officially announced the greatest and most terrible single change in the American situation that has taken place in all our history. Yet our publication of the Lincoln Report's dark substance was treated as quite unworthy of serious notice by all the newspapers not carrying our column, and even by the great press associations with their claims to absolutely comprehensive national reporting. "Time" noticed it, but made a contemptuous joke of it.

Defense reporting, then, is not a branch of the trade that the average American editor as yet regards as essential. Our national situation, which is now so fluid, is still largely taken for granted as being perfectly solid. Otherwise every newspaper in America would have demanded to know more about the Lincoln Report, just as they always demand to know more about any report of mink coats, or vicuna coats, in the White House. Barring exceptional circumstances such as the sputniks created, our press is generally content to leave defense problems to the Generals, the Admirals and the members of the National Security Council. The official administration line is published, and so are the competing claims of the services; but that is about all.

We followed a quite different policy, however. We even got into a good deal of hot water by making something of a specialty of independent defense reporting. Our reasons are best suggested in the history of the failure of "Operation Candor." We think the moment when "Operation Candor" failed was also the precise moment when the Eisenhower administration began to go very wrong, and thus, in our opinion, it was a great and tragic turning point. Yet "Candor's" history is little known, even today; and it deserves to be retold.

It begins long before Eisenhower was elected, in 1951-52, when the Truman administration experienced what may be called its third awakening. The first awakening was caused by the Czechoslovak coup d'état; and it produced Jim Forrestal's aborted effort to rebuild our defenses. The second awakening was caused by the Korean war; and it produced the decision that a massive American defense effort was permanently needed. The third awakening, in contrast, was produced by no single, dramatic and alarming event. It simply resulted from the gradual accumulation of intelligence showing the rapid advance of Soviet weapons-technology.

Even after Korea, the Chiefs of Staff and just about everyone else in the Pentagon had continued to cherish the happy delusion that the

Soviets were technologically backward. It was admitted that they were militarily formidable in a crude way. It was agreed that heavy investments in American and Western defense were therefore unavoidable. But it was hopefully believed that the Soviets could never match the United States in output of the modern, total weapons, because they were supposed to lack the famous American "know-how." Meanwhile the intelligence reports unfortunately said that Soviet "know-how" was quite equal to American "know-how" in any area where they wished to mobilize their scientific and productive resources. And from mid-1951 onwards a small and daring group of government officials, typified by Paul H. Nitze of the State Department's policy-planning staff, remorselessly nagged the Generals, the Admirals and the civilian chiefs of departments to pay more attention to the intelligence reports.

The first result was a series of high-level study projects—among others, Project Lincoln which produced the Lincoln Report. The final result was the third awakening we have already referred to. It was gloomily acknowledged, on the highest governmental level, that the Soviets were threatening to draw ahead of the United States in development, and even in production, of the more advanced weapons. The last great policy paper of the Truman administration was therefore a new directive of the National Security Council, calling for further intensification of our defense effort in order to maintain the American lead.

Like so many time bombs, this NSC directive, and the Lincoln report, and several other papers of a comparable nature, were all waiting on the President's desk when Dwight D. Eisenhower moved into the White House. No documents could have been more unwelcome to an administration of big businessmen, pledged to a balanced budget and longing for a Harding-esque "return to normalcy." In those days, however, Dwight D. Eisenhower had not yet become the willing captive of George Magoffin Humphrey. His natural instincts had not yet been totally anaesthetized by Humphrey's argument, so wonderfully reminiscent of the days of Chamberlain and Baldwin, that an unbalanced budget was far more dangerous than all the armed might of the Kremlin. So Eisenhower did not ignore the unwelcome documents that he found waiting for him, as he was later to ignore other documents of this sort. Instead, he ordered a further series of high-level studies—to the best of our recollection there were no less than five in all. To each succeeding study group of scientists and experts, he gave the same commission—"Say it ain't so." Each group successively replied that it was so, however; and this peculiar process in turn produced the plan for "Operation Candor," which was sketched out in the summer of 1953.

A good deal of the credit for "Candor" must probably be given to Allen W. Dulles, head of the CIA. It was a simple, sound plan. The President was to tell the nation the ugly, concealed facts of the national situation contained in the highly classified papers he had inherited from Truman. He was to give a summary of the Lincoln Report, which had aroused no one when published by us, but would have electrified the nation if presented by Eisenhower. He was to give the grim data on Soviet progress in guided-missile development, and atomic and thermonuclear weaponry, and many other related fields. He was to point out the resulting need for vastly greater American efforts to maintain our narrowing lead. And he was to ask the nation to support these efforts.

The nation's response was easily predictable. It could be foretold from the response of the Congressional leaders, who were actually called to the White House and briefed in preparation for "Candor." Senator Styles Bridges of New Hampshire emerged from the meeting with the comment, "We have been told terrible news." But this was really an admission that even the rightwing Republicans of the old Taft group were unhappily preparing to vote the large additional appropriations which they had been warned would now be needed. Unfortunately, however, a concerted siege of the White House was organized by the administration's budget-balancers, headed by Secretary of the Treasury Humphrey, and the secrecy-addicts, headed by Admiral Lewis Strauss, and a group of the President's personal advisers, headed by the secretary of the Security Council, Robert Cutler. All these joined together to abort "Operation Candor." The President yielded to their mass attack and abandoned "Candor." His already-scheduled first speech to the nation was transformed into a mush of platitudes. The ugly facts were kept in concealment. The necessary efforts were not demanded. From that moment onwards, there was a lie in the Eisenhower administration's soul.

With wonderful fatuity, Cutler later boasted about what had happened. "The thesis was," he wrote in an article, "that the American people could take bad news; officially apprised of the facts . . . they would be more self-reliant, more understanding, more ready to bear the costs of defense. . . . Things progressed so far as sketching out an operation known as 'Candor.' . . . But other and, I think, wiser counsels prevailed." Cutler has also suggested that reporters who defy these "wiser counsels," and insist on trying to "apprise" the American people of the facts of their national situation, are guilty of treasonable behavior. It is an interesting question, this question of the nature of treason in a modern democratic society; and we shall examine it a little later. It is enough to say here that we have always believed that the American people have an absolute, unqualified right to know exactly where they stand at all times. We have further believed that it is the reporter's highest function to add, if he can, to the American people's knowledge of where they stand. This is precisely why we have always made a specialty of defense reporting.

It has always been necessary to *report* rather than accept the hand-outs, for the quite simple reason that the hand-outs of every administration tend towards fakery. This tendency has never before been carried to the extremes of misrepresentation practiced in the last six years. For the nearest parallel to the Eisenhower years, one has to go as far afield in space and time as the Baldwin-Chamberlain cabinets in Britain during the period of Hitler's rise to almost unchallengeable power. But in the fortunately briefer era when Louis A. Johnson was Secretary of Defense, the Truman administration was also flagrantly guilty of the most mendacious complacency-mongering. And even in the early days when we began to write our column together, the fatuity of Robert Cutler was already forecast by the odd innocence of George F. Kennan. Kennan used to argue that democracy must be reformed. National policy-makers, he said, were experts, like doctors, and their prescriptions ought to be accepted without undue argument or inquiry by the Congress and the people, just as doctors' mysteriously scrawled prescriptions to cure belly-aches are generally accepted by persons with belly-aches.

The truth is that the official impulse to conceal "bad news" (to repeat Cutler's own wonderfully revealing phrase) has existed since governments began, and all governments since history began have yielded to this impulse in varying degrees. But there is another natural official impulse which never mastered the American government until just the other day. This is the impulse to harass and penalize and spy upon and threaten those who dare to publish news that officials do not want published. When the senior member of our partnership entered the newspaper business, anything of this sort would have caused a really unparalleled national uproar. We in America had not then felt the thin end of the wedge, which was the wartime censorship. Above all, the success of the Manhattan District Project had not yet clothed secrecy-for-secrecy's-sake with powerful public sanctions. In sum, no American then supposed for a minute that the democratic process could go on working after the people's right to know essential facts had been severely limited, on the largely false pretext of withholding information from the enemy. Thus Franklin Roosevelt, at the very height of his enormous power, would never have dared to question the people's right to know, as it was daily questioned by the most fat-faced and obscure subordinates of Secretary of Defense Charles E. Wilson. Above all, Franklin Roosevelt, even at his most arrogant, would never have dared to take punitive measures against reporters who insisted upon the people's right to know. Yet both the Truman and the Eisenhower administrations have regularly taken such measures. This is a wholly new development in the American democratic process, and it needs to be much more widely known about and much more widely thought about.

Curiously enough, the pioneer of this new development was Dean G. Acheson. As Secretary of State, Acheson courageously opposed the Truman-Louis Johnson disarmament policy that caused the Korean war. Yet Johnson, who had so much to hide, was just an old-style American politician; he never thought of setting the flatfeet on reporters who challenged his concealments. Acheson, on the other hand, had nothing to hide; but he was afflicted with imitation-English views about secrecy. In reality, it has always been easier for responsible and informed reporters to get frank briefings from the Foreign Office than from the State Department. But Acheson had a largely imaginary ideal picture of placidly expert Foreign Office officials, placidly treading their way through all the intricacies of British diplomacy behind the tough screen of Britain's official secrets act. He was a great Secretary of State, but he had not given enough thought to the peculiar character of the American political system. In particular, he had not given enough thought to the peculiar nature of the national debate that makes our system work, and to the special role of the press in this vital debate. Hence Acheson's State Department was where "security investigations" of reporters, and harassment of officials suspected of being too frank to reporters, first became regular practices of the American government. By now, these practices have spread so widely that they might be called governmental SOP.

So far as we have been able to count, we have been honored with no less than six security investigations, sometimes with results that have made us wonder whether we were still living in familiar America. There was the time, for instance, when one of us paid an office-visit to Robert A. Lovett, who was then completing his brilliant and dedicated career of public service as Secretary of Defense. For a talk between two very old friends, the conversation seemed oddly constrained. The constraint was finally explained when Lovett led the reporter into the Pentagon corridor—evidently the Secretary of Defense's own grandiose office was not immune to listening devices—and whispered the tip that the Alsop Bros. were once more being investigated. It was like the warning a friend might give a political suspect in a very different kind of country.

Again, there was the even more unpleasant occasion when Trevor Gardner came to dinner. This singular man, who looks rather like a "New Yorker" drawing of a Martian, is one of the unsung heroes of the Eisenhower administration. As assistant Secretary of the Air Force, Gardner waged the stout fight that produced the Eisenhower administration's quite inadequate guided-missile program—without him, there would have been almost no program at all. He also dared to warn of the effect of the Oppenheimer case on American science, when Admiral Strauss was busily organizing his star-chamber proceeding at the AEC. He further dared to go on pressing Defense Secretary Wilson for an adequate missile program, after the President himself had firmly decided in favor of inadequacy. So Gardner had to go in the end, because he was not a "team-player"; but he was a most useful and courageous public servant while he lasted. He used to talk to us about the guided-missile problem, although only in the most general terms and without any disclosure of classified information. Simply because we knew he was putting up a stout fight on what we thought was the right side, we admired him and were his friends. Hence there was nothing out of the ordinary in Gardner's coming to dinner. What was rather out of the ordinary was Gardner's refusal to enter the house. Instead he beckoned his intending host into the street, announced that he himself would give the dinner downtown, and offered the following explanation:

"I've just heard your house is all bugged up. In fact, they're running an investigation of you two to end all investigations. And I'm not especially anxious to make a sound recording in the Alsop library."

Once, during the Truman administration, one of these so-called security investigations went so far that we received a long visit from two smooth, polite young gentlemen from the FBI. Once, during the Eisenhower administration, a remarkably crude and vulgar attempt to intimidate us was made by Attorney General Herbert Brownell. At a large party attended by several newspapermen, Brownell remarked, with careful casualness, that the Justice Department was examining our case with a view to prosecution on security grounds. He knew, of course, that the remark would be relayed to us within hours. He hoped, no doubt, that we would tremble and obey, at least to the extent of ceasing to print uncomfortably bad news that such men as Robert Cutler thought the country should not be apprised of.

Of course we were not impressed by Brownell's relayed threat. No reporter in his senses would be deterred by this sort of threat. In the first place, if a reporter has paid decent heed to the genuine requirements of national security—as we have always tried to do—he can be sure an American jury will not convict him for publishing the politically inconvenient truth. In the second place, all the security investigations to which we have been subjected started in mare's nests, with only one exception. The exception occurred when a very odd chapter of accidents put into our possession a fragment of the actual language of a cable from Ernest Bevin to Dean Acheson. Acheson was then boasting to Washington's always-echoing dinner parties that he had shut off all our sources of information, and we were pretty angry about it—quite justifiably, as we still think. So we published the quotation from Bevin's cable in a spirit of "Now we'll show him" —quite wrongly, as we now think. A reporter should not only refrain from examining any classified document, in the unlikely case that one is shown to him. He should also refrain from reproduction of the language of any such document, in the very rare cases like the one just cited, when the actual language may be repeated to him. If you do otherwise, you are trenching upon the necessary privacy of the policy-makers.

On the other hand, the two most intensive investigations that have been visited upon us were both the results of mare's nests of the most comic sort. The first, which culminated in the visit from the two young gentlemen from the FBI, was caused by a column we wrote in answer to one of Louis Johnson's more remarkable distillations of poisoned soothing syrup. Long after all the evidence was in concerning the Soviet atomic tests in September, 1949, Johnson kept spreading the word that the Soviets probably did not have an atomic bomb after all; and Senator Owen Brewster finally echoed Johnson in a public speech. In answer, we printed the evidence that the Soviets quite certainly had a bomb—evidence which was common knowledge in the whole American scientific community. As it happened, President Truman himself was mulishly reluctant to believe the American atomic monopoly had been broken, because this event destroyed the sole excuse for the Truman-Johnson disarmament program. Therefore (as we finally learned a full two years later) just the same evidence that appeared in our column had been assembled, in about the same way, in a paper intended to convince Truman; and this paper inevitably carried the topmost security classification. The wholly accidental similarities convinced the President that our column had been cribbed from his precious secret paper. He grew furiously angry, and personally ordered an immediate investigation. So all our affairs were winnowed by the flatfeet for months on end, and finally the flatfeet paid us a charming personal visit, because of the President's conviction that we had seen a paper which we had never even heard about.

The other case was still more laughable. It happened after the intelligence had revealed the Soviet intention to launch an earth satellite, when the Eisenhower administration was convulsed with controversy about the desirability vs. the expense of an American satellite project. We dragged the controversy into the open. By so doing, in fact, we probably helped to force the eventual decision to go ahead with an American satellite—the decision which was then negated by Charles E. Wilson's pound foolish penny-pinching. At any rate, the moment when President Eisenhower had to decide the issue was just at hand, when we published a column containing two imaginary headlines of the future—SOVIETS CLAIM SUCCESSFUL LAUNCHING OF EARTH SATELLITES and U. S. RADAR CONFIRMS EXISTENCE OF SOVIET SATELLITES. The column suggested what the event disastrously proved, that such headlines would be highly damaging to the U. S. world position, if we had not got there first with an American satellite. The partner who wrote the column had used the argument of the headlines in a dinner table discussion of the issue a good many days earlier. A high official charged with studying the pros and cons of an American satellite was struck by what he heard. He used the remembered headlines almost verbatim, no doubt forgetting the source, in the NSC paper he had to prepare (as we learned, as usual, about two years later). For once in a way, the President read his newspaper on the day our column was printed; and then, with awful fatality, he read the NSC paper. Perhaps rather naturally, he did not suspect that this was a case of an NSC paper quoting the Alsops, rather than the reverse. The result was another fearful fit of Presidential temper, which produced another security investigation of extreme severity. The investigation never unravelled the mystery because, of course, security rules prevented anyone from telling us why on earth we were being investigated, or indeed, even officially admitting to us that an investigation was afoot. This is never admitted, unless the last grave step of a visit by the FBI is to be taken; and so you commonly learn that the flatfeet have hit the trail again because all your friends begin to be harassed by them.

The accident of the NSC paper that quoted the Alsops was pretty funny, but such an accident's consequences to the reporter are not at all funny. He is not personally hurt in any direct way. But with remarkable cowardice and considerable success, the American government now strikes at reporters indirectly, by persistent persecution of reporters' friends in government. It takes a lot of guts, nowadays, for a government official to maintain an old friendship with any reasonably honest and effective reporter. We have already remarked that we always avoid discussing matters in their particular areas of official interest with our two closest friends in Washington, simply because we do not wish to confuse these friendships with our trade. Yet one of these men has been called on the carpet five times and more than once threatened with loss of access to classified information—the official equivalent of castration—for the sole reason that he is known to be our friend. These interrogations occurred, these threats were made, remember, without the faintest evidence that the victim was guilty of the faintest indiscretion. There could not have been any such evidence, because of the rule we observe with this friend of ours. To us, this seems a dirty way for an allegedly democratic government to do business. Furthermore, it is a way of doing business that tends more and more to prevent the American people from learning what they ought to know and have a right to know. All officials, at all levels of the government, are now aware of the new rule of guilt-by-association-with-reporters. Hence it is increasingly difficult for reporters in Washington to get at the facts that show where the country really stands. For this very reason, American public opinion is quite visibly beginning to suffer from an anemia of essential information. Although someone always ends by publishing every major new fact, the press as a whole does not regularly carry enough essential information to cure the anemia.

The matter seems to us very important, so perhaps we have gone on too long about this new governmental technique for impeding the flow of vital facts to the American people. At this point, indeed, one can imagine the justifiably irritated reader demanding how these harassed, persecuted and possibly self-pitying reporters ever manage to get any facts at all, and particularly any defense facts which are not provided in the hand-outs.

As far as defense reporting is concerned, the first part of the answer is extremely simple. You go to school. You have to go to school, in order to be able to ask the right questions about such recondite matters as critical size, range of radioactivity, inertial guidance, initial thrust and velocity of re-entry. No matter how arcane the subject, enough has always been printed about it in non-classified publications to give you a general idea of the right questions. Our most painful school sessions, for instance, took place in 1946, when we spent months mugging up all the published data on atomic reactors and atomic weapons. Thus we came across the wholly unclassified paper in which an Austrian physicist first announced the possibility of a thermonuclear bomb. That suggested a pretty important question, which we continued to ask until, some four years later, we got the first news of the great and solemn debate between the advocates and the opponents of an American H-bomb. Our columns on the H-bomb debate incidentally earned us the compliment that pleased us most among the few we have received. Writing in the "New Yorker" about President Truman's announcement that the United States would make an H-bomb, Richard Rovere remarked:

". . . The Alsop brothers, in one of the most remarkable journalistic performances of recent years, forced the hydrogen bomb story into the open . . ."

Again, the administration in general and Admiral Strauss in particular made extraordinary efforts to withhold the tremendous problem of nuclear fall-out from H-bombs. To be blunt about it, the American government told a pack of glib lies on this subject. But we had studied the published data on fall-out, radioactive by-products and so on; and one of us was therefore instantly alerted and astonished by a remark that a fairly high official plaintively dropped into a discussion of the U. S. Army's equipment program. The reporter had suggested that it was a bit dangerous for the army to carry on with so many weapons and so much equipment left over from World War II, when the Soviet army had been entirely re-armed and re-equipped. (This is now a doubly valid point, by the way. The Red Army has now been re-equipped and re-armed virtually throughout for the second time, putting it two laps ahead of our army.) The official said that perhaps the reporter was right, but any new equipment program would have to wait until the General Staff had figured out the right infantry tactics for an H-bomb war. And really, he added, he could not imagine what the General Staff's answer would be, since the area of "lethal fall-out could be anywhere up to several thousand square miles, and the direction of fall-out was so much influenced by the wind too."

Working as he did on quite different problems, the official probably did not know he was saying anything surprising about fall-out. Having done his homework, the reporter knew that fall-out of the indicated dimensions far exceeded anything expected by the actual inventors of the H-bomb, who had pooh-poohed the fall-out danger during the earlier controversy. So the reporter went home, first to have a knock-down drag-out fight with his brother, who had done the same homework and had been convinced by it; and then to have a second bitter argument with the well-known physicist, Dr. Ralph Lapp, who was even more sure there was a mistake somewhere. After that, all three of us did a great deal of checking, asking, for instance, for the results of the Eniwetok H-bomb tests obtained by the independent, non-classified scientists who make a hobby of watching the upper air with their own Geiger counters. After that, we broke the fall-out story in our column. Our friend Lapp later got the whole credit for the news-break, and this, to be honest about it, has always rather rankled.

Experience also counts in these matters, sometimes as much as homework. By 1954, for example, we had had a good deal of experience of the queer results of our government's queer system of making intelligence estimates. So far as we understand this system, the CIA generally gets it about right at the outset. But the final estimate is not made by the CIA; it is made jointly by representatives of the CIA, the three armed services, the State Department, the Atomic Energy Commission and the FBI. The final estimates, on which the American government bases its policy, are thus produced by wrangles in this "Inter-Agency Committee" on intelligence. Where Soviet weapons developments have been concerned, the final estimates have always been two to three years wrong. The first Soviet atomic test took place in 1949, when 1951-52 was thought to be the first imaginable but unlikely date; and so it has gone, again and again, in numerous comparable and subsequent cases.

This experience was very much in our minds in 1954, when certain indications in the Soviet press led us to make a rather intensive study of the available data on the Soviet missile program. We discovered at once that the alleged Soviet dependence on German experts was a pure myth; Russian science in fact had a long record of success with rockets, dating back to before the first world war. We of course knew that the Soviets had begun an all-out missile development effort in 1946, and we also knew that even in 1954, the United States was not making anything like an all-out effort. So we began asking why on earth the Soviets were not likely to fly an inter-continental missile before our own first scheduled test of an ICBM, which was then officially forecast for 1959. "Oh no," came back the defensive answers from a long series of officials, "1959 was the very earliest date when the Soviets could put such a bird in the air, and even this was very unlikely." 1959, then, was clearly the American government's estimated first feasible date for a Soviet ICBM test. If we had not already learned to expect a built-in two-year error in such estimates, we should have accepted 1959 as a valid date. Instead, as all our information bleakly pointed to still another error, we boldly published a warning that "the Soviets were quite probably ahead of the U. S." in the missile race. Correcting for the expected error, we also offered a prediction of "first tests in 1957-58" of "guided missiles of inter-continental range." We were bang on the nose, alas.

Besides knowledge and experience, defense reporting further requires something of the reconstructive imagination of the paleontologist, who can take a rear molar and a bit of fossilized femur and some other scraps, and combine them to make a reasonably accurate picture of the whole animal. In the spring of 1957, one of us picked up the equivalent of a rear molar when an official asked him, with seeming casualness: "What do you think the public reaction would be in this country, if it became known that the Soviets had tested an ICBM?" The reporter already knew that the American intelligence had means of radar-tracking the upper trajectories of Soviet tests of medium-range missiles. Plainly, the same radar could track the test of an intercontinental missile. As above-noted, we ourselves already expected that such a test would take place in 1957; so all the factors combined to arouse suspicion of the official's seeming-casual question. Surely it must mean that a Soviet ICBM test had indeed been radar-tracked. News of this kind is customarily hidden from the country, but it always spreads fairly fast in the fairly large circles of expertly interested technicians and scientists and industrialists and the like. The right question was therefore asked in the right quarters; and the reporter's melancholy suspicion was at once confirmed. In July, 1957, the reporter published the story on page one of the "New York Herald Tribune" that the Soviets had quite certainly tested an ICBM. The "New York Times" countered with an "authoritative" report (the "authority" was most probably either Secretary of Defense Wilson himself, or Under Secretary Donald Quarles, so one cannot altogether blame the "Times") to the effect that the Soviets had not even passed the "very early motor-testing stage" in their intercontinental missile program. But the "Times'" authority had lied. In August, the Kremlin itself announced the success of the Soviet ICBM tests. The Pentagon was then forced to give reluctant confirmation. And in October, the first sputnik showed that the Pentagon's mumbled confirmation had again quite grossly under-estimated the Soviet achievement.

It should be noted that not one of the foregoing very big defense stories was "leaked" to us in the accepted sense of that silly word. In each case, we got a more or less well-defined clue. Just getting the clue took a lot of hard work, because in this respect reporting is like police work: scores of interviews are needed to produce a single clue of any interest. Spotting the clue for what it was took a lot more hard work, done in advance. Following up the clue took still more hard work. Yet in each case, the indignant cry went up that there had been a "leak"—meaning that some miscreant within the charmed circle of the Q-cleared had given us the story, complete in all its details, as a kind of pre-Christmas present. It is a little strange and more than a little insulting to the press, this belief in "leaks." It implies a total disbelief in reporters' energy, intelligence and power to acquire knowledge on their own behalf. But the belief in "leaks" is an unvarying article of faith among all officials of every administration, from the President downwards; and reporters have to swallow the implied insult and learn to be amused by it. Sometimes the results can be very amusing indeed.

For instance, if we have ever rendered any public service at all, showing up Louis Johnson was our most useful service. It has even been said that "the Alsops got Louis Johnson," which is nonsense. The facts got Johnson, when the facts were underlined by the needless tragedy in Korea. We only published the facts that showed the total phoniness of Johnson's claim to be "cutting defense fat without cutting muscle." Our sole boast is that we angrily persisted in publishing these facts because we thought they were important, although readers and editors were bored and irritated by our persistence, and we even lost papers because of this boredom and irritation. At any rate, Johnson was religiously convinced that our facts were being "leaked" to us by his enemy, Secretary of State Acheson, and by his subordinate, Secretary of the Air Force Stuart Symington. As it happened, we were then hardly on speaking terms with Acheson; and although Stuart Symington remained a friend of ours, we saw him only at the rarest intervals. But one day one of us actually called on Symington in his office, to get the answer to a question entirely within the public domain, concerning the total air-frame weight currently on order by the Air Force.

The question was quickly answered from published data, when the corridor door of Symington's office opened, and the bulky figure of Louis Johnson appeared. (We later learned that he had ordered the girls at the Pentagon reception desks to warn him immediately if either of the awful Alsops set foot in the building.) Johnson closed the door, and stood there, saying nothing, nodding his huge bald head up and down with the air of a virtuous husband who has at last caught his erring wife *in flagrante delictu.*

Symington broke the unhappy silence by attempting an introduction, in which he rather slurred over the Alsop name—it sounded something like "Ollup," or perhaps "Ulp." "Yes," Johnson replied, "I know MR. ALSOP," and he pronounced the hated name loud and clear. There was another long, uncomfortable pause, while Johnson continued to nod his head up and down, grinning horribly, before at last he turned and left. Symington and Alsop thereupon collapsed into undignified giggles.

All the while, Johnson ought to have known that neither Symington nor anyone else needed to tell us the facts we were regularly publishing to show that Johnson's boasts were empty untruths. Louis Johnson himself had told us those facts. We simply used the detailed line-budgets which Johnson submitted to Congress, in order to prove his heavy cutbacks in Air Force wings, Navy sea and air units, and Marine divisions.

The same line-budget is of course the principal source of the Kremlin's information about the American defense effort. By putting enough teams of analysts to work on the data from the budget, the Soviet intelligence must each year learn a great deal more about our defense effort than our own people are ever told. Great masses of the information thus acquired by the Soviets must further be in areas classified with utmost strictness in this country; for if real experts in the art know where your money is going, they can tell pretty exactly what kind of missiles or airplanes or radar mechanisms you are making. None the less, anyone engaged in defense-reporting has to ask himself two questions before he publishes any defense news that the government has not already published. The first is simple: Do the Soviets know it already? If the news is certainly known to the enemy, then the American people have a right to know it too. The second question is more complex: Does the news raise an issue of such profound importance that democratic procedure demands public debate, without regard for security? Our inner answer to this second question decided us to drag the controversy about making an American H-bomb into the light of the front pages. We of course knew that Soviet physicists must already be thinking about H-bombs and preparing to make H-bombs. There was nothing secret about the theory of fusion, or about its potential applications in weaponry. We were not so certain that our government's inner debate was known to the Kremlin; but it seemed to us that the issue being debated involved a very great national decision, of the sort that the whole nation ought to join in. So we went ahead and published the story, and even harped upon it for some weeks with the result indicated by Rovere, until the final decision was made.

In borderline cases, moreover, we have always made a practice of

asking the responsible official most directly concerned whether publication would do harm. For instance, we were not only the first to
get the news that the Soviets were testing ballistic missiles of medium
range on a very big scale. We were also the first to learn how these
tests were known to the American government, by the radars em-
placed in Turkey that were capable of tracking the missiles' upper
trajectory. We further knew that these specialized missile-watching
radars had scanning surfaces of enormous size. Thus it seemed to us
highly unlikely that the Turkish radars could have passed unnoticed
by Soviet agents or Soviet upper-air-reconnaissance planes. But we
were still leery of the story, and we took it to the able and always
sensible Allen Dulles. He asked us not to reveal the existence of
the Turkish radars, on the ground that the Soviets might just possibly
not have detected them. So we sat on that part of our story—the part
most certain to excite general interest—for another two years. But
we went ahead and published the news of the Soviet missile tests, first
because this would hardly be news to the Kremlin, and second, because we thought this was news directly bearing on our own national
situation, which ought to be generally known.

In the sequel, one of the very best defense reporters in the business,
Robert Hotz of "Aviation Week," finally broke our story of the Turkish radars. He too had been sitting on it, but he finally lost patience
when the Pentagon high command, for the umpteenth time, publicly
lied about the relative stages of Soviet and American missile-testing,
in order to defend a further reduction in the American program. Hotz
wanted to show that the Pentagon was indulging in conscious untruth,
as it was. The egregious Robert Cutler then made an hysterical speech
to a rally of big businessmen, suggesting that Hotz was no better than
a traitor. He failed, however, to assign an appropriate moral category
to the liars of the Pentagon high command.

In our opinion, it is an honor to be denounced by the kind of
official who condones and even promotes governmental lying and
grows indignant when the inconvenient truth is published by reporters.
We ourselves have received a great many unintentional bouquets of
this kind; and we are proud of them. In our twelve years of partnership, we have cooperated at all times with men in government like the
enlightened former chairman of the AEC, the late Gordon Dean—the
men who always want the American people to know all the facts that
security will reasonably permit, because they have a due respect for

the democratic process. In the same period, we have not feared to defy the men in government like Dean's successor, Admiral Strauss—the men who never want the American people to know where they stand, for one interested reason or another. If we have the good opinion of the Deans, as we like to think we have, and if we have the bad opinion of the Strausses, as we also like to think we have, it suits us very well indeed. It proves, in fact, that we have done our defense-reporting job as we have wanted to do it.

At the end of our road together, we are further convinced that 99/100s of the American government's secrecy has no other purpose but official convenience. The two most obviously explosive governmental secrets we ever ran across were the true stories of the interventions by American secret agents in Iran and Guatemala, which at least temporarily halted the drift towards Communism in both those countries. We neither spoke nor wrote one word about this information which came to us, in both cases, by peculiar accident. But we might, so to say, have saved our silence to cool our porridge. In the 1956 election, it was necessary to prove that the U. S. really had a "dynamic new foreign policy" which had truly "recaptured the initiative," so these super-secret operations in Iran and Guatemala were publicly boasted about in a campaign speech by the President of the United States himself. In truth, when publicity serves convenience, publicity is sought, and the classification stamps go out the window. Most often, publicity serves convenience when the government knows what it ought to do, has the guts to do it, and wants the country to know the reasons and to support its policy. By the same token, secrecy most often serves convenience when the government either does not know what to do, or lacks the guts to do what is obviously necessary. Then the facts are hidden, and the classification stamps are mobilized in fullest force.

So far it has not done much good, in these secretive governmental periods, for the very small band of serious defense reporters to go on dragging the facts into the open. Jim Forrestal's defense program was rejected, and Forrestal died of it, although all the reasons for a contrary course were fully published. The Truman-Johnson disarmament policy remained in force until Korea, despite many anguished warnings. When "Operation Candor" failed, this country still stood at the head of the world, and today we stand in the deadly danger officially summed up in the Gaither report. Yet throughout the intervening

years, the facts indicating the onset of this danger were fully venti-
lated by ourselves and a few others.

That word "few" is the key. This kind of thing could not happen
if the vital facts were reasonably accessible to the entire American
press, instead of being accessible only to the few aroused specialists
who are willing to do battle for the facts, and to run considerable
personal risks to publish the facts. As it is, one is inclined to say,
"Why bother?" since serious defense reporting is both immensely
bothersome and not immediately productive of results. Yet the answer is that one must go on bothering, because it is the reporter's job
to get and print the facts that matter.

V

Last Walk-and-Talk

O NE OF THE MOST instructive legends in the Senatorial folklore of the older Washington concerns the walk-and-talk of Albert C. Beveridge of Indiana and Frank Brandegee of Connecticut. The posturing, expansive, relentlessly oratorical Beveridge belonged to the Bull Moose wing of the Republican party. Brandegee was everything Beveridge was not,—bitter, taciturn, neurotic (he ultimately killed himself) and an extreme Republican rightwinger. One day, the ebullient Beveridge offered to walk home with Brandegee from the Capitol; and as Brandegee did not actively object, Beveridge duly accompanied him. Beveridge spouted unceasingly all the way, about the need for a rejuvenated, progressive, forward-looking Republicanism, and Brandegee answered never a word. When they reached Brandegee's door at last, Beveridge wound up a little lamely: "But Senator, you haven't told me what you think of my ideas." Brandegee replied, thin-lipped: "I think you ought to keep them to yourself."

The legend is apposite, because you can make a good case for the view that reporters also ought to keep their larger ideas to themselves.

As practitioners of a humble, useful trade, they have no call to set up as political philosophers. But we have now finished our twelve-year stint together. We are also on the point of finishing this essay that is intended to introduce the results of that twelve-year stint. In fact this is really our last joint chance to offer some ideas that are, so to say, perilously above our station, but are not wholly irrelevant either, because they are the ideas that have largely guided us in our work as reporters. Hence we shall plunge remorselessly onwards, with the understanding that readers who feel as Senator Brandegee felt may cease to accompany us at this point.

For twelve years, then, we have been engaged together (as we are now engaged separately) in following the complex twists and turns, the breath-taking ups and downs of a great historical drama— the drama whose last scene will announce this planet's future, when the scene is finally played. The drama's theme has been, and is, the grim, relentless struggle between the free and un-free halves of the world. In all that we have written together, this contest for the world between freedom and un-freedom has been the main plot. All else has been sub-plot, whether the squalid-sinister antics of Joseph R. McCarthy, or the dignified power-plays of George Magoffin Humphrey, or the tragic episodes of Anthony Eden's fall, or the ruthless maneuvers of Nikita Khrushchev's rise. When we began to follow this vast, absorbing, ever-changing drama, we had no doubt about the final outcome. The cause of freedom, we thought, might take many a hard knock; the leaders of the cause of freedom might indulge in many a costly folly. But freedom, we were sure, would win in the end. Now we are by no means so sure; and the question we now wish to examine can therefore be summed up as follows: *Can the free societies survive, and if so, how?*

In the last three centuries or so, since the great nations began to divide themselves into free and un-free societies, the free have always won in the end, in all their contests with the un-free. Most people, therefore, will think our question either ridiculous, or impertinent, or both. But the question exists, all the same, and the answer is no longer at all certain, for the very simple reason that our world is no longer the same place that Pitt and Lincoln and Woodrow Wilson and even Winston Churchill knew. The great process of change that began with Britain's industrial revolution has gone forward, by a sort of geometrical progression, until every familiar landmark of the past has now been swept away. Most of us suppose the landmarks are still there, because they *look* the same. But in fact technology has abridged geography. Technology has created a unitary world economy. Technology has altered, and is still altering every established world power-relationship. Technology has entangled the fate of the Eskimos (via our DEW-line) in the remote relationship between Washington and Moscow. For all these reasons, all the rivers of history have now flowed together, into one huge, storm-tossed stream. The most majestic, ancient and isolated national stories, like that of China; the most sluggish, obscure and savage tribal annals, like those of the still-neolithic peoples of West Irian—both these and all the rest have now been merged in a single world-story.

In this radically novel situation, several altogether novel and quite practical handicaps have been imposed on the free societies. For example, free nations, freely associated together, are far from well equipped to solve some of the economic problems that must now be solved without undue delay, such as the problem of the pressure of exploding populations on our planet's limited stock of natural resources. Again, the free nations are even more ill-equipped to solve the new strategic problems that now confront them. In the past, they always won their great wars with the un-free in the same costly, cumbersome way—by mobilizing their huge reserves of civilian manpower and economic power after the war had started, and so attaining the needed margin for victory after perilous years on the brink of defeat. No one can suppose that this belated mobilization will work again in another great war beginning with an exchange of H-bomb attacks. Force-in-being counts now, and not reserves. Yet the free nations are still finding it just as difficult as they have always done to match, or even halfway match, the military force-in-being maintained by the un-free.

These new handicaps that history has now imposed upon us must be taken very seriously indeed. And even the new and heavy handicaps we have cited, which may be called *external,* seem to us considerably less grave than an equally new *internal* handicap. For it is now very clear that the alleged march of progress is also noxiously affecting the actual inner working of every free society, most conspicuously including our own.

The right way to gauge this effect is to look back to an earlier, simpler time, and to compare the inner working of the democracies as it was then, and as it is now. Up to a certain moment in history—1914 is the date we would suggest—the problems nations had to solve, the challenges nations had to meet, were still on an approximately human scale. (We use the phrase in the sense given to it by Bernard Berenson, who once explained to one of us that Paris was the most beautiful of the world's great cities because it was "still on a human scale.") Until 1914, in other words, the nation's problems could be crudely understood, the nation's challenges could be common-sensibly responded to, by any average serious citizen who read a decent morning paper. In the free societies, in these circumstances, really gross errors at the top were fairly rapidly self-correcting—and this was then another advantage of the free over the un-free.

In the 1914-18 war, however, the old landmarks began to be progressively swept away, although they went on looking as though they were still there—which made it worse. Thus the problems nations now have to solve have grown inhumanly complex. The challenges nations now have to meet originate in areas more and more remote from normal human experience. Thus the decent citizen who reads a decent morning newspaper cannot any longer be automatically counted on to understand the problems, or to respond to the challenges. This *"hypocrite lecteur, mon semblable, mon frère,"* who is all of us rolled into one, now needs to be briefed about the problems and the challenges by his leaders. The leaders in turn need to be briefed by platoons of scientists and companies of experts and battalions of intelligence analysts.

If the leaders of a democracy are rightly briefed, and if the leaders rightly brief the people, the system still works with marvellous vigor and flexibility. Think of the American response to the challenge of the second world war, after Franklin Roosevelt had decided that a response was necessary. Or almost better still, think of the first Truman administration, which so boldly laid the foundations of American post-war foreign policy, mobilizing the nation to force a long series of wholly unprecedented and costly measures through a hostile Congress dominated by Robert A. Taft. The greatest legislative manager of his time, James F. Byrnes, said it could not be done. But it was done, and this was a main source of Byrnes' quarrel with Truman. In truth, what the democracies can do today when they are well led is no less than what the democracies could do in the most glorious periods of the past. Let the President of the United States go to the people of the

United States tomorrow morning, and let him say: "Here is this very great national problem, touching even our survival. Here are the facts of the problem, as they have been analyzed and set out for me by the experts. Here is what I think we must do about it. Do you agree?" If the President has a halfway decent case, then the people's affirmative response will be heard the day after the President has spoken. That, indeed, was why "Candor's" failure was so genuinely tragic.

Everything is different, however, when the people are wrongly briefed about the nation's problems and the challenges confronting it. In a democracy, wrong briefing by the leaders invariably takes the form of counseling the easier, more comfortable, pleasanter course. It cannot take any other form. A President or a Prime Minister dare not ask the people he leads to make this sacrifice, or to run that risk, if the weight of the facts is against his proposal. Just because his proposal is uncomfortable, the facts will be found out somehow, and his proposal will be defeated. But a President or Prime Minister can quite easily ignore the weight of facts, so long as he is saying "we do not need to make this sacrifice or run that risk." When it really matters, only the narrowest circle of experts outside the government will understand the weight of the facts being ignored. For in our times, in the early stages of great processes such as Hitler's German rearmament or the guided-missile race, the more significant facts are almost always remote and unfamiliar and quite largely classified. Yet this early period is the period that really matters, because the choices that influence the outcome always have to be made early. The crucial choices are therefore made, nowadays, before the mass of people can understand the nature of the choice, and often before the mass of the people can see that a choice exists. Nowadays, therefore, the free societies have become desperately vulnerable to weak leadership.

One saw this vulnerability in its full development and for the first time in Britain in the 1930s. With all his eloquence, the greatest man of our era warned his people again, and again, and again, that they were heading straight for national disaster. But from the beginning of German rearmament until the time of Munich, the great majority of Englishmen were content to think, or hope, that Winston Churchill was a super-annuated mountebank with alcoholic tendencies. To be sure, the British majority did not quite believe the smooth, platitudinous promises that all was well, which they meanwhile heard from the leaders of the government. Churchill's magnificent and anguished warnings stuck in their minds, as crumbs stick in beds, creating the same sort of slight *malaise*. But the policy pursued by Baldwin and Neville Chamberlain was more immediately pleasant, more immediately risk-free, more immediately tax-free. "After all," said everyone, "*They* have the responsibility. *They* get the intelligence reports and the embassy telegrams. *They* must know best; so why should we argue with them, if they say we can relax and be comfortable." In this manner, the policies of Baldwin and Chamberlain were supported by the British nation until they had taken Britain into the very jaws of final catastrophe. Only then were Churchill's warnings remembered with a thrill of love and admiration. Only then could Leo Amery rise in the House of Commons, to strike down Chamberlain with Cromwell's cruel words: "You have sat too long there for any good you have been doing. Depart, I say, and let us have done with you. In the name of God, go!"

In this manner, gross errors at the top have ceased to be self-correcting in the democracies, at least until it is already much too late. In this manner, in fact, a kind of leadership-principle, a *fuehrer-prinzip,* has now been introduced into the workings of every free society, conspicuously including our own. It is a *fuehrer-prinzip* in reverse. It only works when the leader of the society plays down and muffles and misrepresents the hard facts that demand hard action, and instead urges his constituents to be comfortable and relax and enjoy themselves. But it always works in these circumstances, in just the way it worked in Britain in the 1930s; and it works precisely because the more important hard facts are now too far removed from the ordinary experience of the average citizen. To see how profoundly important this is, you only have to suppose the contrary. Suppose, for instance, that the facts of the missile race had been within our people's range of average experience. No one can then imagine the American people saying: "Really, we'd rather lose the missile race to the Soviets, because we quite agree with the former president of M. A. Hanna and Co. that something called 'our free enterprise economy' will be endangered, if we pay taxes to pay for missile development." Such a choice by an informed American electorate is in fact unimaginable. Instead of trying to picture the impossible, one's imagination flowers into happy pictures of the American electorate shouting down the arguments of the former president of M. A. Hanna and Company with one, indignant, national-minded voice.

But in reality, the facts of the missile race were infinitely remote from our people's experience. The former president of M. A. Hanna and Co. triumphantly persuaded the President of the United States that raising taxes or unbalancing the budget would be far more perilous than losing the missile race. The nature of the national choice we were making was three-quarters concealed from the people, and the quarter that was revealed was misrepresented. In these circumstances, there was no use hoping for the indignant, national-minded shout that would surely have been heard if the nature of the choice had been even dimly understood. Indeed our American democracy unfortunately suffers from a double vulnerability at the new Achilles' heel of all the free societies. Since Lincoln's time, we have always had a Presidential system, which has always worked very badly when the President was not strong. But nowadays Presidential errors not only misdirect the government. They also utterly mislead the nation, until the dreadful moment when the chickens come home to roost looking, as usual, like vultures.

There is no use pretending that the great choices in areas remote from normal experience do not present the most cruel difficulties, even when the man in the White House is both strong and bold. Harry Truman, for instance, was both bold and strong, for all his limitations. With Byrnes and Acheson and Marshall, Forrestal, McCloy, Lovett and Harriman among the higher policy-makers, and with such men on the second level as Bohlen and George Kennan and Robert Oppenheimer and many, many more, the first Truman administration also boasted a galaxy of talent never equalled, before or since, by any American administration in peacetime. As they all quite clearly understood, two great choices confronted these brilliant and far-seeing men who served Truman. The first and most obvious was the choice of the cold war—whether to make humiliating and dangerous surrenders in order to come to terms with the Soviet Union, or whether to assume the heavy burdens and responsibilities of leading the cause of freedom in the world. That choice was made early, decisively and well, with results that every American can now recall with increasingly nostalgic pride. But the second and more profound choice these men had to make was the choice of the atom—whether to insist upon international control of this terrible new force we had brought into the world, or whether to let history settle the matter in history's own stern, chancy way. An effort was made to establish a system of international atomic control. But when the Kremlin rejected the control-system designed by Dean Acheson, Robert Oppenheimer and Bernard M. Baruch, the choice of the atom was quietly shoved under the capacious governmental rug.

George Kennan, who was a leading advocate of this course of action, later published a most curious defense of it. Ostensibly, he was writing about which facts of the national situation ought to be revealed to the American people and which facts ought to be concealed. With characteristic naïveté (the mixture of extreme naïveté and genuine intellectual brilliance constitutes Kennan's peculiar charm) Kennan frankly wrote that if the American people were told *all* the facts of their situation, they would surely do the most awful and unspeakable things. He was writing before the final collapse of the American atomic monopoly. He did not spell out his meaning; but it was simple enough. He meant that if the American people were clearly warned of the probable meaning to them of great numbers of atomic and thermonuclear weapons in the hands of the Kremlin, they might insist on a preventive policy while the advantage still lay with the United States. This was not the national choice that Kennan favored. Kennan is not and never has been a convinced believer in government "of the people, by the people, for the people." As his friend Isaiah Berlin once remarked, Kennan believes "in government by a nest of brooding Salazars." So Kennan saw nothing wrong about himself and the other members of the sacred circle of officials having "clearance" making the greatest national choice of the postwar years, without even telling the nation in plain terms that there was a choice to make.

We disagree with Kennan, and we have always disagreed with him, both as to the practice and as to the principle. We never believed in preventive war, and we never heard preventive war advocated by a Western leader of any consequence, with the sole, somewhat unexpected exception of Aneurin Bevan. (At the forgotten time when Bevan was furious with his Cabinet-colleagues for not breaking the Berlin blockade with an armored column, he told one of us that preventive war "would of course have to be considered if Soviet steel output ever passed 25 million tons a year!") But while the American atomic monopoly endured, we ourselves always wondered whether it was not desirable to consider a policy of preventive show-down, aimed to force some bearable regulation of outstanding world questions, and above all aimed to secure Soviet assent to the most generous international atomic control system. Such a policy would never have worked, of course, unless we had built up our own strength and made ready to risk war with the Soviets; and war might indeed have resulted. Kennan was convinced war would result, and there is no better judge of Kremlin behavior. But as we look at the world around us, in this year of very doubtful grace, we cannot resist the suspicion that it might have been much better to risk war then, in the conditions then prevailing, than to run the risks we are running today.

Those are our practical reasons for disagreeing with Kennan. Yet the reasons of principle seem to us far more compelling. A democracy in which the officials make the great choices is like a proud household in which the footmen make the great choices. The footmen may be admirable Crichtons, every last one of them—and there are few officials we have admired more than Kennan. But this way of making choices in such a society as ours is morally wrong and inherently bad —"unethical and lousy," if you prefer the classic phrase. It is morally wrong because factors that ought to have no part in the equation are not purged out of the equation before the solution is reached. In the choice we have been discussing, for instance, a not inconsiderable factor was Kennan's own political viewpoint—his distrust of popular government, his positive horror of the Congress, his macabre mental picture of a U. S. Senate intoxicated with the *hubris* that would surely have resulted from a successful policy of preventive show-down.

The Senatorial *hubris* would no doubt have been very awful indeed, but the American people had a moral right to be asked whether they would prefer the *hubris* of the Senate or the *hubris* of Nikita Khrushchev and Mao Tse-Tung. Nor does it end there, either. Kennan's thoughts about this great choice, even if they were the right thoughts, would have been sharpened and clarified and amplified, if he had had to defend his position in the rough and tumble of national debate. Everyone's thoughts would have been sharpened and clarified and amplified. Even if the nation had finally concluded that Kennan's position was correct, the United States would then have gone forward with far more sureness, with far greater awareness of the dangers to avoid and the prices that must be paid, and therefore with a far better chance of making a success of Kennan's own policy.

Officials always tend to prefer secrecy about deep matters for just the same reasons that Mrs. Patrick Campbell preferred "the easy comfort of the marriage bed to the hurly-burly of the *chaise longue."* For the short run, secrecy about deep matters is a great deal more easy and more comfortable for officials and politicians than the rough, rude, clangorous and erratic process of public debate. But nothing but public debate insures the hard facts keeping their bite, and the choices being clearly outlined, and the grave situations being squarely faced. With no brisk winds of public opinion to blow the nonsense out the window, the sacred governmental circle of those having "clearance" is always too airless. Its members too largely live and have their being in a private world; and their contacts with reality are not sufficient to encourage realistic thinking, even when they are very able men indeed.

The results of this airlessness and secretiveness are ten times worse, very naturally, when the members of the sacred circle lack the expert preparation of a Kennan, or suffer from other incidental faults. Consider, for example, the specimen of Robert Cutler's prose and thought, which we have already given. Remember that this man was secretary of the National Security Council during a large part of the first six Eisenhower years. Remember further that he has the temperament of an adoring courtier—almost the kind of courtier whom St. Simon bitingly describes congratulating Louis XIV on the glory of his arms at the very moment of France's worst defeats by Marlborough. Remember also that this man who is so anxious to spare and please the President also had the chief responsibility for preparing the American government's most vital fact-analyses and policy-papers. Remember finally that he performed his duties in such inspissated secrecy, with such priestly care to avoid all contact with the "insecure," that he derived his chief external intellectual stimulus from happy old-Bostonian meetings with Secretary of Commerce Sinclair Weeks. Is it any wonder then, that the hard facts all but liquefied in Cutler's hands; and that the big, ugly choices were somehow made to vanish; and that the harsh realities of the national situation were never squarely faced? It is no wonder at all. It was to be expected.

One does not want to be unfair to Robert Cutler, a generous-hearted, honorable and patriotic man although a disastrous public servant. He was a special case. His quite genuine, wholly disinterested attachment to the President, his wish to make his hero happy, caused him to play the role that St. Simon's courtiers played for interested motives. By the same token, the Eisenhower administration is also a special case. It formed its worst habits in the early years, when

"Time" made the American government's feeblest retreats sound like old-fashioned cavalry charges, and the whole press joined in slathering Eisenhower with the most sickly adulation. Our own trade must bear its heavy share of the blame. The publishers and editorial writers and reporters did the President the greatest imaginable disservice, when they daily echoed the theory of the famous team that all would certainly be well, just because it was well known that Dwight D. Eisenhower could walk on the water-hole at Burning Tree golf course. In much the same way, General MacArthur's courtier-riddled staff used to tell him daily that he was capable of miracles. After his wonderfully brilliant Inchon operation, the General really came to believe that his flatterers must be right after all; and the result was the disaster on the Yalu. Once again in much the same way, the Eisenhower administration ended by believing in the miracles attributed to it during its first four luck-starred years. So when the luck turned as it was bound to do, the administration was caught wholly unprepared, both by the sudden turn of the luck, and by the sudden savagery of many who had been the loudest adulators.

If an administration's thinking is shaped by such men as Robert Cutler, and if the press also abandons its prime function of ventilating the big issues, the results are bound to be unhappy—to use the very mildest possible word. But the point we are chiefly trying to make has to do, not with the Eisenhower administration, but with all American administrations, and indeed with the governments of all democracies everywhere. For all of them, one rule is unvarying and will always be unvarying. Great national problems which are not honestly presented to the nation will either be badly solved; or they will simply be left unsolved until they grow rancid by over-keeping and make a public stink.

There is no escape from this rule in any democratic society, for an almost mechanically practical reason. Really major national problems, whether external or internal, can never be solved without effort and expenditure and risk of some kind. In our times, the scale of effort and outlay and risk required by the major problems tends to be more and more appalling. The nation will not make great efforts, or approve great expenditures, or run great risks to solve a problem, unless the nation knows what the problem is. The nation has to know, before the nation will act. That is the beginning and end of the matter; or rather it ought to be the beginning and end of the matter.

Instead, the positive desirability of the nation not knowing about all sorts of problems is now rather widely accepted. We have already suggested that the resulting airlessness of the decision-making process gravely impairs the judgment of the policy-makers who are cleared to know. In any case, although we may be naive, we have far more confidence in the judgment of the nation as a whole than in the judgment of a Robert Cutler or even of a George Kennan. But suppose that a problem of utmost gravity suddenly arises, which the policy-makers of the sacred circle instinctively judge with the most perfect accuracy. Their good judgment still goes for nothing. For the greatest efforts and outlays are demanded for the solution of the problem. The problem itself is triply classified, so the nation cannot be told about it. It is presented in the dim and muffling language of all official papers (that strange governmental prose, which appears to be produced by masticating clichés and used blotting paper into a uniform mush). Hence the policy-makers first measure the needed efforts and expenditures, and shrink back in horror from so difficult a new departure. Then they look at the classification on the official papers, and shrink back in horror from divulging such precious secrets. Meanwhile there is no stimulus to act from a nation clamoring for action, because the nation does not suspect the need for any action. In the end, therefore, the policy-makers forget their horror. They shove the problem under the rug. And they sink into a complacent lethargy, telling themselves and anyone else who learns that the problem is still there, under the rug, that "really nothing can be done about this particular problem because the country will not stand for it."

We have both been given this explanation for inaction again and again, by officials high and low. The need to act is almost never denied. Usually, it is simply stated that "the country will not stand for" the necessary action, as though this were an ample, penance-purging excuse for the government's neglect to do things urgently demanding to be done by the national interests of the United States. In these often-recurring cases, we grow angry, protesting that no official can blame the nation for not "standing for" a policy, when this same official is busily concealing from the nation the reasons why this policy will serve the national interest. Such officials, in our opinion, are derelict in their duties and faithless to their trust. For in such a society as ours, as we have said, the master is the people, the officials are the servants. A steward would be held derelict and faithless, if he let the

house fall down because he did not wish to show his master the cracks
in the foundations and to ask for money to pay for repairs. The
case of the steward who hopes against hope that the cracks will not
prove ruinous, because he dare not show them to his master, is identical with the case of the official who hopes against hope that inaction
will not prove ruinous, because he dare not tell the nation of the need
for action.

From our youth, we dimly remember a rule of Roman law that
suppressio veri is equal to *suggestio falsi*—suppression of the truth is
equal to disseminating untruth. None the less, one has a certain sympathy with officials and policy-makers who are merely caught in the
suffocating toils of our security regulations, like wretched Laocoon
caught in the toils of the god-sent serpents. But what is one to think
of the politicians and officials who go beyond concealing the facts,
who indulge in actual misrepresentation of the facts, in order to dodge
hard policy-choices and gain cheap and temporary political advantages? Here, indeed, is an interesting moral-philosophical question.
Our own government's behavior in these last twelve years has too
often forced us to think about this question; and whenever we think
about it, we always end by asking ourselves another question: Who
was the worst betrayer of the British people, the man in the tower or
Baldwin and Chamberlain?

The man in the tower, in case you do not remember him, was a
miserable junior army officer who sold wholly unimportant military
secrets to Adolf Hitler's agents. He was a traitor, no doubt about it;
and he was hanged for treason as traitors ought to be. Yet in practical
terms, he did only the most trifling harm. Then what about Baldwin
and Chamberlain and the rest, who lied to their people about the
Nazi menace, and left Britain all but unprotected against Hitler, primarily because doing otherwise was politically and economically inconvenient? No one has ever called them traitors; yet no one can
doubt that they did vastly more harm by hiding the big truth from
their own people than the man in the tower ever did by all his little
dealings with the enemy. So one is forced to the grim conclusion,
that nowadays, in the free societies, the worst treason is deception
of the people by the leaders of the people.

Yet once again, it does not quite end there. The man in the tower
knew he was committing treason, and so deserved his hanging. The
Baldwins and Chamberlains and their more recent American imitators

had no such consciousness of guilt. It is true that they acted from interested motives. Baldwin's motives seem to have been primarily political. (So he was enabled to leave office as just about the most popular Prime Minister Britain ever had, but in 1940, he had to be warned against going up to London, lest he be stoned in the streets.) The much narrower, less worldly and more rigid Chamberlain seems, from the documents, to have lacked Baldwin's political cynicism. But he was an egotist with an overmastering ambition to be remembered as a peacebringer—an ambition President Eisenhower has also shared. His views on what could be done and what could not be done were sharply limited by blinkers of class-interest—for a British rearmament effort that really balanced the German effort would have upset the commercial arrangements and weighed heavy on the pocketbooks of the business class that Chamberlain chiefly represented. For the same reason, the same blinkers limited the views of George Magoffin Humphrey, the real master of the U. S. government in the first Eisenhower years, and of the Secretary of the Treasury's useful ally at the Defense Department, Charles E. Wilson.

In truth, the echoes from the past in the Eisenhower administration have sometimes been all but unbearable, for those few who remembered the past. One recalled, above all, the fury-darkened face of Sir John Slessor,* re-living Lord Simon's actions as Chancellor of the Exchequer years later, in the worst moment of the Battle of Britain. "There he sat," said Slessor, "coolly, smugly running his blue pencil through the RAF budget estimates for squadron after squadron, and when we protested, he would say: 'Gentlemen, what you forget is that Britain's economic strength is Britain's first line of defense.' " One of us told that story, once, to George Humphrey. The sequel, even, was recounted; and it is perhaps worth recounting here.

In brief, one of those who saved Britain from the British Treasury's blue pencil was a half-mad but immensely rich old widow imbued with a passionate, old-fashioned patriotism, and suffering from a sad weakness for the company of handsome young men. Lady Houston was her name; and in the interwar years, when we ran into her once in that former meeting place of all the world, Rosa Lewis' Cavendish Hotel, we both pitied the silly, fat, aged coquette and felt contempt for the young RAF Apollo, hardly more than a third her age, who

* Later Marshal of the Royal Air Force; later still, chairman of the British Chiefs of Staff; and now retired.

was her embarrassed escort. But the RAF Apollo was in fact on duty, ordered by his desperate superior officers to get funds from Lady Houston to finance the Spitfire development, which the British Treasury had cut off. Those Spitfire squadrons that barely turned the balance of the battle in the darkest, most hopeless hours of 1940, were ultimately owed to Lady Houston, whom we had thought so pitiful.

It could hardly be hoped, in 1953, that an American Lady Houston would pick up the tab for the guided-missile race—what £100,000 would do very nicely in the early '30s, $100,000,000 would not do only two decades later. In 1953, moreover, the new leaders of our government had seen Lord Simon's error hideously proven. The greatest war in history had shown that balanced budgets offered small protection against the armed might of power-hungry dictators. In 1953, the businessmen who came to office under Eisenhower also had before their eyes the bleak and warning spectacle of the immense price their own class paid in Britain for the policies of Baldwin and Simon and Chamberlain. But for four years George Humphrey continued to make the identical argument that Lord Simon had made to Slessor. At Humphrey's insistence the NCS's grandiose directives formally subordinated the national defense of the United States to those more popular governmental activities, budget-balancing and tax-reduction. By Humphrey's persuasions, the President himself was finally convinced that unbalancing the budget was a shorter road to Communism than letting the Kremlin win the missile race. Although George Humphrey has now physically departed from the U. S. government, his spirit and his principles still ultimately control the administration's policies as these words are written.

Yet the bills for the euphoric years are already beginning to come in. With a cold chill of horror, one already senses that another 1939 and another 1940 may perhaps be contained in the future that is now rushing down upon us. So George Humphrey is a good test case in our inquiry into the moral responsibility of the deceivers of the people. The man himself gives the answer. As a human being, he was surely the most admirable of all the first Eisenhower "team," just as he was surely the most damaging as a national policy-maker. He was forceful, courageous, intelligent within his limits, and imbued with a natural vitality and love of life. He was not smug, or self-righteous, or even arrogant beyond a certain point—otherwise, he would not have listened to any mere reporter's warnings which he had no intention of heeding. He was a patriot, too, in all he did. And thus, by the simple process of elimination, one is forced to what is in fact the correct conclusion about Humphrey: he joined in deceiving the people because he was himself deceived.

There was a brief moment, to be sure, when the scales all but fell from Humphrey's eyes. In the aftermath of the unfortunate Geneva meeting at the summit, the chairman of the British Iron and Steel Board, Sir Robert Shone, led a delegation of Western European steelmasters to survey the Soviet steel industry. Humphrey was momentarily but deeply upset by the report of these trans-Atlantic friends and equals, these big businessmen whose judgment had to be believed, that Soviet steel technology and Soviet steel production were impressively advanced and powerful. He even interrupted the sacred routine of a National Security Council meeting to announce his "very bad news." But this was precisely the same news that Humphrey had already been hearing, month after month for many, many months, in the intelligence reports. No second Shone mission went to Russia, to renew Humphrey's alarm with another report from men he could not disbelieve. The intelligence reports, far from being prepared by big business friends and equals, came from bureaucrats and long-haired analysts and ex-professors, who could be disbelieved very easily indeed. So the scales on Humphrey's eyes reformed with great rapidity, primarily no doubt because he quite genuinely believed that any adequate American response to the "very bad news" of Soviet power would be dangerous to American freedom, or rather to American free enterprise. When you are convinced, as Humphrey once told one of us he was convinced, "that two more years of Truman budgets would have meant Communism in America," you are forced to disbelieve the intelligence and to deceive yourself in other ways. In such a frame of mind, the consequences of facing the hard facts are really too unpleasant.

The case of Humphrey is also the case of Charles E. Wilson with his detestably smug re-iteration: "Don't press the panic button. The Russians aren't ten feet high." By the same token, the case of Humphrey is also in part the case of Cutler, and it is the case of the various stooges Humphrey planted in the Bureau of the Budget, and of Herbert Hoover, Jr., and of Dwight D. Eisenhower himself. And there are the cases of other, altogether different men, who have also been deceivers of the people for altogether different reasons. One thinks of the later Aneurin Bevan, and above all of Harry Truman in his disastrous

Louis Johnson period. The Truman case, indeed, was the most curious of all. We have long pondered President Truman's strange denial of all that he had stood for until 1948, and was again to stand for after Korea. We think it occurred because Truman was temporarily flown with arrogance by his great victory in the 1948 election, and because he was also full of bitterness against Jim Forrestal and those others like Forrestal, who had not helped in the campaign when help was direly needed.

So it will not be enough to make a new law that deception of the people is just as treasonable as selling secrets to the enemy. For although the deceiver of the people is so immeasurably more dangerous than the seller of secrets, how can you pass a law that a man must not deceive himself? Yet something must be done, we think, unless the free societies are to succumb in the end to their new and awful vulnerability to weak, or untruthful, or self-deceiving leadership. We cannot go on any longer repeating the old pattern—comfortably neglecting the balance of power until it tilts too frighteningly against us; then making a desperate war against the heaviest odds; and finally winning the war by the painful process of calling up all our reserves after the war has started. A war of despair with Spitfires and Stukas was quite bad enough; and a war of despair with H-bombs is really not an acceptable way out. Yet if the free societies will not make the efforts and take the risks to maintain a reasonable balance in the vast world contest with the un-free, a war of despair will finally become the only way out—except submission and the end of freedom.

In these grim circumstances, our answer will surely seem too simple. It is indeed so simple that it can be given in seven words: "Throw out the classification stamps for good." We do not mean it absolutely literally, for there will always be a few technical secrets that ought not to be divulged, and there will always be some intelligence, too, that cannot be divulged without revealing the source. But in ninety-nine cases in every hundred, the effect of secrecy is to keep the truth from the people without keeping it from the enemy. Let the truth be open. Let all the press have easy access to it, instead of forcing highly specialized reporters to fight to get the truth. Then the truth will always be known and will always be debated by the whole nation. Let the whole nation debate the truth. Then the intending deceivers of the people will find their task too difficult. Let prolonged deception of the people again become too difficult. Then gross errors at the top will again be self-correcting, before they have produced irremediable disasters.

It is ironically comic, as well as unbearably painful, to see modern democracy strangling in the paper safeguards that rarely fulfill their purpose of protecting the state's secrets, and always and inevitably limit the people's right to know. For if the people do not know, democracy cannot work. The Soviet system can have secrets, and still work very well. The un-free do not need to know, for they heed the master's lash. But our system cannot work with many secrets; for there is no master's lash, and this is our system's glory and its aim. The glory will dim, the aim will be lost, the system itself will fail, if we do not soon again remember what makes our system work—if we do not soon see to it that the people know, at all times and in entire detail, exactly where they stand.

VI

The Years of Accomplishment

THE FIRST TRUMAN YEARS *were the period when the themes of the postwar story were established, and the foundations of the new American world policy were laid. As one looks back, the accomplishments of these years seem much more wonderful today than they seemed at the time. Americans emerging from the war, as we had just done, rather took it for granted that America should do great deeds; and we were only disturbed because the deeds were not greater, because the new departures were not bolder.*

Our first column was published December 31, 1945. Except for Harry Truman himself and the durable George Allen (now Eisenhower's crony and business partner), the men mentioned are now either dead or forgotten. Events, one must add, proved that the assessment of Truman was far too condescending. He kept his cronies in the White House, for poker and political chores. But he had the humility at the outset, and the self-confidence at the close of his time in office, to seek the biggest men he could find for the big jobs in government. Byrnes, Marshall and Acheson were his Secretaries of State.

96

Forrestal, Johnson, Marshall and Lovett were his Secretaries of Defense. Harriman, W. Bedell Smith, Sidney Souers (the first head of what became the CIA, the first secretary of the National Security Council, and a wise and capable man although very little known), Allen Dulles, David Bruce, Paul Hoffman, John J. McCloy and, one must remember, John Foster Dulles too, were other men on the top level of Truman's administration. Truman indulged in no nonsense about a staff system, but these men were his real staff; and except for Louis Johnson, every one of those listed was a most exceptional public servant.

The reference in this column to Truman's wage-price policy raises another interesting point. Until we looked back over our earliest pieces, we ourselves had altogether forgotten that the Truman of the 1948 campaign, who gave Hell to the "do-nothing 80th Congress" and its "slave-labor" Taft-Hartley act, was really the end-product of a long process of evolution. On labor and other social matters, in fact, Truman at first tended to follow his more conservative advisors, typified by Snyder and Steelman. His final position was in doubt right up to the Taft-Hartley act veto—for over two years more, indeed. Even that veto was preceded by a bitter battle in the White House. The battle ended when Truman chose the 1948 electoral strategy designed for him by his closest personal assistant of that period, Clark Clifford.

WASHINGTON

To those who have returned after four years' absence, the most conspicuous single fact in Washington is Harry S. Truman. In 1941, the White House was a place of power, whose occupant's every word was conned for hidden meanings and deeper implications touching the national future. In 1945, the White House has become the home of an average man in a neat gray suit, who answers questions briskly and is chiefly marked off from his fellows by such habits as folding his handkerchief into four perfectly symmetrical points. It is natural, therefore, to begin by asking the question: "What sort of a job will he do in the difficult times ahead?"

Some months of observation lead to a mixed answer. An average man, honest, well-intentioned, full of average virtues, but shrewd rather than brilliant and hopeful rather than far-sighted needs a strong staff if he is to solve complex problems. Thus the most important factor on the minus side is the poverty of Truman's personal staff. The need for stronger assistance is felt by Truman himself, who complains constantly of his inability to secure first-class men for the Government. Efforts have been and are being made by Bob Hannegan, among others, to introduce into the White House such men as the exceedingly able young Chairman of the Federal Communications Commission, Paul Porter.

Yet the gaps remain unfilled. Truman keeps about him his private cronies—George Allen, Captain Vardaman, the unfortunate Brigadier General Vaughan—men of the sort to be conspicuous good fellows at a State convention of the Legion. For business purposes, however, Truman's staff consists almost wholly of his old Missouri friend, OWMR Director John Snyder. Snyder's intimacy with Truman rests on the foundation of strong similarity in background, viewpoint and character, so that Snyder more reinforces than supplements Truman. Besides Snyder there are only Judge Rosenman, soon to leave, and the Labor Department's former director of conciliation, John Steelman, a new figure.

Nor is it true that Truman can dispense with a strong staff because he has reverted to cabinet government. He has not. Matters of foreign policy, to be sure, are left wholly to Byrnes. But in the past month, the vital labor issue, for example, has been handled so exclusively by Snyder and Steelman that it now seems that Secretary Schwellenbach is consulted only as a matter of form.

It is not surprising that an average man, dealing with vast problems, with minimum assistance, should sometimes seem less than sure in his touch. Neither is it surprising that this average man, crushed down by complex responsibilities, should sometimes groan that he never wanted the job—as everyone now knows Harry Truman does. What is more significant is that the Truman Presidency has recently passed into a new phase, not lacking in encouraging features. The first phase was the delusive honeymoon, when Truman entered the White House. The second was the phase of drift, when Truman tried to ease a whole New Deal program through Congress by the simple expedient of being amiable to reactionary legislators. The third is the present phase, in which the President has faced the facts—perhaps not quite all the facts, but a good many of them.

The turning point was the October 30 speech in which the President announced his wage-price policy, and first attacked Congress for inaction. The speech left lasting scars on the Administration, inflicted by Truman's acceptance of Snyder's advice to hold a balance between labor and industry, instead of siding with labor in the Roosevelt manner. It also marked out the way Truman would go.

Since that speech, Truman has tried his best to save some shreds of the Roosevelt program, by using the biggest man in the domestic side of his administration, Secretary of the Treasury Fred Vinson, as liaison with the Hill; and by backing Vinson to the full. He has put forward a program of his own—the labor disputes, health insurance, housing, price control and British loan bills. He has secured acceptance of the UNO Act and UNRRA appropriation. And he has labored endlessly to prevent labor disputes from halting reconversion. It is a reasonable record, made more hopeful by the indication that both Truman and his close advisers are constantly learning from experience.

Certain labor leaders and some of the old New Dealers are so discouraged that they are talking third party seriously. Some of the more reactionary businessmen appear to feel they can now discount the Government. Both groups in fact assume Truman's failure. Yet it is still an open question whether Truman can master his job. On his failure or success depends the answer to a question far more fundamental—whether the American machinery of government can any longer be controlled by an average man.—December 31, 1945 (JA & SA).

The shape of things to come was surprisingly visible, even in January, 1946. We still do not know, by the way, whether we were right about the danger of chemical and bacteriological warfare noted in the following column. We were trying to learn about it then; we were terrified by the little we learned; but we have been unable to learn much since. At any rate, its effects cannot be so terrible as the effects of H-bomb fall-out on a big scale. This was then, of course, unforeseen.

WASHINGTON

Even now, after the discussion of the atomic bomb, no one has grasped the fullness of the change in world power relationships wrought by scientists of World War II. Take, for example, one of the important reasons why a faction of the general staff advocated besieging rather than invading Japan. It was the invention of a chemical poisonous to plant life, a tablet of which, dropped in a rice paddy, was enough to kill the rice. A few B-29s dropping these chemical tablets were calculated to be sufficient to destroy upwards of half of the Japanese rice crop and thus to force surrender by the threat of imminent starvation.

Take also the carefully muffled developments in biological warfare. Nothing precise has leaked out. Yet it is known that the scientists who spent some 50 million dollars on this problem developed means for producing epidemics which it was expected would almost imitate the black plague, epizootics which would attack an enemy's cattle and other food animals and violent plant infections to attack food crops.

These things, like the atomic bomb itself, must radically alter all power relationships and therefore all political relationships.

The fact has been recognized by the first authoritative study of the strategic meaning of the atomic bomb and other new weapons, which now has been completed by the operations and plans division of the War Department. In view of the department's ingrained reluctance to educate the American people in the grim realities of their situation in the world, the paper will no doubt be withheld from publication.

Yet the paper's general conclusions, as reported on high authority, should be the subject of anxious, sleepless consideration by every thinking American. The main points are as follows:

1. The primary offensive weapon is now the air, with long-range rockets substituting for aircraft later on. The composition of the ground forces must be changed. The main component will be airborne troops, to land in enemy territory where opposition has been beaten down by a barrage of atomic explosives. Ordinary ground troops would be provided mainly for occupational and police duties.

2. The speed of modern attack, combined with the terrible, almost total destructive force of the atomic bomb, makes surprise the decisive factor. The nation which attacks first will be nearly sure of the victory. The United States is especially vulnerable to surprise attack, in view of the concentration of our people in great cities and the concentration in those cities of our war-making potential. In fact, when the new weapons are available to all nations, the United States will be the most dangerously placed of all the great powers.

3. Since the governmental structure of the United States deprives this country of the use of surprise in its initial defense, the only sure defense of the United States is the political defense. By the political defense, the strategists of the OPD mean the maintenance of world peace.

In other words, if we permit the world again to reach the condition in which war is likely, we may expect to be destroyed as the result of our own easy negligence and complacency.

That makes bitter reading in conjunction with the events in London so obviously foreshadowing the possible breakdown of the U. N., the political defense so toilsomely constructed during the past three years. It makes bitter reading also in conjunction with our postwar relapse into national weakness and complete demilitarization, which has already vastly reduced our power to influence the course of world events. . . .

No thinking official in Washington shirks the conclusion which must be drawn. A dependable world peace must be established, by whatever means. Possibly, when they are sufficiently alarmed, the men in the War Department, the Navy Department and the State Department who now discuss their fears in private will feel called upon to speak out in public. Then thinking will be somewhat more realistic. —January 29, 1946 (JA & SA).

January 18, 1946—and here already, is the cold war upon us. The Azerbaijanian crisis began our education in Soviet aims and tactics. What we wrote about it was unpopular—we were "premature anti-Stalinists." In this column we underestimated the potential of American pressure—which finally led to the Soviet withdrawal from Azerbaijan. We also got ourselves a calling down from an impeccably Republican publisher, who said we were too suspicious of the Kremlin. The publisher later dabbled in McCarthyism for a while, which made us laugh.

WASHINGTON

It is difficult, here in this country, to lie awake nights worrying about a bleak and distant nation with a backward population and a frowzily corrupt government. Such a nation is Iran. Yet it must be recorded that the official American observers interpret the Iranian crisis in a manner which is downright spine-chilling. If the experts are correct, it is urgent to grasp the issues which were raised when the Iranian representative, with the timidity of man conscious that he is being tactless, placed before the UNO Assembly his country's grievance against Russia.

First, what are the facts? Many months ago the Soviet Union indicated long-term ambitions in Iran by requesting an "oil concession."

The terms of the request were such that granting it would have meant virtual cession to the Soviet Union of most of northern Iran. The Iranians hastily announced that they would grant no concessions to anyone, including the United States, which had also asked for oil rights of a more conventional sort.

But the Russians did not let the matter rest there. The Iranian people are easy targets of agitation, being oppressed by a landlord-ridden government. In Azerbaijan, one of the northern provinces, a local front movement was organized and rebelled against the central authority. The Azerbaijani rebels were protected by the Russian occupying force, which forbade Iranian government troops to enter the area and put down the rebellion. With this assistance the rebels have now consolidated control of Azerbaijan. There are already strong indications that the process is about to be repeated in two other northern provinces, Meashead and Mazanderan, which will give the Russians about what they asked in the first instance. If the matter were to end there, however, it would concern only the Iranians, and those who believe that the UNO should protect its member states from such misfortunes.

Unfortunately, it seems extremely unlikely that the matter will end there. Opinion among the technicians at the State Department, based on the reports of our Teheran and Moscow Embassies, is virtually unanimous that the true Russian objective is the Iranian government itself. From their controlled northern provinces the Russians can send to the Iranian Parliament a solid bloc of deputies. This bloc, assisted by Russian pressure, and perhaps by the other forms of persuasion which are notoriously acceptable to Iranian politicians, will be enough to throw out the present Iranian administration. A new, Russian-dominated regime for all of Iran will then be installed.

If and when that is permitted to happen, illimitable perspectives of trouble will be opened out. The new Iranian government can transfer to the Russians the Anglo-Persian oil concessions which are vital to the British economy. They can bring the Russians down onto the Persian Gulf, a state of affairs which has been the nightmare of British imperial policy for 100 years. They can serve as a base for further pressure against Iraq and elsewhere in the Middle East. Perhaps most important of all, by the mere fact of being Russian-dominated, such an Iranian government could not avoid inflicting a mortal blow to British prestige throughout the whole Middle and Far Eastern colonial area.

The threat to the British imperial position will, of course, be redoubled if Soviet pressure on Turkey is renewed after the UNO meeting. Equally, the UNO's difficulties will be vastly increased, for the Turkish government is united and determined, where the Iranian government only weakly demands redress. In short, two things are at stake in the Iranian crisis and related Turkish problem. First, failure to find a sound solution will demonstrate the impotence of the UNO, almost at the moment of UNO's birth. Second, it will drastically alter the world balance of power by undermining Great Britain where it will hurt most.

Neither the effectiveness of the UNO nor the world balance of power can be considered matters of indifference to this country, although one may question the soundness of a power balance partly founded on imperialism. On the contrary, they are vital problems, directly affecting the national future.

Unhappily, it is hard to know what we can do. As a nation, we are rather in the position of one of our own leading officials, who tried to visit the scene of trouble in Azerbaijan. Every facility was promised him by the Soviets. But somehow the Soviet officer who had to stamp his passport had such a bad cold that no passport was issued until the American had to leave for home. Our ineffectuality seems to have been recognized by our top policy makers. They hope, at best, that some window-dressing will be applied to the accomplished facts by an Anglo-Russo-American commission of inquiry, which the Iranians have thus far refused to accept. At worst, they would not be heart-broken by a straight, old-fashioned Anglo-Russian deal for the partition of Iran in all but name. In the opinion of the technicians, however, neither of these solutions would permanently prevent the disastrous consequences which they foresee.—January 18, 1946 (JA & SA).

Here is a first report on the strange post-war peace-making process which, as predicted, made no peace. The column was a reaction to a scene—herein described—and an evening—not described. Ben Cohen, Chip Bohlen and the reporter went to dinner at Larue's. There, sitting on the dusty red plush banquettes, drinking cham-

pagne that Larue had hidden from the Nazis, the reporter heard
Bohlen give a full and honest forecast of the results to be expected
from the conference in Paris and the others that would follow it.
Cohen acted as a Greek chorus, keening, as it were, over the sad
future, while a pouch-eyed, elderly waiter looked on in melancholy
alarm.

PARIS

In the spring of 1941 it was natural for a man abandoning the newspaper business to resolve to attend the peace conference which would,
as one said then, mark "the end of all this." As a sort of sentimental
journey, your correspondent is fulfilling that resolve. It is necessary to
add, however, that no sensible man in the pompous precincts of the
Luxembourg Palace supposes for a moment that this meeting marks
either the end or the beginning of anything at all.

At best it will be a rather dull interlude in the new great power
diplomacy. At worst it will be a squalid public exhibition of the deterioration of international relations in our time. The Byrnes-Attlee
discussions of the Palestine problem are of far more functional importance.

Nevertheless, this meeting has its meaning, if it is viewed in the
correct perspective. It is not surprising to anyone accustomed to the
public speech of politicians and/or statesmen that the setting supplies
a far better perspective than anything being said on the floor of the
old French Senate Chamber. The park around the Luxembourg Palace, the last ecstasy of the old-fashioned French gardening, is in brilliant perfection. The trees display their green in ordered ranks. The
beds of flowers approximate the ideal of every French gardener, which
is to make nature look like a Turkish carpet. And in the graveled
walks the children still roll hoops while their parents (nurses are
expensive and therefore rare) talk of the two great themes of modern
Europe, the black market and the likelihood of war.

As for the palace itself, it was built for Marie de Medici at the
moment when the fruit of western culture was beginning to reach its
final ripeness on the sunny wall of France. And in the gross ornamen-
tation of the much later Senate Chamber, built into the ancient fabric,
one can perceive what overripeness does. It is very suitable that all
the little men in dark suits, waiting in boredom to speak themselves
or to listen to their chiefs, should be enshrined amid the coarse gilding, heavy crimson plush and vulgar plaster fantasy that first bespoke

decline. Without, in the balmy afternoon, there are those who want peace. There is even a suggestion of what peace can be. Within, in the stuffy atmosphere of the palace, there are the little men in their official chairs. They are the delegates to a peace conference, which they have little hope will bring peace.

If this meeting achieves anything, what will the achievement be? It will be a registration of the previous decisions of the Council of Foreign Ministers. And what will that registration accomplish? A little, the wise men answer. The Trieste settlement may establish the semblance of a governmental structure in that troubled area. Italy may at least be told where she stands and on what slender foundations she must attempt to build her future well-being. Balkan treaties may at least be signed. And the exhausted foreign ministers may at least be able to assure themselves that one group of questions has been stricken from the crowded agenda. That is something, even though it is not peace.

How little it is can best be judged by comparing the realities in the Balkans with the fine words of the treaty texts. The Soviet Union has engaged to evacuate the Soviet forces from Bulgaria within ninety days of the ratification of the treaty. But that will hardly be until next spring. Meanwhile, the little men in the plush chairs whisper to one another that the Soviets have already organized a wholly dependable Bulgarian secret police and are about to expel the non-Communist Minister of War and purify the army. With the opposition liquidated, the secret police in their hands and the army under Communist control, it will not matter much whether Soviet forces are in Bulgaria or out of it.

The same process is going on more slowly in Romania and Hungary, but there the Soviet armies will remain until the distant date when an Austrian treaty has been signed. At this writing the little men in the plush chairs are inclined to write off Romania, never notable for political independence, while they have hopes for Hungary. But as the destruction of the Hungarian economy continues, and as concession after concession is offered to Rakosi, the Communist leader, they also ask where it all will end in Hungary. Or one supposes that through the eyes of the Soviet delegation, who seem somehow harder and more solid than the other occupants of the plush chairs, Romania appears to be almost dependable while anti-Soviet wreckers are still permitted to survive in the streets of Budapest.

It is these realities which tell the truth about this conference. It is not such a meeting, even, as the unhappy conference at Versailles. It is a mere episode in the contest between two vast systems, one controlled by the Soviet Union, the other intermittently led by the United States. Every move by the chiefs on both sides has behind it the thought that ultimately the contest may lead not to peace but to war. It is still not too late to find some accommodation. But it hardly seems likely that an accommodation will be found if the occupants of the plush chairs do not begin to discuss their problem in realistic terms. Without leaders who will speak out as Litvinov did in the old days at Geneva, and without nations determined to support their words with deeds, the future may be hard for the children rolling their hoops under the sunlit trees.—July 31, 1946 (JA).

The most difficult trick in all reporting is to get the time-scales right, and to make sure you have covered all the bases. The time-scale in this column is very wrong, because we had not then covered a major base. In other words, we had not then done enough homework to know the primary importance of the means of delivering nuclear weapons, in any calculation of nuclear striking power. In the interval, the Soviets have acquired as many nuclear weapons as they need; but they are only just now, as these words are written, beginning to acquire superiority over us in the means of delivery. The reasoning of the column therefore has a vivid, present interest. But we are not so sure any longer that the original title of the column, "Must War Come?" was well chosen. The title should have been, "Must War or Surrender Come?"—but we had not envisioned the possibility of American-made Munichs in those early, proud and hopeful days.

WASHINGTON

When there is danger—even remote danger—of war, it is necessary to give prayerful consideration to the time factor. What situation will usher in the crisis, and how long will it take for that situation to arise? This is another of those questions which the men in Paris, who are debating peace and thinking of war, do not permit to creep into their public speeches. But it can be said on ample evidence that the question has not been banished from their minds.

The key to the time factor can be given in three words—the atom bomb. Atomic armaments are now of value to us, in blunt language, because they give us time in which to seek an understanding with the Soviet Union. Until the Soviet Union is equipped with atomic armaments, war is unlikely. Although they have largely concealed it from their people, the Soviet leaders know the meaning of the bomb. At Potsdam, when the secret was disclosed to him, Stalin dropped his guard and showed visible dismay for the first time in the history of the wartime meetings. Much more recently Molotov is known to have admitted to certain of his non-Soviet confederates that the bomb gave the Western powers "temporary" military superiority.

For the present, therefore, there will be crises. There will be thrusts to test our strength and firmness. There will be underground and indirect aggression. But there will be no final clash unless the Soviet leaders misjudge a situation and go too far to withdraw. Eventually, however, the successful manufacture of atomic armaments will restore to the Soviet leaders the military confidence which they now lack. And if in the interval the West has not surrendered, and no understanding has been achieved between the West and the Soviet Union, war will then be almost certain. Then the military advantage will be all on the Soviet side.

This is something that it is vitally important to grasp. The quickest way to grasp it is by studying the British position. These reports have referred before to the official estimate of Britain's situation, prepared some months ago for the Cabinet by the British chiefs of staff. Its known findings were: first, that the British Isles could not be successfully defended against atomic weapons and, second, that since the British Isles were indefensible, consideration should be given to transferring essential war manufactures to the dominions and colonies.

Recently, a man well qualified to speak with authority put the point rather more vividly. He was discussing the strategic meaning of the long-range rockets that the Soviets have been showering over Scandinavia from centers in Germany. These centers, incidentally, in themselves constitute a flagrant violation of a solemn treaty. He pointed out that the rockets already in use were capable of subjecting Britain to a hideous ordeal, comparable to what she would have had to withstand if Hitler had been ready to use his V-2's in mass in 1942 or 1943. "We are now the Malta of the next war," he remarked wrily. "And when an enemy can put atomic warheads into those rockets, I'm afraid we shall be the Pantelleria."

What Britain lacks, and what the Soviets have, is space. Space is vital, because dispersion is the only real defense against atomic weapons. In the United States we too have space. What we lack, and what the Soviets have, is the kind of society which permits space to be used for defense. Our essential industries—and our population—are heavily concentrated in our great urban centers. In the strategic studies prepared by our own Army General Staff and approved by the Joint Chiefs of Staff, it is estimated that mass bombardment by long-range projectiles with atomic charges would kill or disable something like 40 per cent of our people.

It would naturally destroy a far higher proportion of our industrial potential. Next to the establishment of an enormous, costly and permanently alerted war machine, our first defensive measure would have to be re-planning our urban pattern to disperse population and industry. That would call for virtual abandonment of all our great cities. We could not conceivably take this and the other needed defensive steps without changing the very basis of our society. Freedom would have to go first.

It is no use attempting to forecast a future which is still mercifully distant, at least by a number of years. But it would be foolish not to take note that the Soviet offensive against Britain began only a few months after the close of the second world war. In the current phase it is concentrated in the Middle East and it is being waged with the weapons of political warfare and the warfare of nerves. Yet it is no less an offensive for all that, and no less clearly discloses future Soviet aims. It would also be foolish to forget Brooks Atkinson's wise observation, that Soviet policy is motivated by a passion for security, but that the Soviet leaders will never feel secure so long as the United States and Britain are dominant powers. If Soviet policy is already expansionist when Soviet military power is inferior, what will Soviet policy become when Soviet power passes that of the West?

It is a grim question. The experts are all but unanimous, however, that mass production of atomic armaments will be an effort of years for the war-ravaged, never complex industry of the Soviet Union. The time is not so short as many people suppose. Furthermore, if the atom bomb is like a time bomb, which must explode into war if it is not defused by realistic peacemaking, it is also the best hope of peace that we have.

This is true, not because the bomb is a threat, but because the simple act of internationalizing control of atomic energy will constitute a sort of permanent peace insurance. Previous systems of international co-operation have always broken down because they have contained no element outside and above competing national sovereignties. The atomic development authority proposed in the Baruch report will be precisely such an element, giving to the United Nations a special strength no league or federation in history has ever had. If Soviet policy really changes, the first sign will be acceptance of the Baruch report. And if ever an atomic development authority is established and a measure of disarmament is agreed upon, the world can live without fear. It is toward that goal that the American policy makers are patiently plugging away.—September 25, 1946 (JA).

This column from Athens was written after the younger member of our partnership had been confidentially informed of Attlee's message to Truman, announcing that Britain would have to lay down the burden she had been carrying in Greece and Turkey. The senior partner in Washington did not know the background; but the tone of the lead so struck him that he hurried to the State Department. And there he found assistant Secretary of State Will Clayton somewhat distractedly involved in the preliminary studies of the Truman doctrine and the Greek-Turkish aid bill.

ATHENS

The United States has got to fish or cut bait not only in Greece but throughout the whole area. In a rather crude nutshell that is the opinion of every experienced observer in Athens. It is also the conclusion which has been independently reached and dispatched to Washington by both Mark F. Ethridge, head of the American delegation of the United Nations commission, and Paul A. Porter, chief of the American economic mission to Greece.

The conclusion is in essence this: Either the United States makes a determined effort to bring some sort of order out of the political and economic chaos in which Greece is now wallowing, or Greece is mathematically certain to become another Soviet-Balkan puppet, with the profoundest effect on the whole world balance of power.

If the United States decides to make this effort, Porter and Ethridge will be initially, at least, the two chief instruments of the radically new American policy. Their jobs will be cut out for them. A brief glance at the present internal situation of Greece is enough to show why.

In the first place Porter has found himself confronted with an economic crisis which threatens to blow the whole of the Greek economy sky high within two to four weeks. If that happens Porter and Ethridge might just as well have stayed at home.

The crisis springs from the fact that the Greek drachma has been held in some sort of wobbly equilibrium for a number of months only by offering sovereigns minted from the pre-war stock of Greek gold in exchange for paper money. Now the Greek government is scraping the bottom of the barrel and already the warier Greek merchants are refusing to deal in drachmas in large sums. If nothing is done the drachma will again litter the Athens streets within a month at the latest, and all hope of bringing order out of the Greek economic mess will have come to an end.

In these circumstances Porter's first objective has been to buy time, a commodity which only the United States government can now afford. His first effort met with a rebuff when the Federal Reserve Bank rather haughtily pointed out that the technique he advocated was contrary to its charter. Yet Porter is a determined man and it is probable that some expedient will be found. Even so, he will not really have begun to do his job; he will merely have made it possible to do a job at all.

The Greek political situation and the Greek economy are in effect one and the same problem. The guerrilla fighting in the north is a terrible strain on the feeble Greek economy, a fact of which those who organized and control the guerrillas are fully aware.

Intelligence reports indicate that the guerrillas have recently greatly expanded their area of control so that the fighting threatens to take on the character of a full-scale civil war. The guerrillas, commanded by the Communists, are ably abetted by the Communist-Leftist coalition, the E.A.M. They support the guerrillas with adroit propaganda, which they are willing to carry to remarkable lengths.

On one recent occasion they planted a corpse for a junketing M.P. to trip over, with the idea of convincing him of the merciless terror of the Greek "Monarcho-Fascist" regime.

More important than the Communist propaganda have been their secret organizations, of which the most successful is the Kossa, established to infiltrate and weaken the Greek Army. No one knows how many Kossa men there are. When uncovered they have always been found to be those soldiers who had saluted most sharply and clicked their heels most enthusiastically. The Greek Army contemplates an all-out drive against the guerrillas in the spring and it will then become clear just how effective the work of the Kossa has been.

As for the Greek government, it has often been described as Fascist. Its main characteristic seems to be rather its total incompetence. There is no doubt that it was elected fairly and by a huge majority and there is also no doubt that it has allowed complete freedom of speech and of political action, at least in Athens. But at the last elections, the Greek people, revolted by the excesses of the Communists, turned in terrified reaction to the Right.

The result is a government largely dominated by a small group of rich traders and merchants who religiously avoid the payment of income taxes. These men are totally incapable even of discussing the kind of sweeping social and economic reforms which alone could counteract the quite natural attraction of Communism in this misery-ridden country.

There are a few capable men in the government and a few tired old men of good will, like Maximos, the new Prime Minister. But most Greek politicians have no higher ambition than to continue to taste the profitable delights of a free economy at American expense. To the skirts of politicians clings a vast mass of civil servants, astonishingly inefficient, who are guaranteed by law a life-time place at the public trough.

There is some Fascist talk in the smart bars in Athens, but the real failure of the Greek government is better typified by American luxury goods bought with precious dollars, visible in the windows of rich shops, while small boys beg at the doors of the foreigners' hotels.

But more tragic than government incompetence is the new and bitter hatred between Greek and Greek. Neither American economic aid nor the implacable bloodletting of Soviet rule will soon end that. Certainly Porter and Ethridge have their job cut out for them, but it is only necessary seriously to consider the alternative to realize why so many competent experts here are convinced that it is a job which must be done.—February 24, 1947 (SA).

Under the sharp stimulus of the Greek-Turkish problem, the bipartisan foreign policy was now taking the shape that endured through the great, creative years, until Arthur H. Vandenberg's death. Senator Taft later told us that he disliked the small share in the machinery that Vandenberg insisted upon giving him. In fact, Taft thought, as he always used to say, that the "opposition's job is to oppose," on foreign and defense policy as well as other matters. But the nation was told, in clear, bold terms, about the national problems; and Taft, for all his extraordinary mastery of the 80th Congress, could do nothing to obstruct the measures that he detested, like the Marshall Plan and the resolution that laid the foundations for the later-voted NATO alliance.

WASHINGTON

Two men will largely determine how the Republicans respond to the President's presentation of the world crisis at his White House conference with the leaders of Congress. And since the President needs Republican help to get any kind of measure through the House and Senate, these two men share the heaviest responsibility for the crucial decision, whether the United States will now shoulder the burdens of world power. The pair to whom fate has given this choice—which may come close to being a choice between national survival and non-survival—are Arthur Hendrick Vandenberg, of Michigan, and Robert Alphonso Taft, of Ohio.

Under the circumstances, it is important to know whether there is any truth in the recurrent reports of dissension and rivalry between these two chieftains of the Republicans in the Senate. Currency has been given to these reports by their recent open differences, in particular on trade agreements policy and on the confirmation of David E. Lilienthal. The reports have gained further color of probability from the tendency of the more progressive Senate Republicans to line up behind Vandenberg, while the extreme conservatives look to Taft for leadership, despite the marked differences between his viewpoint and theirs.

For the present, however, it can be said that Vandenberg and Taft are still working together and still anxious to continue to do so. Both are conscious that a wedge can easily be driven between them, and both are aware of what such a personal split would do to their party. Accordingly, they are both now going rather farther out of the way than in the past to keep their relationship in working order. During the last week, in recognition of the danger in which they find themselves, each has acted to acknowledge the claims of the other.

For his part, Vandenberg notified the White House after the first conference that Taft and the official Senate majority leader, Wallace

H. White, of Maine, should always be invited. This, to be blunt about it, was a development which the White House had been anxious to avoid, considering Taft resistant to bipartisan co-operation in general and Administration foreign policy in particular. Under the circumstances, however, the White House could only yield, so that Taft hereafter will share part of Vandenberg's authority in the foreign policy field. He cannot help but do so, if he is also to be acquainted with the same confidential facts which are imparted to his co-leader.

In the same fashion Taft almost simultaneously acted to have Vandenberg join in the meetings of the Republican steering committee of the Senate. From the time of his elevation to the Senate presidency pro tempore Vandenberg had not been a working member of this body and the committee had lacked any expert on foreign affairs. On Saturday he joined the committee for a long session, at which the developing world crisis was discussed in some detail. Partly as a result of this it was arranged that he should make a presentation of the problem to the Republican conference following the White House meeting of Congressional leaders.

But while Vandenberg is still a foreign policy expert his return to the Republican steering committee will also give him a voice in domestic policy.

These developments are important in themselves, since they indicate that Vandenberg and Taft have grasped the obvious fact that foreign and domestic policy cannot be kept in entirely separate compartments. In order to avoid any rivalry Vandenberg and Taft originally staked out separate claims. Vandenberg was to lead the Republicans in foreign policy matters and Taft was to be supreme in the domestic field. That plan of organization has now broken down under the impact of the world crisis. If large appropriations are needed—as they unquestionably are—in order to finance the job of restoring economic and political stability in such troubled areas as Greece, then Taft's cherished program of domestic economy is immediately endangered.

That is the immediate cause of the breakdown of the divided leadership, which was bound to run into trouble sooner or later in any case. A new system is now being improvised. Most probably Vandenberg will remain predominant, but cease to have the only casting vote in the foreign field. The same dilution of authority will be accepted by Taft in the area of domestic policy. And as a result the Republican leadership of the Senate will assume a greater collective responsibility. This is a healthy change.

Meanwhile, it is natural to ask how the pair will react in their present difficult situation, in which they must choose between the inherent necessities of the Vandenberg foreign policy and the announced objectives of the Taft domestic policy. Although Vandenberg's final word is yet to be given (and will no doubt depend on his opinion of the detailed plans offered by the President and the State Department) no one feels much doubt about how the Michigan Senator will answer the question now being put to him. In essence, it is simply a question whether he is willing to surrender the largest part of the world to Soviet domination.

Like President Truman himself he has so far deferred demanding the active but costly preventive measures which the situation so long required, yet Vandenberg's answer to such a question is not hard to anticipate.

With Taft, the puzzle is infinitely harder to solve. Recently he has given some indications of approval for aid in the Greek emergency; and has even suggested that a broader program could be excused as necessary to "finish the war." If Taft decides to work with Vandenberg, a radical change will come over the American political scene. But if he pulls back at the last moment (as his instincts will surely urge him to do) anything can happen, from an open war between Republican factions to a constitutional crisis.—March 10, 1947 (JA).

The "logical conclusion" of the Truman Doctrine was, of course, the Marshall Plan. The next piece was written when we had in fact learned of the anxious discussions in the State Department between those who said it must be done, and those who said it could not be done. The strongest voices in the first category were Dean Acheson and Paul H. Nitze. They convinced General Marshall; and when Marshall said: "Mr. President, this is in the national interest," Truman, to his eternal credit, squared his shoulders and agreed.

WASHINGTON

If the "Truman Doctrine" of containing Soviet political imperialism is to succeed, it must be followed to its logical conclusion. And if it is to be followed to its logical conclusion, the United States must have some new technique for implementing it financially. One reason why this is so may be sensed from the remark of one experienced British diplomat in the Middle East. The Americans had made a hard choice in the Greek-Turkish aid policy, but the only possible choice. "But my God," he added, "what a way to go about it!"

No doubt in the back of his mind was the startling contrast between the British financial approach to the Greek problem and the new American approach. So quietly was it done that only after the Greek crisis came to a head did it become known that since the end of the war, counting all expenditures, the British had poured into Greece the fantastic total of $760,000,000 in the pound-sterling equivalent. Thus it is not surprising that the British (very few of whom have ever really grasped how the American political system actually works) were genuinely surprised and shocked to find that a request for one-third of this amount from the American Congress was accompanied by an enormous hullabaloo and that the policy of aid to Greece was made to seem hardly less than a declaration of war on the Soviet Union.

This British reaction is interesting only in that it serves to demonstrate the basic weakness inherent in the present technique of implementing American economic foreign policy. The British themselves, as their leading economists in Greece were willing to admit, made a vast miscalculation in handling their economic policy in Greece; they attempted unsuccessfully to buy time in installments, and without any master plan, against an over-all world settlement. The United States cannot afford to make the same mistake on a world scale.

For it is obvious that what is true of Greece and Turkey is likewise true in many other parts of the world; in Korea, in China, in the Middle East as a whole, possibly in Italy and France. If the "Truman Doctrine" is to work it must be applied, according to a well thought-out master plan, in these and other parts of the world. But no master plan is possible if there is to be a piecemeal approach. And above all, world peace will hardly survive a long series of Greek crises, with the Congress being bludgeoned and frightened every six months or so into sticking a costly finger into some new hole in the dike.

Yet no instrumentality now exists for pursuing any other course. The chief financial instruments are the Export-Import Bank and the World Bank. One is American, the other international (although as the biggest investors in the World Bank the American influence there is evidently preponderant). Aside from the fact that neither institution has much left in the kitty, both suffer from the same limitation. A reasonable certainty of the return of money lent is a requirement for both. Thus the operations of the Export-Import Bank and of the World Bank must necessarily be concerned with good financial risks. Yet the areas of the world most closely threatened by Soviet political imperialism are precisely those which are bad financial risks. The United States is thus in the position of having committed itself to a policy and of having at the same time no way to make this policy work.

Reduced to its simplest terms, the reasoning behind the developing American policy runs like this: As long as the present post-war economic misery continues, the opportunity for world-wide expansion of the Soviet Union through the medium of its political instrument, the Communist parties of the world, continues. Therefore, just as it is in the interest of the Soviets that this misery go on, so it is in the interest of the United States to make a determined effort to get the war-wrecked economy of the world back on its feet. There is nothing academic in this assessment.

Two recent developments underline the urgency of the crisis which threatens the Western World. One is the growing monetary crisis (in Western Europe) described in a recent report in this space. The other is the mounting evidence that the Communist party line is about to make one of its historic shifts. The real meaning of the French crisis is that there is now a strong likelihood that in those countries where their hold over the labor movements is tight, the Communists may soon discard their policy of off-again-on-again collaboration with governments of which they form a part, and use their power in the labor movements to reduce the slowly recovering national economy to chaos.

In this situation the United States has a choice. Either we can withdraw nervously into continental isolation, close our eyes and cross our fingers, or we can follow the "Truman Doctrine" to its logical conclusion, with the hope that in a reasonably stable and economically sound world situation a true world settlement with the Soviet Union can be made. If the latter choice is the American choice—and it is the only choice which does not lead either to surrender or to an American version of Fascism—it has a real chance of success, but only if certain conditions are fulfilled. One condition is a working partnership agreement with a recovering Great Britain. Another is a practicable master plan based on the grim realities of the world economic situation rather than the present method of attempting feverishly to snuff out fires al-

ready well started. A third is the authority—and the money—to carry
this master plan through to completion. And the last is a determination
of the American people, in the dark days which are surely coming, to
see through to the end of what they have now started.—May 16, 1947
(SA).

At the time, the following column about Czechoslovakia caused us
to be widely denounced as scaremongers. But "within a few months"
the iron curtain did indeed "clank down with finality." Poor Masaryk!
The reporter had seen him in Paris and had been shocked by his
frivolity. But no doubt he was making jokes then to distract his mind
from the fate he saw already rushing down upon him.

PRAGUE

In contrast to the rest of Europe the surface of life here is wonderfully bustling and prosperous. Prague's baroque palaces and modern
suburbs could still do with a lick of paint. But the shops are full of
goods. The streets are jammed with traffic. And the people are downright fat.

Beneath this happy surface, however, an ominous and tragic fact
is only half concealed. Czechoslovakia is in the grip of a creeping
terror. Since the end of the war this has been a show place for optimists. It has been the place where Communists ruled like democrats,
where East and West could meet without an intervening iron curtain,
where human freedom survived in the shadow of Soviet power. That
period is coming to an end. Within a few months, unless drastic coun-
termeasures are taken, the iron curtain will clank down with finality.
The terror, now creeping underground, will be open and unashamed.
Czechoslovakia will know the fate of Hungary, of Poland, of Romania
and Bulgaria.

It seems incredible that a freedom-loving people, Western in habit
and tradition, should accept such a fate when there are no Soviet troops
in Czechoslovakia. But the Czechs bear deep scars of national neurosis
from the experience of the last eight years. All of them are conscious
that the Soviet armies in Germany are deployed along their borders.
As for their government, President Benes, the beloved link with the
past, is aged and ailing. The Foreign Minister with a great name, Jan
Masaryk, is a paunchy man who makes jokes. And since the last election the real control has been in the hands of the Communists led by
Prime Minister Gottwald.

Long ago the Communists made their preparations for the event that is now occurring. At the head of the army they placed General Svoboda, commander of the Czechoslovak corps in Russia during the war, rumored holder of a party card and, in any case, a man who knows which side of his bread is buttered. Almost without exception he has passed over Western-experienced Czech officers and promoted those who have Russian associations. Above all the army's counter-intelligence corps, which is really a secret service, has come under the domination of Communists or men who will do their bidding.

The army is infiltrated and neutralized. The Information Ministry, in overtly Communist hands, is ready to blare propaganda through Soviet-style loud speakers in every town. Most decisive of all, the Ministry of the Interior, headed by the Communist Nosek, has transformed all branches of the national police into service organizations of the party. With complete control of the labor unions and a considerable number of armed partisans, the Communists thus hold all the trumps for any game of coup d'etat.

To be sure, these trumps have long been in Communist hands. But until recently even the more Western-minded Communists, like Prime Minister Gottwald and the Deputy Foreign Minister Klementis, seem to have believed that their role was to play the game the Western way. Czechoslovakia is economically dependent on its links with the West. When the Marshall plan was announced, Czech Communists and non-Communists alike voted unanimously to send a delegation to the preparatory conference in Paris. This occurred, interestingly enough, after the Czechs had been assured by a visiting group from Warsaw, including influential Communist members of the Polish government, that Poland would do likewise.

As every one now knows, the Czechs learned their error from Stalin in person. At Moscow Gottwald had his head washed by the generalissimo. Under the implied threat of rupture of the Czech-Soviet alliance the whole Cabinet voted unanimously to reverse its previous unanimous vote. In the streets of Prague people talked of "the new Munich." The incident showed the Czechs how far their independence was impaired. What was far more important, it also showed Moscow that some spirit of independence remained at Prague. The order is now known to have gone out at once "Put the screws on." The screws are on today. The major manifestation of this fact so far has been the arrest of a large number of members of the Slovak Democratic party on charges of collaboration with "Fascist refugee wreckers."

The atmosphere of terror is already tangible. Already leading non-Communist Czechs are known to be considering flight. And this is only the beginning of the story. All competent authorities here, foreign and Czech, have privately agreed that the end will come with the open suppression of Czechoslovakia's hardly rewon independence unless those who love their liberties act in the interval in self-defense. They must do so before next spring, the time of the elections, for which the present terror is intended to prepare.—November 5, 1947 (JA).

This was the first unqualified and public warning of the Berlin blockade.

BERLIN

Every new arrival in Berlin complains of a sense of unreality. Against the impossibly melodramatic backdrop of the ruined city, the life of the American community in the undamaged suburbs, complete with hot dogs, country clubs, Coca-Cola and Saturday night hops, seems totally unreal. Yet behind the unreality there lies one terrible reality: if war is to come, it may well start here. For the Russians, who completely surround the city, are determined to force the Western powers out. There is no doubt at all about that. The only question is how much the Kremlin is willing to risk in the process.

Unfortunately, many observers here believe that the Russians are willing to risk a great deal, for two reasons. First, despite every effort of the Soviets, Western influence still seeps out from Berlin to the Russian empire to the east. The Western presence here thus no doubt appears a malignant cancer which must be cut out. Second, and perhaps more important, Soviet plans for employing a revived and controlled German nationalism as an instrument for eventually bringing all Germany within the Soviet sphere can never really succeed while the Western powers remain in Berlin.

The Soviet campaign to correct this situation by forcing the Westerners out is, of course, already well under way. There has been nothing official. Indeed, Russian General Sokolovsky (a personally likeable man who admires Jane Austen) has never even so much as hinted to American General Lucius Clay that he would be glad to see the last of him. Yet Russian actions, in forcing the Americans to take to the air to supply the American contingent, in stopping road convoys and in cutting off shipments from Berlin to the west, have spoken a great deal louder than words.

Under the firm, wise leadership of General Clay the Americans nevertheless remain, as do the British and French. It must now be clear to the Kremlin that if this infinitely dangerous game of cat and mouse is to be played to the end more drastic action will be necessary. Such action, in the opinion of qualified observers here, could take either of two forms.

The first alternative is the obvious one. As one American officer put it, "They can load us on cattle cars bound for Siberia any night they want." The Western response to the use of force is equally obvious—war. It is possible that the Kremlin may have concluded that war is inevitable, and that it is better fought now than later. But this appears increasingly improbable and is really no longer feared.

The second possible Soviet move is less obvious, and the appropriate Western response is anything but clear. This move is simply to cut, whether overtly or under some pretext, the civilian supply lines from the Western zones to Berlin. For example, the vital Magdeburg bridge over the Elbe might suddenly break down, while fortuitously sunken barges made the canal network into Berlin impassable. The results are entirely foreseeable. The two million people in the Western sectors of Berlin would soon begin to starve. For although the Americans here are supplied entirely by air, it is impossible to supply the Germans in the Western sectors except by rail and canal shipments from the Western zones.

As the starving Berliners rioted, the Soviet authorities might then approach the Westerners, note that the situation was deplorable, and offer to assume the task of feeding Berlin. They would attach one condition: that the Western powers, having no business in Berlin anyway, evacuate the city.

What should the Western powers do then?—June 2, 1948 (SA).

We include the following for two reasons. It recreates the atmosphere of the most hectic convention we can remember. And it also illustrates the still slightly patronizing attitude towards Harry Truman —then widespread—that led us to make the biggest bloomer we ever made. This was flatly predicting and positively assuming that Truman was hopelessly doomed from the start. We and many others were still patronizing towards Truman then, because we thought the big successes of his administration were owing to the big men in the Cabinet —Marshall, Forrestal, Lovett and the others. But it is the rule that a President must always be given final credit for *all* his administration's successes, and final blame for *all* its failures.

PHILADELPHIA

"He's stopped trying to be President. He's being Truman now." A close observer of the President made the remark a little sadly, in the ghastly early hours of the morning, while the President was shouting his defiance of the Republicans before the sweating delegates to the Democratic convention. The most striking thing about the President's speech was his final abandonment of the rather stilted, elevated tone which he has thought suitable to his office. He was campaigning for re-election as a county Sheriff in the Ozarks might campaign.

The drama and interest of the whole episode were more genuinely intense than is usual in politics. There was, first of all, the inescapable feeling that the President was venting on the Republicans some of the resentment which he feels against the Democrats who opposed his renomination. It was known that his congratulatory telephone call to Senator Alben Barkley, the previous evening, had been rapidly transformed into a philippic against his enemies within the party. From the rear steps of Convention Hall, where the President waited for hours to speak, word kept coming back of the sharpness with which he still felt this resentment.

There were, secondly, the circumstances of the stirring decision to call a special session of Congress, which was being bruited about hours before the President at length spoke. The decision was taken at the White House, without consultation with any of the Congressional leaders. Even the President's running mate, Senator Barkley, was not informed of what was afoot at least until late in the afternoon before the convention's final session. Here in Philadelphia Robert Hannegan, James Roosevelt and a group of representatives of the big city leaders had agreed the previous evening that there ought to be a special session, and had passed their view to the White House. But very probably the President himself was not informed of this meeting, since a good many of those present had played leading parts in the abortive anti-Truman coalition. Truman and his advisers—most conspicuously Clark Clifford—took the decision by themselves, to all intents and purposes.

Then there were also the decision's motives. The President beyond question sincerely believes in the social and economic objectives which he set forth in his speech. It is also important to note that he and his advisers have sincerely convinced themselves, as threatened politicians so often can, that the victory of their opponents will inevitably usher in a total triumph of reaction and perhaps of Fascism. These two beliefs provided the atmosphere of the decision.

In this connection, it is vitally important to distinguish between the effects of the call for a special session and the motives for the call. The Republicans in Congress richly deserve what they are getting. The President was entirely correct in almost every word he said about their handling of social and economic measures, no matter what you may think of the tone in which he said it. The Republican platform may, and probably does, represent the views of Governor Dewey and Governor Warren. But the platform's kind words for enlightened social policies do not correctly represent the Congressional majority.

It will be incredibly costly and dangerous to have the whole country set by the ears, and all the dirty linen of our politics publicly washed, in a time of dreadful danger abroad. But it will also be useful to have the wide difference between the Republican candidates and the Republican Congress aired during the campaign. And certain badly needed legislation may even be passed before the special session ends.

So much for the effects. As for the motives, no one who is not very naive can suppose that securing passage of needed social measures was a predominating influence in the President's decision to call the session. The decision was taken with the clear knowledge that tremendous risks were involved. Yet the real reasons for the decision were obviously political. First, a special session provides the President with an inexpensive form of electoral campaign, which is helpful in view of the present state of Democratic party finances. Second and more important, holding the session will be a much more effective way to campaign than a straight debating match against such a powerful adversary as Governor Dewey.

All these assorted facts, so complexly inter-related, in turn say something about the President himself. Even the majority of his oldest and closest friends now agree that he is a man who, although decent, patriotic, honest and courageous, has been terribly overburdened by the responsibilities of the Presidency in such a time as this.

At first, he seemed to hate those responsibilities. Then he began to cling to them, as men in such positions will. And now that the campaign is ahead, and defeat looms up, he is "being Truman now" in the sense that he is fighting for re-election on a sort of no-holds-barred system, without any of those claims to the grand style which he used to try to make. It would have been better if he had fought for his program in this manner from the first. As matters stand, one must admire the President's courage. One must hope that those who deserve to be shown up in the fight are in fact thoroughly shown up. But one cannot help but fear the consequences of an all-out political free-for-all in the United States of 1948.—July 16, 1948 (JA & SA).

Even before McCarthy, the seeds had already been planted. This pre-McCarthy forecast of McCarthyism's effect on the government service was to be lamentably substantiated by events.

WASHINGTON

There is not the slightest doubt that in these times the American government must have the right to protect itself from attack from within. The immensely delicate and difficult problem of national security exists and it must somehow be solved. No sensible man believes that J. Parnell Thomas's headline hunts can solve it. And any one who believes that the solution is to be found in the present loyalty program should consider certain questions which the conduct of the loyalty program has posed.

First, there is the whole troubling question of guilt by association. Obviously, a man who has constantly associated with Communists and promoted Communist fronts should not have access to state secrets. But how far should this principle be carried?

Take the recent case of a State Department employee. He was charged with having associated with ten persons, all presumably suspect. He had never heard of five of them and had had only the most casual contacts with four. But he had known one of the ten intimately for several years.

This man was a banker, and stood high in the banking community, a community not conspicuous for its radical tendencies. The State Department man could only defend himself by defending the banker, and neither he nor the banker had any notion why the banker was suspect. It finally developed that the banker had lived briefly in Albuquerque, N.M., several years before, and that an anonymous landlady had reported to the F.B.I. that he kept Communist literature in the basement. On further inquiry, it was established that the Communist literature consisted of accumulated copies of "The New Republic" which the banker had discarded.

This sort of thing is making the loyalty program a pretty sour joke. Moreover, the case of the State Department man is typical in that in the great majority of cases of guilt by association, at least half the supposed associates are wholly unknown to the accused.

Second, it seems obvious enough that an intellectual pro-Communist, who accepts unhesitatingly the Communist dogma, should hold no sensitive position—this was the sort of individual who figured conspicuously in the Canadian spy case. But, again, how far should this principle be carried?

Here are a few verbatim quotes from recent loyalty hearings: "What type of books did your associates have—any on political or social economy?" "What kind of books, by title, did you purchase, what kind of literature?" "How many copies of Howard Fast's novels have you read?" "Do you read 'The Newspaper PM'?" "Have you a book by John Reed?"

All government employees know that such questions are asked in loyalty cases, and the assumption that any kind of intellectual or political curiosity provides grounds for suspicion is inevitable. If this country wants a government service in which ignorance is at a premium, it will doubtless get what it deserves.

Third, does it really matter in America whether a man's maternal grandparents came over from Poland, or whether all his ancestors landed decorously on Plymouth Rock? There have been countless instances when, during loyalty hearings, individuals have been asked where their parents and grandparents were born. An entirely American response would be that it was none of the loyalty board's damn business where a man's forebears came from.

Finally, there is the question of confrontation. Take the case of a man who has one item of "derogatory information" in his dossier. His file notes that F.B.I. source X-32 has said that the accused is known to have attended a meeting of high Communist leaders in Seattle. The accused man hotly denies it. The loyalty board has no way whatsoever of knowing whether X-32 or the accused man is lying, and the board knows nothing at all about X-32.

It is the F.B.I. position that to allow those charged to confront their accusers might compromise F.B.I. sources. This seems logical enough. It is also the F.B.I. position that F.B.I. agents should not be allowed to make estimates of the trustworthiness of their sources, and this too seems logical. Yet surely loyalty boards which must decide cases certain to affect the whole future of government employees should know the identity of the sources of their information. They should also, in case of necessity, be able to confront and cross-question such sources in secret.

Obviously there is no easy solution to the problem of national security. But a government of drones and boneheads and toadies hardly contributes to national security. And if the sort of thing outlined above is allowed to continue indefinitely, that is the kind of government we shall get.—August 22, 1948 (JA & SA).

This column announces the decision—then unreported elsewhere—which was the real prelude of the Korean War.

WASHINGTON

The early evacuation of the American zone of Korea was quietly voted by the National Security Council about a month ago. The more honest State and Defense Department policy-makers frankly admit that the decision's ultimate effect will be to throw all of Korea into the expanding Soviet Empire. Under the circumstances, this remarkable decision, taken without any public discussion of the grave issues involved and only now disclosed, deserves rather careful study.

Superficially, the decision is in order. Under the U.N. settlement, the United States and the Soviet Union are to withdraw their troops from their Korea zones within ninety days of the establishment of working governments in each zone. But in fact, both the recent decision of the National Security Council, and the American management of the Korean problem in the U.N., were the result of a debate among the strategists and planners over whether Korea was worth holding at all.

The conclusion that Korea was not worth holding was reached on three grounds. The occupation costs in the American zone of Korea amount to between $200 and $300 million a year. The Army can ill afford the 24,000 troops now on garrison duty in Korea. And from the standpoint of straight military strategy, Okinawa and the Japanese islands are positions of equal, if not greater value.

These are practical considerations of high importance. They are not very frankly admitted, however, A good many of the responsible policy-makers even speciously argue that perhaps the South Korean regime of Dr. Syngman Rhee will be able to maintain its independence after all. Certain measures to this end are being taken. Before the final evacuation, for example, the American garrison will recruit and train a South Korean constabulary of 40,000 men or more. When the American garrison departs, it will leave its arms behind. And the South Koreans may perhaps be assisted by an American military mission.

But the facts show that these measures are mere gestures, which one suspects are primarily designed to save face. The South Korean government is relatively feeble and troubled by a serious problem of Communist infiltration. In North Korea the Soviets have set up an efficient puppet regime. This regime has at its disposal no mere constabulary, but a full dress army variously estimated to number from 60,000 to 250,000 men. The best guess is that the North Korean forces actually total 125,000.

Furthermore, as the expense of our occupation indicates, South Korea is not economically self-sustaining. The South Koreans cannot hope to feed themselves. With the exception of one small power plant, their entire power supply comes from North Korea. Obviously no government can sustain itself against a strong rival government which controls the main food resources, owns the power plants and possesses three times more military force. After the American evacuation, the Kremlin can take South Korea if and when it chooses, without moving a single Russian soldier.

Then if one digs deeper into the background of the Korean decision, another significant group of facts emerges. The American abandonment of Korea will have an immediate, disastrous psychological and political effect on all the forces of resistance to Communist expansion throughout Asia. Particularly, this will be true in adjacent China, where the National government of Generalissimo Chiang Kai-shek is perilously close to collapse.

Yet this politico-psychological factor was only lightly weighed in the Korean decision, and for a very simple cause.

Not in Korea only, but in China, Burma, Malaya, Siam, Indo-China, the Netherlands Indies and the Philippines, the local Communist parties are hard at work in the open. Their armed efforts in China, Burma and Indo-China, at a minimum, seem quite likely to be successful unless counter-pressures are soon to be applied. But palsied impotence marks the present approach of the American policy-makers to this whole huge Asiatic problem, mainly because of the hang-over from the petty vanity, political folly and crass disregard for obvious American interests which characterized American Asiatic policy in war time.

The main objection to the Korea decision is simply that the issue, whether palsy is our only possible Asiatic policy, is going to bulk large in the coming political campaign. The Republicans, who are so obviously likely to win, at least want to try to do something about Asia. Perhaps they may fail. Perhaps the evacuation of Korea might even be included in a constructive program. But it seems outrageous to take this crucial decision now, in the prevailing atmosphere of dank defeatism, when such decisions are quite likely to prejudice any future attempt to turn the tide in Asia.—August 30, 1948 (JA & SA).

How long ago it seems now when we were breaking the Berlin blockade. And with what nostalgia one now reads of this moment when all the West gave thanks for the greatness and the courage of the U. S.!

BERLIN

At Wiesbaden this morning, a steely haze hung very low over the steel-cold ground. On the swarming airfield, the German workers clapped their chapped hands to warm them, as their truck moved away from Big Easy 103. Thirty-five minutes earlier Big Easy 103 had come in from Tempelhof. Now the C-54 was loaded again with another Berlin cargo—ten tons of dried apricots, canned applesauce, cement and roofing paper.

"We're ready to roll," said the pilot briskly.

Pilot, co-pilot and engineer performed the complicated ritual of starting the engines and warming them up. The big airplane lumbered down the field and took its place in the line of other waiting C-54s at the end of the runway. Take-offs were spaced only three minutes apart, and it was not long before the pilot called the tower.

"Hello, tower. Big Easy 103 in No. 1 position."

"Roger, Big Easy 103. You are cleared for Tempelhof at 6,000 feet, standard departure. You're No. 2 to take off." Then three minutes after the plane across the runway had soared into the air, the final word came: "Big Easy 103 cleared for rolling take-off."

"Roger," said the pilot, and in what seemed no more than a few seconds the big plane was airborne and totally enveloped in the chill gray haze. For ten minutes the trio in the cockpit worked with concentrated precision, flying the prescribed three sides of a rectangular course that would bring Big Easy 103 into the flight path to Berlin.

Then the turn into the flight path was made. We were above the clouds now, between the pale sunny blue of the winter sky above and the serrated, brilliantly lit expanse of white wool below. Ten miles away and a thousand feet below us there was a speck which was another C-54 carrying another ten-ton load to Berlin. And ten miles behind and a thousand feet below us, the chatter on the radio announced the presence of still another. The co-pilot picked up a Tempelhof announcement that the ceiling there was 200 feet and visibility was half a mile.

"It's away below minimum now," said the pilot. "But it will probably get a little better before we get in. We can make it with GCA."

Once in the flight path the trio in the cockpit relaxed. History and the Air Force had casually assembled them—Captain Clinton Hankins, from Humboldt, Iowa; Second Lieutenant John B. Duvall, from Fennville, Mich., and Sergeant Kermit Green, from Los Angeles— for the job now in hand. On the Berlin air lift no crew assignments are permanent, but the three had flown together often enough to be friends. They smoked and talked, mostly of the lift itself, and Green paid his respects to the press by doing a cruelly funny imitation of an "extreme Left-Wing newspaper man" who had flown into Berlin with him last week.

"He wanted me to tell him I was oppressed," said the sergeant, with rich scorn. " 'Mister,' I said, 'do I look oppressed, do I talk oppressed, do I act oppressed?' That fixed him."

Over the Fulda beacon, the first report went from Big Easy 103 to Tempelhof Airways. Fifty minutes out of Fulda, the pilot again called in. The city was utterly invisible beneath the overcast, but we were nearing Berlin. Tempelhof replied that the ceiling was now 600 feet, and visibility was "about to the end of the runway—about to the end of the runway." A moment later we were cleared down from 6,000 to 2,500 feet.

"Roger," said Captain Hankins, "Big Easy 103 descending."

Again the trio in the cockpit got down to serious business. The altimeter needle revolved rapidly until the 2,500 point was reached, and Captain Hankins reported: "Hello, Tempelhof Airways. Big Easy

103 over Tempelhof range at 2,500." Tempelhof Airways replied with an order to "go over to jigsaw," which meant to begin taking orders from the Ground Control Approach controller.

On the radar scope in his instrument-packed trailer, the GCA controller, by some incomprehensible magic, found the little blip that was Big Easy 103. The heavy-laden C-54 was sent by the controller around three sides of a small square and at last commanded: "Big Easy 103 on No. 12 beacon—No. 12 beacon—for your final approach. Now go over to final controller." And in an instant, the wonderfully calm and soothing voice of the final controller, who guides every airplane to the ground in bad weather, began on the radio.

"Big Easy 103, steer right to a heading of 190 degrees." The pilot answered and a staccato exchange began, Captain Hankins announcing his position and the final controller correcting his course, until the triumphant announcement: "Two hundred seventy-five is now your heading. Your glide path will be half a mile. You're coming into the center line very nicely and you're two and a half miles from touchdown." The exchange continued until the big plane broke through the overcast and almost simultaneously touched the Tempelhof runway.

Then Captain Hankins thanked the final controller. Big Easy 103 taxied up to its place in the long line of C-54s on the grandiose Tempelhof apron. As the plane reached a halt, a truck backed up to its side and discharged fifteen shivering Germans, who flung themselves upon the cases of apricots and sacks of cement as though their life depended upon speed—as indeed it does. And another air cargo had been delivered to the beleaguered city of Berlin.—December 29, 1948 (JA).

VII

Return to Normalcy

THE SECOND TRUMAN ADMINISTRATION *opened with Harry Truman's abortive try for a Harding-like "return to normalcy." This chiefly took the form of throwing into the discard the program of American and Western re-armament that James V. Forrestal had painfully hammered out after the Czechoslovak coup d'état had convinced the leaders of the West of the danger of weakness. The Truman-Louis Johnson disarmament program was only interrupted by the Korean War, which was a direct consequence of our disarmament plus one other event of the period, the Communist victory in China. The test of the first Soviet atomic bomb, the H-bomb debate in America, the rise of Senator McCarthy, were other events of these years. They were not very happy years for the United States, although they were marked by the greatest American action of the post-war period—the bold response to the challenge in Korea.*

As reporters, we have two great regrets about our work together. We regret, first and most of all, that neither of us went back to see what the Korean fighting was like after the delusive long dragged-out truce negotiations had been started. Neither of us really understood what was happening in Korea in this period until one of us went out to take stock after the truce was signed and sealed. We doubt whether the country understands, even today, what happened in Korea in the time between the Chinese intervention and the final truce—but of this matter, more will appear later.

Secondly, we regret that neither of us went to the Far East in the decisive post-war years, when the Communist victory in China was being prepared. One reason for the omission was the simple fact that America's attention was centered on Europe in the years just after the war. The other reason was personal. The older member of our partnership had had his belly-full of China's politics in wartime, when he played an active and fairly significant role there.

For these two reasons, our first Far Eastern journey was made by the younger partner in 1949. He saw the last agony of the old regime on the Chinese mainland—and it was not a pretty sight. He also saw that all China's neighbors would begin to be in danger just as soon as the Communist victory in China had been consolidated. On his return, he wrote a series of columns on this point. It was regarded as a very odd point to make by very large numbers of persons in those days. A high State Department official with a large share of responsibility for Asian affairs made us very angry with the comment: "The trouble with you journalists is that you are always dealing in theoretical eventualities." But the eventualities have turned out to be the opposite of theoretical; and these old columns today only seem to belabor the obvious. Nowadays, instead, it is hard to believe that "American power and influence" were "paramount" in Shanghai only a few years ago. So we reproduce a portrait of this great city in its death throes. A comment on the administration of American aid to China is omitted.

SHANGHAI

It is no wonder that in distant Washington the low gun rumble announcing the onset of disaster sounds less loud than the click of typewriters, the high whine of axes being ground and the noisy bustle of politics. For even here, in disaster's very shadow, the surface of life in this great doomed city seems normal enough.

From the suffocatingly crowded streets to the famous long bar of the Shanghai Club (where the gimlets are as good as ever) life in

Shanghai appears to go on without change. Then one begins to notice certain signs that the city is besieged.

There is, for example, the wooden fence which surrounds the city, which is universally believed to have netted a certain Nationalist general a handsome profit in contracts, and which has no military meaning whatsoever. There are the sad Nationalist soldiers wandering glumly in the streets or perched with machine guns on the tops of the highest buildings to shoot into crowds if there are riots. There are the factory workers, who have been paid in kind because there is no money to pay them, trying to sell bolts of silk or tennis shoes in the streets so that they can buy rice.

Yet more striking than such visible details is something invisible —the thick, heavy atmosphere of a frightened city. Fear is everywhere, whether cheerfully masked at the diplomatic cocktail parties, or almost tangible in the dim, silent streets after curfew.

The fear springs from the two facts of which every one of the six million people in Shanghai, from the most prosperous American businessman to the hungriest coolie, is thoroughly aware. The first fact is simply that the Communists are coming in and that nothing will stop them from coming in. The city awaits their coming, living on like some animal from whose brain an experimental surgeon has removed the higher centers.

The second fact, almost as certain as the coming of the Communists, is that there will be famine, and that famine will be followed by riots and bloodshed. The only question people ask here is whether the final descent into chaos will occur before or after the Communists come.

For the moment, this city, in which American power and influence have been paramount and are soon to be wiped out, is still being kept alive by the United States. Without American food and American cotton and fuel oil for the industries, most of Shanghai would already be starving. But even if American aid continues, chaos may come before the Communists.

The reason is simple. Money has virtually ceased to have any meaning. Only the American greenback and the Chinese silver dollar still have value, but there are not nearly enough to keep the wheels turning.

Thus Shanghai presents the incredible spectacle of a huge, modern city without any valid medium of exchange at all. The factories have no money to pay the workmen, the workmen have no money to buy food from the rice stores, the stores have no money to buy food from E.C.A., and E.C.A. itself has not had the money to pay men to move the food and goods from the docks.

Shanghai today would doubtless be a fascinating case study for an E.C.A. economist, but it is not a pleasant place to be. For, as the economic machinery grinds to a stop, it becomes always more certain that the hungry people will take matters into their own hands. Every day the army publicly shoots a few more people through the base of the skull as a graphic object lesson. Even so, there have already been a few minor flare-ups. Soon there may be something a great deal more ugly.

That is why one often has the odd experience of hearing solid American and British businessmen saying, "The sooner the Commies come, the better." It is true that looting and riots have ended with the Communist occupation of cities in the north. But Shanghai is different, and it is difficult to see how the Communists can prevent chaos here.

Old China hands here are also fond of explaining, "the Communists will ruin Shanghai and Shanghai will ruin the Communists." It is certainly true that Mao Tse-tung and his followers, accustomed to guerrilla leadership in the back country, will face a hard test in the administration of such a city as Shanghai.

Yet it is also true that sufficient ruthlessness can solve even such a problem as this. And the fact remains that Shanghai is a symbol. This huge, rich, productive megalopolis, fourth largest in the world, is now to pass within the Soviet sphere. So is most if not all of a country with one-quarter of the world's population. No amount of rationalizing, no multiplication of complex excuses by the little men behind the desks in Washington can alter the hard, plain, unpleasant truth that this means a very great disaster for the United States and the whole non-Soviet world.—May 13, 1949 (SA).

1949 was a very curious year. After China went down the drain at last, the British experienced the most severe of their recurrent monetary crises. This led George Kennan to propose the creation of an Anglo-American economic-strategic community, probably also including Canada, Australia and New Zealand, as the best way out. (Kennan's suggestion came to nothing, but the effects on Britain of the developing Middle Eastern catastrophe are now quite likely to force us down the road Kennan proposed so long ago, unless we prefer to see the final breakup of the Atlantic alliance.) Meanwhile, the year's domestic politics was petty stuff, with one exception to be shown later. And despite the gathering avalanche of troubles abroad, Harry S. Truman was obstinately experimenting with his own "return to normalcy," with the enthusiastic help of Louis Johnson and the crony-Secretary of the Treasury, John Snyder. Even Acheson at the State Department did not object really strenuously to the Truman return to normalcy until the event recorded below, which was a critical turning point. Note an optimistic and mistaken assumption that Truman would soon change course. Note the error of intelligence-estimation, too. In our gloomy way, we had written two weeks before that a national policy based upon the expectation of prolonged American atomic monopoly was "moronic nonsense." But we had still supposed that the monopoly would last a little longer.

WASHINGTON

The chief American political and strategic policy-makers are now working on plans to deal with the new situation created by "the atomic explosion somewhere in Russia." Their directive from President Truman has been to evolve a program which will provide genuine security for this country, regardless of other considerations.

According to those who should know, the President has responded to the challenge of the Beria bomb with the courage that marked his sponsorship of the draft bill two years ago. If Truman does not weaken, and his advisors do their jobs honestly and well, there can be only one result. The country will shortly be presented with a program going considerably beyond all our previous great measures to solve the problem of Soviet imperialism.

No hint of this fact has yet been given for two reasons. First, the program is not ready. Second, the President has calculated his timing very carefully. In order to avoid accusations of scare-mongering, he purposely delayed announcement of the Beria bomb until the Senate had safely passed the military-aid program for Europe. In the same manner, in order to avoid accusations of war-mongering, he is waiting now until the Soviets have proved once again that they will not accept true international control of nuclear energy.

When this proof has been given, as is inevitable, the President may be expected to issue a rallying call for greater national effort. What will be asked for will unavoidably constitute a compromise between peace-time practicalities and cold war necessities. The reasons why even a compromise of this sort will demand intensified national effort are inherent in the basic security situation.

As was first disclosed in this space, all defense planning of the Joint Chiefs of Staff has long been founded on the expectation that the Beria bomb would be produced in 1952. But the first Beria bomb has now been tested in 1949 (and is considered by our scientists to have proved as powerful as our Nagasaki bomb, and therefore better than the bomb that destroyed Hiroshima). This in turn both violently contracts, and gives dire urgency to, the whole defense timetable.

On the basis of the 1952 date, the Joint Chiefs of Staff allowed five years for our defense buildup, counting three years until the Soviets produced a bomb and two more for them to accumulate a decisive stockpile of their new weapon. The job for which five years was formerly allowed must now be done in two years at the outside. To take one specific example, the Joint Chiefs had projected expenditures of $1.8 to $2 billion annually for European rearmament, intending to complete this vital program at a total cost of $8 to $10 billion at the end of the five-year period. Logically, therefore, Western European rearmament ought now to be completed in two years, at an annual cost of around $5,000,000,000.

This rule will hold for almost all defense spending. Moreover, mere physical defense is by no means the only problem. While this country is presently beyond range of mass attack from Soviet bases, Europe is within easy range. A decisive stockpile of Beria bombs is defined as enough of these weapons to break all European resistance. And these grim facts will ultimately have sharp political effects upon our allies.

Unless we choose to confront an expanding Soviet empire in naked isolation, we must therefore move forward on the political and economic fronts as well as on the defense front. Hard solutions must be found for all the Atlantic community's pressing problems, such as those revealed by the British economic crisis. Even with this kind of strong American support, our allies will need great courage not to desert the united front against Soviet imperialism. And if we fail our allies in any respect whatever, we must expect our allies to fail us.

There are many other things to be done, in the Far East, for instance. Indeed, the effort which logic demands undoubtedly goes beyond the effort which is really feasible, as is suggested by the case of Western European re-armament. It will be criminal, however, if not enough is done to convey to the Kremlin a lively sense of the determination and mobilization of the Western world. Less than this will court disaster. And even as much as this will be both costly and difficult.

Precisely because the effort demanded is so great, the implications of the Beria bomb are already becoming dirty words, unmentionable in polite society. Perhaps the President will after all avoid any crude public statement of the new facts of life in the world, or any troublesome attempt to deal with those facts. But one must hope that he will live up to the expectations of some of the best men around him; for the facts are facts none the less, and will exact their penalty if ignored. —September 30, 1949 (JA & SA).

Taft began his fight for re-nomination to the Senate a full year early; and in a comment on his tireless campaigning, the pattern of the Republican future was pretty well forecast. Eisenhower was our hope. Yet much as one might disagree with him, one always had the feeling about Bob Taft that "he nothing little did nor mean"; and this feeling was justified except in one instance—Taft's support of Joe McCarthy as the man to run interference for the Republicans in the 1952 campaign. Despite this, there was never a moment when both of us did not like and admire Bob Taft as a man. Over one of us, he exercised such fatal charm that a meeting with Taft almost had to be followed by de-brain-washing, in order to remove strong Taftian tendencies. The cuts in the column eliminate an analysis of the Ohio politics of that period which has no interest now.

WASHINGTON

Senator Robert A. Taft's first Ohio speeches indicate a vital fact. Taft evidently believes that an out-and-out isolationist campaign is the best way to make his crucial fight for re-election to the Senate. This is not only the appeal he will make to the Ohio voters. It is also the appeal by which he hopes to win the Republican Presidential nomination two years after the Ohio voting.

Obviously, if Taft is victorious next year, the strong isolationist tendency of the right wing Republicans will be immensely fortified and intensified. And in part for this very reason, the stand Taft has taken is tending to raise up powerful opponents against him. . . .

There is no use trying to forecast the outcome of the most important and most disputed state election in a great many decades. Whatever other results may ensue, a Taft victory in Ohio can be counted on to stimulate very powerfully another major Republican development.

To put it bluntly, those who know him are convinced that General of the Army Dwight D. Eisenhower will be infinitely more receptive to the Republican nomination if the party's only other alternative is the out-and-out isolationist, Senator Taft. There is no need to expatiate on the depth and strength of General Eisenhower's belief in the critical importance of American world leadership. Any one who knows him and his record is aware that he thinks a revival of isolationism will doom the cause of freedom in the world.

Of late, moreover, Eisenhower has shown signs of increasing political interest, both in his speeches, and in the attention with which he has been following the national situation. And it is not insignificant that a number of the same men who financed the Willkie and Dewey campaigns for the Republican nomination, in 1940 and 1948, are reported to be lining up for an effort for Eisenhower.

Undoubtedly, of course, the idea of seeking the nomination has not as yet even crystallized in Eisenhower's mind. But it is also undoubted that if Senator Taft is the leading contender, Eisenhower will hardly be able to resist the resulting political and moral pressure to make the race. Last time, besides his strong argument that no officer should go straight from the Army into politics, Eisenhower often pointed to would-be supporters that there were plenty of strong alternative contestants. He used particularly to mention Senator Arthur H. Vandenberg.

Now, however, there is no longer any question of Senator Vandenberg leaving his present great position to try for the Presidency. Equally, although Thomas E. Dewey may wish to be a king-maker, and would find Eisenhower an easy king to make, the New York Governor must be credited with good enough sense not to seek the top place a third time. As for Harold E. Stassen, he is in the uncomfortable position of being pretty well debarred from political progress in his adopted Pennsylvania, unless he makes an abhorrent alliance with the prehistoric Grundy-Owlett faction. The other possible Republican contenders all suffer from comparable handicaps. Thus, if Taft wins in Ohio, the chances are that Eisenhower will have to choose between stepping down from his non-political pedestal or letting Taft take over the Republican party by default.

All this is perhaps peering too far into the future. But these long-range speculations both have some foundation in the present, and serve to emphasize a vital point. The Ohio election was already sufficiently important before Taft made his isolationist choice. It is now not exaggerating to say that the national future may hang on the outcome.—September 16, 1949 (JA & SA).

Mr. Vishinsky, who denounced us as "rapists" as well as "congenital murderers," stimulated us to describe our "inner picture of the world."

WASHINGTON

Perhaps Andrei Vishinsky was showing unusual knowledge of American criminal history when he denounced these correspondents as "congenital murderers" at the United Nations last week. A century or so ago poor Dr. Webster undeniably dismembered rich Professor Parkman, and stuffed the pieces into the Harvard physics laboratory furnace. And poor Dr. Webster was undeniably the great-great-great-uncle, or first cousin nine times removed, or some such relation, of these correspondents.

Once this rather moldy old fact is known, everything naturally follows from it. Has not the great academician Lysenko already announced the sacred theory of the inheritance of acquired characteristics? And is not the inheritance of a great-great-uncle's genes and chromosomes a mere minor miracle, by the standards of Soviet science? The case is proved, beyond a doubt.

In short, there is no use arguing the major charge of the Soviet Minister of Foreign Affairs. Mr. Vishinsky went on, however, to describe these correspondents as "bandits of the pen"—a phrase borrowed from the pages of "Pravda," which probably means the same thing as such epithets as "alarmist," "interventionist" and "warmonger," as used by many worthy persons in this country. It may thus be permissible for these correspondents to forget, momentarily, the normal rules of the reporter's trade, and to explain why they write in a way to get themselves called such hard names.

Every reporter has, after all, an inner picture of the world, which makes the day's events seem important or unimportant, serious or comic. One reporter, with one kind of inner picture, will be solemn about the curious charge of Guy Gabrielson, chairman of the Republican National Committee, that President Truman was trying to steal the headlines from the dim little Republican farm conference by announcing the Soviet atomic bomb. Another reporter, with another inner picture, will be equally solemn about the worst maunderings of Henry A. Wallace.

The views of these particular reporters lie somewhere between these two extremes. Once this has been said, however, it is then necessary to inquire how seriously a reporter takes the processes of history; and, if he is an American, what role he gives America in the historic process.

In the case of these particular reporters, the answers to these questions are simple. It would be pleasant to pretend that we are living in the secure and happy world of our grandparents. It would be soothing to believe that the remorseless advances of science and technology are not, by indirect effect, constantly increasing the importance and extending the frontiers of state power in society. But these are aspects of the historic process which cannot be wished away.

In this new world of increasing state power, it would also be far more agreeable if two sharply different forms of society had not emerged. But this is also an aspect of the historic process that must be faced. In the free world, with all its multiformity and all its faults, the total power of the state may grow and does grow with every month and year. But the rule of the free world is that, no matter how much state power may grow, the state is there to serve the individual, the citizen, the man in the street. And in the slave world, on the other hand, the man in the street is the mere serf of the impersonal machinery of the state.

In this difference, moreover, lies the seed of an irremediable struggle between the free world and the slave. It was the struggle that was waged against Adolf Hitler—and which culminated in war only because the free world was weak. It is the struggle that is being waged against the Soviet Union. And in this titanic convulsion, the aftereffects of the second world war have forced upon the United States the role of indispensable leader of the free world.

Finally, it is necessary to inquire how you believe this country should exercise its leadership. Proudly, confidently, with untiring effort, and with certainty of victory, would be the answer of these reporters. Nothing is more sure than victory, in this great struggle between slave world and free, if this nation will but bear its leader's part with boldness, with generosity, and with wisdom. Nothing is more certain than the power of our people, if they are but told the honest truth.

On the other hand, nothing is more sure than defeat if this country falters, or weakens, or wanders into self-indulgence. And nothing is more certain to promote such folly than any attempt, by political leaders or business leaders or ordinary reporters or others having some responsibility, to gild the harsh colors and soften the grim outlines of the facts of our time. In short, if plain reporting of plain facts makes you a "bandit of the pen," these reporters take it as a title of honor.—December 4, 1949 (JA & SA).

This was the first column in a series we wrote on the secret debate on the hydrogen bomb. The series generated a major furore, which was ended a few weeks later by Truman's publicly announced decision to go ahead with the hydrogen-bomb project. In the rest of the series, we insisted that the U. S. could not shrink back from producing thermonuclear weapons, because it was certain that no such shrinking could be expected from the Soviets.

WASHINGTON

If you want to know where we stand at this macabre half-century mark, you will be interested in a debate that is now troubling the highest level of the government. The issue is, very simply, whether to launch an effort comparable to the war-time Manhattan District Project, in order to produce what is referred to as the "super-bomb."

This is the weapon, with approximately 1,000 times the destructive force of the bomb that fell on Hiroshima, that Senator Ed Johnson of Colorado recently described to his television audience. Its power will derive from the nuclear explosion of hydrogen. It will have the estimated capability of devastating, in one detonation, an area of 60 to 100 square miles. Its theoretical feasibility is well established.

Indeed, none of those now arguing the problem doubts for a moment that this hideous weapon will be built eventually. That will be taken care of by the ordinary work of the Atomic Energy Commission —for it is the peculiar triumph of our time that we are already very close to achieving the weapons of ultimate destruction. The question is, rather, whether to appropriate the money and mobilize the man power to build such a bomb in perhaps two, or three, or four years.

Interestingly enough, the same issue was first debated immediately after the war, before the Atomic Energy Commission was set up. The theoretical possibility of a hydrogen bomb was as well understood then as now. A great effort to produce one was urged in certain quarters. President Truman then referred the problem, for study and recommendation, to Dr. Vannevar Bush and President Conant of Harvard.

As reported by competent authority, Bush and Conant found, first, that the problem of building a hydrogen bomb was quite as big, complex and difficult as the original problem of building the Hiroshima bomb. By the same token, they also found that the project would demand the same over-riding priorities, the same mobilization of resources and man power that made possible the success of the Manhattan District.

At that time, there was no question about our monopoly of the uranium-plutonium bomb. The power-for-dollar return on the investment did not appear to justify a vast peace-time effort to produce a hydrogen bomb. Conant and Bush returned an adverse report.

When the Atomic Energy Commission was organized, therefore, its primary task was to continue and expand the Manhattan District's work. As a matter of course, studies and experiments looking to the eventual construction of a hydrogen bomb were also undertaken. Good progress has been made, by ordinary standards. Yet no rapid success can be achieved by the present sort of effort, if only because huge, highly experimental and immensely costly installations must probably be built for the later stages of the work.

In this situation, the explosion of the Soviet atomic bomb last September inevitably led to the present debate among the policy makers. As soon as Marshal Lavrenti Beria broke the American "monopoly" of the uranium-plutonium bomb, the desirability of a great special effort to hasten production of a hydrogen bomb began naturally to be urged.

The arguments of the proponents of this special effort are too obvious to need setting down. The case of the opponents is more complex.

Some, like David E. Lilienthal, who has no taste for being a merchant of death, have been visibly influenced by moral revulsion. In the main, however, the opposition has based its case on the arguments originally advanced by Conant and Bush. It is pointed out that a bomb

1,000 times more destructive than the Hiroshima model is far from being 1,000 times more useful. And it is asserted that the strength to be gained from possessing a hydrogen bomb will not be proportional to the anticipated outlay to build it. In short, it is argued that there are more fruitful ways to invest the same resources in the national defense.

Policy planners, war planners and governmental scientific advisers are to be found on both sides of the argument, although most soldiers are "pros," and there is a higher proportion of scientists among the "cons." Discussion and study of the problem have now reached the highest level, and a policy decision will presumably be made before long.

Thus dustily and obscurely, the issues of life and death are settled nowadays—dingy committee rooms are the scenes of the debate; harassed officials are the disputants; all the proceedings are highly classified; yet the whole future hangs, perhaps, upon the outcome. It will no doubt cause irritation, it may probably provoke denials, to bring the present debate out of its native darkness. Yet this must be done, since deeper issues are involved, which have been far too long concealed from the country.—January 2, 1950 (JA & SA).

Immediately after the explosion of the Soviet atomic bomb, we began a long series of columns exposing the real effects of the Truman-Louis Johnson disarmament policy. We made no personal attack on Johnson, however, until the winter of 1950. Finally, the endless repetition of phony defense claims drove us to write a column which we wanted to call "Mr. Johnson's Lies." The "Herald Tribune's" lawyers insisted that we change "Lies" to "Untruths," which we still regret. The column is mainly interesting as a political-historical item, because it and the others like it ended by influencing later events. The first paragraphs alone are worth preserving:

WASHINGTON

"It is a grave act to charge a high official with deliberately misinforming the nation. But it is graver still for the nation to be grossly and persistently misled about vital matters, as we are now being misled by Secretary of Defense Louis Johnson's smarmy misrepresentations. The time has come to call a spade a spade. Johnson has not been telling the truth about the national defense.

"Specifically, on Dec. 7, Johnson told the National Association of Manufacturers that his savings in the defense budget were being made "without any reduction in our state of preparedness." He then reiterated this claim in his official annual report, stating that we are "obtaining greater national security at less expense." All precautions are being taken, he said, to "increase rather than diminish the over-all combat capabilities of the armed forces." Many other similar statements of the Secretary of Defense might also be cited.

"Only a few of the facts that flatly and utterly refute these claims of Johnson's can be compressed into the space of a newspaper column. Yet even these few facts are sufficient to prove that the Secretary of Defense has been practicing what amounts to a confidence trick upon the nation."—February 13, 1950 (JA & SA).

What followed was a detailed listing of Johnson's cuts in marine, naval and air force units. It gives you a nostalgic feeling to read, nowadays, for the era of Truman-Johnson disarmament seems downright cosy, compared to the present era of the "missile lag." But the details are still pretty boring, so we omit them. For the same cause, we do not offer any other specimen of the dozens of columns we wrote in this period, exposing the weakness of our defense policy. The reasoning behind these columns alone makes them important today. We reasoned, in brief, that Western military weakness constituted an unbearable temptation to which the Kremlin would yield in the end by exploiting its own military strength.

By the winter of 1950, we were correctly convinced that Western disarmament was inviting Soviet aggression; but we followed the more realistic leaders of the Western governments, such as Attlee and Acheson, who also foresaw aggression but mainly feared a frontal attack in Western Europe. Until Korea, Louis Johnson pretty well managed to limit the newly formed NATO alliance to a paper organization; but there were a series of important planning conferences, at the Hague, at Brussels and at London. At London, Dean Acheson actually offered a forecast of a Soviet attack on Western Europe in 1953-54. In our gloomy way we did not exclude the possibility of an earlier attack by satellite armies—the exposed position of Jugoslavia especially impressed us. At about this time, George Kennan also sent out a whip to the armed services, asking for the Pentagon's choice of the most likely victim, if Stalin decided to order a satellite army to cross a border. Korea, it is ironical to recall, was the one possibility absolutely excluded, on the basis of General MacArthur's G-2 estimates of the relative strength of the North and South Korean forces. The following gives a good summary of the mood of those who saw trouble surely coming, but did not foresee the trouble that came so soon. Some military details are omitted.

PARIS

There is one single, simple explanation of the sudden growth of tension, the seemingly unaccountable attack of nerves that is overtaking the Western world. We are imperceptibly passing into another period of acute crisis, comparable in some ways to the crisis period that produced the Marshall plan.

One cause of this new crisis is the tempo of Soviet rearmament. At London, it can now be disclosed, Secretary of State Dean G. Acheson gave the solemn opinion that the Kremlin's war preparations would at least reach a preliminary climax in 1953-54.

Acheson's time estimate was accepted by his fellow Foreign Ministers, despite some wishful tendencies in certain quarters. The time schedule for the Western defense effort under the Atlantic pact was thus defined and established.

The other cause of the crisis is the sudden realization of the present weakness of the West. During the last two and a half years, Western unions and Atlantic organizations have been formed; imposing headquarters have been established; reams of top-secret paper have been turned out by platoons of inter-allied brass. Most people were lulled by all this activity.

Then, at The Hague, at Brussels and at London, the bleak reality was progressively unmasked. The governments of the Atlantic nations suddenly woke up to the fact that in an emergency, they would have almost nothing to throw into the breach except the platoons of brass and the reams of top-secret paper—"and a damn good thing, too," one statesman remarked a little peevishly.

The contrast between Western weakness and rapid Soviet war preparation has in turn produced the new crisis, which is essentially a crisis of will and leadership in the West.

Immediate war, it must be understood, is not the danger. It will be three years, after all, before the Soviet rearmament program is completed. For the present, our atomic weapons and strategic aviation, our troops in Germany and other factors still continue to serve as decisive deterrents to Soviet aggression. The danger is, rather, in the future, when the existing deterrents will cease to operate because of the great growth of Soviet armed strength.

What must be done, therefore, is to build up balanced and solid Western forces. Only thus can we continue to deter the Kremlin from military adventures, after the Russian war program has come to fruition. This job must be begun now if the needed weapons and men are to be ready in time. But doing this job with 1953-54 as the target date will require greatly increased national expenditures and other politically uncomfortable sacrifices. Hence the crisis of will and leadership in all the governments concerned, and most conspicuously in our own.

The crisis is rendered more agonizing, both by the inevitable difficulty of preventive action in democracies, and the scope of the job to be done. For example, the Soviets will have both a strategic air force and a respectable stock of atomic weapons by 1953-54. Yet Western Europe is now virtually without any effective air defense whatever. There is simply nothing here, worth mentioning, beyond the air warning net and fighter squadrons in the British Isles. . . .

Again, since all France's professional army is pinned down in Indo-China, there are no combat-worthy ground forces in Western Europe except the two British and two American divisions in Germany, a Belgian division and other bits and pieces. Incredibly enough, in fact, the Swiss and Jugoslav armies are by far the most powerful in Europe today. Meanwhile, the Atlantic nations need somewhere between thirty and forty divisions in Europe—the estimates vary. . . .

Three points must be emphasized in conclusion. The foregoing is an entirely defensive and pacific program. . . . Second, while the cost will be great, it will not be unbearable. Additional outlays of from three and a half to five billion dollars a year by the Atlantic community as a whole should be sufficient, if there are simultaneous economies by suppressing non-essentials. Third, if the job is done, there will be no great reason for alarm.

This is the essential point. The Soviet war program will not be a great danger, if it is confronted by solid defenses. But it will be hideously dangerous if great Soviet power is confronted by a virtual military vacuum. We still have time, as Stanley Baldwin had in 1935, to determine which of these two conditions shall arise in the future. If the leaders of the Western world now once more make Baldwin's choice, one must conclude that the West does not deserve to survive. Nor will it survive.—June 5, 1950 (JA).

It is generally forgotten now, but at the time this column was written it was assumed by Eisenhower and most of his supporters that he could have the Republican nomination without lifting a finger to get it. In the end, he had to fight for the nomination with everything he had. As the last sentences in this column suggest, we then admired the General, perhaps rather extravagantly. It should be added that a large part of the political community and press treated the Eisenhower candidacy as a pipe-dream at this time. Again, political trivia that have lost their former interest have been excised.

WASHINGTON

Rightly or wrongly, those who have talked to General Dwight D. Eisenhower in recent weeks are convinced that he has now pretty well made up his mind that he wants to be President. He is reported to have told at least one close friend that, provided there were no deals or compromises involved, and provided he did not have to campaign for it actively, he would accept the Republican nomination if offered to him.

Others close to him are convinced that he will co-operate with any organization set up to promote an Eisenhower boom at least to the extent of not actively opposing his own nomination, as he did in 1948. All this may be wishful thinking on the part of those who are searching desperately for a way to beat Senator Robert A. Taft for the nomination. But it is at least true that the Eisenhower backers are already planning the broad strategy of an Eisenhower campaign.

The first move, according to the strategists, must be for Eisenhower firmly to announce his Republican affiliation sometime shortly before the November elections. This would be designed to mollify the regulars, who point out that Eisenhower has never even said he is Republican, and most of whom would prefer Taft anyway. It would also be designed to give influential Republicans second thoughts about jumping on the Taft bandwagon which is sure to get rolling if Taft is decisively re-elected in Ohio.

The second move would be to set up an effective, well-heeled Eisenhower organization, staffed with professional politicians, working for Eisenhower delegates in all key states. As far as money is concerned, there would be no difficulty—for example, one of the fabulously rich Southern oilmen has already let it be known that he would be willing to contribute personally a quarter of a million dollars to get Eisenhower nominated and elected.

The general's only part in such an organization would be the entirely negative one of simply not repudiating the efforts on his behalf. Finally, at some strategic moment shortly before the convention, Eisenhower would formally acknowledge his availability.

All this may be a pipe dream, since everything depends on Eisenhower, and it is always easy to mistake general expressions of interest in politics for a personal willingness to run. But the purpose of the strategy outlined above is of course clear. It is, in the words of an Eisenhower backer, "To get Ike off the ground before Bob Taft can get the nomination in the bag."—April 9, 1950 (SA).

"War through weakness" began the night the following column was published; and as far as the United States was concerned, it began in the garden of the older member of our partnership. He was giving himself a party, to celebrate his own homecoming from Europe. Justice Frankfurter was there, and the Secretary of the Army, Frank Pace, and the under Secretary of the Air Force, John McCone, and the Assistant Secretary of State for Far Eastern Affairs, Dean Rusk. The night was marvellously beautiful. The talk on the terrace under the stars was growing lively. But it was interrupted by a servant rather plaintively announcing a "telephone call for Mr. Rush." Dean Rusk being identified as the probable call-ee, he went indoors to the telephone, and came out a few minutes later as white as a sheet, to beckon Pace and McCone into the house with him. A few minutes later still, they left for the State Department, explaining that "there had been a rather serious border incident in Korea." The party settled down to argue whether *this was it*. We were pro that point of view and many others were con. The next morning's papers told the news of the Communist army driving towards Seoul. The record of the division of opinion in Washington on the very eve of disaster is interesting— and instructive. We did not know it when we wrote our column, but Louis Johnson had just issued orders to the armed forces to cut another billion dollars out of the next year's budget.

A great subterranean struggle is now going on in Washington. The chief actors in this silent drama are Secretary of State Dean Acheson and Secretary of Defense Louis Johnson. The struggle revolves about a life-and-death issue whose real meaning has been analyzed in recent reports in this space. The issue is this: Will a serious effort now be made to place the Atlantic community in a posture of defense against the time when Soviet re-armament will be complete? Or will the present sham effort be continued indefinitely?

The inner history of the Acheson-Johnson battle on this issue goes back to the time when President Harry S. Truman announced his decision to go ahead with the hydrogen bomb. Immediately thereafter, Truman ordered Acheson and Johnson to make a joint over-all review and re-assessment of American foreign and defense policy, in the light of such events as the loss of China, the Soviet mastery of atomic energy and the prospect of the hydrogen bomb. The State Department's policy planning staff was assigned to do the spadework on this global policy paper. Immediately, the policy planners struck a large, stubborn snag.

On the one hand, every responsible official in the State Department, from Acheson on down, was convinced that the American response to the challenge of mounting Soviet strength was inadequate. For some months, this conviction has been reflected in all of Acheson's public statements, in which he has been calling for "total diplomacy," for "creating situations of strength" and for "mobilizing our total resources."

Yet on the other hand, this Acheson prescription, translated from generalities into hard realities, would make nonsense of Johnson's "economy" program. Johnson would thus be forced to reverse himself in the most embarrassingly public manner. And for obvious reasons, Johnson has no intention whatsoever of allowing this to happen.

Thus those charged with writing the global report were faced with the problem of reconciling two entirely contradictory views. This situation was dealt with in a wearily familiar way. A paper was produced which called for an increased foreign and defense policy effort by the United States. But the paper was couched in such vague and general terms that it committed no one to anything.

Johnson accepted this watery version, and it was accordingly submitted through the National Security Council to the President. Truman immediately turned it back to the N.S.C. He rather tartly and quite accurately pointed out that it was pointless to talk vaguely of a stepped-up American effort to win the cold war. He demanded precise answers to the obvious questions—Where? How? How much?

The attempt to answer these vital questions in real, dollars-and-cents terms has precipitated the great, invisible struggle which is now going on. Occasionally, the struggle becomes briefly visible above the surface. This happened, for example, early this month, when first Acheson and then Johnson testified on the Military Aid Program before the Senate Foreign Relations Committee.

On June 2, Acheson said that the only "honest answer" he could give was that the scale of expenditure under M.A.P. would have to be increased in the future. Three days later, Johnson, while blandly disclaiming any disagreement with Acheson, flatly disagreed with him. Asserting that "I think I have been living a little more closely with this field of military expenditures than Acheson," Johnson "guessed" that the rate of expenditure could be progressively decreased in coming years.

It is impossible to find any informed official in Washington, in uniform or out, who sincerely shares this Johnsonian view, or who believes that the current level of expenditures will provide in time even a skeleton defense for Western Europe. Yet partly because of Johnson's undeniably effective bullying, and partly because of the tradition of paramount civilian responsibility, the Joint Chiefs of Staff now seem prepared to go along with Johnson. If they do, this will render Acheson almost powerless, simply because the final responsibility for making an essentially military assessment obviously rests with the Joint Chiefs.

Yet Acheson has not lost. The Joint Chiefs themselves are perfectly aware of the probable outcome if Western Europe is still nakedly defenseless and the United States half disarmed when the Soviet rearmament effort reaches its peak in 1953-54. There have been increasingly audible murmurs of revolt in the Pentagon. And Acheson has important allies elsewhere, including N.S.R.B. chairman Stuart Symington, E.C.A. chief Paul Hoffman, and now Averell Harriman, who, as the President's Man Friday, will occupy a central position.

Finally, there have been signs (like his appointment of Thomas Finletter as Air Force Secretary, an appointment very far from welcome to Johnson) that Truman himself is not entirely happy about

Johnson's business-as-usual policy. And it is Truman who must make the final decision. This is not a light responsibility. For it is almost mathematically predictable that Truman's decision will lead in a few years either to peace through strength or to war through weakness. —June 23, 1950 (SA).

Three sample columns follow from the Korean war reporting of the senior member of our partnership. In a strange way this was, for him, the best time of the post-war years—partly because he made the interesting discovery that he could do this sort of job (which he had never done), but mainly because in Korea, in this uncomplicated opening period of the war, one felt really hopeful about the future and deeply proud of one's country's performance in the present.

WITH U. S. FORCES IN KOREA

"We're pretty far forward. The 1st Battalion holds this side of the valley up ahead. The 2d Battalion has the other side. The South Koreans more or less hold the flanks. We pushed in here easily, but the enemy have been building up since then. They have three divisions at least in the area now, and I expect a big attack tonight."

This summary of the local situation was cheerfully offered by the brilliant young commander of the 27th Regiment, Col. John Michaelis. It did not seem exactly ideal. Yet the scene appeared singularly peaceful when this reporter entered the valley of Chanpyongdong a few minutes later, to become the guest of the 27th Regiment's 1st Battalion for some days.

A lowering sun gilded the eastern slope of this temporary home of these few hundred men, who have seen much of bitter fighting and hardly won much honor in the Korean war. In a clear, rocky brook among the green rice paddies and cotton patches, half a dozen young soldiers were luxuriously bathing. On the road, one company was lining up for supper, and the smell of good food hung in the clear, bright air. Farther on, beyond a solitary scar of charred, still smoking thatched huts, the valley opened, funnelwise, upon a glowing prospect of distant hills and sky.

It was hard to believe that no-man's-land began just down the road, or that the occasional snicking sound above the chow line was really a rather inefficient sniper to whom nobody paid much attention. The battalion commander, Lt. Col. G. J. Check, a short, wiry, businesslike man, who once worked for the Agriculture Department and "just stuck" in the Army after the war, welcomed his guest like a hospitable suburban householder.

This peaceable illusion was broken soon enough, however, when the meal ended and Col. Check's young executive and operations officer, Capt. Don Hickman, set off to see to the dispositions for the night. The 81-millimeter mortars covered both the valley approach and the flanking mountains. Tanks squatted heavily by the roadside and the stream bed, menacing the prospect with their guns. In near-by foxholes, men nursed 3.5 bazookas. And the positions of the battalion's three rifle companies, Able, Baker and Charlie, bristled along the valley's fringing hills.

Over Baker Company's command post, Persimmon Grove, overlooking no-man's-land, dusk was already falling and there was a sharp rattle of small arms fire from the South Koreans defending the mountain crest far above.

"It sure sounds good," said one officer at length. "But it makes me mad when their tanks won't come up far enough. I like to get them with bazookas."

Here was the heart of the matter. The whole little valley had been efficiently transformed into a grim trap for the enemy armor and infantry that had to come this way to gain the main road to the South Korean provisional capital, Taegu. In a few minutes, just as we reached the battalion command post in a rocky gully, the enemy announced his intention to test the trap. There was a loud whistling sound and a tremendous crash on the flank above. Col. Check, sitting on a rock in a tangle of telephones, grunted happily.

"That's the mortar preparation," he said. "We ought to clobber them tonight."

Darkness fell. The whistling and crashing of the incoming mortar fire went on interminably. Suddenly the radio, astonishingly clear, spoke insistently, "Able Charlie to Amazing Able, over. Able Charlie to Amazing Able, over." It was Charlie Company, two hours' time up this mountain, reporting both that the telephone line was out and that there was noise of tanks at the end of the valley. Capt. John L. Beard, the liaison officer of the 8th Field Artillery, called his forward observers, got an estimate of nine tanks and much enemy infantry, and then directed his rearward batteries of 105-millimeter howitzers onto the target. Our guns commenced a slower whistling and a more distant booming. The battle was joined.

With infinite incident, with endless uncertainty, the fighting continued all through the night. At one moment the South Koreans on the mountain crest called for support, and our big mortars spoke. At another, the forward observers reported a tentative enemy advance, Col. Check ordered flares, and as our firing testified, the attackers hastily retired, peevishly blasting away with their flat trajectory guns. Linesmen went out to repair broken communications among the dark precipices; runners came and went. The noise of fighting rose and fell.

Yet not even the wisest was sure what was happening—whether the artillery really had knocked out its target; whether the enemy really had turned back or were creeping across the rice paddies; whether the South Koreans still really held the mountain crest on the exposed flank. In night fighting, an infantry battalion is like an organism with an inadequate central nervous system, which survives because all its well-trained members rapidly and correctly react to local stimuli.

The time for these reactions to be fully tested came at last about 3:30 a.m. after a long lull. Suddenly the forward observers reported the enemy's full advance. They had passed the crossroads. They had passed the village of Chanpyongdong. They were still coming on, and two tanks were already within Charlie Company's perimeter. While Capt. Beard's artillery roared away and the enemy answered, the men of the 1st Battalion held their fire until the flare went up.

There followed a curious coughing crash from all our mortars, all our tanks; then, after a few minutes, an explosion like a giant firecracker blowing off; and after that, for half an hour, the wild rattle of machine-gun and rifle fire. At 5 a.m. when the pale dawn was just beginning, the whole North Korean force took flight. The battle was over. In the command post, men lay down to doze on the hard rocks.

The sun was hardly up, however, when Col. Check set off to find the results of the night. A confusion of wrecked and smoking vehicles with two tanks among them, just where the road emerged from Chanpyongdong, announced the artillery's success. By the stream, where they and their men were happily shaving, Lt. Jessie F. Van Sant, of "Alma" and Sgt. Howard Ezell of "Ida" (all our tanks bear incongruously girlish names) told how they had got three more of the

enemy's tanks at point-blank range, while the bazooka man picked off
a big self-propelled gun. The three rifle companies reported few casualties, but when the Colonel went farther forward there were North
Korean bodies sprawling everywhere in the rice paddies. Five tanks,
the guns, the road trucks, several hundred dead—the night's score
was good. The trap had worked. The immediate commentary was
supplied by Capt. L. V. Merchant, whose Fox Company of the 2d
Battalion had shared the enemy's infantry attack with Baker Company of our battalion.

"Col. Check, sir," said Merchant, grinning triumphantly, "I want
you to tell Baker Company that their machine gunning was beautiful,
just beautiful. The gooks left arms and weapons and ammunition all
over those damn rice paddies. It was just beautiful."

You form, it seems, a new but understandable concept of beauty
in the infantry.—August 28, 1950 (JA).

WITH U. S. FORCES IN KOREA
Baker (B) Company of the 27th Regiment's 1st Battalion was break-
fasting in a cheerful mood. The morning was sunny but almost cool,
and the men crowded hungrily into their front-line mess hall—a little
rocky draw that gave protection from sniper fire. When the young
company commander, Capt. Gordon Jung, joined the chow line he
was greeted with comments on the good night just passed.

"Yes, we had a quiet day altogether," Jung reflectively replied.

Possibly Baker Company's standards of quietness have been influenced by their experiences in Korea. In their first action, more
than six weeks ago, they were overrun by six enemy tanks and more
than 1,000 infantry. Rallied by Capt. Jung, they held their position
until they could retire in good order, and help the rest of the battalion
wipe out the attackers. That day Capt. Jung earned a recommendation
for the Distinguished Service Cross, and Baker Company learned that
"we was better than they was," as a beardless Pfc. succinctly explained.

At any rate, the reader must judge of this quiet day, which this
reporter spent as Baker Company's guest. The day began at sun-up,
after an agreeably successful little night battle during which a Baker
Company bazooka team polished off an enemy self-propelled gun
when "they were looking right down our throat," while the rifle
platoons decimated a North Korean infantry battalion charging across

the rice paddies just before dawn. And for the first hours of the day it really was pretty quiet.

To be sure, a constant rattle of firing came down from the high mountain peak on the left flank, which the South Koreans were holding. To be sure, our mortars and the enemy's sometimes rather languidly lobbed shots back and forth. But in Baker Company's command post, in a leafy persimmon grove overlooking no-man's land, there was comparative peace.

While those on duty maintained the alert, most of the company's 140 men and five officers slept on the hard ground, or gossiped of past fighting, or cleaned their weapons. The day's real work began rather disconcertingly in mid-afternoon.

The firing on the flanking mountain peak had long been growing less intense when suddenly South Korean troops began to filter through Baker Company's line. With a strong enemy force moving onto the heights above, the position instantly became critical. While more and more starveling South Koreans drifted in, the battalion was notified; a full alert was sounded, and a South Korean officer was rounded up. The young Korean lieutenant haltingly but defiantly explained that his men had been "too many days" on the mountain without enough food or water or even ammunition. Meanwhile, Charlie (C) Company, farther down the line, reported enemy infantry already attacking them.

The battalion spoke. All companies were to rally all South Koreans in their positions, offering food, promising heavy artillery support, urging them to retake their mountain peak. With infinite difficulty and patience, Jung explained all this. The Korean lieutenant nodded curtly, called to his men, and led them back up the hill. Our mortars began their screaming in dead earnest, the 155 mm. howitzers boomed angrily, and the mountain peak was veiled in silvery and brown puffs of white phosphorus and high explosives. There was a long, anxious wait. At last the enemy fled. The flank was secure again.

By then supper was over. Capt. Jung, his face a little drawn, gave his instructions to his platoon leaders. The battalion had just rather grimly announced a heavy enemy attack on the artillery batteries and main supply road in the rear. But the threat of being cut off seemed to worry Jung much less than the danger on the mountain above—"If the flank goes again, we've still got to hold the front; we'll just skeletonize the rifle platoons to reinforce the heavy weapons platoon on the hill."

Meanwhile, 1st Sgt. George S. Hearn, a massive man with a fresh shrapnel dimple in his cheek who learned ground fighting as a lieutenant in Merrill's Marauders, passed out grenades and ammunition with a running commentary. Hearn allows liberties to those who know their business, like the lean Sgt. George Bass of the first platoon, who likes to argue that war would be more enjoyable if fought with clubs. But the younger soldiers Hearn instructs——"now, you Prokov, you're a messenger tonight. Regardless of what's afalling you've got to get out to the platoons on order. But you'll be all right if you'll just learn where the platoons are at."

As dusk fell, F-80s roared down the valley under towering thunderheads, rocketing and strafing the enemy position. Jung walked along Baker Company's Hill, saying a quiet word now and again to the men in the foxholes, pausing at his forward platoon to watch a jewel-like kingfisher zigzag down its brook in terror at the rocket explosions. Then it was time to button down for the night.

At the command post, Sgt. Hearn and the communications men were already in their foxholes. As Jung returned, the thunderheads burst. Swearing briefly, he stretched a poncho above his own night's refuge, settled down and telephoned his forward observer, Lt. P. C. Rodgers. Rodgers reported an enemy force with two tanks at the far end of the valley. Incoming mortar fire suddenly crashed round about. And so the good night began.

It was a good night because Baker Company and the other men of the 1st and 2d Battalions had hit the enemy so hard on the three nights preceding. Its goodness consisted in the failure of the discouraged North Koreans to attack in force again. But all night the attack threatened. All night the firing continued, culminating in a heavy fusillade from the enemy tanks just before dawn. And all night the rain fell, filling the foxholes, freezing the men. In the infantry, you get a queer idea of a good night.

As the sun rose, Baker Company began the new day. Sgt. Hearn crept down the line, to steal the rifles of any sleepers and thus teach them to remain alert. The cooks arrived with breakfast, and three men whose wounds had healed reported for duty again. A messenger from across the valley reported that one of the enemy tanks' shells had landed in the midst of a Baker Company bazooka team, severely wounding all four men. The news was accepted, not indifferently, but as a matter of course.

"If they didn't attack all night," Capt. Jung summed up, "I guess that means we are through here. I'm glad. I like going after them better than having them go after me."—August 30, 1950 (JA).

TOKYO

One of the odder rules of war seems to be that all the good people are at the front and all the odious people are at higher headquarters. Besides the gratitude of the civilian to the fighting man, the observer also feels curiously grateful to the men in the lines for their unvarying hospitality. On leaving Korea for a few days, this reporter therefore proposes to write a sort of bread and butter letter to the members of the 1st Battalion of the 27th Infantry Regiment, who were his hosts for some time when they were brilliantly winding up a very tough job.

What makes a good battalion, is the letter's theme. Wherein lies the secret of such a fighting team? "In the men themselves," is the obvious first part of the answer.

In the 1st Battalion, there is, for example, Capt. Logan E. Weston, now wounded but lately commander of Able Company. When Able Company was attacked by a heavy force of night-infiltrating enemy infantry, Weston rallied his men. He rushed two enemy machine guns single-handed and destroyed them with grenades. Although sorely hit, he continued to command the fight until ammunition ran short. Under heavy fire, he sought the ammunition bearer. Wounded again, he plunged back into the struggle. And only when the enemy fled at last did he collapse from loss of blood.

. Or there is Cpl. Arthur Prater, who got the Silver Star in the battalion's first action for carrying rations and water to a company that was cut off. Prater has bad feet, but prefers staying with the outfit to accepting a medical discharge. Or there is Acting Supply Sgt. Clurion Grigsby, who drove into the middle of an enemy armored column when he was bringing equipment from the rear. Grigsby seized a bazooka, leaped from his weapons carrier and got a North Korean tank at ten yards range.

Or there are many scores of others, in this small outfit of a few hundred, who are not so very different from those who have been named. At first, these men of the 1st Battalion impress you as individuals, some clever, some less clever, some mature, some incredibly young, but almost all lean, hard, good tempered and businesslike about their task of fighting. Then, as you listen to the talk among them, you are struck by the way that shared experience knits them together.

Of experience also, the 1st Battalion has had a generous helping in only six short weeks. On their first day on the Waegwan front, when Prater got his decoration, the battalion was attacked by no less than 2,000 enemy infantry, moving forward in columns behind six tanks. Baker Company's position was utterly overrun. The lead tank was halted almost at the entrance of the battalion command post.

But the battalion stood firm and shot it out until the North Koreans ran; then rapidly regrouped to meet a night attack on its flank and covered the rice paddies with North Korean dead. That, they tell you, was how the outfit was made.

Or there was the long reconnaissance in force, when the whole battalion drove into enemy territory for twenty-seven miles beyond Chindong, was cut off for twenty-four hours, and briskly fought its way back. That time, two tank drivers were killed. Volunteer replacements were called for. Two men who had once driven bulldozers stepped forward. And the tanks rumbled back into our lines with a cook and a medic at their wheels.

Or there were a score of other skirmishes and actions each variously memorable, all matters of pride. Hearing these discussed, watching still another fight that would also be recalled, one gradually realized that there was yet one more ingredient in this puzzling entity, the 1st Battalion. And this ingredient, of course, was good leadership.

From the wiry, unpretentious little battalion commander, Lt. Col. G. J. Check, down to Baker Company's massive, fatherly 1st Sgt. George S. Hearn, the 1st Battalion's leaders sedulously avoid any appearance of panache, preferring a good salty joke to any military heroics. But by the hard, poorly rewarded, unremitting work of these men, the battalion's companies organize each new position as though by instinct; the rifle platoons flinch from no shadows but are always ready, day and night; the tank crews and the mortars coolly aim their fire, whether the battle goes well or ill; the bazooka teams, lonely in their forward foxholes, keep vigil until the time comes for their task. By leadership and training, with courage and experience, the battalion does its job.

Such then is the 1st Battalion, no assemblage of saints and when on occupation duty rather notoriously the opposite, but a fighting team that will go forward without counting costs; will hold an exposed position against heavy odds; will uncomplainingly endure great hardships; will see its own men fall and quietly close the ranks. Many have fallen. When this reporter watched the blanket-covered litters being brought down the mountainside, he found himself recalling Simonides's great epitaph on the Spartans at Thermopylae. It was inscribed on the monument erected in the pass by the Lacedaemonian state. The dead speak:

"Go stranger and in Lacedaemon tell
That here, obedient to the laws, we fell."

But these men were not Spartans, drilled, beautiful and unthinking. They were Americans, fighting not for iron laws, but for a good life and a good society. And if perchance the good life and the good society survive in this now-darkening world, it will be to such men as these, simple perhaps, inarticulate perhaps, but bold, tough, ingenious and free, that the great debt will be owed.—September 11, 1950 (JA).

The portrait of Bob Taft on the stump makes the following worth preserving. The reporter omitted two things in his campaign assessment—the American electorate's enthusiasm for strong character, even strong character travelling in a direction that by no means evokes the same enthusiasm; and second the power of really lavish campaign financing to beat down a feeble opponent, such as Taft had. The Taft 1950 campaign set a money record for Senate campaigns which still stands, to this day. Once again, the political trivia of the period have been dropped.

VERSAILLES, OHIO

The energy and endurance displayed by the sixty-two-year-old Senator Robert A. Taft in his campaign for re-election must be seen to be believed. The hour Taft spent in this small, pleasant, rural town in southwestern Ohio gives some idea of the sort of campaign Taft is waging, all day, every day.

The first thing you see as you enter the town is a large truck, patriotically draped in red, white and blue, drawn up in front of the main square. Gathered around the truck are perhaps two hundred and fifty people: students from the local schools, looking self-consciously serious; the high school band, magnificent in scarlet costumes; local business men (many of whom look as though they might be the candidate's brother) and their wives; well fed farmers from the flat rich land round about.

As Taft appears, in the back seat of the open light blue limousine of a local Republican bigwig, there is a little whisper of interest, and some desultory clapping. There is nothing in the scene to suggest that great issues depend on the fate of this particular candidate—the future course of the Republican party, the direction of American foreign policy, the success or failure of the Truman administration's alliance with organized labor, perhaps even the identity of the next President.

The scene suggests, instead, a cheerful Sunday school outing, presided over by a rather irascible schoolmaster. Here, as in the United States Senate, there is between Senator Taft and his audience something of the relationship between teacher and taught. Taft mounts the truck, removes the wilted grey felt hat which appears to have been worn, and sat on, by generations of Tafts, and looks about him. You get the feeling that he is not going to take any nonsense from his pupils. Then Taft smiles.

It is the charming smile of an essentially shy man who does not smile easily. But it is the last smile his audience gets. There are no jokes, no casual chitchat in the speech which follows. It is a formal set speech, and a long one—too long, indeed, for a standing audience, and there are signs of restlessness before it ends. Yet on the whole, the people of Versailles listen attentively.

Senator Taft is no great shakes as an orator. But an audience will always listen to an angry man, and Senator Taft is clearly a very angry man indeed. When he has finished, there is certainly no wild excitement, but there is obvious sympathy and even some enthusiasm. With a rather limp hand, Taft acknowledges the clapping, and he is off to make much the same speech all over again, in the tiny town of Russia, some miles away.

For ten weeks now, this scene has been repeated with minor variations, nine or ten time a day. With Nov. 7 looming near, Taft is now making as many as fourteen speeches in a single day, exhausting whole platoons of assistants and reporters. And the astonishing energy of Taft's campaign—for which even his enemies admire him—has its significance. For Taft is "running scared. . . ."

Taft concentrates not on the prosperous present, but on an awful vision of what the future will hold if the Truman administration is not confronted by "an independent Congress."

This vision of the future sees the British version of Socialism triumphant in the United States, and Russian Communism triumphant everywhere else. The United States will be shackled with Socialism because Harry Truman has become the captive of the C.I.O.-P.A.C. And Communism will be allowed to triumph elsewhere in the world because the Administration has repeatedly demonstrated a "strange sympathy for Communism"—as demonstrated by the fall of China, the "invitation" to attack in Korea, the "whitewash" of the McCarthy charges, the Hiss episode, and the Truman veto of the anti-Communist bill.

Nov. 7 will show whether this is effective strategy. But it must be said that this vision of the future—a Socialist America in a vast Communist sea—is somehow a little unreal in the atmosphere of friendly comfort which pervades the main square of Versailles, Ohio, as it basks in the gentle autumn sun.—October 23, 1950 (SA).

At the time of the total failure of General MacArthur's intelligence, and the ensuing great defeats of our forces in North Korea by the Chinese, we published a column beginning with Thucydides' description of the Athenians receiving the news of defeat at Syracuse: "The citizens mourned and the city mourned; they had lost the flower of their youth, and there were none to replace them. Whichever way they looked there was trouble; they were overwhelmed by their calamity, and they were in fear and consternation unutterable." Sometimes one wonders now whether the defeat on the Yalu, and above all what happened afterwards, really did not play the role of Syracuse in the Peloponnesian war—the role of the moment after which the road was largely downwards, even though the descent was not at first perceived.

President Truman's first response was to seek a final showdown with the Kremlin; and on December 6, 1950, eve-of-general-war warnings were actually sent out to our armed forces all over the world. But the President's advisers, and above all British Prime Minister Attlee, who flew to Washington for the purpose, finally succeeded in muting and diverting the President's initial impulse. It was a curious episode, for the British had far more that was directly at stake in the Korean outcome than the United States. The process that began with President Eisenhower's final acceptance of concealed defeat in Korea has now begun to strike, with fearful power, at all the ex-colonial positions overseas that Britain needs to nourish her economy and feed her people. The Middle Eastern catastrophe is only the latest result. The division of Indo-China, the shaky situation in Malaya, the still worse situation in Indonesia—all these are also part of the price of not winning the Korean war.

The following column shows how close we were to a showdown policy. Note that it was written a week before the eve-of-general-war warning above-mentioned.

WASHINGTON

We have come to the end, or very nearly to the end, of the dark road of the post-war years. Perhaps the best symbol of how much has ended was the President's response to the first news of the fearful disaster in Korea. The always cheerful Truman, always so confident of peace, who had always said he would see Stalin in the White House and nowhere else, now actually proposed that he cross the ocean, meet with the Soviet dictator, and "lay it on the line."

The "it" referred to was, of course, the atomic bomb. The choice to be offered Stalin was, of course, the choice between peace and war. And if our mad folly had not left us with nothing but the atomic bomb to "lay on the line," the President's advisers might not have labored so hard to dissuade him from his project.

The episode, which may be denied but is undeniably authentic, means that we in America must look back upon the roaring '20's, and the hopeful '30's, and the victorious '40's, and say "good by to all that." It means that we are entering an iron decade, perhaps an iron half-century, in which all our accustomed pleasures, from television to partisanship, from juke boxes to self-delusion, must be sacrificed to the stern requirements of independence and survival.

Any one who doubts this needs only to consider the broad tendencies already manifested in the anguished meetings of the National Security Council. Although the President was dissuaded from doing the job the simple way, it is deeply significant, for instance, that the early drafts of Secretary of State Dean G. Acheson's solemn speech to the nation actually contained something very like a conditional declaration of war, with the scope of the war left undefined.

We have now asked the Chinese, in somewhat milder language, to "come to their senses." But there are few reasons to hope that they will do so. Their contempt for the United Nations was sufficiently displayed in Ambassador Wu Hsiuchan's first outburst at Lake Success.

Their obedience to the Kremlin was revealed in Wu's faithful parroting of all Vishinsky's favorite phrases. And their long advance planning and preparation was indicated by the mere size of the Chinese military trap into which Gen. MacArthur has walked.

In these circumstances, it is worth recalling a report from Tokyo that appeared in this space some weeks ago, stating that the Chinese would not intervene in Korea "unless the Kremlin actively desired to plunge the world into a third great war." At that time, the American experts were unanimously convinced the Kremlin would take no such risk. But the experts were wrong. And the fact that the Acheson speech was softened in its later drafts does not diminish the danger.

The reason for this is, in part, the same reason why the masters of the Kremlin have propelled their Chinese puppets across the Korean frontier. Nothing could be more dangerous or damaging than for the United States to become involved in a costly struggle with the Chinese people, whose country does not even offer profitable targets for our only major weapon, the atomic bomb; whose divisions out-number ours by a ratio of twenty to one. Until three days ago you would not have found a single high official in Washington who did not prefer a showdown with Moscow to a war with China.

Even today, when weaker spirits are quailing before the brutal facts, the same sentiment generally prevails. There is no sentiment at all for mere feeble submission under the Chinese attack. If we refuse to submit, if the Chinese will not withdraw, if we reject a limited war with China, then the showdown with Moscow looms as the only eventual alternative. President Truman's instinct was not very different from the instinct of his advisers, even if the method of his project for a showdown drew protests from the men around him.

At this instant, when the enemy's response is unknown, when the degree of defection among our allies cannot be forecast, there is no way to read the future. The broad Administration attitudes to each of the major alternatives—surrender, limited war with China, and showdown with Moscow, can be discerned as suggested; yet all is too dark and doubtful to make it possible to guess whether the alternative that is most or least favored today will in the end be chosen. Only one fact is clear.

This is the fact that the world struggle has moved into a wholly new phase. Even if this new phase does not include open world war, mobilization of the United States is ultimately inevitable. If time is granted to us before war comes, that time will now be used for an effort to build strength in the free world going far beyond anything that has been discussed or imagined before this moment. We are paying today for our failure to begin that effort long ago. Whatever happens, nothing must stand in the way of that effort now.—December 1, 1950 (JA & SA).

The new year began with our first "security" investigation—but not our last.

WASHINGTON

The other day a new experience—a visit from the F.B.I.—came to these reporters. It was a surprisingly sociable, indeed a downright genial, meeting. The two agents representing the bureau were decent, intelligent young men. They neither blustered nor talked nonsense. A shrewd but friendly inquisition merged, almost insensibly, into a friendly parting. Nothing could have been more painless.

In the background of this jolly chat, however, lurking, as it were, behind the curtain of amiability that inclosed the conversation, there were one or two things that were decidedly disagreeable to think about.

To be specific, the misdeed being investigated was no sinister subversive activity. It was the publication of the proof that the Soviet atomic explosion was the planned explosion of a workable atomic bomb, and the disclosure of the best estimates available of the stock of atomic bombs accumulated by the Kremlin since the seismographs picked up the earth tremor in central Siberia. This was the crime that led President Truman to order a "security investigation." It would have been more fitting to investigate why the leaders of this nation failed to impart such vital information to the American people on their own initiative.

The twenty to thirty bombs now in the possession of the Kremlin, the hundred or more atomic bombs the Kremlin will have in another eighteen months, are not all pretty baubles by Fabergé. Their mere existence intimately, directly and deeply affects the world position of the United States, the future of the free world, the individual future of every American citizen. Their existence, in short, is one of the three or four salient facts that must influence every decision of national policy.

In Russia, no doubt, such knowledge may be closely guarded. But ours is a free society, whose masters are the people of the United States. The great decisions of national policy are made by the people, and not by the President or the Secretary of State, or any other temporary office-holder. In order to decide wisely, the people must be informed. And it is the most sacred trust, the most important single duty of the highest public servants to inform their masters, the people, so that the decision of the people may be wise.

As Winston Churchill brilliantly proved, facts which are matters of life and death can always be presented honestly to the people, even in circumstances of great delicacy and danger, without giving aid and comfort to the enemy. Suppression of such facts is not a sign of prudence. It is a sign of leadership that is feeble, or dishonest, or both.

If the leaders wish to represent a disastrous program of disarmament as "cutting fat without muscle"; if they desire to bemuse the people about the meaning of such a great event as the Soviet atomic explosion; if they are pretending that the chances "were never better for peace" with Korea just around the corner, it is only natural for everything to be classified except the toilet paper. Such is the rule that has been followed in Washington, more or less consistently, for the last two years.

In these circumstances, it becomes the duty of every self-respecting reporter to dig out, not any facts which are properly secret, but the essential facts which affect the national posture and welfare. It is a risky business; for reporters and editors cannot know what is known to Presidents and Secretaries of State—exactly how to present these vital facts so that no harm is done. But if the press lets itself be transformed into a mere machine for transmitting the doctored handouts of shabby politicians, the press has abdicated its chief function.

There are other points besides the foregoing that are raised by the recent visit of the young men from the F.B.I. A whole chapter might be written on the shocking but increasing use of these "security investigations," not only as a weapon to muzzle the press, but as a weapon of intra-departmental bureaucratic war.

Another chapter might be devoted to the methods used—the broadside inquiry which in these reporters' experience at least never hits the target; the wholesale harassment of innocent men on the method of "who knows whom"; the unashamed official practice of the very same guilt-by-association which is considered so shocking when indulged in by Sen. Joseph R. McCarthy. Something more might even be said about the scrupulosity of the F.B.I. as compared with the State Department's special agents, who have done things in the last

two years that must have made Secretary of State Acheson's great
master, Mr. Justice Holmes, turn in his honored grave.

But there is no space here to go slumming in these purlieus of the
American government. The point here is very simple indeed. In a free
society, secrecy is not security. National ignorance is the shortest road
to national annihilation. And this "security investigation" caused by
the publication of information most vital to the national future shows
how great is the confusion and the danger.—February 19, 1951 (JA
& SA).

The rehearsal for the later tragic drama in the Middle East began
in Tehran, and was presided over by Dr. Mohammed Mossadeq.
Some time after the column below was written, in the most acute
stage of the Iranian crisis, a plan of military occupation of Southern
Iran was actually presented to Washington by London, by Ernest
Bevin's successor at the Foreign Office, Herbert Morrison. The fact
is amusing to remember, in view of the Labor Party's subsequent
trumpetings about Suez, and in view of the further fact that the Cabinet which approved Morrison's project included most of the present
Labor leadership. As one now looks back, the distinguishing feature
of this first rehearsal for the drama in the Middle East was the extreme prudence of the Soviets. "Hands off the Middle East" was
Stalin's rule. The rule would no doubt have been broken if Morrison's
plan had been carried out. For this reason, the State Department
strongly opposed the Morrison plan. But as it was, after years of
nervous travail, the Iranian crisis finally sputtered out in a settlement;
and the final Middle Eastern crisis only began after the Summit meeting in Geneva in 1955.

TEHRAN

The first point the American and British negotiators have passed
over in their meaningless communique from Washington is the extreme seriousness of the Iranian situation they have been so nervously
discussing. By a long course of flaccidity and folly, Iran and the Middle
East in general have been brought close to the point of explosion. The
decision of the Iranian Majlis to nationalize the Anglo-Iranian Oil
Company is merely the slow match that may touch off the explosion.

The American tendency to assume an air of conscious rectitude,
and to hint that this is a nasty imperialist mess with which we are not
concerned, can only be compared with the similar (and even less ex-

cusable) British tendency in dealing with the Far Eastern crisis in recent months. In fact, American interests are as inextricably tangled in this Iranian problem as are British interests.

If no sensible compromise on the oil question is found, the first consequence will be general imitation of the Iranian example throughout the whole Middle East. The American oil properties here will also be involved. What is far worse, loss of control of her Middle Eastern oil, which is all the oil Britain has, will promptly reduce Britain to the status of a secondary power. Thus the whole huge American post-war investment in maintaining Britain as a major power ally will be flushed down the drain. Interruption or reduction of Middle Eastern oil supplies will be crippling, in truth, to the strength of all of Western Europe.

En route to Tehran, this correspondent touched base in London. There he received the strong impression that the British government will not accept defeat in the long hard struggle to rebuild Britain's power position and economy. Instead, if worst comes to worst they will dust off the plan the Cabinet actually approved during the previous Iranian crisis of 1946.

At that time, it will be recalled, British occupation of southern Iran was hurriedly prepared for in order to protect the oil property from the Soviets. If the British now move troops to Iran, Soviet occupation of the rest of the country under the 1921 treaty will become virtually inevitable. Even if the British shrink back at the last moment from such desperate measures, a general effort by the Middle Eastern governments to take over the oil companies can only lead to political chaos throughout the whole region. The companies are actually larger organizations than the governments themselves. The process of takeover will unleash unimaginable political tensions. One way or another chaos will be unavoidable.

Chaos in the Middle East, in turn, will compromise the whole position in the eastern Mediterranean. The American Mediterranean fleet, which is now much larger than the British fleet there, and especially the Anglo-American air bases in Cyprus, Cyrenaica and Tripoli, are now among the chief deterrents to Soviet aggression. If the air bases alone cease to be available—and the British will hardly be in a mood to permit their use if deserted by us at this juncture—the effect will be the same as losing one-half or more of the American Strategic Air Force.

In short, this business in Iran is *potentially* more serious for the Western alliance than anything but naked Soviet aggression in a critical area.

This does not mean that the decision of the Iranian Majlis to nationalize the Anglo-Iranian Company is the result of a Soviet plot. It does not mean either that Dr. Mossadeq and the other Iranian nationalists who have taken the lead in this matter have consciously wished to cripple the Western alliance; they are comparable, rather, to the American isolationists of the Wherry stripe, who also wish to bring the whole world down in ruins because they cannot see beyond their noses.

Finally, just because the problems created by this business in Iran are so immensely grave, it does not mean that these problems cannot be solved. The slow match in fact can be extinguished.

Grasping the immensity of the stakes in the game, however, is the essential first step toward an understanding of how the game must be played. What has happened could have been prevented by wise Anglo-American action long ago. Instead, the British in the Middle East have pursued a policy of business as usual, the standard of business as usual being established by the conditions that prevailed before the shattering changes of the second world war. Meanwhile, the Americans have been flabby, uncreative and unwilling for many reasons to take firm initiatives.

Thus Anglo-American influence, which is still potentially very great, has gone for nothing or has been downright pernicious. And this has created a situation in which heavy immediate risks must be run in order to avoid the certainty of eventual disaster.—April 16, 1951 (JA).

This was the year when witch-hunting began in earnest. In addition to disliking witch-hunting in principle, we were obliged in practice to go rather further than reporters generally go in their response to ugly public phenomena. The favorite victims of the witch-hunt were the officials who had helped to make our wartime China policy; and the older member of our partnership had been very intimately involved in all those policy battles of the past. He thought, and still thinks, that he was right to fight against the American officials and military officers who were hostile to the Chinese Nationalists and deluded by the Chinese Communists. But he was also conscious of having fought with no-holds-barred. As an officer in uniform, he had even drafted the Generalissimo's telegram demanding the recall of General Joseph Stilwell; and although Stilwell's recall certainly saved China for a while, it was at least a little unconventional for a very junior officer under Stilwell's command to join in preparing a document of quite this character. In short, he was conscious that he had been guilty of impropriety in China, if anyone had.

In these circumstances, we not only fought the witch-hunt with our typewriters to the best of our ability; we also intervened in a more personal manner on several occasions. The brilliant John Paton Davies had been the leading back-room boy on the other side of the fight in China. When his marathon loyalty investigation began, the older member of our partnership therefore volunteered to appear for Davies. The column we published about this experience won us the largest volume of complimentary mail, and the most civilized complimentary mail, that we have ever received—maybe because people like columnists to admit past errors. As recounted in our chapter on political reporting, the older member of our partnership was also able to disprove the charge made by the ex-Communist Louis Budenz, that Henry A. Wallace had been "under Communist guidance" during his wartime mission to China for Franklin Roosevelt. Again, this involved an appearance on the witness stand, before the super-witch-hunting committee headed by Senator Pat McCarran of Nevada.

What infuriated us most in this period was the partial character of the witch-hunt. General Douglas MacArthur's insistence on the need for a massive Soviet military effort to defeat the Japanese armies on the Asian mainland had been the strongest spur to the American negotiators at Yalta. Senator Wiley of Wisconsin, then a member of the Taft wing of the Senate, had publicly said that he hoped our diplomats at Yalta would not be "lily-fingered" about paying any price the Kremlin might demand, in order to save expenditure of the lives "of American boys" to defeat Japan. From General MacArthur's headquarters had emanated another project calculated to give the greatest aid and comfort to the Chinese Communists—a project for General Stilwell's return to China with a force from Okinawa, with the specific mission of linking up with the Communist armies in North China and supplying them with American arms in large quantities. But all this was forgotten, and the targets of the witch-hunt were people like Davies, John Carter Vincent and poor silly Wallace. Worse still, the same powerful publications that had followed the Davies-Vincent line in wartime now forgot their own past errors and either failed to come to the defense of the accused, or even joined in condemning them. The following column records our resulting exasperation:

WASHINGTON

Perhaps the strangest characteristic of our time is the distortion of the sense of history. Because they uttered sentiments in war time that were widely shared by irreproachable, church-going, Republican-voting, tax-paying, payroll-meeting citizens, unfortunate people are now hauled before Senatorial bars to answer the charge of pro-Communism.

By way of contrast, a man like Philip Jessup, who took a thoroughly pernicious part in the "America First" movement, proudly drapes the "America First" mantle around his shoulders to prove that he is not a Communist. And far from suggesting that an extreme America-Firster may not have the kind of judgment needed for a post of high responsibility, everybody wags his head and says, "Ah, that's a strong point in Jessup's favor." The whole business has become nonsensical.

These reflections are inspired by this reporter's curious experience of sitting for long, weary hours, waiting to take his turn on the stand, while Robert Morris, counsel of Sen. McCarran's Sub-committee on Internal Security, grilled Henry A. Wallace on selected tiny morsels from the distant past. One of the main subjects of inquiry was a rather silly pamphlet Wallace wrote for the Institute of Pacific Relations in 1944, called "Our Job in the Pacific." Morris treated this unrepaying ten cents worth as though it were a red-hot bomb, concocted in the secret cellars of the Kremlin.

The pamphlet did not mention American arms for the Chinese Communists. It did not mention coalition in China. Indeed, it did not even touch upon the Chinese Communists at all, while it included a glowingly laudatory reference to Chiang Kai-shek. These points were not remarked upon. The pamphlet was also anti-colonial in general tone. An American who sympathizes with colonies struggling to be free is not by definition pro-Communist. Yet as far as this implication could be left upon the record, Morris left it.

The great point that Morris made, however, was that poor Wallace was pro-Communist in a series of waffling expressions of hope that the Soviets would be nice after the war. In brief, Wallace had written that the Russians had shown good faith by not previously interfering in Chinese affairs (which was wrong, since Marshal Stalin was the first to give active aid to Generalissimo Chiang Kai-shek in the war against Japan). He had written further that he believed the Russians had no imperialist aspirations, and that he hoped the Russians, Chinese and Americans would all be able to co-operate cosily in the postwar world.

As Morris droned on with his accusatory questions, this reporter automatically sought distraction in an article in the well known fellow-traveling publication, "Amerasia." This article turned out to contain generous quotations from two other papers, by the Morris system also by inference fellow-traveling, "Life" and "The New York Times." In the spring of 1944, a "Life" editorial had commented on an unusually venomous attack on Generalissimo Chiang Kai-shek's government by the Time-Life correspondent in China, Theodore White. Reproducing a few of the more choice White epithets, the "Life" editors remarked:

"The United States cannot ignore the fact that if China's government should become a fascistic, power-hungry, repressive, land-lords'-and-usurers' government, it is all too likely to get into trouble with Russia; whereas a government which stands for freedom, reform and international co-operation is not. Under no circumstances would the American people ever wish to be embroiled with the Soviet Union in a struggle in which they would feel politically on the wrong side."

This "Life" editorial, so closely paralleling Wallace, except that he was genial toward the Generalissimo, closed with the prediction that if the Chinese would only be "freedom-loving, progressive," there would be no trouble with the Soviets. As for "The New York Times," in the fall of 1944 its editorial page ringingly called upon President Roosevelt to "make it clear to Chiang that his prestige will be enhanced, not diminished, if he takes certain steps." Among these steps were ceasing to "hold a great part of (his armies) on guard duty against his political opponents" (the Chinese Communists); making "a genuine truce with the Chinese Communists"; and consenting "to take into his government members of the representative groups and parties."

Here, in "The New York Times," was strong stuff indeed. Here was open advocacy of several points that the eminent professional ex-Communist Louis Budenz had testified on oath belonged to the Communist party line. Here was worse than Wallace, with a vengeance. But who was on the stand? Why, Wallace of course, under charges of pro-Communism. The reader can find his own language to characterize this sort of thing.—October 21, 1951 (JA).

The indecisive end of the Korean war was coming into sight—but it was still a long way off, none the less. We learned a little later that secret negotiations with the Soviets, looking to an end to the Korean war, had already been initiated by George Kennan on instructions from Dean Acheson when this column was written. Hence the "smell in the air."

WASHINGTON

It may be that Secretary of Defense George Marshall's sudden, unannounced flight to Tokyo and Korea has no political significance at all. This is the official line, and no official will budge from it. But in connection with Secretary Marshall's trip, it is at least interesting that secret diplomatic negotiations looking to an end to the Korean war have certainly been seriously considered, and may already have been initiated.

A little more than three weeks ago, this reporter described "a sort of smell in the air in official Washington," which for the first time suggested that a truce in Korea was a serious possibility. The air has now cleared sufficiently so that it is possible to define more precisely the sources from which this odor emanated.

One source was the very faint indications from the direction of the Kremlin that a reasonable settlement of the Korean war might be patched up. These indications were never strong enough to be described as "peace feelers." But the first signs of a switch in the Kremlin's policy are never much more obvious than a twitch of the eyebrows or a clearing of the throat. And because these signs were followed by a sudden inspired Communist campaign for a Korean truce, especially in "The New York Daily Worker," they were taken entirely seriously by those best qualified to judge.

A more important source of the smell in the air three weeks ago, however, was the simple fact that about that time the United States government finally made up its vast collective mind on just what it wants in Korea. The National Security Council recommended, and the

President approved, a policy paper calling for a cease-fire no further south than the 38th Parallel, followed by a staged withdrawal of all foreign troops under the surveillance of the United Nations. The United States would refuse to discuss either the disposition of Formosa or the admission of Communist China into the United Nations as a prelude to such a cease-fire.

This is what the American government wants simply because it is pretty unanimously agreed in the Pentagon and the State Department that this is the best the American government can get, bar a general war. This is also, of course, what the British government has wanted all along. The question remains how both governments are to get what is wanted.

This vital question has been the subject of prolonged conversations between Secretary of State Dean Acheson and British Ambassador Sir Oliver Franks; more recently between Gen. Omar Bradley and the British military chiefs in London; and between American and allied officials at various levels. Acheson's statements on Capitol Hill, outlining the terms which this government would be prepared to accept, were of course carefully prepared in advance, and constituted in themselves an obvious "peace feeler."

But what happens next? The situation is terribly complicated by the fact that the Soviets, whose intentions will determine the outcome, are not officially engaged in the Korean war. It is further complicated by the ancient Soviet tendency to interpret any overtures whatsoever as a sign of weakness.

As far as can be determined, no final decision on how to deal with this situation has been made. But what seems likely is an overt, official approach through the United Nations to the Chinese and North Koreans, probably coupled with some sort of secret, diplomatic approach to the Kremlin. A truce offer to the Chinese and North Koreans could come either in a report to the United Nations by President Truman, or in a declaration by the sixteen nations with forces in Korea.

The precedent for the direct, secret approach to the Soviets is found in the infinitely delicate, infinitely dangerous negotiations conducted by Dr. Philip Jessup, which led up to the end of the Berlin blockade (a great service for which Jessup was rewarded by being called a Communist by the Congressional Neanderthal men). Something of the sort may already, indeed, have been initiated. If so, it is quite properly wholly secret. And whether it has started or not, it must be said with all possible emphasis that those who know place the chances of a peaceful negotiated settlement of the Korean war at no better than even.

The chance of peace is placed this high only because the Soviets must know that the United Nations forces cannot now be defeated in Korea without direct Soviet participation, which would lead to world war. They must also know that if there is not a settlement quite soon, this country, to quote Gen. Bradley, will undertake "other measures" to end the war, rather than accept an endless bloody stalemate. These "other measures" will confront the Soviets with the choice between abandoning their most important ally, or accepting the extreme probability of world war. Thus the final choice, as it has from the beginning, rests with the Soviet sponsors of aggression. And thus the world, in the early summer of 1951, quivers on the knife edge between war and peace.—June 11, 1951 (SA).

In 1951 Nasser was not foreseeable, but what produced Nasser sprang to the eye in Cairo. At this time, of course, the fat Farouk still sat on his throne.

At the conclusion of his Middle Eastern journey, the reporter wrote: "Through all the complexities of what is happening in the Middle East, this one fact stands out—the United States, the powerful leader of the Western alliance, is not greatly influencing the course of events in this vital area. And while the U. S. stands thus paralyzed, the Middle East is displaying almost all the symptoms of disintegration which China showed before China fell." That judgment still holds.

CAIRO

On leaving such a city as this, it is difficult not to give way to a sense of despair. For here, in this curious, unpleasant atmosphere (the air has a sweet cloying smell, rather like a baby's diaper), it sometimes seems that the isolationists are right: that we should retire into our continental Gibraltar, eat our lotus leaves while we may and await our inevitable end.

Given a good deal more shrewdness and foresight than London and Washington have customarily displayed in these parts, the situation might be glued together here, so that it can be rendered more or less manageable for a time. But only for a time—and what happens after that?

The plain fact is that this is an essentially revolutionary situation. It is true that Americans are apt to be overly horrified by the fantastic contrast between wealth and poverty in such places as Egypt (a contrast to which those from the "capitalist, reactionary" United States are far less accustomed than Europeans). It is true that this contrast has existed since the time of the Pharaohs. Yet the essential fact remains.

The structure of society here—the ruthless exploitation of the many by the very few who own all the land and therefore all the wealth—simply cannot stand up indefinitely. For all sorts of technological and political reasons, some sort of basic and probably violent change is inevitable here. In such a situation, those who stand for violent change are likely ultimately to profit, while those who seem to stand for things as they are will surely lose.

Under the above formula, the Soviets will profit and the West will lose in the present world struggle in such areas as this. Yet the dilemma of the West is obvious. If only to keep the situation glued together, it is tempting, and indeed for a time it may be necessary for the Anglo-American partnership to use something very like the technique of influence which the British used here and elsewhere for many years and with considerable success.

The British, in effect first created the ruling class of pashas and then controlled this class by bribes of one sort or another. The British needed the pashas simply because they needed a handle through which to exercise their power in Egypt. British power was sometimes thus exercised by subtle and indirect means. Often the means were most simple and direct.

When, for example, Ernest Bevin perhaps unwisely put a stop to the practice, the Egyptian politicians and journalists whose palms had been regularly greased by the secret funds of the British Embassy were honestly indignant. They have since become professional Britain baiters to a man.

Because the handle still exists, in the form of a small and by no means incorruptible ruling class, this technique or something like it seems logical, and it might work for a time. But it cannot work indefinitely, as the experience of the British all over this area has shown. The fact is that the present ruling class cannot rule for very much longer and only rules now by going to any lengths whatsoever to distract the attention of the ruled from the misery of their condition.

Although it is easy to state the dilemma, it is impossible clearly to see the way out of it. Yet two points may be worth considering.

In the first place, we ought to stop talking nonsense about democracy. Talking about democracy is talking nonsense as concerns countries like this, where the great majority of the population lives rather below the level of their animals. Democracy here means simply that politicians must outbid each other for the support of the street mobs. This in turn leads straight to the most vicious extremism—"kill the Jews" yesterday, "kill the British" today, "kill the Americans" tomorrow. A wise Anglo-American policy here could bolster the moderates for a time, but if the moderates are not assassinated anyway, the extremists will always overtake them in the end.

The second point follows from the first. What is needed in this sort of situation is a reasonably enlightened dictatorship. The model is Turkey's Kemal Ataturk, who, by making basic changes, transformed a crumbling, corrupt and anarchic society, much like Egypt's today, into a modern state. Tough though it may have been, Ataturk's dictatorship laid the groundwork for the democracy which now functions so surprisingly well in Turkey.

The problem, of course, is to find your Ataturk—in a pinch, we should certainly settle for a Reza Shah Pahlevi. It is hopeless to expect a stooge of the West to exercise power—no stooge of the West could rule. Any stooge of the pashas, moreover, would in the long run spell victory for the Soviets, since what is needed is precisely the sort of change, including land reform, which the pashas most fear.

At any rate, it is time to strip ourselves of our illusions. It comes hard for any American to find himself advocating authoritarian rule anywhere. But the fact remains—the kind of rational dictator who will interest himself in the defense of his country and in the basic change which his country needs to survive as an independent state is the best we can hope for in such places as Egypt. It is also a great deal better than anything we are likely to get.—November 12, 1951 (SA).

Our own reaction to the first Soviet atomic bomb had been an intensive study of the peculiar Soviet economy, with its delusive surface weaknesses and its remarkable power to mobilize immense technological and productive resources at all points regarded as critical by the masters of the Kremlin. As early as November 2, 1949, we wrote that "the intelligence services of the Western powers have now proved to be just as wrong about other Russian technical capabilities as they were about the time schedule of the Russian atomic energy program. This means, very simply, that the other grounds for Western complacency are going the same way as the American atomic monopoly." We published a long series of columns on this theme, but as they were all chiefly devoted to breaking the news of Soviet technological advances which everyone now takes for granted, they have lost their current interest. One abbreviated specimen will suffice. It retains its interest even today because it shows that the military effort of the Western nations, even at the peak of the past Korean rearmament, never caught up with the military effort of the Soviet Union.

WASHINGTON

It is time to face up to a simple, bleak fact. The Soviet Union is currently outproducing the United States, and by an incredibly wide margin, in modern combat planes. Since air power is certain to be the decisive factor if war comes, this is frightening, to put it mildly.

Yet it is easy enough to prove that it is a fact. The air war of the future will be fought with jet-powered planes. And here the figures tell their own disturbing story.

First, take jet interceptors. Soviet output of the MiG-15 jet fighter, plus newer models, reached during the last year according to the most reliable estimates an annual production rate of between 5,500 and 6,200—a really astonishing achievement of the Soviet aircraft industry. American production of the older F-84 was in the middle hundreds, and of the F-86 in the low hundreds—the very low hundreds.

The MiG-15, it must be added, is a first-rate, modern jet interceptor, which has already outdistanced the F-84. Pilots who have fought F-84s against MiG-15s in Korea report that combat between the two planes is murder for the F-84s. Thus the F-84 is now considered obsolescent, and the newer F-86 is rated the only American plane capable of holding its own in combat with the MiG-15. And American production of truly modern jet interceptors will not have reached a thousand by the end of this year, while Soviet production is still on the increase. Thus, even by the end of this year, the Soviets will have an enormous six-to-one advantage, at least in the jet fighter field.

The comparable figures on jet bombers are hardly more reassuring. During the past year, the Soviets are reliably estimated to have attained an annual production rate of about 750 jet-powered medium bombers. They have approximately 450 such bombers actually in combat groups.

Last year the United States produced considerably fewer than fifty B-47 jet bombers—this is the only American all-jet bomber actually in production. The British (who are concentrating on commercial jet carriers) produced one jet bomber, which crashed. During the coming year it is believed that more than 300 B-47s will come off the assembly lines, plus a handful of British jet bombers. This means that hoped-for Western production for the *coming* year will still represent less than half the production rate reached by the Soviets during the *last* year.

Nor do even these somber figures—at least six-to-one for jet fighters, at least two-to-one for jet bombers—tell the whole story. The supersonic plane is the plane of the future, which will make subsonic planes obsolete as surely as the jets are rendering obsolete the reciprocating engine. According to highly rated intelligence, the Soviets now have actually in production a combat plane which will fly faster than sound. The American Air Force hopes to get such a plane—but not before 1954.—February 1, 1952 (JA & SA).

The following column marks the beginning of our only old fashioned crusade, against the hired informers that the U. S. government then had in its employ. Louis Budenz, the subject of this column, was certainly the best of them. He testified falsely—that we proved—but he was led on to do so because the McCarrans and McCarthys tempted him with a stirring public role. His motives were complex; we doubted, even, whether he knew what he was doing; and he was certainly not animated by a simple desire for cash.

Cash was the prime motive, however, of the worst of these paid professional witnesses that the U. S. government used to turn on and off, like taps, in its anti-subversive and immigration cases. Most of the people they testified against were about as bad as the government witnesses, but it seemed to us that even such people, if American citizens, had a right to a fair trial. So we kept hammering on the hired informers for a long time. The climax came in the Eisenhower administration, when we were able to force the reluctant and enraged Attorney General Herbert Brownell to order an investigation of perjury by the most wretched of these creatures, Paul Crouch. Next

Brownell had to order two more investigations of perjury by government witnesses who had testified in a loyalty proceeding against Dr. Ralph Bunche. After that, the hired informers were quietly dropped.

As you cannot charge a man with perjury without careful documentation, all our columns on this theme make rather pernicketty reading. Hence we preserve only one, about Budenz, in which we first sounded the call for an investigation of these people.

WASHINGTON

The Congressional investigating process has been so warped and twisted that the really important issues involved in any given inquiry are quite likely never to be mentioned at all. That is certainly true of Sen. Pat McCarran's Internal Security Subcommittee of the Judiciary Committee, which has just finished beating John Carter Vincent over the head with its verbal substitutes for a rubber truncheon.

In all the brutal questioning of this high State Department official, not one word was said about the veracity of Vincent's sole accuser, the professional ex-Communist, Louis Budenz. Yet as a witness before the Tydings committee, and as the pet witness of the McCarran subcommittee, Budenz has literally charged several scores of other Americans besides Vincent with being Communist party members. And surely this mass production of charges of treason to the United States is no light matter.

Furthermore, even before the Vincent case, it was pretty hard to take Louis Budenz at his own valuation, as one of the "most truthful people in the world." The facts, indeed, speak for themselves.

Budenz left the Communist party in October, 1945. Not long thereafter, he began to work with the F.B.I. He has said himself that "no (other) American has given so many hours to the F.B.I., and at all hours of the day and night, and at any time . . . eighteen hours a week . . . every week holiday and the entire Christmas holidays and all the other times I could be reached." He has further estimated that between the end of 1945 and the early spring of 1950, he dedicated an over-all total of 3,000 hours of his time, or the equivalent of 375 eight-hour days, to this voluntary labor as an F.B.I. informer.

You might have supposed that 375 eight-hour days would have given Budenz enough time to search his memory for the name of every lurking traitor, however insignificant, as to whose Communist party membership he could testify with confidence. But you would have been quite wrong in any such supposition.

While Budenz usefully assisted the F.B.I. in preparing cases against such Soviet agents as J. Peters and Gerhard Eisler, he somehow forgot, for rather more than four years, about John Carter Vincent and the other men he is currently accusing. It was not until March, 1950, when Senator Joseph R. McCarthy let loose his first bellows about fifty-seven, or eighty-one, or 205 "card-carrying Communists" and sympathizers in the government, that Budenz's memory suddenly acquired its astonishing built-in pick-up. He went to the F.B.I. to denounce Owen Lattimore as a Communist for the first time in the same week of March, 1950, when McCarthy declared that this silly, fellow-wandering Johns Hopkins professor was the "top Communist agent" in the United States.

As it happened, Budenz had already twice denied that Lattimore was a Communist, once to a State Department investigator in 1947, and again, in the most categorical terms, to an editor of "Collier's" magazine, Leonard Parris, in 1949. In the same fashion, when appearing before the Tydings investigating committee to make his public accusation against Lattimore, Budenz firmly refused to accuse John Carter Vincent as a Communist, saying he had to be "careful." But a week or so later he went to the F.B.I. again, and now denounced Vincent as a Communist for the first time.

These peculiarities of his memory were never explained by Budenz. He admitted he had lied to the State Department investigator and the "Collier's" editor because, he said, he preferred to do all his talking to the F.B.I., but the best reason he could offer for his failure to accuse Lattimore or Vincent during 3,000 hours of previous work with the F.B.I., was that he and the F.B.I. agents had been too busy talking about other things. He also half-admitted links with Senator McCarthy through his close friend in the China lobby, Alfred Kohlberg, who was one of McCarthy's original inspirers.

These facts alone would be enough to cast the gravest suspicion on Budenz's testimony in any normal court of law. Then in the Vincent case, Budenz for the first time broke his most curious rule. Always before, he had stuck to the naked and hearsay accusation, based on his own alleged recollection of the six or eight or ten-year-old statements of other Communists, who could not be called to the stand. Never had he tried to substantiate his charges with any evidence that could be checked against historic facts.

In the Vincent case, however, Budenz made the checkable statement, that Vincent "guided" Henry A. Wallace "along the paths" of the Communist party line in China in 1944. The strongest documentary and other evidence was at once produced, to show that Vincent's influence on Wallace had in fact been profoundly anti-Communist.

Neither Budenz nor the McCarran subcommittee could produce a jot or tittle of solid counter-evidence, either to prove Vincent's pro-Communist influence on Wallace or to show Vincent's Communist party membership. With Vincent's appearance before the McCarran subcommittee, all the testimony is now in; and the disproof of Budenz's first checkable statement stands absolutely unimpaired. Under the circumstances, Louis Budenz would seem to be the man to investigate.—February 6, 1952 (JA & SA).

In the Democratic camp, President Truman had decided to comply with the curious memorandum he wrote to himself in 1950, setting out all the reasons why he should not become a candidate again. The obvious Democratic white hope was the able and eloquent Governor of Illinois; but when Truman called him to Washington and asked him to become a candidate, Adlai Stevenson refused to do so—mainly, one now suspects, because he did not wish to be Truman's personal nominee. Here is Stevenson in the aftermath, putting on the public wrestling match with his own soul that was impressive at first, and then became tiresome and even disturbing by dint of sheer repetition. Political details which have now lost interest have been omitted.

WASHINGTON
An extraordinary human drama is now being played out in the Governor's mansion at Springfield, Ill. Ever since President Truman's surprise withdrawal at the Jefferson-Jackson dinner, Gov. Adlai Stevenson, in the intervals of attending to the 14-hour-a-day task of governing his big state, has been wrestling with his soul. Will he or will he not co-operate in the strong movement to draft him for the Democratic nomination? Such is the question he is seeking to answer.

According to personal friends who have witnessed Stevenson's private wrestling match, it has been downright painful to watch. Gov. Stevenson has gone through a series of phases. Immediately after the

President's announcement, he was about ready to "chuck the whole thing" by announcing that he was not a candidate and would not accept the nomination if offered.

Twenty-four hours later, after a day in Washington in which he was showered with assurances of support from important political leaders and cogent arguments from friends that it was his duty to run, he seemed to have changed his mind. On the television program on the Sunday night after the President's announcement, he certainly sounded like a receptive candidate, if not like an active one.

Back in the huge, rambling Governor's mansion in Springfield, however, torturing indecision again seized Stevenson. At first he was very strongly inclined to pretend, in effect, that nothing had been changed by the President's withdrawal. He intended merely to sit tight, to get on with his business as governor, and to say nothing at all about the party nomination. Then he found himself besieged, by telephone and in person, by hoards of leading Democrats, all urging him to make the race.

His close friends advised him that he must somehow clarify his position, and to this he has now agreed. Again, his first inclination was to make a statement on the famous General Sherman pattern. Last week, he was actually within a hair's breadth of removing himself once and for all from consideration. Only the importunities of friends and admirers, who have been rather in the position of men hanging on the coattails of a would-be suicide, prevented him from doing so.

The reasons for these hesitations are understandable. Gov. Stevenson is a man cursed with an excess of imagination, only too capable of foreseeing what would await him if by chance he should be elected President. Moreover, he has what he considers a "difficult moral problem." He has persuaded all sorts of able men to throw up their private jobs in order to serve the Illinois state government, on the explicit understanding that he would run again for governor.

He fears—and here most Illinois political observers agree with him —that another Democrat cannot beat the powerful and well financed Republican machine owned by Col. Robert R. McCormick. Thus he thinks his withdrawal may mean turning back the state government, in which he has become passionately interested, to the sleazy crowd which ran it before his election in 1948. He has, also, little desire to run against General of the Army Dwight D. Eisenhower, whom he admires, and whom he considers the most probable Republican choice.

Finally, he is in some ways a rather diffident man, and he has a mortal fear of seeming presumptuous, of other people thinking that he considers himself "an indispensable man."

Because of these strong feelings of Gov. Stevenson's, there is little or no chance of his becoming an active candidate in the manner of Sens. Estes Kefauver and Robert Kerr. The issue involved in the drafting of his forthcoming statement is not whether to announce he will chase the nomination, because he has no intention of doing so. The issue is, rather, whether to discourage the major state leaders who desire to join in a draft-Stevenson movement, as these words are written, the betting is reported as 50-50 either way at Springfield. —April 14, 1952 (JA & SA).

There were two really crucial episodes in the Republicans' pre-convention maneuvering. One was the New Hampshire primary, when a huge and unexpected Eisenhower vote stopped Bob Taft's bandwagon before it really got started. That, really, was how Sherman Adams got his start. The other was the Texas convention, which provided the issue on which the Eisenhower strategists won the day at Chicago. The senior member of our partnership went to Mineral Wells for two reasons. He had been warned of what would happen there by Henry Cabot Lodge Jr. And he knew that the press association reporters and Bill Lawrence of the "New York Times"—the only others going to see the show—would be required to call a spade an agricultural implement in all that they wrote. Being free to call a spade a spade, he thought he might be able to focus greater attention on "the Texas delegate steal," as the story of Mineral Wells subsequently came to be called. So it turned out—"Time's" story on Mineral Wells, for instance, picked up whole paragraphs of the columns written from there. Cabot Lodge, who was Eisenhower's floor manager at Chicago, subsequently thanked the reporter for "creating" the issue which was so important at Chicago.

The earlier pieces in the series, written at Mineral Wells, described the delegate-steal in painful detail—for you cannot charge theft without proving it. The following wrap-up of the story, written just after the Mineral Wells convention had ended, has rather more survival-value, because of its portrayal of the ham-fisted comic characters who tried so hard to serve the cause of poor Senator Taft.

What has happened here in the Republican party in Texas confronts the national Republican party with two of the gravest issues it has had to face in many years. Indeed, the longer one works to sort out the impressions left by the incredible Texas Republican convention at Mineral Wells, the bigger and uglier and more important these issues come to seem.

The first issue is simple enough. With Sen. Robert A. Taft, of Ohio, in the lead, the Republicans have been justifiably denouncing the corruption that has crept into the American government. But honest government depends on honest politics. And the first issue presented by the recent events in Texas is the issue of honesty in politics.

As to this, there can be no doubt. A powerful popular surge for Gen. Dwight D. Eisenhower gave his adherents a heavy majority in the Republican state convention, which in turn chooses the delegates to the national convention at Chicago. No one has argued, no one has even suggested, that this pro-Eisenhower majority in the Texas Republican state convention was elected illegally or improperly. Under the law and the rules, the Eisenhower faction had won the fight in Texas before the Mineral Wells meeting was convened.

But Texas national committeeman, Henry Zweifel, already had promised that Texas would be in the Taft column at Chicago. Mr. Zweifel solidly controls both the Republican state committee and its executive committee. The executive committee of the state committee, in turn, has the power to draw up the temporary roll of the state convention, making a preliminary choice in all contests for seats and seating those they choose on the convention floor. With this power, forty seedy old-guard politicians set aside the expressed will of a three-to-one majority of many thousands of legitimately enrolled, deeply enthusiastic Republican voters.

When the temporary roll was drawn up by Mr. Zweifel's henchmen, all the illegally chosen Zweifel-Taft supporters were seated, while nearly 600 Eisenhower supporters were denied their places on the convention floor, which were theirs by right of the ballot box. Armed deputies were brought in the next day, to make sure the Eisenhower faction did not attempt to seize what was legally theirs. The phony majority in the state convention was then employed—perhaps the rawest touch of all—to vote that it was not phony. And the phony convention thereafter elected the "official" pro-Taft delegation to Chicago.

The only thing that can be said for Zweifel and Company is that they at least had the grace not to pretend that these transactions were either savory or honest. The case was put rather plainly by the state chairman, an amiable old gentleman named Orville Bullington, whose war cry is, "To hell with foreign policy." He told this reporter:

"They'll barrelhouse 'em through. Whoever controls the committee can always barrelhouse 'em through. You'll see; it'll be the same at Chicago."

By the same token, when national committeeman Zweifel was questioned on the subject, he made no attempt to deny that the other side had the real majority. The reminder made him look a bit more shifty than usual, but he did not argue about it. And when he was asked whether majorities did not matter in Texas, he replied irritably and belligerently:

"They don't in the Democratic party in Texas either."

This peculiar explanation, that trampling on popular majorities was just an old local custom, like yodeling or tossing the caber, was nicely annotated by the state vice-chairman, Mrs. Burk West. Mrs. West admitted that the pro-Eisenhower faction "did comply with the law to some extent." She added, however, that "The law is one thing, but the law does not govern a party's policies." The final word was said by L. J. Benckenstein, who ran the Zweifel-Taft steam roller— a task for which he is admirably fitted, being a vast man with a vast oily smile and a fist like a ham.

"On its face," said Benckenstein, "it looks wrong. There's an explanation, but I can't give it to you. Maybe I will if you'll call me up some time."

Such are the men and women who organized the steal of the Texas Republican delegation, with the on-the-spot encouragement of Taft national managers David Sinton Ingalls and Brazilla Carroll Reese. The second issue raised by this steal ought to transcend even the issue of common honesty in politics, at least in the eyes of those practical-minded Republicans who would like to win an election for a change.

This reporter cannot of course gauge groundswells here in Texas, but the political experts of the leading Texas newspapers, who were all gathered at Mineral Wells, may be considered impartial and sound judges. These experts were unanimous on several points. First, Texas wants to get rid of the Democrats in Washington, and this sentiment entered very largely into the Eisenhower surge. Second, the Eisenhower surge here was a true popular movement, as is evidenced by the fact that in the biggest counties, more people turned out for Eisenhower at the Republican precinct meetings than attended the Democratic precinct meetings.

Third, Texas might also have gone for Sen. Taft in the national election, but will never do so after the ugly business at Mineral Wells, unless the Senator repudiates the actions of his local agents. And fourth, if Eisenhower is nominated by the Republicans, there is an excellent chance that the 1952 election will start a genuine two-party system in this state.

Zweifel and his crowd, and Ingalls and Reece too, for that matter, have defended themselves on the ground that many of Gen. Eisenhower's supporters were ex-Democrats and independents, only recently converted to Republicanism. The defense seems a bit odd, since this supposedly sinister infiltration was in fact the bright hope of the Republican party in Texas. The national Republican party will have to consider the issue, whether their hope is to be utterly extinguished.—June 1, 1952 (JA).

The following column, written just after Eisenhower's return from Europe, records the impression he then made on both of us. The event was to show that the impression was quite remarkably incomplete. But the surface of the man, as herein described, continues to please and reassure the American people. It is still the President's greatest single asset.

ABILENE, KANSAS

Dwight D. Eisenhower's first three days as an active Presidential candidate have made at least one thing entirely clear. His is the most effective political personality to emerge on the American scene since the death of Franklin Delano Roosevelt.

The impact of a political personality is impossible to define, but very easy to recognize, in the tingling expectancy of a crowd, in the electric undercurrent of excitement which a man's mere presence conveys. The secret of this very rare political magic differs with different men. Eisenhower's secret seems to be that he really is what he seems to be, and that he really means what he says.

At his press conference today he was obviously nervous at first—

as he had every right to be. Perhaps because of this his face, which is so mobile as to be downright rubbery, assumed an extraordinary variety of expressions. At one moment, he would purse his lips and peer intently at the ceiling of the movie theater in which the conference was held, as if he found the hideous decorations there absorbing. Then he would grin ruefully, rather like a little boy found with his hand in the cookie jar. Then he would frown, with ferocious concentration. Then he would smile his famous, astonishingly infectious smile.

There was nothing at all actorish or fake about all this. When he peered at the ceiling, he was quite obviously asking himself, "Now how in the world will I answer that one?" The occasional rueful grin was a silent tribute to the more shrewdly phrased have-you-stopped-beating-your-wife questions. And when he smiled the famous smile, he was honestly amused. The Eisenhower magic derives from the fact that he is essentially a simple and uncomplicated man, who really believes the not very startling and not very profound things he says, and who has never learned to assume either the synthetic manners or the synthetic opinions of so many professional politicians.

The quality of being what he is and meaning what he says came out strongly in Eisenhower's first short speech here, when he laid the cornerstone of an Eisenhower Memorial, to be built on a vacant lot next to the house in which he was brought up. He talked mostly about his parents, and about what they believed in and taught him to believe.

The "home and mother" theme has been pawed over so mawkishly by so many time-serving politicians that it has become almost a mark of political dishonesty. Read in cold print, this Eisenhower speech might seem to contain a good many kernels of corn—it even included references to "my mother's knee"—yet somehow every word rang true. Partly, perhaps, this was because of the nostalgic atmosphere of this small city, once "the sinfullest town in the West," now a pleasant community of wide lawns and white houses with big comfortable porches. Its total effect is more Penrod than Tom Sawyer. But mostly it was because Eisenhower really did feel deeply about the simple sentiments, so shop-worn in other hands, which he expressed.

This quality saved his major speech yesterday from being rather embarrassing anti-climax. His domestic political views were what every one wanted to hear, and his vaguely phrased denunciations of disunity, inflation, bureaucracy and excessive taxation would have been a monument of dullness in the mouth of any other living American politician. But there was an odd freshness to what Eisenhower said, simply because he so obviously earnestly believed it, although a full generation of politicians have been saying the same things in almost the same words.

All this is not to say that Eisenhower is a wide-eyed political innocent, unaware of the political realities of the situation in which he finds himself. The answers he gave at his press conference were certainly most carefully considered in advance, with a shrewd eye to the political effect not only on the Democrats but more especially on the conservative wing of his own party.

Yet the fact is that these answers were also perfectly honest and true, or so they seemed to this reporter. They landed Eisenhower rather precisely in the middle of the political road, and one has the impression that this is where Eisenhower belongs; that the middle of the road is where all his political thinking has taken him. He was frequently a little vague, but he was never really evasive and never sly. He answered one question, about farm parity, with the politically unheard-of phrase, "I don't know," and one sensed that on a number of domestic matters he had quite simply and unsurprisingly never worked out a detailed position in his own mind. Again and again as he spoke one had the feeling that "he really means this." And this in turn lent a curious freshness and authority to what he said.

In short, Eisenhower's personality, the publicly visible nature of the man himself, is a tremendous political asset to Eisenhower. It is also the greatest political asset which has been available to the Republican party in many years. An effective political personality, of course, does not necessarily determine the outcome of a nomination or an election. There are other powerful influences at work—like the control of the party machinery at convention time, or the price of corn at election time. But after three days of watching Eisenhower in action, this reporter is convinced that he will be a remarkably hard man to beat, whether in July or in November.—June 6, 1952 (SA).

Our campaign reporting in 1952 was our last effort in the old style —on the trains with the candidates, and off the trains with the local political leaders. Since the results are only too well known, no specimen is worth preserving except this one, which added a word to the American language. The "rising young Connecticut Republican," by the way, was our brother, John. He is also the author of Alsop's law of political oratory: "The important thing is to be able to say, 'Most oranges are round,' and sound as if you meant it." Stevenson's inability to fulfill Alsop's law was his real weakness. He was always remembering, he was even hinting to his audience, that no orange is absolutely round, that oranges only seem round, that they have pores on their surfaces, and so on and so on. The effect was beautiful, but in the end it lacked mass-impact.

SPRINGFIELD, ILLINOIS

Aside from their obvious devotion to Gov. Adlai Stevenson, the young political amateurs of the small staff which Stevenson has gathered here share one striking characteristic. They are all what the Europeans would call "intellectuals"—they are interested in ideas and in the words used to express these ideas. As a result, the atmosphere of Stevenson headquarters here rather reminds the visitor of a small university town.

The kind of campaign being waged by Gov. Stevenson clearly reflects this atmosphere, so unusual in a political headquarters. The Stevenson campaign, quite aside from the merits of the issues, is obviously the most intellectual and literate of any waged since the days of Woodrow Wilson. This raises the question—is intellect good politics?

After Stevenson's serious and rather difficult atomic energy speech in Hartford, Conn., this reporter remarked to a rising young Connecticut Republican that a good many intelligent people, who would be considered normally Republican, obviously admired Stevenson. "Sure," was the reply, "all the egg-heads love Stevenson. But how many egg-heads do you think there are?"

How many indeed, and how many people, not egg-heads themselves, admire and would vote for such an obvious egg-head as Adlai Stevenson? The Stevenson aides here, egg-heads to a man themselves, were at first overjoyed by the quality and reception of Stevenson's speeches. But now they are beginning to worry and wonder—especially since the recent performance by Sen. Richard Nixon.

The Nixon performance was certainly not calculated to appeal to the intellect. Indeed, certain of Nixon's assertions, like his claim that he was really "saving the taxpayers money," were hardly complimentary to the intelligence of his audience. Yet it was a brilliant performance of its kind, as the Stevenson staff here ruefully recognized. Nixon tapped, in a new way and almost for the first time, the vast store of accumulated skills of the entertainment and advertising industries.

With its convincing picture of the struggling, idealistic young lawyer and his devoted family (even including "Tricia's little dog"), the Nixon performance had all the emotional impact of, say, "Mr. Smith Goes to Washington." And emotional impact is just what the brilliant Stevenson speeches seem to lack. As the Stevenson aides who listened to both broadcasts here were well aware, Stevenson's Baltimore speech, following on the eve of the Nixon talk, seemed cold, impersonal and pallid by comparison.

Such polished phrases (to choose two from the Baltimore speech) as "like a new fog bank rising from a troubled sea" or "we shall survive with sacrifice or perish cheap," read very well on paper. But the Stevenson staffers are beginning to wonder if such well chosen words are worth votes. It is a symptom of this growing self-doubt that some Stevenson aides now believe that the Nixon episode may turn out to be a net asset to the Republicans. A basic reason for this growing lack of confidence lies in the evident affection and respect accorded Gen. Dwight D. Eisenhower by the large crowds which are greeting him on his whistle-stop tour.

Eisenhower's little whistle-stop homilies are certainly not profound, nor are they couched in deathless prose. But the crowds obviously respond warmly to the sincerity and essential goodness of the man, in a way that Stevenson's notably smaller crowds do not respond. Stevenson leaves his listeners amused or thoughtful, but he does not seem to stir their blood.

Another symptom of self-doubt in Springfield is the fact that the forthcoming whistle-stop tour by President Truman, once the forgotten man of the Stevenson campaign, is now being viewed here with enthusiastic anticipation. Truman, it is thought, may supply the missing ingredient—a direct, simple appeal to the voters' emotions and self-interests—which Stevenson, for all his brilliance, has not seemed able to achieve.

Yet the American voter is an unpredictable creature, and here it may be worth recounting an episode which followed Stevenson's remarkable speech in Richmond, Va. In this speech Stevenson, to the blank astonishment of some of his listeners, dwelt at length on such subjects as the literary achievements of Ellen Glasgow and William Faulkner. In the crush which followed the meeting, this reporter found himself squeezed between two elderly Southern ladies. The following exchange ensued:

First elderly Southern lady: "That was a funny sort of political speech, wasn't it? More like an address, you might say."

Second elderly Southern lady (with obvious pride): "Well, you see, Gov. Stevenson knew he was speaking to a specially intelligent audience."

And so, who knows? Being an egg-head may be shrewder politics than any one realizes, provided the egg-head talks as though every one else were an egg-head too.—September 26, 1952 (SA).

The day after Eisenhower was triumphantly elected, we published a piece that opened with the remark: "the new President of the United States is going to have to make just about the hardest decisions for the future any President has ever been called upon to make." Our main reason for this depressing forecast was simple enough. We had learned about the re-evaluation of Soviet military-productive power and technological proficiency that the Truman administration completed in its last year in office. The new findings, which have been substantiated by events, demanded a greatly intensified American effort to maintain a reasonable balance of power in the world. We had no doubt, then, that Eisenhower would do whatever might be necessary. But from the moment when he chose a Cabinet of "seventeen millionaires and a plumber" (we were the first to put this label on it) we began to be apprehensive. As Eisenhower had been a genuine hero to both of us, we went on hoping for the best. Yet a good deal of the shape of things to come, and the more important human reasons for it too, appeared in the following.

WASHINGTON

The Eisenhower Administration is going to be predominantly a business man's administration, and this can be one of the healthiest and most hopeful aspects of the new era. Nonetheless, after having a good look at the way the new administration is taking shape, it seems prudent to point out a serious danger that may lie ahead.

The best way to suggest the nature of the danger is to point out what has happened in Britain. Business influence in British politics was a more gradual and later growth than in America. The governments of Stanley Baldwin were the first in which the British business leaders had anything like an equal voice, even in the Conservative

Party. The government of Neville Chamberlain was the first, and last, British government truly dominated by business men.

Chamberlain's failure has all too often been attributed to evil motives. In reality, it was no more than the result of exaggerated concern for the domestic economy, and insufficient understanding of growing dangers abroad. The note was most clearly struck by the Chancellor of the Exchequer, Sir John Simon. He once justified crippling slashes in the budget of the Royal Air Force on the ground that the diplomats and service chiefs were worrying far too much about Hitler's Luftwaffe, and were forgetting that "the strength of the British economy was Britain's first line of defense."

From every standpoint, then, there are real risks as well as great reasons for hope, in Eisenhower's decision to form a business man's administration. The fact needs to be noted now, even before the administration has had a chance to try its hand, because one can already see a pretty sharp division of opinion about policy priorities. With one group of Gen. Eisenhower's new men, the domestic economy comes first; with another, the perils of the world situation are given first consideration.

The division declared itself on board the Helena, when President-elect Eisenhower was returning from Korea. Naturally enough, the incoming Secretary of the Treasury, George Humphrey, stood forward as the champion of the domestic economy; while the future Secretary of State, John Foster Dulles, argued that it was no use safeguarding the domestic economy while allowing the world situation to go to pot.

The difference that developed then has not been settled yet. With the next budget as the main bone of contention, the debate continues in Gen. Eisenhower's inner councils.

This is, of course, the psychological point on which President-elect Eisenhower has got to assert his authority to Congress. If he vigorously insists that all real foreign and defense requirements must be met in full, he will carry the day and establish his authority for a long time to come. If he seeks to appease the Republican isolationist faction of Congress, they will run away with the budget, and with American foreign and domestic policy too. After that, Gen. Eisenhower's authority can only be restored—if it is restored at all—when the nation is confronted with the grim consequences of a Congressional isolationist field day.

These facts of political life are not apparent to all of Gen. Eisenhower's new advisers. Many of them exaggerate the sums that can be saved by economical administration, and underrate the time it takes to sweat off fat without losing muscle. The new President has promised Sen. Robert A. Taft to "aim for" a budget cut down to $70,000,000,-000. In some measure, Gen. Eisenhower himself shares the excessive apprehensions of his friend, Gen. Omar Bradley, who publicly supported Secretary of Defense Lewis A. Johnson's totally disastrous "economy" program because he honestly thought the United States could not afford to defend itself.

Meanwhile, John Foster Dulles is reported to be arguing that it can be disastrous if this country merely *seems* to shrink back from its world responsibilities. Mr. Dulles is right that the slightest hint of American retreat can cause the Western Alliance to disintegrate. And he has to press, in addition, for the means to tackle such urgent but neglected problems as that in Indo-China.

The worst aspect of the whole situation is the time factor. Given time, such able men as future Secretary of the Treasury Humphrey would learn soon enough, by hard and even bruising contacts with world fact, about the necessary priorities between national survival and a lower national tax bill. But there is no time. In these circumstances, one can only place one's faith in the proved wisdom of the man who must make the ultimate decision—Dwight D. Eisenhower. —December 31, 1952 (JA & SA).

VIII

The Wrong Turning

1953 and 1954 were the formative years of the Eisenhower admin-
istration. We kept hoping that the new President would fulfill our own
image of him, as a moderate conservative about domestic matters, and
a believer in strong defense and foreign policies. The record shows the
outcome.

The opening months of 1953 were perhaps the most peculiar period the American government has ever passed through. The new
President's rule for dealing with Congress was, "I speak my piece,
and then it's up to them." His "piece" was very largely determined
by the views of Senator Taft; for until his last illness struck him
down, Taft in effect exercised a power of veto on all the administration's actions. This situation did not make Eisenhower at all happy;
as we were the first to report, he gradually became so disgusted with
his own party that he began to talk in private of the need for a new
party, vaguely formed of men-of-good-will. But the President's un-
happiness was never remedied in the usual way, by a firm assertion
of the great powers of the Presidency.

193

One of the consequences was the squalid, continuous appeasement of Senator Joseph R. McCarthy, in the face of the clearest evidence that McCarthy was the enemy of Eisenhower and everything he stood for. The first McCarthy rule, strongly supported by the passionately partisan Taft, was "no holdovers from Truman." Its enforcement produced at least one good story, when the secretary of the NSC, Robert Cutler, reminded W. Bedell Smith, then Secretary of State, that the rule had to be enforced. Smith remarked that he was himself a "holdover" from the Truman years. Cutler mumbled something about Smith being an exception. "Well," said Smith sardonically, "I can tell you another exception."

"Who's that, General?" said Cutler, nervously.

"Dwight D. Eisenhower," replied Smith, still more sardonically.

The worst center of appeasement of McCarthy was none the less the State Department. The foreign service of a government without a foreign policy—such as the American government until 1941—is not likely to be well adapted to such terrible new challenges as the American foreign service had to meet in the war and postwar years. By the time John Foster Dulles took office, however, the germ of a very great foreign service of the future already existed, in the form of an inner group of brilliantly able and courageous men who were the acknowledged leaders and the models of their colleagues. With the help of W. Scott McLeod, the road-company McCarthy whom he named as his own assistant, Dulles proceeded first to crush the hopeful germ that might have given us a better foreign service; and then to reduce the survivors to a sort of grey human mush. Even today, we find the episodes of this process, which publicly shamed the United States in every world-capital, too painful and too humiliating to recall in detail. So we offer only the following, our farewell to George Kennan, whom Dulles simply refused to employ any further.

We still consider the U. S. invitation to the Soviets to join the Marshall plan the most remarkable single stroke ot American diplomacy. It gained us an immense advantage all over Europe. Yet if Kennan's forecast of the Soviet response had proved wrong, the Marshall plan could never have passed the Congress—as both Kennan and Secretary Marshall well knew.

WASHINGTON

The best way to illustrate the real meaning of the retirement from government service of George S. Kennan is to go back to an incident which occurred in mid-summer, 1947. The Marshall plan, which was to save Europe, was in the final incubation stage. A last, crucial question remained to be answered. Should the Soviet Union be invited to join?

Asking the Soviets to join presented certain very great political advantages abroad. Yet, if the Soviets accepted, they could wreck the plan from within. Secretary of State George Marshall was puzzled and disturbed. Finally he called on his chief policy planner, George Kennan, for advice. Without hesitation, Kennan advised Marshall to ask the Russians to join. There was not, he said, the slightest chance that they would do so.

Marshall decided to accept the risk—and the Kremlin's violent refusal and savage disciplining of the Soviet satellites helped to solidify the West. This was one of this country's first major post-war diplomatic victories.

There are many such examples of the extraordinary prescience which Kennan has repeatedly displayed. Kennan also warned Marshall and others, for instance, that a strong Soviet reaction to the Marshall plan was inevitable—and he said that this reaction seemed to him very likely to take the form of a Soviet-engineered coup in Czechoslovakia. Precisely that happened.

After the Inchon victory in Korea, as these reporters can personally attest, Kennan was almost wholly alone in predicting flatly that either the Russians or the Chinese Communists would intervene openly if the United Nations' offensive were pressed close to the Sino-Soviet borders.

More recently, when Kennan was American Ambassador in Moscow last summer he reported in cables to the State Department the existence of a powerful inner group in the Soviet government, which favored a major change in tactics toward the West. He outlined in substance precisely the change in tactics which the new Soviet regime has now introduced.

This ability to sense beforehand the course the Kremlin is likely to adopt is not mere crystal-gazing. It derives from a lifetime of experience and study. Perhaps Kennan's most enduring contribution was his brilliant analysis of the nature of the Soviet state, contained in his now famous 8,000 word cable from Moscow in 1946.

This, remember, was still the time of the great illusion, when it was still fashionable (notably among those who now make a political living denouncing others for "softness toward Communism") to regard the Soviet Union as a sort of awkward and over-grown, but lovable and good-hearted, democracy.

In his long cable, which he sent as charge d'affaires of the American embassy in Moscow, Kennan warned that the Soviet government, "a conspiracy within a conspiracy," was "committed fanatically to the belief that there can be no permanent *modus vivendi* with the United States." He warned that this Soviet government wished to see "our traditional way of life destroyed," and that it would seize any "opportunity of extending Soviet power."

This cable, which is summarized in the Forrestal Diaries, is one of the great state papers of our time. By the same token, it is a measure of the loss to the American government in Kennan's retirement.

In the State Department's announcement, it was implied that Kennan retired by his own wish. This is true as far as it goes, for Kennan, a quiet and contemplative man, is perfectly content to return to his studies and his writing. But it is only part of the truth. The whole truth is that Kennan would certainly have accepted a responsible post if one had been offered him—but none was offered.

This is no doubt understandable. Through no wish of his own, Kennan became a political symbol during the recent campaign. Much semantic nonsense was then spoken and written about the "policy of containment," with which Kennan's name was identified, versus the "policy of liberation."

If Kennan had been nominated for an important post, the Congressional know-nothings would doubtless have attacked him as an "Acheson stooge"—despite the fact that Kennan resigned as chief State Department policy planner largely because he disagreed with certain basic Acheson policies.

With the bitter battle over Charles E. Bohlen fresh in their minds, it is no doubt natural that the Administration leaders had no wish to repeat the experience. Yet the unequaled knowledge of the Soviet state and the intuitive brilliance of George Kennan are assets which the American government cannot replace at any price.

And it will be a sad day when the expert non-political government servant must give his loyalty, not to the government which he serves, but to the political party he thinks most likely to win the next election.
—April 12, 1953 (JA & SA).

Outwardly, what some people called "progressive conservatism" was the dominant theme of the early Eisenhower period. Within the administration, however, a vastly more portentous theme, terrible in its character and terrible in its consequences, was debated continuously for the first nine months. This debate, which received very little public attention except in our column, concerned the series of reports on defense problems and the new defense directives left behind by the Truman administration. The story is told at length in our chapter on defense reporting.

It is enough to say here that the Truman administration had belatedly waked up to the ugly fact that Soviet weapons technology and Soviet military-industrial mobilization were beginning to threaten the famous "American lead" that we used to boast about. The most important single news story we ever published was a by-product of this awakening—a summary of the so-called "Lincoln Report" showing that the United States, for the first time in our history, was becoming nakedly vulnerable to devastating foreign attack because of the growth of Soviet air-atomic power. But this is not news any longer, and it is only worth recording the following paragraphs—the first of the sort, so far as we know, ever published in the U. S.—from the series on the Lincoln Report:

"(There) are some further unpleasant facts. A long-range guided missile with atomic warhead, probably a two-stage version of the German V-2, is now known to be eventually possible. In their search for such a missile, the Russians are using many of the best German missile experts captured at Peenemunde. Most of the best American judges think that the Soviet investment in a long-range guided missile program is very heavy indeed. Our investment is relatively light, for the long-range missile project is only one among twenty-seven projects in a Pentagon missile program with an appropriation of about one billion dollars.

"Furthermore, we are not merely running the risk of falling behind Soviet development of these dreadful weapons, which in themselves may decide the world power struggle. We are not even making the effort to find out all we can about Soviet progress."

Later on, it is worth noting, the American missile-tracking radar system which showed us Soviet progress was established (in the teeth of most bitter opposition from Donald Quarles, the present Under

Secretary of Defense and the chosen idea-man, unfortunately, of Defense Secretary Neil McElroy). But in the winter of 1953, one could not foresee Quarles and the others of his kidney. At this period the Eisenhower administration's final response to the documents Truman left behind him was still in doubt. The following records the "great debate," as we called it, which then went on in the U. S. government's most secret inner circle.

WASHINGTON

In the 1930s, a wrong order of priorities destroyed Britain as a great power and all but destroyed Britain as a nation. The British leaders of the period—men of the highest attainments and best possible intentions—genuinely believed their own catch phrase, which excused their long neglect of Britain's defenses:

"We must remember that Britain's first line of defense is Britain's economic strength."

Unfortunately, the event proved that a balanced budget would not stop a Panzer division or a Heinkel bomber, as it cannot be counted on today to stop a Soviet TU-4. It is at least highly significant, therefore, that the same order of priorities seems likely to be officially established by the Eisenhower administration.

The debate has been going on for three months. In the somewhat airless chamber of the National Security Council, the President and the key members of his Cabinet have been wrestling continuously and prayerfully with the same problem of priorities on which Britain foundered. The tentative result—and it must be emphasized that it is only tentative—is a decision that "economic destruction" is just as much to be feared as national destruction in the more literal sense of the phrase.

This debate has been the real, unseen drama of the Eisenhower administration to date. The issues in dispute were first raised in September, 1949, by the explosion of the Soviet atomic bomb.

To begin the policy story at its very beginning, the Soviet atomic explosion resulted in March, 1950, in a National Security Council policy paper known as NSC-68. Previously we had relied on our atomic monopoly as our sole defense. NSC-68 for the first time established the principle that Soviet military power must be in a measure matched by American military power.

President Truman and Secretary of Defense Johnson signed NSC-68 in March, but continued their contrary policy of American disarmament until June, 1950, when the Korean aggression taught them the error of their ways. The Korean war brought NSC-68 into force with a vengeance.

As early as 1951, however, a re-examination of NSC-68 was launched in the inner circle, largely on the motion of Secretary of Defense Lovett. This further study by the National Security Council revealed much that was deeply disquieting.

Despite the heaviness of our own defense burden, the Soviet military-industrial effort was still on a greater scale than ours. Meanwhile, the growing Soviet atomic stock and strategic air force were beginning to constitute a very serious threat to this country. Over-all, America, once invulnerable, was becoming very vulnerable indeed. Such were the findings.

These findings led to a revision of NSC-68 known as NSC-141, calling for considerable intensification of the American defense effort in certain important spheres—especially in the sphere of air defense. This was Truman's legacy to Eisenhower.

NSC-141 and its supporting documents, such as the report on Project Lincoln's investigation of the air defense problem, were waiting for the president when he took office, like so many skeletons in the White House closet. The question was—and is—what to do about these skeletons, which in effect gnashed their ugly jaws and demanded a reversal of the President's campaign promises about the budget and fiscal policy.

The argument about this issue first broke out on the cruiser Helena, with Secretary of the Treasury Humphrey pleading for conservative fiscal policies, and Secretary of State Dulles arguing for a national effort adequate to safeguard the American future. This has been the main division ever since. Secretary Dulles has been supported by Mutual Security Administrator Harold Stassen and Under Secretary of State Bedell Smith.

According to credible reports, Vice-President Nixon, who is playing a remarkably useful part behind the scenes, also took this side. And the President himself was also much impressed at first by NSC-141, and insisted that every Cabinet member give the closest study to this paper, its facts and its conclusions.

In the last analysis, however, any Cabinet member usually wins an argument mainly concerning his own department. In this instance Secretary of Defense Wilson, the chief party at interest, strongly sided with Secretary Humphrey. Hence the new doctrine, which is reported to be in process of official formulation by the Security Council, that we must fear "economic destruction" just as much as air-atomic devastation.

The biggest problems raised by NSC-141, such as the air defense problem, were not seriously tackled in the Truman defense budget, huge as this Truman budget was. Hence the President's cuts of the Truman budget do not absolutely preclude these problems being dealt with. Then too, the wisest men in the Administration pardonably argue that they cannot tackle gigantic new problems until they feel themselves in full control of the vast, unfamiliar government machine. Yet the indicated order of priorities is still wrong; for if worst comes to worst, who would not rather be a bankrupt American than an atom-bombed American or a defeated American?—May 5, 1953 (JA & SA).

The last Truman year had ended with the fearful roar of the American H-bomb test at Eniwetok. We were the first to publish the news of the new bomb's hideous power, and the first to announce the existence of the problem of H-bomb fall-out. These are now twice-told tales. In a later, analytical piece on the H-bomb, we further posed the following questions, which are worth re-printing because they are still unanswered by any in authority (although they are being answered by events).

"But we must also consider the future time, when the American hydrogen bomb will be matched by a Russian peoples' democratic hydrogen bomb.

"Which way will the balance tip then? Who then will be the gainer —the United States, which cannot launch a surprise attack, or the Soviet Union which can attack by surprise as soon as the rapidly growing Russian strategic air force is ready for the task?

"Or what will be needful, if we prefer to rely on what Winston S. Churchill has called 'the peace of mutual terror'? What must be done to make the terror truly mutual? If we wring out the budget now, shall we not later be wringing our hands? and can our kind of society exist in a condition of perpetual, life-and-death alert?"

All that winter and spring, what we had learned about the H-bomb continued to haunt us, and finally, when we heard a friend of ours in government glibly talking about "megadeaths," we published the following outburst, which we entitled: "They talk of megadeaths!" It is, alas, just as true today as it was in the spring of 1953; and if people have become hardened to living with the problem, it is a sign of their folly.

WASHINGTON

Who has heard of megadeaths? Can you define a megaton? And would you know a megabuck if you saw one?

In this strange aftermath of the Korean fighting, these questions are relevant, and for a curious reason. If a truce comes, it will wind up what we are likely to remember—if there is any memory—as the last serious war on something resembling a human scale.

The scale would indeed have surprised the great commanders of the past. On a quiet day on the Korean front, settling nothing, leading nowhere, the casual expenditure of ammunition must have been perhaps ten times the terrible fire of Napoleon's artillery in the inferno of Austerlitz.

Yet the scale of the Korean fighting was wholly human, for all that. The outfits, the commanders, even the soldiers in the ranks still somehow retained their individuality; still showed and made their individual marks against the bloody background of the war. For one who went from the inhuman, gigantic intricacies of world politics to the dusty, doubtful front in Korea, as one of these reporters did, the reality of the war was very nearly a relief, very nearly a refreshment.

One could cheer for those who won through, as men who had met a great challenge, and not as mere automata who had somehow escaped the blind brutality of destiny. And those who fell could also be remembered as men, as individual human beings, no different, despite the GI fatigues, the comic books and the bazookas, from all the men who have fallen bravely fighting for their countries in all the centuries of history.

In the peace, if peace comes, mere men, mere citizens, mere soldiers will hardly count, however. The Medal of Honor winner and the engineer from Pusan, the battle-worn GI and the mechanic who tended a jet on Taegu Airfield, will all be merged and lost and forgotten, along with all the rest of us, in the great mass of people who do not know about megatons and megabucks and megadeaths. History will return to the sole charge of the special sect of officials who know about these things.

It is perhaps time to answer the questions with which this report opened. What is a megaton? It is a measure of the explosive power of an atomic or thermonuclear weapon—a bomb of one megaton has the explosive power of a million tons of TNT. What is a megadeath? It is the death of a million human beings—as in the phrase, "a saturation attack resulting in eight megadeaths." And what is a megabuck? It is a million dollars—as in the sentence, "It will cost so and so many thousand megabucks to deliver (or to prevent) an attack of X-megaton power, which may be expected to result in Y-megadeaths."

The simple fact that such words as these have become part of the arcane jargon of the few hundred men who know speaks volumes about our time and our condition.

One should not be surprised, no doubt. This inhuman inflation of the historical process began long before the atomic bomb. Europe and America rocked with indignation in the early '90s when the first George F. Kennan reported on the plight of the Russian political exiles in Siberia. There were less than 400 of them in those days.

But almost twenty years ago, the second George Kennan, great-nephew of the first, could report from Moscow that the political exiles now numbered in the millions. The second Kennan might, if he had chosen, have estimated in his dispatches that there were now at least ten megaslaves under the orders of the Soviet political police. And when individual men and women are utterly lost in the faceless, lifeless mass of the megaslave, it is hard to feel the indignation that was aroused by the first Kennan's stories of Blok, Kropotkin and Vera Figner.

And it is not only this loss of the power to feel that is a danger to us. There is also the loss of the power to understand, which threatens the very foundations of the free societies. As Robert Oppenheimer remarked in his article recently summarized in this space, "I do not think a country like ours can survive for very long if we are afraid of the people."

That remark was, in some sense, a fragment of a private conversation between Oppenheimer and the rest of the tiny sect of those who know. He was, in effect, pleading with his fellow-initiates to pass on their knowledge—to tell the people the story that has grown stale and unreal in the air-cooled government offices remote from busy reality. He wanted the loss of power to understand that menaces our society to be overcome by disclosure and by knowledge.

But that is too much to hope for. The rest of us will go on not knowing. The sect of those who know will carry on their private conversations about our destiny. In the poem which will look well on the grave-markers of these men who know, W. H. Auden astutely said:

"The last word on how we may live or die
"Rests today with quiet
"Men, working too hard in rooms that are too big,
"Reducing to figures
"What is the matter, what is to be done.

"A neat little luncheon
"Of sandwiches brought to each on a tray,
"Nourishment they are able
"To take with one hand without looking up—
"From problems no smiling
"Can dismiss."

For such as these, a megadeath has lost all human meaning, being reduced to a mere statistic in papers so top secret that they are carried from office to office in locked brief-cases by men of the rank of major or over, who are worried by their receding hair-lines and the doubts about their promotions caused by their dull assignment.—June 22, 1953 (JA & SA).

In judging the wholly inexperienced Eisenhower's performance in the White House, it is unwise to forget that he had difficulties with his own party that might have daunted a seasoned political professional. Noah Mason, the proud reactionary, was a rather extreme case, but there were a lot of other men like him in Congress in those days; and as long as Senator Taft survived to lead them, they could cause infinite trouble for the President.

WASHINGTON

President Eisenhower's problem with his own party is agreeably symbolized by Noah Mason, one of the unreconstructed members of the House Ways and Means Committee who are fighting the Administration on the extension of the excess profits tax.

This small, brisk, genial, silver-thatched old man thinks that Eisenhower is a great President. In the chatty weekly letter that he writes to his Illinois Congressional District, Mason has sternly berated the American business community for "just giving the President passive support." But ask Mason where he has stood on the main items of that rather small Eisenhower legislative program, and you get some odd answers:

How did he vote on the Foreign Aid bill?

"I've been against all these give-away programs from the start, and I was against that one."

How about the renewal of the President's government reorganizing powers?

"I was against that too."

And the Pakistan wheat bill?

"Another give-away. I opposed it."

And the one-year extension of the Reciprocal Trade Act?

"I'm proud to say I've voted against every extension of reciprocal trade since I came to the House nearly seventeen years ago."

How about statehood for Hawaii? Surely he was for that?

"Nosirree. I was dead against that, too."

But had there been any bill the President wanted, which the House had so much as bothered to argue about, that he had voted for?

"Just can't think of any right now."

In other words, Noah Mason is a lifelong Republican from a rock-ribbed Republican district, who has an unblemished record of continuous opposition to the first Republican national Administration in two decades. There are a good many others like him in the House, from the Mid-West and the country districts of the East. He is a phenomenon of some significance, worth having a look at.

In a kind of way, to begin with, Noah Mason is the American dream come true. His family—he was the twelfth of thirteen children— emigrated from Wales when he was a child; and his father went to work in one of the now-played-out Illinois minefields. He did not have a soft childhood in the little coal town, and he went to work himself, on a farm his father had moved to, at the age of fourteen. But his proud, ambitious Bible-reading mother, who lived to be ninety-seven, wanted her children to be something better than miners and farmhands.

She drove Noah to get himself an education that was perhaps a bit haphazard, but good enough in those days for a school teacher.

Before very long young Noah was Superintendent of Schools in Oglesby, Ill.; then Town Commissioner; then State Senator; and finally, member of the House of Representatives from the 15th District.

"If I'd stayed in the old country," he says with a note of pride, "I suppose I'd have been a mason, which was my father's real trade, or I'd have gone into the mines." All the same, Noah Mason is not in favor of the American dream coming true any more—he strongly supports Sen. McCarran's brand of immigration legislation. "We've got to keep America American," he explains.

In the House of Representatives, taxation has become his specialty, and he has considerable say about it as a member of the Ways and Means Committee. He wants, as he frequently remarks, to "relieve the overtaxed by taxing the untaxed." By this he means reducing income and corporate taxes, while levying a manufacturers' sales tax, taxing co-operatives, and depriving the churches, charitable foundations and universities of most of their existing exemptions.

More generally, Noah Mason would like to repeal every item of social and economic legislation of the last twenty years. (Another favorite plan is to balance the budget by selling all government power projects on the open market.) He is 100 per cent protectionist, 100 per cent isolationist. His twin heroes are Sen. McCarthy and Gen. McArthur. And he thinks that "the Communist threat from within is much worse than the threat from without."

"When I was sixteen, seventeen, eighteen," he says, with a characteristic twinkle, "I was almost a liberal. I took a nibble of everything new. But now, some people might almost call me a reactionary."

Withal, Noah Mason is not at all like the bitter old men and cheap young demagogues who form the majority of his Republican faction. He is kindly, friendly, unassuming and altogether sincere in his peculiar beliefs. None the less, the question remains—and it is a pressing question—whose party is it, Noah Mason's or Dwight D. Eisenhower's?—June 29, 1953 (JA & SA).

"Kremlinology," as this strange art is called by its practitioners, is an extremely chancy art for reporters to attempt. But some memento is required of the death of Josef Stalin, since this was the biggest piece of luck the new administration enjoyed. It caused Stalin's heirs to "stop bucking the line and start throwing forward passes"—the phrase, which was George Kennan's, is from a column we wrote just after Stalin died, in which we also noted Kennan's prediction that Stalin would some day be attacked by his own heirs as "an arch-traitor to the revolution."

The end of line-bucking in turn permitted the false peace in Korea. The administration leaders had looked at the price of actually winning the Korean war. They had at first been tempted by a new policy that was called "disengagement." It meant building up the South Korean army, to permit the phased withdrawal of the American units in Korea. It would surely have ended in disaster, if the war had gone on.

In the end, when the risks of "disengagement" were acknowledged, noises began to be made, particularly by Secretary Dulles, that sounded as though we were going in to win in Korea. Contrary to most observers, we are both convinced that this was a politically feasible thing to do. We are sure, in fact, that the American people would have responded strongly, if the President had told them: "I promised I would end the war in Korea, and there is only one way America has ever ended a war—in victory; so I am now ordering national mobilization." But we were then divided, and we are still divided on the other vital question; as to whether this was the right thing to do. Going all-out for victory in Korea would surely have involved a risk of general war, not only with China, but with the Soviet Union as well. It would also have caused sharp inter-allied contentions, and it might even have disrupted the Western alliance. Indeed, the objections to this course were many and grave. The older partner believed that even if an all-out showdown was necessary for victory, it was better to have a showdown at once, when the United States still enjoyed a considerable preponderance in air-atomic striking power. He further believed that a compromise in Korea would have many evil consequences, and would probably lead to the necessity of a showdown later on, under vastly less favorable circumstances. The younger partner agreed on both points. He further believed, however, that the United States and the other Western Allies were too utterly unprepared for the risks involved in a showdown policy—to name just one, a world war in which Western Europe would be over-run. On balance, he preferred the other alternative—a compromise settlement in Korea, if that could be honorably obtained.

At any rate, when the Korean truce was signed and sealed, we both believed, and we still believe, that the administration was highly disingenuous in presenting this compromise to the American people as a glittering political-strategic triumph. Neither of us is sure to this day whether the noises about winning in Korea that Foster Dulles made that winter represented a serious intention or were mere bluff.

They never went further than a flat warning, given Jawaharlal Nehru by Secretary Dulles, that we would seek a full Korean victory if we could not get an early peace. This was of course passed on to Peking by Nehru's ambassador there, K. M. Panikkar.

Long before this, while Stalin still lived, the Chinese had already rather desperately tried to end the Korean war behind Stalin's back. In December, 1952, Peking had in fact made an independent try, through the Indians, to settle the outstanding issue of prisoners of war. Stalin had then stamped upon them, with great brutality. With Stalin dead, however, the Chinese had a stronger voice in Moscow. Indeed, Chou En-lai spoke the words that promised eventual false peace in Korea as he descended from the airplane that carried him home from the dead tyrant's grandiose funeral. For reasons that will be indicated later, the Chinese very badly needed the truce we so eagerly granted them. But all this was not apparent to us, until one of us went out to the Far East to see the results of the truce there.

The following Kremlinological item is our chosen memento of Stalin's death for three reasons. It records the item of evidence that first suggested the theory, now accepted by almost all experts, that Stalin himself was really murdered. It hints at the first great throat-cutting among Stalin's heirs, the execution of Lavrenti Beria, which ensued in a matter of days. And it is a reminder of the brave and tragic East German uprising of 1953, which first showed up the total phoniness of the promised "Liberation" policy of John Foster Dulles.

WASHINGTON

A fortnight before the announcement of Stalin's illness, a curious announcement appeared in "Pravda." A certain Maj. Gen. Kosynkin was stated to have met with "an untimely death." Kosynkin had never been heard of before, but his death notice revealed that he had held a key post—commander of the Kremlin guard.

Even so, no one would have attached particular significance to the death of Kosynkin if it had not been for the subsequent death of Stalin. Then the most widespread suspicions were aroused by Stalin's death, the astounding explosion of the famous doctors' plot, and the subsequent reversals of so many Stalinist policies. It seemed very clear indeed that an important faction in the Kremlin not only had disagreed with the aging dictator, but also had feared they would soon be victims of another purge on a great scale.

From these facts, a deduction was drawn, which is now accepted as logical by a very large number—perhaps a majority—of the ablest students of the Soviet enigma. If this deduction is correct, Kosynkin died in the performance of his highest duty, to protect the person of Stalin. One can imagine the pattern of the episode—the gathering of the plotters; the overpowering of the Kremlin guard; the impotent fury of the suddenly naked old dictator.

Lavrenti Beria, chief of the secret police, and those who were allied with him, both had the means and were thought to have the motives to arrange such an episode. Then, within a few days after the death of Stalin, the old man's chosen heir, Premier Georgi Malenkov, began to lose ground.

Starting with the exposure of the doctors' plot, projects sponsored by Malenkov and personalities close to him were dramatically attacked or actually liquidated. The reorganization of the Communist Party Secretariat, the purges in the governments of Georgia, the Ukraine and Latvia, and certain shifts in the official party line, were all obvious blows to Malenkov's position.

Malenkov's name all but vanished from the Soviet press. While Malenkov's power seemed to decline, the policies and supporters of Lavrenti Beria appeared to carry all before them. As Beria had been suspected of doing away with Stalin, so the master of the secret police was now again suspected of having removed Malenkov from the scene. By last week, Malenkov was rumored to be dead.

At this juncture, what pass for the social columns of the Moscow press supplied a sharp corrective. An announcement appeared that the whole leadership of the Soviet state had honored last Saturday's evening performance of the opera, "Dekembristy," at the Bolshoi Theater. Malenkov's name headed the list, but the name of Beria alone was not included. And this absence of Beria from the theater party on Saturday has now started speculation on a new line, that Beria is in trouble rather than Malenkov.

This feverish summary is by no means intended to reflect upon those who seek to unriddle the Soviet enigma. On the contrary, it is altogether probable that Stalin was murdered. It is quite certain that the other Soviet leaders have been hard at work cutting Malenkov down to size. And it is even possible that the non-appearance of Beria at the Saturday opera has a significance not visible on the surface.

What this summary is intended to indicate, rather, is the extreme fluidity and doubtfulness of the present situation in Moscow. And now, in the midst of this doubtful situation in the Kremlin, a bombshell has exploded, in the form of the uprisings in East Germany, in Czechoslovakia and elsewhere in the satellite area.

Any such disaster invariably has the widest political repercussions in the Soviet system. The Soviet doctrine is that the system itself is never to blame—that individuals are always at fault. Under the best circumstances, therefore, scapegoats would now be driven out; human sacrifices would be offered, because of the set-back in Eastern Europe. But this set-back, the worst the Soviet policy has met with in a very long time, has now occurred in the midst of an envenomed struggle for power within the Kremlin.

Inevitably, therefore, the set-back and the struggle for power will get mixed up together, as it were. Some of those engaged in the struggle for power will be placed on the defensive; others will be strengthened, and the set-back itself will become an issue in the struggle.

Precisely this is now thought to be happening. What is much more important, the Kremlin is also thought to be taking a new look at the policies evolved since Stalin's death.

On the one hand, the Kremlin cannot carry on its peace offensive with any hope of success while engaging in a campaign of iron repression throughout Eastern Europe. On the other hand, Eastern Europe may be in danger if iron repression is not resorted to. The Pilsen steelworkers, the construction gangs of the Stalinallee, may well have upset the Kremlin's best-laid plans, and have given a new twist to history. Unwittingly, they may have created conditions in which the peace offensive will have to be abandoned.—July 3, 1953 (JA & SA).

That summer, the younger member of our partnership went to Europe. He had a lot to report, about the effects of Foster Dulles on the American foreign service, for instance. (Having observed the flatfeet operating in the Bonn embassy, a German friend asked him, in deep alarm, whether this was "the beginning of Nazism in America.") From Paris he also pointed out that France was beginning to have "no stomach for the Indo-Chinese war," although the Korean peace had transformed "the defense of Indo-China (into) the heart of American policy in Asia."

But mostly he tried to analyze the signs that had been left behind by the great East German rising of June, 1953, which foretold

Hungary, and Gomulka's return in Poland, and so much else besides. Until this rising in East Germany, the solidity of Eastern European Communism had been widely taken for granted. After careful study, he now reported that the Communist system would collapse in every satellite if the Red Army were withdrawn; but he added that no satellite resistance movement could ever succeed while the Red Army remained. The following commemorates the brave men who risked their lives to prove these points to the outside world. These two got away, but many died.

BERLIN

What has been happening in East Germany has transformed the whole world situation. The best way to understand what has been happening is to consider in some detail certain recent events in the small industrial city of Bitterfeld, in the Soviet Zone of Germany, as seen through the eyes of two brave men.

These men are Wilhelm Fiebelkorn, a school teacher who looks like a high-strung, unhealthy, very intelligent American Indian, and Horst Sovarda, a skilled electrical worker who looks like a genial, ham-fisted football tackle. Fiebelkorn and Sovarda arrived a few days ago in the safe haven of West Berlin, after being condemned to death by the East German Communist regime. For Sovarda, the worker, and Fiebelkorn, the intellectual, were the leaders of a revolt which actually seized and for a time exercised power in the city of Bitterfeld.

Sovarda tells the first part of the story. Toward the beginning of June, when the Communist regime was announcing all sorts of "easements for the population," the workers in the big Bitterfeld electro-magnetic combine learned that their "production norms" were to be increased. Already, Sovarda and other workers' leaders had organized an elaborate cell system in their plant, precisely patterned on the Communists' cell system in capitalist countries. The time had come, they decided, to risk everything. The order to strike was passed through the cells, and on the morning of June 10 the whole plant closed down.

Sovarda and the others, expecting arrest, cannily refused to meet the Communist functionaries who came to the factory. Then on June 11, the Communists capitulated completely and astonishingly. All the workers' demands were met, and the men went back to work.

For three days the workers quietly absorbed this evidence of the regime's weakness. On June 15 they struck again, with increased demands, and again the factory closed down. Again, the regime failed to react with the expected violence. Then, on the evening of June 16, RIAS, the American radio station in Berlin, carried word of the construction workers' strike in East Berlin, and the word spread rapidly throughout Bitterfeld.

Until then, the strike had been confined to the electro-magnetic plant. Now every factory in the Bitterfeld area struck, and on the morning of June 17 the workers filled the streets of the city. Here the German instinct for order asserted itself. A mass meeting of workers elected Fiebelkorn, favorably known as a "militant intellectual," as chairman of the "Bitterfeld District Strike Committee." In a methodical manner, the committee set about organizing the city.

The Communist mayor was quietly evicted from his office. The workers took over the headquarters of the Communist party, the secret police, and all public buildings. Eighty-six political prisoners were freed from the jail, while six criminals were firmly re-locked in their cells. The workers took over the telegraph office, where Fiebelkorn drafted and dispatched two remarkable telegrams.

The first was addressed derisively to the "so-called Democratic peoples' government in Berlin." It contained a list of eight curt demands, including free elections, the release of all political prisoners, the dissolution of the "so-called peoples' army," and the dissolution of the government itself.

The second was addressed to "the honorable Semyenov." This message to the Soviet proconsul was most polite: "We respectfully request that you will lift the siege in Berlin and proclaim your solidarity with the workers in the Eastern Zone. We hope that you, sir, will act in accordance with our wishes, so that we can believe that you are the champion of peace, international understanding, and democracy. With the greetings of the strike committee of Bitterfeld." Unlike the telegram to the government, this included space for a prepaid reply, as a further mark of respect.

The reply came, of course, in the form of Soviet troops and tanks. By early in the evening of June 17, all public buildings had been occupied, martial law had been declared and Fiebelkorn and Sovarda had been condemned to death as "criminal saboteurs." So ended Bitterfeld's great revolt.

But has it really ended?

Asked how such things could happen in a supposedly monolithic police state, Fiebelkorn shrugs his shoulders and replies that it is as though "a lighted match were thrown on a haystack." The haystack, he explains, is the universal hatred of the East German people for the puppet regime which has ground their lives into misery. The match is the weakness of the regime which the workers began to sense soon after Stalin's death, and which they sensed with certainty with the sudden adoption of the policy of "easement for the populace." The haystack and the match—hatred and contempt—are still present.

What happened in Bitterfeld happened in almost exactly the same way in more than seventy-five other German cities (though Fiebelkorn's telegrams were unique). As this is written, moreover, it looks as though the haystack were again beginning to smolder. Seventy thousand workers in East Berlin have proclaimed a sitdown strike, and the movement is beginning to spread to the Soviet Zone. "We know now that they can't kill all of us," Sovarda says.

It would be very wrong to imagine, as some officials in Washington like to do, that a few blasts on the propaganda trumpets will now bring the whole Soviet empire crumbling down. The Soviet tanks which crushed the Bitterfeld revolt are still very much present. It would be equally wrong to imagine, as other officials are able to do, that what has happened here is an interesting but not very important phenomenon. It might well be, instead, a great turning point in world affairs.—July 10, 1953 (SA).

The "great debate" about defense and budgetary policies came to a head inside the Eisenhower administration in the autumn of 1953, when the next year's budget—the first Eisenhower budget—was being prepared. An expert committee headed by Mervin J. Kelly of Bell Laboratories had meanwhile been commissioned to examine the Truman administration's reports showing the impending loss of the American lead. A whole series of other, lesser committees had checked the conclusions of the Kelly committee. All had said the same thing—that much greater efforts were needed to maintain our lead. So the President almost, but not quite, defied his Secretary of the Treasury, took the American people into his confidence, and did what should have been done. The rest of the story appears in our chapter on defense reporting. This records the moment of highest hope, soon, alas, to be disappointed:

After interminable wavering, the Eisenhower administration has at last decided to tell the country some of the truth about the national situation. The decision was taken before the Kremlin tested its first hydrogen bomb, but this event has further strengthened the hands of the advocates of "Operation Candor," as the project is called in the administration's inner circle.

The President will do the talking. The time, the place and the medium are now under discussion. The method most favored at the moment is an informal television talk, or perhaps a combination of a television talk with a full-dress radio speech.

Such is the final upshot of a debate that has been going on inside the American government since the final period of the Truman administration. Certain officials of the old psychological strategy board were the first to insist that it was dangerous to keep the country in ignorance of the threat to national survival implicit in the steadily growing Soviet air-atomic capabilities. They were also the first to argue that a frank White House briefing was the only way to get the truth across to the country.

Hence the problem was on the National Security Council table, so to speak, when President Eisenhower took office. Active discussion of "Operation Candor" began as early as mid-winter. In the spring, at least one major meeting of the National Security Council was devoted to the subject, and Drs. J. Robert Oppenheimer and Vannevar Bush were invited on this occasion to make the case for being candid.

None the less, the wavering continued into mid-summer. And even now there are certain leading members of the administration who hope that the Security Council decision—for such it is—may yet be reversed.

The argument most often used by the opponents of frankness is the highly specious one "that the country knows everything but the real military secrets already." It is true, of course, that the real national situation is well understood by a small number of persons who have struggled to find it out. It is also true that some of these persons have done their best to make the hard facts more widely understood.

But this is not only specious; it is also irrelevant. The country as a whole does not yet understand the country's situation, because the country's leaders have thus far persisted in concealing or misrepre-

senting the hard facts known to the experts. In difficult and unpleasant technical matters, the country does not listen to every chance
voice. The country's leaders must inform the country, and no one
else can do so.

The proof of this has just been given, in dramatic form, by the inquiring Dr. Gallup. The experts know very well that the Soviet Union
already possesses the atomic bombs for a crippling attack on this
country. They know also that the Soviet long-range air arm is entirely capable of delivering the bombs. They know further that unless
drastic measures are taken to improve our air defenses, the Kremlin
will be able to make a totally devastating air-atomic attack on the
United States within eighteen to twenty-four months.

But the country at large plainly does not know about all this. In
fact, when Dr. Gallup's pollsters asked their victims whether they
thought their cities could be destroyed by Soviet atomic bombs, less
than a third thought there was much risk. In short, three-quarters of
the people of the United States are living in a dream of false security.

Those who have wished this dangerous dream to be prolonged fall
into three categories. There are the neurotic advocates of "maximum
security," common in the Pentagon and now gaining ground at the
Atomic Energy Commission; there are the State Department officials
—George F. Kennan used to be one of them—who fear that the
American people will demand all kinds of dangerous and impulsive
remedies if they are told the plain truth; finally, there are the high
administration officials who think high taxes are more dangerous than
atomic bombs.

This last group is of particular importance. They think that if the
truth is told, a strong demand will immediately be felt for heavier
defense outlays on air defense and for other purposes. In this they are
undoubtedly correct.

Maybe the promised Presidential candor will not be so very candid
after all. But if he is fully candid, it can be taken as certain that the
current approach to defense problems will no longer be tolerated. And
it is hard to believe that the decision to be candid does not imply a
further decision to make a different approach to defense.—September
9, 1953 (JA & SA).

In the autumn of 1953, it was the turn of the senior member of our
partnership to undertake a rather longer foreign journey, to see the

effects of the Korean peace in the Far East. He saw many things that deeply stirred him—for instance, the evacuation of the last Chinese nationalist troops from their refuge in North Burma, where they had settled after their wholly abortive, now-forgotten, American-aided attempt to re-invade South China. He made a good many discoveries, too, such as the sleazy fakery of the administration's policy towards Formosa, which was proven by events in the year that followed.

For the long run, his most important discovery was simply the sheer power of Communist China. The Korean war had utterly transformed and modernized the huge Chinese Communist armed forces, increasing their real strength many times over. Stalin, one suspects, had never intended to undertake this immense modernization program for his Chinese partners; but he was forced into it when his own Korean gamble went wrong. He made the Peking leadership pay for their new strength at a very dear rate, however; and the whole Chinese regime was strained to its foundations when President Eisenhower obligingly granted the Korean peace. With the Korean strain removed, the new Chinese power was rapidly consolidated. Hence a wholly new Asian power-balance was created. We have not yet seen all, or half, or even one-quarter of the results of this new balance.

It was very evident then, however, that the first results would appear in Indo-China. It is tempting to reproduce some of the reports of this period on operations with the French army, partly because the experiences themselves were vivid, and partly because they help one to understand the role that the French professional army has now played in the change of government in France. But the following column is even more interesting, because it gives the practical reasons for the eventual outcome in Indo-China—reasons which the American government was then resolutely ignoring:

HANOI, INDOCHINA

This is a war in which you do not see very much of the enemy unless you stick around for a long time. It is easy enough to hear the enemy's bullets whistling round your ears. Unless you are careful, you are quite likely to step on one of the enemy's mines. If you are lucky, you may even catch sight of dark, remote human specks craftily maneuvering through distant rice paddies. But a young lieutenant who was in the big hand-to-hand fight at the end of the Mouette operation put the position very neatly.

"It was a real privilege," he remarked cheerily, "to see those fellows face to face."

Yet what has to be realized, none the less, is that this usually invisible enemy is generally somewhere in the immediate neighborhood. There may be a company of the Viet Minh hiding under water in the muddy canal by the road side and breathing through bamboo tubes. There may be a Viet Minh battalion concealed in the marvellously camouflaged holes that they dig by night, waiting a chance to rush your camp. Or the peasants humbly toiling in the fields may simply have laid away their guns under the pale golden shocks of rice straw.

This omnipresence of the enemy is the real heart of the problem in the Indo-Chinese war. Consider the fantastic disposition of forces here, and you will quickly see why.

In brief, the main prize both sides are fighting for is this rich and strange Tonkin Delta. The delta is a triangle about 100 miles long on each side. It is a huge lake in summer, remains a fertile marsh in the dry season and supports an incredible population of 8,000,000. The delta, which is formed of Chinese soil deposited over the ages by the Red River, also lies conveniently close to the frontier of China. If and when the Communists get a firm grip on the delta, it will be only a matter of time until the rest of Indo-China falls under the Viet Minh yoke.

At present the main body of Communist regular troops is outside the delta, in the surrounding wall of steep, jungle covered mountains and in the rich and important rice growing region of Than Hoa, just to the south. This main body of the Viet Minh strength comprises five infantry divisions and one artillery division. One of these divisions has been badly mauled and the enemy's current plan of attack has been distinctly unset by the offensive-defensive effort, Operation Mouette, which Gens. Navarre and Cogny have now successfully completed. None the less, the enemy's main body is expected to attack the delta pretty soon, probably from the north.

The delta is the main French base. The superb French army could await the enemy's attack on the delta with some confidence if it were not for one rather unfortunate fact. In several respects, the Tonkin Delta is also the main Viet Minh base. At least 80 per cent of a map of the delta shown to me by Gen. Cogny was painted bright red, meaning that the villages in these regions were under Viet Minh control.

This wildly eccentric situation has existed since 1951, when large bodies of Communist troops infiltrated the delta, destroyed the village militias, and set up a secret Communist administration considerably more efficient than the Viet Nam government administration that the French support. This Communist administration of the delta rests primarily on force and terrorism. By terror and force, it boldly levies heavy taxes of rice which feed the main Viet Minh army. It calls up the recruits that maintain the army's strength. And it otherwise bends the suffering peasants to its will.

The authority of this Viet Minh administration of the delta is in turn sustained by regular units of the Viet Minh army, regularly armed with light weapons, mortars and machine guns, which are stationed underground—often quite literally underground, in nests of hiding holes, within the delta provinces. The Viet Minh command has tidily divided the whole area into three sectors. Each sector has a regular sectoral regiment; plus one regular battalion for each of its several sub-provinces, which we should call counties; plus a regular company for each of its scores of districts, which are still smaller administrative units. In addition, there are the guerrillas, who are used by the Viet Minh command as reinforcements.

In sheer number, then, this Viet Minh force behind the French lines in the delta is very large. But its size is none the less not so important as its invisibility and flexibility. Villages that would like to get rid of this heavy incubus dare not collaborate with the Viet Nam government and the French army, because the regular provincial forces of the Viet Minh will visit a heavy punishment upon them. And while they terrorize the countryside into submissiveness, these Viet Minh forces also carry on a continuous guerrilla war against the Franco-Viet Nam forces.

I myself have seen the supply of a whole French regiment that was already seriously short being held up for more than a day by a Viet Minh frogman breaking a bridge. That same night, while the bridge was being broken, a couple of Viet Minh companies attacked the militia of a village that had not submitted to them. And if they had not been discovered in their holes by a fortunate accident during the previous day, a Viet Minh battalion would also have tried that night to rush the French post nearest to the bridge.

By night operations and in other ways, the French do their best to overcome their handicaps. Yet their heavily armed units, and indeed the regular units of the Viet Nam army too, are creatures of the towns and the strong points. The Viet Minh forces, although regularly organized and regularly armed, have the inestimable advantage of being creatures of the rice paddies and the villages.

It is remarkable, in these discouraging circumstances, that the outfits here retain such a superb spirit. Wherever there has been the combination of a good local governor and strong French and Viet Nam units to protect the local people, it has proved possible to clean the area up, step by small, difficult step, village by village. The able Gov. Tri, the overlord of Tonkin, has greatly improved conditions. But the forces to protect the villages from the Viet Minh are all too often insufficient.

The plain truth is that the French command just does not control enough armed power for the two urgent tasks—cleaning up the vital delta base and opposing those six enemy regular divisions that are always threatening the delta from without. For reasons which will be examined later, it is also rather questionable whether the growth of the Viet Nam government's army should be counted on to provide the needed extra power. At present, in any case, one of the two urgent tasks is always having to be sacrificed to the other.

Meanwhile, the Viet Minh strength is also growing. Only last month the Viet Minh artillery division received a complete new regiment, and the results of the Korean truce have not yet appeared.

In short, unless the American government wants to risk losing all of Asia by losing the war here, it is time to take a wholly new and very much bolder look at the situation in Indo-China. Such brilliant and implacable organization as Ho Chi Minh and his Gen. Giap have achieved is not to be beaten by the kind of half-hearted effort the free world is making here. Gen. Navarre's and Gen. Cogny's men have plenty of courage and resourcefulness; but courage and resourcefulness will not do the job forever, when there are not nearly enough men and those men do not have nearly enough backing.—November 16, 1953 (JA).

After Indo-China, the Asian journey continued through Thailand and Malaya, Indonesia and Burma. Everywhere, in varying degrees, one saw the same phenomenon—the pressure of the Chinese mass to the north upon the more or less fragile Southeast Asian political structures. Semi-final results can now be observed in Indonesia.

Malaya was the scene of the ghastly jungle patrol described elsewhere in this book. After the patrol came a long day with General Sir Gerald Templer, the brilliant officer who then commanded in Malaya. Templer voiced the opinion, and the reporter agreed, that his long, hard struggle against the Communists in the jungle was within about eighteen months of final success. Templer added, however, and again the reporter agreed, that all the gains already made would instantly be lost, and rich Malaya would finally be doomed to domination by the Communists, if the French in Indo-China either gave up or suffered defeat.

Paris was the last stop on the way home from the long Asian journey; and there Foreign Minister Georges Bidault squarely confirmed the reporter's suspicion that the French would not carry on much longer in Indo-China without direct and full American military support.

Three largely forgotten factors influenced one's judgment of the results of a Communist victory or a negotiated settlement in Indo-China. First, it was the official doctrine of the American government, publicly enunciated by John Foster Dulles himself, that a Communist victory at this highly sensitive point would be rapidly and unavoidably followed by other Communist victories in every other country of Southeast Asia. Second, this was a high point of the post-Korean period of Chinese Communist aggressiveness—a period that did not end, indeed, until the next year, when the Kremlin switched its policy-hose, so to say, to wash out the Western positions in the Middle East. Third, it did not then seem possible, for excellent reasons that will appear later, that any negotiated settlement could endure for very long in Indo-China. Such a settlement seemed likely to produce just the same result, in fact, that was produced by the first cessions of Czechoslovak territory to Adolf Hitler.

For these reasons, the time factor of the forecasts in the last paragraphs of the following column has been proven to be quite wrong. But we greatly fear that in the future—perhaps the not too far distant future—the forecasts themselves will turn out to be correct, for precisely the reasons here given. What is more interesting is the fact that the long, lamentably accurate analysis of the Indo-Chinese problem itself, made by a single newspaperman on the basis of his own on-the-spot observations, was then angrily and scornfully rejected by the entire American government. The complacency and will to self-delusion in Washington were then such that we found ourselves, in this matter, a minority of two. The column was written at Avon because there was a reunion at the family farm for the returning traveller.

AVON, CONNECTICUT

Judging by the optimistic sounds that fill the American air, this is going to be a minority report. The country is being told by all and sundry—most recently by the President himself—that "we have recaptured the initiative" in the world struggle against Communist imperialism. Speaking very mildly, the traveller abroad finds mighty little evidence for this hopeful view.

Certainly there is nothing to suggest that we have recaptured the initiative in Asia. In Asia, where this reporter has just made a journey of nearly four months, all the signs suggest the exact contrary. And this is vitally important, since the Kremlin's obvious current strategy is to talk sweet in the West, while continuing to press the attack on the free world's vulnerable flank in the Far East.

The blunt truth is that the situation in Asia has been deteriorating ever since the Korean truce, which was signed in such haste, just when the strain in Korea had brought the Chinese Communists close to the breaking point. This deterioration shows in two quite different ways.

First, the center of strategic interest has been abruptly transferred from Korea to Indo-China, and at the same time the problem in Indo-China has grown far more difficult.

On the spot, to be sure, real gains have been made by the new French military team of Gen. Navarre and Gen. Cogny. So long as these fine leaders stand at the head of a superb French professional army of 185,000 men, there is no immediate possibility of Communist victory in Indo-China. But there is no possibility either of a French victory in Indo-China, either now or in the foreseeable future. Herein lies the first danger.

After seven years of it, the French were already growing tired of the Indo-Chinese war when we made our truce in Korea. The American example set Paris on fire. Since then, the impulse has been steadily growing, both among the French political leaders and French people, to wind up the Indo-Chinese war at all cost. Ho Chi Minh, Radio Peking and Radio Moscow are all encouraging this French impulse by cooing about a "negotiated settlement."

Any imaginable "negotiated settlement" will mean a Communist take-over the day the French expeditionary force is withdrawn from

Indo-China, if not long before. Yet recent trifling and strictly local Communist successes in the Laos country filled Paris and the French government with a positive fever to start negotiations without further delay. Any future French reverses—and these, alas, must probably be expected—will cause the fever in Paris to mount still higher. It may well become irresistible during this winter or next spring.

There is only one kind of inoculation against this danger in Paris that the French, as they always say, "will do what you Americans have done already." This is to give the French real hope of victory. Unfortunately the crying need in Indo-China today is not for more equipment, but for more bodies in the fighting line. More generous American material aid will help, but it will not help enough. Unless we are remarkably lucky, there will come the bleak question, whether the American government will also help with troops.

To make matters worse, Gen. Vo Nguyen Giap, the military chieftain of the Indo-Chinese Communists, has just the opposite problem from Gen. Navarre. Giap has plenty of men, but not nearly enough supplies. With the strain of the Korean War at an end, the Peking government should easily be able to increase the supplies for the Viet Minh from the present level of about 1,000 tons monthly to at least 4,000 tons monthly.

When and if this happens, the strength of the Viet Minh will increase greatly. Thereafter the French are likely to suffer no mere local reverses, but really serious defeats. Furthermore, there is not the slightest safeguard against such an increase of strength for the Viet Minh in Secretary Dulles' repeated but somewhat meaningless warnings that we shall go to war if the Chinese Communists intervene directly in Indo-China after the manner of Korea.

Such is the situation at the weakest point in the dam that holds back the Communist flood in Asia. Meanwhile, the second and perhaps more important effect of the Korean truce has been to allow the water pressure behind the dam to begin to increase very rapidly. In other words, the powerful military build-up of the Chinese Communist armed forces, which was already going on during the Korean fighting, is now becoming a serious matter for all of Asia.

Hitherto, the flower of the Chinese armies have been pinned down in Korea, and the whole military investment has been concentrated there. But the Korean truce, plus the new Russo-Chinese military-economic aid agreement, have changed all that. Within a couple of years, instead of fifty-eight modern Chinese divisions in Korea, Peking may have as many as 170 modern divisions to deploy where they will do the most harm. The effect on Communist China's weak and divided neighbors to the south is not hard to foresee.

Indo-China has already taken on the role of an Asian Czecho-slovakia—the position that cannot be let go without disastrous con-sequences. If Indo-China is allowed to fall, while the Chinese power build-up continues without interruption, we shall almost certainly have to make the kind of choice in Asia which Neville Chamberlain's follies finally forced upon him in Europe. And even if this quite probable worst does not happen in the end, just where does the present picture in Asia show proof of a recaptured initiative?—January 13, 1954 (JA).

Senator Joseph R. McCarthy was still continuously increasing his political power, by the rather simple system of continuously forcing the administration into new appeasements and humiliations. The White House was angrily complaining that the press was "building up McCarthy"—which was nonsense, for the simple reason that any man is news who can regularly blackmail the President of the United States. Meanwhile, it also seemed to be the policy to make McCarthy-ism respectable by proving that the American government could be quite as unscrupulous as the celebrated Senator from Wisconsin. This was the first exposé of the sleazy "numbers racket," uncovered by the younger member of our partnership. It was published, remember, at the time when the Bricker amendment to forbid the United States from having any foreign policy very nearly passed the Senate. Such was the contemporary atmosphere, in which the following exposé aroused no public indignation at all.

WASHINGTON

Since he returned from France to seek the Presidency, Dwight D. Eisenhower has been sold a good many lemons in the name of "smart politics." But about the worst lemon he has been sold yet is the strategy, worked out by certain of the Administration's amateur Mach-iavellis, for dealing with the "Communist issue."

As an example of this strategy in action, take the Administration's repeated boasts about the 1,456—now 2,200—people who have been fired from the government as "security risks." The privately admitted purpose of these "security firings" has been to "grab the Commie issue away from Joe McCarthy."

The idea has been to undercut McCarthy by broadcasting the notion that the new Administration found the government crawling with subversives, promptly fired the lot and thus left McCarthy with nothing further to do but twiddle his thumbs. The story of the State Department's security firings demonstrates how this was to be accomplished.

A grand total of 306 State Department security firings has been announced. According to reliable reports, this impressive—even frightening—total was arrived at in the following manner. In the first place, the word was passed down through Scott McLeod's Security and Personnel Offices that what was wanted was the largest possible total of such firings.

Two techniques—both palpably dishonest—were therefore used to swell the total. The files of those State Department employees who were in the process of resigning—always a considerable number, since there is a constant turnover—were carefully scrutinized. In the raw files of any government worker who is not a zombie, there is pretty sure to be some morsel of gossip which can be labeled "derogatory information." Wherever the raw files provided the slightest excuse for so doing, the names of those who were resigning anyway were added —without their knowledge—to the grand total of State Department security firings. About half the State Department total was arrived at in this way. If the same proportion holds throughout the government, there must be more than a thousand government workers who have resigned with a clear conscience and what they thought to be a clear record, and who were nevertheless listed officially as having been fired as security risks.

The second technique was just as dishonest. Large numbers of people were being transferred from the administrative control of the State Department to Harold Stassen's foreign aid outfit and to the newly independent Information Agency. Many of these people were transferred "with the warning flag up" and then listed as State Department security firings—although the great majority were cleared on further investigation, and never fired at all.

In the vast majority of these cases there was no question whatsoever of disloyalty or pro-communism. In about nineteen out of twenty cases, the reason, if any, for the firing was heavy drinking, temperamental unsuitability, or the like. Where there was some pro-Communist charge, it was often on the order of the charge against one female government worker, who was accused of "sympathetic association" with her husband. This woman appealed the charge, and on further investigation her husband turned out to be a rather mousy fellow, who had never taken an interest in politics.

In short, there was not a single case of actual subversion in all the State Department's security firings—and it is doubtful if there was one such case throughout the government. Yet to ninety-nine out of a hundred people, the news that there have been a large number of security firings means that this number of Communists and subversives have actually been uncovered in the government.

Under the circumstances, it is surprising that any self-respecting person will work for the government at all. What is even more surprising is that any one should have thought that this amateurish political fakery should not be exposed for what it is. Apparently it never occurred to the geniuses who thought up the scheme that some one might ask for a breakdown of the security firings. Thus when reporters asked Civil Service Commission Chairman Philip Young for such a breakdown he could only reply fatuously that he was "not interested" in such matters, and did not believe the "average person" was interested, either. The story of the State Department firings makes the reason for this awkward evasion perfectly obvious.

But what is downright incredible is that any one could have supposed that this sort of slick numbers game was an effective way to undercut McCarthy. McCarthy has already, or course, profited heavily from the whole business—much as he profited heavily from Attorney General Brownell's attack on ex-President Truman, which was also supposed to steal the show from McCarthy. McCarthy has used the Administration's fake figures to "prove" his own ancient discredited charges against the State Department.

According to report, the President himself, and chief Presidential aide Sherman Adams, are beginning to realize that they were sold a lemon, and are by no means pleased by the realization. If so, this may help the Administration's amateur Machiavellis to understand that they are no equals to Sen. McCarthy, when it comes to slick political flim-flammery.—January 20, 1954 (JA & SA).

Some months earlier, the Eisenhower administration had decisively taken what we fear may yet prove a truly catastrophic turning. For the last time, the President and his highest subordinates had squarely faced up to the harsh strategic realities of the H-bomb era; and then they had been appalled by the efforts and expenditures those realities demanded, so they had quickly looked the other way again. This was when "Operation Candor" was abandoned. The result was the so-called "New Look" at American defense policy, which was really a decision to have almost no defense except the nuclear deterrent, and then to neglect the nuclear deterrent so badly that the American lead in this most vital area would also be lost later on. There were still a few officials who felt the future aching in their bones; so we learned the story of this final turning point in all its details. Because this column mentioned an NSC paper (which we had of course not seen) it brought on a particularly nasty "security investigation" of the Alsop Bros. We knew it would, but we wanted to record the American government's official opinion of the national strategic situation, because this was the best commentary on the subsequent choice of the "New Look." The conclusion of the column, set forth in the last paragraph, turned out to be ludicrously over-optimistic. NSC-162 was in fact simply forgotten.

WASHINGTON

No decisions of the Eisenhower administration are more in need of understanding than the great strategic decision of the New Look at American defense. And the best approach to the many problems of the New Look is to see how it originated.

The time was Oct. 13, the place a meeting of the National Security Council. The chairman of the Joint Chiefs of Staff, Adm. Arthur Radford, had been invited to the meeting to present the results of what is usually regarded as the Joint Chiefs' new look, which was not the real New Look at all.

Three months earlier, on July 10, the President had instructed the new Joint Chiefs to re-examine the whole design of American defense in the expectation of a "long period of tension" and danger. The chiefs had done many weeks of hard work. Adm. Radford now gave the Security Council the results in the form of proposed forces levels for the Army, Navy and Air Force. Through Radford, the chiefs asked for bigger armed forces—somewhat bigger than we have now and substantially bigger than we shall have in 1955.

Big, immediate cuts in the defense budget were wanted by most of the men at the council table. When the controller of the Defense Department, W. J. McNeill, put an annual price tag of $43,000,000,000 on the forces levels Radford proposed, Budget Director Joseph Dodge and his allies were vocally horrified. Adm. Radford answered their protests with an historic little speech.

The civilians, Radford said, had never told the military what sort of war to get ready for—whether a conventional big war or an atomic big war, an old-fashioned small war or an atomic small war. After Korea, there was every reason to doubt that use of the new weapons would ever be permitted in any war, yet the new weapons were our real strength. Preparing for every imaginable kind of war was necessarily costly.

Tell us what kind of war to fight, Radford in effect summed up, and then the Joint Chiefs can have a real New Look and no doubt save you some money as well.

Not long after the Oct. 13 meeting, therefore, the National Security Council directed the Joint Chiefs to plan on using the new weapons wherever and whenever these would be effective. The Joint Chiefs then jettisoned the historic American defense concept of balanced forces. They substituted the new concept of a national defense entirely built around American air-atomic striking power.

This single change, from conventionally balanced forces to forces primarily designed to exploit the new weapons, is the strategic essence of America's New Look at defense. The change required larger investment in air power, allowed sharp cuts in the Army and Navy, with resulting over-all economy. Over the protests of the Army and Navy chiefs, Gen. Matthew Ridgway and Adm. R. B. Carney, the new concept was adopted, and the budget based on it was approved at a Security Council meeting on Dec. 15.

The decision to make this very far-reaching change of concept must also be judged against the background of the long evolution of the Eisenhower administration's defense thinking. This has been complex indeed. Back in January, 1953, the leaders of the new team had only two aims. The first was to end the Korean War at all costs. To achieve this aim, it can now be revealed, the President was getting ready, last March, to order national mobilization and an unlimited effort to win a final victory. Then came the Chinese truce offer (probably stimulated by word of the President's decision passed on by Pandit Nehru). That opened the way to the new team's second aim, which was to balance the budget at all costs.

Yet the Soviet air-atomic threat was rapidly growing. The budget-balancing drive immediately raised a very serious question: which was to have first priority, the nation's military security or the nation's fiscal stability? At first, men like Secretary of the Treasury Humphrey and Secretary of Defense Wilson tried to pretend the conflict did not exist, with unhappy results apparent in last year's defense budget. Then the big question was squarely tackled last spring in an informal debate of the highest Administration policy makers, called together by the President in the top-floor sun room of the White House.

This debate gave birth, by the President's order, to the elaborate National Security Council study known as "Operation Solarium." Solarium went on through the summer. The explosion of the Soviet hydrogen bomb in August clinched the decision. The Solarium findings were summed up in the Security Council policy paper known as NSC-162, which was approved on Oct. 7. NSC-162 defined the threat to the United States as "total" and gave first priority to the nation's military security.

The New Look really began a week later, at the council meeting of Oct. 13, when Adm. Radford made his little speech, but the prelude was the approval of NSC-162. Thus the budgetary spur may have caused the New Look—but only after the Administration leaders had unanimously agreed to give first priority to the national security. In short, the new approach to defense planning is not mere penny-pinching—it is a sincere attempt to adapt American defense concepts to the revolution in weapons development.—February 22, 1954 (JA & SA).

That winter everything seemed to be coming to a climax, all at once. The true climax of the McCarthy era in American political history was the row between Senator McCarthy and well-meaning, rather chuckle-headed Secretary of the Army Robert Stevens. It was the climax because it finally forced the White House to turn and fight McCarthy, albeit in a somewhat cornered-rat-like manner. McCarthy was not yet quite big enough to take on the President of the United States himself. Thus the Senate censure resolution of the next autumn, and McCarthy's subsequent descent into oblivion, were the inevitable sequels of the Army-McCarthy hearings.

We played a minor role in this climactic episode, in two different ways. In the first place, Stevens' unfortunate General Counsel, John S. Adams, was a friend of ours; and he gave us all the disgusting facts in his report to Stevens about the Nazi-like bullying of McCarthy's aide Roy Cohn, the outrageous attempts to get special treatment for Cohn's friend in uniform, David Schine, and the peculiar behavior of McCarthy about this matter. The report, now forgotten, was a flaming issue at the time. The Administration had denatured the published version. We printed what had been left out, thus inflaming the issue still further—which was just what we intended, because we wanted to close off the administration's avenues of retreat from a head-on fight.

Then too, in Germany in 1946, we had both observed that the President, as supreme commander in Europe, had tolerated or been victimized by many known Communists in our military government of Germany. By Eisenhower's own directives, indeed, about half of the West German press and radio was at first handed over to the Communist Party. When we now checked back to confirm the remembered details, we found McCarthy's spoor on the same trail. It was quite obvious that if McCarthy won his battle with the Army, he would then at last be big enough to take on the President. It was also obvious that he meant to do precisely this. By a McCarthy-style presentation of the German story, the President could be made to look much "softer towards Communism" than ninety-nine per cent of the wretched victims of his administration's numbers' racket, just as John Foster Dulles could be described as much "closer to Alger Hiss" than any of the unfortunate people whose careers he broke to appease McCarthy.

The older member of our partnership therefore requested his first and only appointment with Sherman Adams. The German facts were laid before Adams. It was somewhat grimly suggested that it would be better for the German story to be published in our column at once, than to let McCarthy make it a nine-months-wonder later on. Adams was then asked, point blank, whether the administration now meant to fight McCarthy all-out, in which case, it was added, there was no reason for us to publish the German story. After a long silence, Adams swore that the White House now meant to fight McCarthy without giving or asking quarter. After a further silence, he inquired: "Do you believe in God?" The reason for this peculiar question is not yet apparent to either of us, and the question itself seemed exceptionally impertinent. Hence the answer was: "I believe in the United States." And so this somewhat uncomfortable encounter ended.

The following column suggests how the White House balance wobbled, at the climactic moment, between another retreat and a firm line. The men who chiefly tipped the balance, incidentally, were Henry Cabot Lodge, Jr., General Lucius D. Clay and John J. McCloy. Among them, only Lodge had a post on the White House staff; and his office was later moved to the State Department, away from the President's immediate neighborhood, because he had stuck his neck out. The next column describes an exploit of our brother John's, of which we are still proud; and it also helps to convey something of the atmosphere that was dispelled by McCarthy's eventual defeat.

When the first column appeared, it should be noted, Cohn's attempt to bully the Army into giving special treatment to Schine had not yet become a special issue. The issue that touched off the Army-McCarthy row was McCarthy's shocking public bullying of General Zwicker, whom he blamed for the promotion of an army dentist called Peress. It seems strange, now, but the promotion to an Army majority of a pinko dentist really convulsed the whole country in those days.

WASHINGTON

As an awful object lesson, the real story of the McCarthy-Stevens imbroglio is worth recounting in all its peculiar detail. Here are the inside facts, which divide themselves naturally into scenes of a drama:

SCENE I: After being told he is unfit to wear a uniform by Sen. McCarthy, Gen. Ralph Zwicker calls his superior officer, Lieut. Gen. Withers Burress. "I don't have to take this stuff," says Zwicker in effect. "I quit." Gen. Burress tells Gen. Zwicker to keep his shirt on; then telephones the Army Chief of Staff, Gen. Matthew Ridgway, that Zwicker has threatened to resign his commission.

SCENE II: Gen. Ridgway calls a meeting of senior Army officers, who agree that McCarthy is endangering the morale of the Army. The generals then present their views to Secretary of the Army Stevens. Stevens immediately agrees that it is his duty to protect the men in uniform. He thereupon issues his celebrated defiance of Sen. McCarthy.

SCENE III: The White House, President Eisenhower's vacation headquarters at Palm Springs, the Office of the Secretary of Defense and the rest of official Washington, learn of Stevens' action from the press tickers, for he has consulted no one. Presidential Press Secretary James C. Hagerty announces that Eisenhower is "standing aloof." It is arranged that Stevens and McCarthy are to confront each other at a public hearing. These developments throw the two great Administration factions, the appeasers of McCarthy and those who would stand firm, into frenzies of activity.

SCENE IV: The appeasers, who include the President's Congressional liaison officer, Wilton B. Persons; the Attorney General's assistant for political intrigue, William Rogers, and one or two more, first seek to defer the date of the McCarthy-Stevens confrontation. This is accomplished Monday. Their next purpose is to bring Stevens together (in private) with McCarthy and Sens. Mundt and Dirksen. This is accomplished Tuesday afternoon, when Stevens agrees to lunch with the Senators on Wednesday. The Vice-President is informed of this.

SCENE V: The White House group that favors standing firm places the whole situation before the President on his return from Palm Springs. They do not tell him of the coming luncheon at the Capitol, because they do not know about it. They believe that all is in good train, and so does Eisenhower. He asks them to send a message to Stevens, assuring the Secretary of the Army of all-out Presidential backing.

SCENE VI: McCarthy and friends pass the word at the Capitol Wednesday that Stevens is coming to luncheon, for they want the maximum audience for the triumph they already anticipate. Meanwhile, poor Stevens, who has been pledged to secrecy, says nothing of his engagement to his associates at the Pentagon. He spends most of the morning discussing strategy for the public confrontation with McCarthy, now scheduled for the next day. He is bold and confident. He leaves, saying only that he has a luncheon date. Just after he departs—too late, too late—comes the message from the White House promising full Presidential backing.

SCENE VII: Over the luncheon table, three of the toughest customers on Capitol Hill hold poor Stevens' feet to the fire for two long hours. McCarthy thrice threatens to leave the room and split the Republican party wide open there and then. Battered and bewildered, Stevens at last approves the so-called "Memorandum of Understanding." This he oddly regards as a simple, neutral document, although it concedes every point McCarthy wants.

SCENE VIII: After the first grand announcement, McCarthy informs his favored journalistic supporters that Stevens could not have surrendered more completely, "if he had gone down on his knees." For more public consumption, he offers wanderers in the Capitol corridors Army commissions if they want them.

SCENE IX: Stevens returns to the Pentagon to announce that he has avoided an open fight, yet saved the principle he was fighting for. (Mundt and Dirksen had apparently promised the unfortunate man that McCarthy would be nice if he were given precisely what he wanted.) Gen. Ridgway thanks the Secretary with emotion. Then the text of the "Memorandum of Understanding" produces a sharp disillusion. Under Secretary of Defense Kyes and general counsel Struve Hensel tell Stevens the worst. He does not believe it until that evening, when McCarthy's boasts are repeated to him. Thereat he begins offering to resign.

SCENE X: In Washington the next morning, the atmosphere suggests Berlin after the Reichstag fire with Stevens in the role of Van der Lubbe, the dullwitted Dutchman who committed the arson; with Eisenhower as the aging Hindenburg and with Hitler played by you-know-who. Horror seizes the White House. The President, who had welcomed the showdown with McCarthy, and prepared to back Stevens all the way, is enraged to find himself placed in such a position —namely, be it noted, by the busy activities of the appeasers on his own staff.

SCENE XI: On the Hill, a desperate effort is made to persuade McCarthy to agree to a statement saving Stevens' face, which McCarthy of course resists. At the White House, meanwhile, a Stevens statement is drawn up and issued, saying what the President had meant to have said all the while. It undoes some of the harm, by making the President's position reasonably clear. But the worst of the damage is irreparable.—February 28, 1954 (JA & SA).

AVON, CONNECTICUT

It is better to say at the outset that this is going to be a rather personal report, since it concerns Avon, Conn., the small New England town where this reporter was born and brought up. The most stirring event in the history of Avon took place a few days ago in the auditorium of the Towpath School.

My father, who was Republican first selectman of Avon for thirty-five years, for a long time strongly opposed the building of the Towpath School. He said it would cost too much money. When it was pointed out that the old school was a firetrap, my father replied that it was a low building, and in case of fire the children would jump out the windows if they had any sense.

But in the end the new school was built (at vast expense to the tax-payers, as my father had predicted). Last Thursday night, 350 of the town's registered Republican voters met in the school's modern auditorium to vote on a resolution reaffirming support for Dwight D. Eisenhower, and sharply repudiating Joseph R. McCarthy.

As Avon's Republicans gathered in the auditorium, there was the traditional neighborly chat, sometimes disconcertingly frank, after the New England manner ("Why, Stewart, I just didn't recognize you—your face sure has fleshed up."). There was also a certain tension, unusual in an Avon Republican caucus. The fact is that when three Republican town committeemen, Phil Bauer, Bob August and my brother John Alsop drafted the anti-McCarthy resolution they didn't know what they were getting in for.

It would be too much to say that Avon became a center of national attention. But the nation at least caught a glimpse of Avon out of the corner of its eye, for the first time in Avon's long history—and Avon is not used to Klieg lights and television cameras. Moreover—incredible as it may seem in these days of careful political stage-managing—no one knew what might happen. My brother John thought it quite possible that the resolution would be beaten.

He led off with a masterful speech, clearly challenging—or so it seemed to me—Sir Winston Churchill's claim to supremacy in the field of oratory. His theme was the preamble to the resolution: "We deplore and vigorously denounce Sen. McCarthy's methods and, what is more, we sincerely question his motives and objectives. We are convinced that his activities are placing the Eisenhower program in jeopardy and damaging the reputation of the Republican party. We believe that Avon's Republicans are in agreement with us."

My brother was ably seconded by Bauer and August, and then it was the turn of the town's leading McCarthyite, Fiske Ventres. Fiske is a pleasant-mannered man with an owlish face. Like John, he once represented Avon in the State Assembly. He made a pretty good speech of its kind.

His theme was that "the Army brass has been awfully blind to the Communist menace" and that only McCarthy could prevent America "being sold down the river to the Russians." He spoke with passionate conviction, and the speech was going over rather well until Fiske made a fatal mistake. "Sen. McCarthy and President Eisenhower," he said, "are working hand in hand."

This remark was greeted with a roar of good-natured laughter, as sweet and sane a sound as this reporter has heard for a long, long time. That laugh was the turning point. When Fiske ended his speech, there was polite applause, some more desultory discussion, and then Avon's Republicans voted for the resolution, 350 to 1.

Does this vote mean anything? My brother John thinks that it means a lot. "A while back," he says, "McCarthy had a lot of support in Avon, and now, almost over night, this support seems to have crumbled away." Avon is a typical farming-manufacturing-commuting small town. Perhaps Herbert Brucker, wise editor of "The Hartford Courant," was right when he remarked to my brother: "It's another case of the people being way ahead of the politicians." At any rate, throughout the evening of the caucus, I kept thinking of my father, who had presided over so many Republican caucuses in his thirty-five years as Avon's first selectman. My father was a conservative if there ever was one. He abominated the New Deal and never could see any good reason for labor unions. But he also despised sham and cheap trickery, and he loved the old unspoken traditions of Avon, and of America—the traditions of free choice, and friendliness, and simple, open-hearted tolerance.

For these reasons, before he died last spring, my father had come to despise Joe McCarthy and everything he stood for, perhaps the more bitterly because McCarthy called himself a Republican. My father would have disliked the Klieg lights and the ruckus but, if he had been present in the auditorium of the Towpath School the other night, I think he would have been proud of Avon.—March 22, 1954 (SA).

On January 27, 1954, we published a piece entitled, "Where is Dienbienphu?" It was the first full account of the Dienbienphu operation to be printed anywhere, including the French press; and it concluded with the suggestion that the battle that was just starting at Dienbienphu might well turn out to be "the Yorktown" of Indo-China's revolutionary war. By April, this unhappy forecast was coming closer and closer to final substantiation.

It was a desperate period. The American government seriously considered a carrier-borne air strike with atomic bombs to relieve Dienbienphu from the pressure of the encircling Vietminh battalions. The National Security Council actually decided to send American troops to Indo-China—and this decision was even communicated to the nation in a speech made by Vice President Richard Nixon. If the British had been ready to support the activist group in the administration (headed by Secretary Dulles, Admiral Radford and the Vice President) we have no doubt that the already prepared draft resolution authorizing the President to send our forces to Indo-China would have been presented to the Congress. But the British government, after a gingerly promise to cooperate, rather suddenly and very firmly set its face against the plan the NSC had approved. The first Soviet H-bomb had been tested shortly after our first H-bomb; and it proved to be a somewhat more advanced design. As Sir Winston Churchill frankly and sadly confessed, the H-bomb in the Kremlin's hands was already beginning to influence British policy. "Remember, we *live* in these small islands," he would tell people in those days.

The British position in turn tilted the balance in Washington in favor of George Humphrey and the other budget-balancers, who opposed decisive action for their usual reasons. The Vice President did not give up without a struggle, but Secretary Dulles never fought really hard for the position he had taken; and one gathers the President was positively delighted to have a pretext to reverse the NSC decision above-noted. The sequels were the triumph in France of Pierre Mendes-France (not in itself at all a bad thing), and the pre-summit Geneva meetings which divided Indo-China in the Korean manner. We called this a "Munich" in Asia, and we still think it was, although the full effects we then anticipated have not yet appeared.

In those months, we printed a good many more fragments of this remarkable story (which is still incompletely told) than anyone else printed. The foregoing in fact summarizes a long series of columns. But we prefer the following piece about the French commander at Dienbienphu, as our reminder of this grim business. We called it "Remembering De Castries."

WASHINGTON

The early sun was already baking hot when Gen. René Cogny pushed aside the dusty tent flap, and entered the forward operational headquarters of Christian de Castries.

In those days last autumn, the heroic defender of Dienbienphu was already, as he used to point out somewhat sardonically, "the only colonel in the world commanding a division—at least it's something to be unique." Yet De Castries' headquarters would have horrified an

American divisional commander, and indeed displeased the colonel of any well found United States regiment.

A tent, a couple of desks, a map board, half a dozen officers—that was all there was to it, set down in the midst of the dusty disorder of truck park, tank park and ammunition dumps. There was something businesslike, all the same, in the way the slender De Castries moved to the map board, as soon as the greetings were over and Gen. Cogny asked for a situation report.

De Castries spoke quietly, almost nonchalantly, pointing out his dispositions with waves of his smart riding crop. The picture painted was reasonably hair-raising, for his nine battalions were strung out in line down a narrow valley, with the enemy in heavy force in the hills on either side. The last battalion, of Moroccan Rifles, was about to be committed in the drive on the final objective, the little town of Phu Nho Quan.

"They're ready for the jump-off?" asked the general.

"Yes," said De Castries amiably, "they should be jumping off now."

"But you will have no reserves," said Gen. Cogny.

"Well," replied De Castries, still amiably, "we've had to do without reserves before. It would be better to have some, but we can manage if we must."

That was how I met Dienbienphu's defender. An hour or so later, after Gen. Cogny had ordered a battalion of paratroopers flown to De Castries from his own slender central reserve, I joined the Moroccans in the attack on Phu Nho Quan. What happened there, except that Phu Nho Quan fell to us on schedule, is no longer at all important. What is still important is how his men and his fellow officers talked about Christian de Castries.

He was one—almost the last one in Indo-China—of Gen. de Lattre de Tassigny's famous "fighting colonels," those brilliant men of war whom the brilliant De Lattre used to restore the fallen morale of the French forces in Indo-China. He had nineteen battlefield citations. He had the largest collection of horse show prizes in Paris—for he is a celebrated jump-rider. He had a wonderfully beautiful wife; and when he was not in the field with his men he and Mme. de Castries defiantly lived in a large, highly vulnerable country house in a countryside crawling with Viet Minh guerrillas.

So went the stories about Christian de Castries, all of them, as I later found, quite true. A courage that would have been close to madness if it were not always cool; a nonchalance that might almost have been negligence if the man's eye did not casually take in every detail of importance; a sardonic humor that might have been unrelieved cynicism, if he had not believed very deeply in a few things, such as France—these were the more striking qualities of this man.

The picturesque, the dashing, the stylish leader is a rare animal in modern war—some people would say an out-of-date animal except in such a war as that in Indo-China. De Castries was all that, and he did not seem out of date. The last time I saw him was at a grand dinner at Gen. Cogny's, celebrating his victory in the Mouette operation, which I had joined for a while. He was enormously gay, enormously ribald, enormously witty, telling stories and drinking toasts and making those around him roar with such loud laughter that Mme. de Castries looked a bit quizzical at the other end of the big candlelighted table.

It is a long way, a horribly long way, from that happy dinner party to the inferno of Dienbienphu, where the outcome hangs in the balance as these words are written.

One can imagine De Castries cursing the intelligence, who had not counted on the post-Korean increase of supply for the Viet Minh, and did not believe the enemy would have heavy artillery. One can picture him making his night and morning rounds, as was his custom, snapping his riding crop easily against his boot in a thunder of enemy fire. One can see him, above all, encouraging his men to the most desperate resistance by the best of all methods, his own superb example.

It is good now, and it is only just, to remember Christian de Castries. For you may think as you please of the politicians in the Chamber of Deputies; but the free world owes to De Castries and the other French soldiers of his sort in Indo-China a debt that the free world is unlikely to repay. The debt should be acknowledged; that is the least that can be done.—April 5, 1954 (JA).

That was a horrible spring and summer, when the only solid consolation was Joe McCarthy's step-by-step decline from power. In late spring, we began dragging into the open the dread facts about H-bomb fall-out, which Admiral Strauss was trying, as usual, to conceal from the country. (We wanted to title one column about the biological hazards, "Whose Gonads Are They, Admiral?" but the

"New York Herald Tribune" would not let us.) By now, however, the fall-out facts are too well known, so we reproduce none of our columns on the subject. One of the unseen spring events was a decision in the Pentagon that intercontinental ballistic missiles were feasible after all. Previously, the Pentagon specifications for such missiles had required a degree of accuracy that really was not feasible at such enormous ranges—a hangover from the grave errors made in this field by the Truman administration. Now, the immense area of destruction of an H-bomb warhead forced a change in the specifications. In May we published a glum piece beginning with the sentence: "The development of the hydrogen bomb is now expected to lead on, by the peculiar logic of destructive science, to the early development of guided missiles of intercontinental range."

In July after collecting all the data we could, we followed up with a column describing what is now euphemistically called "the American missile-lag." Once again, the column's present interest lies in the curious fact that the government of course possessed vastly more data on the same subject, all of which pointed to our conclusion; and yet the "missile-lag" was tolerated. We omit the column's last paragraphs, concerned with the air defense lag.

WASHINGTON

In the year 1960, by the agreed estimate of the Pentagon's official analysts, the Soviet Union will fly its first intercontinental ballistic missile.

That sentence may sound innocent enough, but it is not. The intercontinental ballistic missile, or I.B.M. as the experts call it, will be an accurately guided rocket, comparable to a giant V-2, capable of carrying a hydrogen warhead over a range of 4,000 to 5,000 miles.

Such a weapon will marry the ultimate in destructiveness with the ultimate in striking power. There will be no defense against this ultimate weapon, nor any warning of its coming. And this is what the most highly qualified American experts now expect the Kremlin to possess within six short years.

It must be noted, furthermore, that our official experts have consistently underrated Russian weapons development. In every major case from the atomic bomb down to the new long-range jet bombers, the Soviet developers have always beaten the American official forecast by at least two years.

There are no reasons to suppose that our forecasters are not making the same mistake all over again. There are also many reasons why they may be wrong.

In the guided-missile art, great strides have recently been made toward solutions of the two most knotty problems, accurate guidance and atmospheric re-entry. The Soviets are in a good position to take advantage of this forward movement.

Since the end of the last war, they have been working all-out to get a long-range guided missile, with the most massive human and material resources going into the effort. In this particular field, moreover, the Russians began with a technology and even a manufacturing capacity superior to ours.

Here in America, by contrast, we have not been going all-out. Even today, the total budget of our ATLAS project is reported not to exceed $50,000,000, and this and other guided-missile projects are complexly entangled in Pentagon red tape. At present, the National Security Council is ponderously mulling over the question whether to make an all-out effort. But for the usual budgetary reasons, the N.S.C.'s answer is just as likely to be "no" as "yes."

In short, it seems entirely possible that the Kremlin will possess the ultimate weapon before we possess it.

Maybe it is foolish to be insistent about such unwelcome facts. Last week, Sen. Stuart Symington, of Missouri, made a brilliant speech on this subject. With all the authority of a man who knows the American defense picture from the inside, Symington warned of the danger described in the present report. His speech, though thoroughly factual as well as grimly ominous, received far less attention than the most recent didos of the McCarthy Committee.

Maybe people in this country are not interested in the facts of life and death, which the Administration so sedulously conceals from them. All the same, it is time—it is past time—to realize that America's traditional invulnerability is not going to last forever, or even for very long.

The era of the intercontinental ballistic missile will be the final stage of the journey into danger.—July 25, 1954 (JA & SA).

All in all, 1954 was an eventful—even a hideously eventful—year. It was the year of the Oppenheimer case, which we had known was coming since late November, 1953, but only wrote about it the day

James Reston of the "Times" also broke the story, and because we knew Reston was going to write about it too. To us, the verdict on Robert Oppenheimer seemed a national disgrace (and it still does), so we took time off from the column for what amounted to pamphleteering, first in "Harper's" and then in book-form.

In the autumn came the election, when the Democrats made important gains. The younger member of our partnership did most of the election reporting, and called the turn with pleasing accuracy. Finally, at the end of the year, the senior partner went off again to have another look at the still tense Asian situation.

The first stop was in Viet Nam. The division of the country into Northern and Southern halves was then going on, and the outlook certainly seemed as dark as possible. South Viet Nam was ruled then, and it is today, by the narrow, obstinate, brave and determined Ngo Dinh Diem. In those days, President Diem, who had originally been appointed by the French, could hardly be said to possess a government, much less an administration. There was dissidence in his army, which did not look very combative anyway, because Diem had just expelled the pro-French army commander, General Hinh. For this and other reasons, the important French element that still remained in South Viet Nam had turned against Diem with really astonishing venom and fury.

In addition, Diem had to solve the problem of the "sects." These were warlord-gangster groups with neo-religious overtones, which the French had used as counterweights to the Viet Minh while the Indo-Chinese war was still going on. As the sects controlled most of the city of Saigon and large areas of the countryside, Diem had to defeat and destroy them before he could possibly establish a Southern government capable of competing with the Northern government. The French were loudly certain that the sects could quite easily defeat any force poor Diem could put in the field. The fighting began when the senior member of our partnership was still in Saigon. He had just had an excellent dinner when the first firing was heard; and he took a pedicab down the Avenue Galliéni to see the opening battle between Diem's troops and the men of the gangster-sect that had got the Saigon concession from the French.

He subsequently made one of the very worst of our mistakes of judgment, writing that "one of the casualties" of this fight was "the American policy of supporting President Ngo Dinh Diem." He was at least in excellent company. The American ambassador on the scene, the able General J. Lawton Collins, was also convinced that the pro-Diem policy had better be washed out; and he actually joined with his French opposite number, General Paul Ely, in a formal recommendation that support for Diem be immediately withdrawn. Just this, indeed, was what the reporter had in mind when he went so wrong.

Meanwhile, however, South Viet Nam was saved, at least for the time being, by about as odd a concatenation of personalities as one can imagine. Largely because of his Roman Catholic faith, President Diem had made two close American friends—Cardinal Spellman and Senator Mansfield of Montana. They formed a combination that Secretary of State Dulles was extremely reluctant to defy by withdrawing support from Diem. Meanwhile, on the scene in Saigon, President Diem also had an American friend, in the person of one of our unsung postwar heroes, Colonel Edward Lansdale.

This astonishing young airforce officer had begun a new career some years earlier, when he was named to routine liaison duties with the Philippine War Department. The post brought him into contact with the Minister of War, Ramon Magsaysay. Lansdale became Magsaysay's most intimate councillor, and in some sense he was the real architect of Magsaysay's greatness. When Magsaysay had been safely elected President of the Philippine Republic, Lansdale was rather ruthlessly transferred to Saigon in an intelligence capacity, with an extremely transparent cover. His new job was to try to save something from the wreck in Viet Nam. It was remarkably exciting, it was downright inspiring, to see this still young, decidedly dashing American officer, helped only by a few untrained and almost beardless lieutenants borrowed from our forces in Korea, yet laboring with utmost vigor and self-confidence to stave off the ruin that so obviously threatened. But it was hard to believe that Lansdale could succeed in his assignment.

In the end, however, he did succeed. He insisted on the need to go on backing President Diem. ("Who the hell else have we got?" he would inquire.) The Lansdale messages to brother Allen gave Foster Dulles the excuse he needed to delay a little longer, and so avoid an open attack from Mansfield and a covert onslaught by Cardinal Spellman. Dulles therefore rejected the recommendation of his own Ambassador, General Collins. Support for Diem continued. As Lansdale had hoped, President Diem then beat the tar out of the sects, got his own army under control, and largely mastered the Viet Minh infiltration of the South. The result was South Viet Nam as it exists today, in continuing but still precarious independence.

At first sight, the problem of Communist infiltration in the South seemed even graver than the problem of the sects. An attempt to investigate this problem at first hand led the reporter into what was certainly his most dangerous, and very nearly his most enjoyable experience as a foreign correspondent. In brief, a prominent Viet Minh sympathizer in Saigon pretended to arrange a journey for the reporter into one of the Communist-controlled *enclaves* that still existed, at that time, in Southern Indo-China. According to this man's story, the Viet Minh high command were going to issue the reporter's *laissez-passer* when he reached their headquarters in the Camau delta. Meanwhile, a young Communist guide was provided for the first stages of the journey. The guide, who had also been deceived, was well known in the Camau *enclave*—he had been one of the three pharmacists who took care of the Viet Minh forces in the region. The guards accepted the guide's assurance that his companion was expected. The long canal journey to the Viet Minh headquarters at the very center of the Camau delta was completed without a hitch. And then it was discovered that no advance approval had been given, that no *laissez-passer* had been prepared, and that the whole journey had been undertaken on alarmingly false pretenses.

Even under house arrest, and although he was extremely doubtful whether he would ever get out again, the reporter managed to learn a lot. Learning, made more vivid by one's inner tensions, provided the enjoyment. He learned, above all, about the cruel, ruthless, brilliant and efficient way the Viet Minh's Communist hard core had turned the decent emotion of Vietnamese patriotism into an instrument for leading half a nation into slavery. The following column is one of those he wrote in Saigon after he had finally escaped from his predicament—escaped quite literally by the hair on his legs, as is related elsewhere:

SAIGON, INDOCHINA

Across the busy canal there was a barracks. One could tell it was a barracks because the Communist chiefs of the Viet Minh army enforce strict, if primitive, rules of personal hygiene, which brought out the whole company of men inhabiting the little palm huts to soap and scrub themselves in the muddy canal water, morning and evening at appointed hours.

The soldiers were preparing for the public ceremony that would take place before their embarkation to join the big Communist armies in the North. There was singing. There was a gymnastic exercise. And the high point was a long, elaborate, propaganda dance miming the fall of Dienbienphu or some other Communist victory.

Of the five-man dance team, three members were graceful, slender Vietnamese. One was stocky, deep eggplant colored and performed his steps with a marked stomp—most probably a French Colonial soldier from the Ivory Coast. And the bright blond head of the fifth dancer marked him as a captured German member of the Foreign Legion who had been successfully "re-educated." They danced well, and passing sampanloads of villagers stopped to watch and applaud.

I was not supposed to be in the independent Viet Minh state, which still survives in southern Indo-China but will soon be moved north. Having got there, I was not supposed to see anything. But I was allowed to take the sun on the little pier in front of where I was being held under a gentle house arrest. And from my pier, I too darted occasional cautious glances at the dancing soldiers.

It was the dance team, perhaps illogically, that first brought home to me the formidable character of the Viet Minh achievement. For where would you find a more threadbare Communist propaganda trick than this too obvious demonstration of the brotherhood of "Peace Fighters?"

And yet where would you find a better proof of the Viet Minh success than these dancers, perfecting their performance with trained enthusiasm, and including two of the mercenaries brought there by the French to Indo-China to destroy the Viet Minh? What careful organization and what power to inspire emotion must have been needed to produce this single trivial result of five posturing, chanting young men, who were so obviously convinced and delighted by their solemn humorless Communist dance!

A far longer report would be needed to describe the Viet Minh methods in detail, but two sets of facts will help to convey their remarkable character. One of the questions I asked the high Viet Minh officials who came to talk with me before deciding to let me go home again, was how they managed to provision the very large army in their zone without making it a burden to the peasantry.

They replied that it had really been very hard until two years ago, when the inflation of the Viet Minh currency had forced the substitution of rice taxes for money taxes. The change over had really gone very well—here Dr. Vinh, the local former secretary of the treasury, smiled as George Humphrey might have smiled over the passage of last year's new tax bill.

The average tax of just over 20 per cent of rice production had not proven too burdensome for the villagers. The inflation had been immediately rolled back, so that the exchange rate of the Ho Chi Minh piastre against the French piastre dropped from 150 down to forty to one. And rice storage, which they had been very worried about, turned out to be no problem at all.

Government granaries were of course out of the question because of the danger of French air attacks. So when the taxes were paid in, the peasants' patriotic associations in each village nominated certain trustworthy villagers to hold the government grain. That way, the treasury, like everything else in the region, was ideally dispersed.

The army too was normally dispersed as well as kept on the move. When a company entered a village, the company commanders simply presented the necessary rice receipts to the village grainholders. The government rice was paid out again to feed and pay the soldiers; and that was that, except when troops were being collected for a big offensive operation. Then the peasants of the surrounding region would be asked to transport extra government rice to the main concentration points.

How primitively simple, yet how marvelously efficient! And what rigid discipline, what general loyalty must have been needed to make such a system work without cheating or pilferage by soldiers or villagers! As to the existence of this discipline and belief, the bleak statistics of the life of the men I chiefly talked with gave proof enough of that.

All might have been living comfortably or even richly as city bourgeois. All were living as poor peasants, although at least two were very high officials of the Viet Minh state. All got approximately the same state salaries—enough rice to eat plus enough more rice to pay for a little fish and vegetables, with an issue of black cloth to make two pyjama uniforms a year. With this much, for years of constant danger, they had been passionately contented.

To them it had been fully worth it. Smiling a little thinly, Dr. Vinh remarked to me just before we parted, "We started from zero in 1945 when I joined the resistance, we had nothing, nothing. And now we have almost everything and it will not be long before all Viet Nam is ours." He was, alas, only too probably bang right.—December 27, 1954 (JA).

IX

The Years of Euphoria

1955 and 1956 were the years of euphoria. Every practical sign, in both the political and military spheres, only too clearly warned of trouble ahead. But the "spirit of Geneva" distilled at the famous summit meeting, plus prosperity at home, plus the administration's habit of concealing the warning signs from the nation, all combined to produce a euphoric mood in America.

The period after the false peace in Korea and the Munich in Indo-China was marked by extreme tension, all along China's borders. All Asians saw the Korean settlement for what it was, a concealed defeat for the West and a solid victory for the Communists. Most Asians further expected a chain reaction of disaster after the cease-fire in Indo-China—just the same chain reaction which had also been predicted by Secretary of State Dulles and the American National Security Council before they decided not to intervene in Indo-China after all. That winter, wise old U Nu of Burma told the older member of our partnership that he already foresaw the absorption of South

Viet Nam by the Communists in the North; the subsequent surrender to the Communists of Cambodia and Laos; and the resulting establishment of a pro-Communist government in Thailand, on Burma's own borders.

In these circumstances, the American government's public presentation of the situation was really unbearably hucksterish. The "Time" cover of John Foster Dulles that was published at this time, with the legend, "He strengthened the outposts," made the whole of Asia laugh and caused every sensible American in Asia to squirm with angry embarrassment. Sheer indignation at this huckstering sharpened the language of the disturbed and rather too portentous columns that were sent back that winter from Cambodia, Thailand, Indonesia and Burma. They described dangers that still exist, and can quite easily take material form in the rather near future. The Asian chain-reaction, in our opinion, has only been deferred, but has not been decisively prevented. All the same, we prefer this chronicle of an escape into pure pleasure—one of those escapes which help to restore the sense of proportion of a reporter abroad who is beginning to feel the pressure of the situation he is trying to investigate.

NONGKHAY, THAILAND

This reporter is currently recovering from giving a New Year's Eve party which perhaps deserves recording on a higher level than the expense account, if only because it was a dinner-dance for 150 people that cost $35.

It was born of a decision to spend Christmas and New Year's Day in this lovely region of Thailand, which is also the most exposed to communist pressure and the most penetrated by fifth columns. When I got here, my friend Rod Hemphill, who runs a local silk factory, said no one could understand Thailand without getting the feel of village life.

It was a pity, Rod added, there was no village party coming up, because going to a village party was the best way to see what a Thai village was really like. And so I asked whether I might give a New Year's Eve party at the Village of the Lotus Lake, where Rod's silk factory is situated.

From there, Rod's charming and intelligent Thai partner, Kun Nom, and the extremely able, tough village headman, Som Si, quietly took over. There were a couple of preliminary crises, about the price of the cow that was to be the main dish, and about the difficulty of obtaining the truly superior brand of local white mule that is made across the Mekong River in Laos.

But Kun Nom and Som Si were as efficient a catering service as any in Washington. On the morning of Dec. 31, they reported that my $35 had provided a cow, half a buffalo, and several ducks and chickens; plus about fifteen gallons of white mule for the common people, with a specially invigorating and precious bottle of white mule mixed with black monkey's blood for the honored guests; plus the most cele-brated player of the ken, a local instrument halfway between bagpipes and pan pipes; plus prizes to persuade the young ladies to dance, which they are reluctant to do without suitable inducement.

Rod and his beautiful wife, Annong, and I set off for the party in the late afternoon. The children of Lotus Lake Village were driving the village buffaloes home from their wallow; the herons were gloriously winging their way back to the heronry by the Lotus Lake; and the lowering sun was gilding the rice straw in the fields. But this perfect atmosphere of pastoral peace was shattered, when we reached the ball-room (Rod's silk factory). Som Si had insisted on installing the power-ful American public address system that the village bought last year to brighten up its festivals.

The noise of alternating records of Bangkok songs, local ballads and arias from Thai classical opera was downright deafening. Besides, half the village was already there. The white mule was already going round. And the conversation was beginning to show that added brightness that always marks the cocktail hour.

The first item on the program was the idea of the village elders—to wind the *bai see* strings which bring good luck on the arms of Rod and Annong and me. The ceremony involved sitting on the floor through an interminable, imitation Pali chant, and being wound with the strings while all those not busy string winding held hands to strengthen the life forces.

After that the party really got going. The white mule circulated rapidly, by an efficient loving cup system. The cow and the buffalo ap-peared in the form of *laap,* which means that they had been chopped fine with the fieriest red peppers available, extra seasoned with spices and rather summarily cooked. With *laap* and curry and salad and white mule in plenty, the usual second stage of every party, when the con-versation almost overtops the music, was easily reached.

Then the ken player took over the microphone. With many a shy gesture, the young ladies took the floor, and the village bucks stepped out for the circle dance. This involves revolving, very remotely, around your partner, making elegant hand and arm gestures. An American buck would find it unexciting, but Thai bucks think differently.

And so we reached the party's final phase, which continued, with louder and louder music and faster and faster circle dancing, until all could wish one another a Happy New Year. There were the usual late party incidents—the headman's son went a bit too far, as headmen's sons so often will. There was also the usual group who could not resist the temptation for "just one nightcap," so the Lotus Lake Village was still ringing with song in the dawn. But as a party it was a clear success.

And what useful information did I garner from this evening, it may well be asked. Well, I learned from all those present that Thai villagers are charming, gay and friendly people. From Som Si and one or two other intelligent and sober elders, I learned they hate the Chinese and Vietnamese with an intense passion, and equate communism with its great Asian converts. And just by listening to the loud speaker, I learned that this was a semi-neolithic community, experiencing a violent impact from Western civilization whose final outcome you could not predict.

And I also learned that Kun Nom was not factually accurate when he promised that Laos white mule mixed with black monkey's blood never gave you a headache.—January 7, 1955 (JA).

The Asian tension reached its climax that winter in the affair of the offshore islands occupied by the Chinese Nationalist forces. The American handling of this matter was the most astonishing case on record of "The good old Duke of York, he had ten thousand men; he marched them up the hill, then marched them down again."

The first action of the alleged "dynamic new foreign policy" of Eisenhower and Dulles had been the alleged "unleashing of Generalissimo Chiang Kai-shek." As we rather indignantly pointed out at the time, this was a totally fraudulent gesture; but it produced one solid and most unfortunate result.

Previous to the celebrated unleashing, the Generalissimo had never made any serious attempt to hold the offshore islands—the Tachens and Nanchishan quite far to the Northwest of Formosa, and the

Matsus and Quemoy, just across the Formosa Strait. There were Nationalist guerilla outfits on the islands, but that was all; and the islands were regarded as expendable. After the unleashing, however, perhaps to give some semblance of reality to the fraud, the American government placed the severest pressure on Chiang Kai-shek to occupy these alarmingly exposed positions in real force. With extreme reluctance, pointing out the risks involved and the blow to his own prestige that would result from a subsequent withdrawal, the Generalissimo yielded to this American pressure. All the islands were occupied; and the Tachens became the main forward base of "Western Enterprises, Inc." (This CIA outfit was certainly the most uncovered covert operation the world has ever seen, having its own housing developments, PXes and social clubs at Taipeh. Its purpose was to stimulate resistance to the Communist government on the mainland.)

Soon after the Korean peace, however, our reconnaissance aircraft spotted increasing concentrations of Chinese Communist troops in Chekiang and Kiangsu provinces, where they threatened the Tachens. Intimations also came from Peking of an oncoming assault on Formosa proper. The administration in Washington responded in three different ways. They passed the Formosa treaty through the Senate. They publicly talked about bombing the Chinese mainland if the Matsus or Quemoy were attacked; and a flat guarantee of Quemoy and the Matsus was given Chiang's government—and then hastily withdrawn. But the administration also quietly re-leashed Chiang Kai-shek, and they began to press him to evacuate the most immediately threatened position—the same Tachens which they had previously pressed him to occupy.

Chiang was justifiably embittered, and he resisted the new pressure as long as he could—until the most northerly island of the Tachen group had actually fallen to a Communist assault. Then the evacuation was ordered, while the world literally held its breath.

Even after this withdrawal under threat, the Formosa crisis dragged on for a long while. The senior member of our partnership took a much too gloomy view of the probable immediate outcome; but he was once again in good company, since the Chief of Staff of the U. S. Navy, Admiral Carney, predicted "war by April 15" in a public speech. Furthermore, the situation in the Formosa Strait has the same pattern today that it had in 1955, with even more explosive potential. As these words are written, in fact, it seems on the point of exploding.

But rather than offer the analytical and straight news columns that are summarized above, we have chosen one about the evacuation of the Tachens, which is more human and better conveys the contemporary emotion.

NORTH TACHEN ISLAND

One of the casualties of the latest free world retreat in Asia is a place called Halfway to Heaven.

Halfway to Heaven perches, or rather used to perch, on the cratered summit of the highest peak of North Tachen Island, some 1500 feet above the surrounding, nourishing sea.

It began a little more than a century ago, when the first harsh impact of the modern world on ancient China produced the Taiping rebellion, which in turn produced a fearful famine in Chekiang Province. Fleeing the famine, a handful of inhabitants of the Chekiang town of Wan Ling found a safe refuge on this island crag, and stayed to build a village, or rather two villages, for the lesser of the two adjoining craters contains Little Halfway to Heaven, and the larger, Big Halfway to Heaven.

For five generations, sons succeeded fathers, gradually clawing new terraces from the crater walls and naked mountain side for their plots of vegetables and sweet potatoes, gradually adding vessel to vessel in Halfway to Heaven's fleet of fishing sampans until there were 130 sampans owned among the hundred families of peak dwellers.

The bitter poverty of the original refugees thus slowly gave way to a kind of crude prosperity. Long low houses of chinked stone, with finely carved, boldly curved ridgepoles were built to cling to the crater sides. A little temple to the Taoist earth godlings gave the villagers some one to pray to when times were hard. The young men fished all year. The elders, the children and the women tilled the terraces.

With salt and cloth from the big settlement on South Tachen Island, with their fish and sweet potatoes and vegetables, with a rare treat of meat from the pigs, chickens, rabbits and goats they also kept, the people of Halfway to Heaven were not ill-content. But for a hundred years no outsider ever saw Halfway to Heaven, except the people from Door of the Wind Hill, the village on the other side of the crag, and the huge, superbly winged fish eagle that had his nest on the cliff below the village graves.

Then President Eisenhower "unleashed Chiang Kai-shek," and the American government pressured the Chinese Nationalist government into occupying the Tachens in force. So the soldiers came, barracks were built, and Halfway to Heaven briefly tasted an unfamiliar, uneasy prosperity. And then again, President Eisenhower released Chiang Kai-shek, and the American government pressured the Chinese Nationalists into abandoning the Tachens; and that was the end of Halfway to Heaven.

In the Chinese way, the end came without undue lamentation. The villagers talked it over and decided that what they had heard of communism from their fellow fisherfolk from the mainland was ugly enough to justify a move. The government said it would help. And so, on the afternoon before the move was to be made, no one was weeping except the wife of the elder of the Leng family. She was deaf and could not read, and she wept because she had grasped that a move impended but no one could tell her why or where.

The elder of Leng, a little, old, gnarled, toothless man like a weathered root, with what must really be the last queue on any Chinese head, was ignoring his weeping wife. He and the elder of Chu and the young men and boys of Little Halfway to Heaven were sitting in the pale, watery sun in the village center, while the women finished their packing. Yes, they said, they were leaving. Yes, it was hard to go, but they did not want to stay. They had swept the graves one last time, and now they were ready.

It was the same in Big Halfway to Heaven, where is found the house of the place's richest man, Cheng, who owned three whole sampans in the fleet that used to sail from the foot of Knife Back Mountain. He had enough capital stored up to open a restaurant when the soldiers came, and his Chinese crullers and hot soya bean milk brought him in the magnificent cash profit of two dollars a day. But Cheng too was leaving without reluctance.

As the dusk fell, the village headman, Lo the Clever, came back from organizing the evacuation of all North Tachen Island—Kwan Yins Village, Bare Rock, the East Village and the rest—which were all to be led by Lo. He had his aged mother to calm and his household to organize, for Lo the Clever is a widower. So he let his deputy, Hung, give the movement orders to the chiefs of the "sections" of fifty or sixty people into which the village, by immemorial Chinese custom, is administratively divided.

The meeting took place in the upper room of the house of Liang, a big house, for the Liang clan was the largest in Halfway to Heaven. A score of men, young and old, stood around the table, their faces work hardened, their black peasant clothes worn, making a picture fit to be painted by a Chinese Breughel in the yellow light of a guttering tallow candle. Hung read the movement order in a brisk singsong.

Departure would be at 9 the next morning. Each section leader would be responsible for his section. Each person would be allowed to carry 100 pounds of personal belongings if he could manage that much.

There were quick questions: How about bad weather at sea, from a weatherwise fisherman; how about pregnant women, would they get medical care on the ships, from a young father-soon-to-be; and so on. Hung dealt with the questions intelligently. And then every one went home for a great feast of all the food that could not be sold to the soldiers, was not worth carrying, and was no longer worth scrimping against a poor season.

Before dawn the next morning, the young men of the village set off down the mountain side, each balancing two enormous packs on his back. At first Lo had a little trouble forming the line to his taste.

Then the last shout was given. Little Liang marched proudly forward. Children shouldered the babies. Men and women, young or old, hoisted up their heavy packs. Even the old bound-feet grannies carried something. But none complained. And so the slowly moving line wound its way up over the crater lip and down the long miles of fearfully curving, fearfully mud-slimed road to Yellow One Beach, where the transports awaited them.

An old nanny goat and her two kids, which had somehow escaped the pot, were being chased by two soldiers when the last of those who had made Halfway to Heaven a living, breathing place of habitation cast his last backward glance into the familiar hollow on the mountain summit. The great fish eagle still magnificently volplaned in the cloudy sky above. But the doorways of the houses were dark and deserted. The muddy lanes were strewn with the rubbish of departure. Halfway to Heaven was dead—killed by forces it did not understand, utterly destroyed because it had been briefly swept, by what strange processes and chances, into the dread vortex of great events.—February 14, 1955 (JA).

The summing up after the long Asian journey still has interest today, because the situation it describes is still there, and is just as dangerous as ever. The reference to "keeping them guessing" needs explanation. Secretary Dulles had been the strongest advocate of drawing clear lines that the enemy must not cross. But even then, when the American lead still existed, Dulles was not willing to commit the American government with absolute finality to a war for Quemoy, so he explained that we must "keep (the Chinese Communists) guessing." As these words are written, one wonders what their guess and our response will be.

TAIPEI, FORMOSA

In order to understand the Formosa crisis, we must try to see ourselves as others see us. And if we make this always-depressing attempt, the sad truth comes out that the Chinese Communist leaders almost certainly believe that America really is a "paper tiger." On this highly significant point, all the on-the-spot experts encountered by this reporter have been unanimous. The expert opinion is not surprising, either. For the Red Chinese theory that America is a paper tiger is rather squarely founded on the facts of the recent record.

In the period since the Eisenhower administration took office, there have been three tests of will and purpose between Peiping and Washington. The first test, whose outcome was the source of all the bristling current dangers in Asia, was the test in Korea.

In January, 1953, America was tired of the Korean War, but Red China was utterly exhausted by it. Since August of the year before half the Cabinet of the Chinese Communist government had been in Moscow to plead for more generous aid, which was not forthcoming. In December, the Chinese had even made an independent peace bid through India, only to be slapped down hard by the old tyrant Stalin.

In the winter of 1953, in short, the Chinese were visibly hanging on the ropes. Whatever errors may have gone before—and this reporter thinks there were many such—the winter when President Eisenhower took office was the ideal moment to mobilize America's resources and go in to win in Korea.

A real victory in Korea would have given the free world at least ten years' breathing space in the Far East. But instead, after long hesitations, the Administration gave the Chinese Communists a truce which both ended the Korean strain on their regime and left Communist China as the unchallenged and predominant military power in Asia.

The Korean truce led directly, inevitably and naturally to the next year's crisis in Indo-China. As though astonished by this perfectly foreseeable consequence of their own decision about Korea, the Washington policy-makers at first resolved that surrender in Indo-China "could not be permitted." This decision of the National Security Council was freely publicized. The Vice-President himself informed the nation's newspaper editors that American divisions might have to be sent to Tonkin, and there was much other big, bold talk by those high in authority.

But in the outcome, the big, bold talk turned out to be meaningless. Protesting only feebly, the American administration assented to the Far Eastern Munich at Geneva. Chou En-lai enjoyed a grandiose international triumph, and the fate of Indo-China was sealed.

The Geneva Munich, in turn, led directly, inevitably and naturally to this year's crisis in the Formosa Strait. Once again, the Washington policy-makers were visibly taken by surprise by the perfectly foreseeable consequence of their own act. Once again, the first reaction was big, bold talk in Washington. And now we are again entering the period when the big, bold talk is to be put to the test.

The Chinese Communist leaders might be less confident of the result if the evidence of the two previous tests of will were not confirmed by the evidence of recent American defense policy. Unfortunately, however, Secretary of Defense Charles Wilson's alleged defense economies have left the United States with less strength in the Pacific than at any time since Pearl Harbor.

Secretary of State John Foster Dulles could say at Bangkok that we had more strength in the Pacific than in the moment of victory over Japan only because we have stocks of atomic and hydrogen bombs that we did not have in 1945. But in simple terms of men, guns, planes and ships, the power we can bring to bear in the Far East has now reached its post-war nadir, being weaker by far than on the dark day when the Korean War broke out.

This state of affairs is given rather lurid importance, moreover, by one of the few wisps of fairly hard information about the Khrushchev-Bulganin-Mikoyan visit to Peiping last October. During this visit, when China's Formosa plan was co-ordinated with the present leaders of Russia, the Russians are reported to have assured the Chinese they need not worry about America using atomic weapons in a Far Eastern war.

There were, obviously, two strong arguments behind this reported

Russian assurance. On the one hand, we did not use atomic weapons in Korea, but instead patiently suffered the Chinese intervention there. On the other hand, our present defense design depends very heavily on the overseas air bases of the Strategic Air Command.

For all-out atomic war, we need those bases. No one can be sure that the use of atomic bombs in the Formosa Strait will not lead to all-out war. Our allies who control our overseas bases will not join a war starting in the Formosa Strait.

Hence the risk of using atomic bombs to defend Quemoy and the Matsus is far greater than was the risk in Korea, when we did not use them. This reasoning is all too persuasive. Furthermore, if the Chinese believe we will not use atomic bombs, they must consequently believe they can attack Quemoy and the Matsu Islands with impunity.

Even if we fight back, our greatly depleted conventional military power in the Pacific is almost surely insufficient to hold the virtually indefensible rocks in the Formosa Strait against a determined Chinese assault.

Such is the practical position as it most probably appears in Peiping's eyes. Hence the tactic of "keeping them guessing" is about the worst we could adopt, for the Chinese are most likely to guess that we shall back down again as we did before.

It must be added that if we do back down again as we did before, the Chinese Communist leaders will inevitably regard America not just as a paper tiger, but as a paper rabbit. And therefore next year's ugly choice will be as much worse than this year's, as this year's is worse than last year's, and last year's was worse than the choice in Korea.— April 17, 1955 (JA).

Much earlier, we had published the first reports of the intra-administration argument about an American project to launch an earth satellite. A chapter of accidents explained elsewhere in this book caused the following rather late column in the satellite series to enrage President Eisenhower. The immediate consequences of the President's anger was another "security investigation."

WASHINGTON

With a determined but not very expensive effort, it should be possible to launch an artificial satellite into space about this time next year. This, at least, is the contention of leading technicians in the missile field who have submitted to the Pentagon plans for launching a man-made heavenly body in about twelve months.

Until recently, it was thought that it would take at least two years to put a satellite into space. But recent technological breakthroughs in the missile art have made it possible—at least in the opinion of some qualified technicians—to halve this estimate.

If the Pentagon approves the project, the object to be shot into space so soon will not be much to look at. The plans call for an object only about nine inches in diameter, of the simplest and lightest possible construction. To save weight and bulk—which is, of course, all important—the little thing will contain no instruments at all, other than a radar-response device to permit it to be tracked by radar on its journeyings around the globe.

The purists in such matters insist that the object will not be a true earth satellite, but rather an "orbital vehicle." The purists are right, in the sense that such an object will not remain forever in space, like the moon. Instead, it will spiral very gradually back toward earth, after some weeks or months of circling the globe, and when it reaches the denser atmosphere close to earth, it will disintegrate.

Obviously, the tiny thing will have no immediate military application whatever. For this reason, a debate has been going on in the Defense Department about whether or not it is worth going ahead with the satellite project. Aside from the prejudices against "frills" held by the supposedly hard-headed business men who now run the Pentagon, there are serious arguments against going ahead all-out with the satellite project.

Although some of the specialists in the art believe that a simple satellite or orbital vehicle can be launched into space for as little as $20,000,000, others strongly disagree. The more skeptical technicians point out that there are many unknown factors remaining, and they have estimated the cost as high as half a billion dollars or even more, and the time as several years.

The most serious argument against the satellite project is that it might divert funds, facilities and talents from other missiles—above all from the Intercontinental Ballistic Missile, the grand prize of the missile race. The technicians who favor the satellite project argue on the contrary that the satellite can be achieved without any sacrifice of time in the missile race; that the satellite is, in fact, a kind of free dividend of the efforts to create an I.C.B.M.

But the most cogent pro-satellite argument can best be understood in terms of a couple of headlines: SOVIETS CLAIM SUCCESSFUL LAUNCHING OF EARTH SATELLITE, and U. S. RADAR CONFIRMS EXISTENCE OF SOVIET SATELLITE.

Two facts suggest that these headlines are not as fanciful as may be supposed.

First, the possibility that the Soviets will launch a satellite is taken so seriously that a satellite-detection project has been established at White Sands, New Mexico, and at Mount Wilson, Calif. A tremendous flap was caused not long ago in the Pentagon when the project identified not one, but two satellites. It turned out that both were natural satellites, never before detected.

Second, the Russians in April announced with a flourish the creation of a "permanent interdepartmental commission for interplanetary communication." Russia's greatest scientist, Peter Kapitsa, was appointed to the commission. Its first task was announced as "the organization of an automatic laboratory of scientific research in cosmic space which would, over a long period, revolve around the earth as a satellite, beyond the limits of the atmosphere."

This bland announcement also caused much dismay, at least among the more sensible men in the Pentagon. For this kind of before-the-fact boasting by the Soviets must be taken very seriously indeed, as the Pentagon has learned to its sorrow, conspicuously in the case of the atomic and hydrogen bombs. Those who oppose the satellite project argue that it would not matter very much if the Russians did get the first satellite into space—it would presumably be as militarily valueless as the proposed American device.

But, as one pro-satellite official put it—"we wouldn't really know it was harmless—all we'd really know is that it was up there." The first satellite will certainly be the forerunner of satellites with enormous military value in reconnaissance, missile guidance and other fields. Moreover, it does not require much imagination to foresee the impression that a successful Soviet satellite launching would make on the world. To knowledgeable men in every foreign office and military establishment, it would mean just one thing—that the Soviet military technicians had gained a commanding lead over their American opposite numbers, in the race for the ultimate weapon.—May 25, 1955 (SA).

This portrait of Lyndon Baines Johnson in action is just as accurate now as it was then. It also commemorates a domestic political development that turned out in the end to be far more important than any other such development in 1955, except perhaps for President Eisenhower's severe heart attack. This so-important development was simply the emergence of Lyndon Johnson as a truly commanding figure in the U. S. Senate.

WASHINGTON

There is always something peculiarly satisfying about watching a genuine professional at work, whether on the baseball diamond or on the floor of the United States Senate. Any one who wants to see in action the best professional floor leader of our time need only visit the Senate gallery at a tense legislative moment, and keep his eye on the tall, lanky, slow-moving form of the Majority Leader as he ambles about the floor below.

Like a great professional athlete, Lyndon Johnson, of Texas, makes no waste motion. A word here and there, a casual, political arm around a recalcitrant shoulder, a brief, companionable colloquy with his opposite number, William Knowland, of California—and the chances are that the bill under consideration will slide through the Senate almost without debate.

Take a few recent examples. The reciprocal trade bill which had generated immensely heavy pressures from back home, was in very bad trouble. It was being freely predicted that it would pass, if at all, only after many weeks of weary wrangling and many crippling amendments. It passed after three days of debate in surprisingly unmutilated form.

Traditionally, the agricultural appropriations act, touching as it does many sensitive farm pocketbooks, is the subject of loud, long and angry argument. It passed, all unnoticed, after exactly an hour of debate. The Colorado River basin reclamation bill involved one of the hottest political issues in the Far West. The bill has often been debated in other sessions, but never passed. It went through the Senate in this session in three days. The Paris accords, which could have been expected at the very least to have elicited a lot of oratory for the folks back home, slipped through in just two hours.

And so on. The fact is that this session of Congress has passed a good deal of important and controversial legislation. But this has been done so quietly, with such a minimum of fuss and pother, that old hands are saying that this is the least exciting session since the '20s. At any rate, it is certainly the most efficiently run session in recent memory. It is interesting, therefore, to visit the Majority Leader, and ask him how he does it.

Now that the White House has been ruined by the modernizers, the Capitol is the last place in Washington with a real smell of the past. Johnson's little office off the gallery floor, with its handsome chandeliers sent up from the White House by Theodore Roosevelt, its turn-of-the-century furniture, and its odd decorations (an old portrait of "Rebecka, daughter of the mighty Prince Powhattan, Emperor of Attaboughkomouck," for example) helps to remind the visitor that the Congress of the United States, after all, is one of the world's most ancient legislative bodies.

The Majority Leader fits well into the atmosphere. The Senate is in his bones and in his blood. And the same thing is true of the committee chairmen who are Johnson's principal lieutenants and collaborators in the business of running the Senate.

When you ask him how he does it, Johnson gives most of the credit to the chairmen. He reels off their names, and appends to each a short political biography, going back to the state legislature and the county judgeships.

"Hell," he says, "every damned one of 'em's an old pro. They've been twenty-five years in Congress, on the average. You wouldn't expect them to get all flustered up about nothing, would you?"

Getting controversial issues thoroughly settled in committee before they ever reach the floor, and before any one has a chance to get all flustered up about nothing, is the most important part of the Johnson recipe for running the Senate. For the rest, the recipe calls for a large, efficient, experienced staff, capable of finding out how each Senator will vote almost before he knows himself; and a thorough knowledge of the complicated rules of the Senate. "No slipperies or trickeries," says Johnson (who has an odd turn of phrase), but you've got to know the rules."

Finally, the recipe calls for something intangible, a special sort of instinct. "You haven't got any business being in my profession," Johnson says, "if you can't smell things coming."

Those who have watched him in action agree that Johnson can certainly smell things coming—especially trouble. His critics say, indeed, that Johnson is a great deal better at making the Senate function smoothly and without unnecessary rows, than in making issues which will help the Democrats win back the White House in 1956.

Johnson himself firmly believes that a well-run Congress and a united party are the best possible assets for next year's Democratic Presidential candidate, whoever he may be. At any rate, Johnson is the kind of man the American system has always had to have—a man who makes the system work.—May 22, 1955 (SA).

The story of the "Moscow overflights," as they were called, typifies the government's approach to the defense problem at this period. In flat defiance of the intelligence, Secretary of Defense Charles E. Wilson had been telling the country that Soviet air preparations were "purely defensive," and were no good anyway. This was his reply, in fact, to the stories we and a few others had published earlier, about the successful Soviet development of the "Bear" long-range turboprop bomber, and the "Bison" and "Badger" jet bombers.

Wilson had just reiterated his happy reassurance to the country, when the Kremlin staged a series of overflights of Moscow city by its big, shiny, very far from defensive bombers. The design of the bombers, with engines having twice the thrust of the best American engines then in production, further proved that the Soviets were far ahead of us in jet engine design. In the face of this evidence, Wilson continued to grumble that the Kremlin's bombers were really only a few "hand-built" proto-types (his idea being, apparently, that a country without General Motors must build everything by hand). All the same, the B-52 program was increased under pressure of the news from Moscow—which is the chief reason why we at least have a serious B-52 force today.

The Moscow overflight story is mentioned in the following column. What makes it really worth preserving, however, is the revelation of the President's curious mental process concerning these matters. Take the two paragraphs in quotes, and put the President himself in the role of the "Soviet leader" therein mentioned. You then have almost the entire explanation of the seeming mystery of our defense policy.

WASHINGTON

In the language of the psychiatrists, the Eisenhower administration is now suffering from a severe censorship syndrome. The worst sufferer seems to be the President himself. The resulting loss of contact with democratic reality is only too easy to prove. Not long ago, for instance, the President complained long and loudly at a National Security Council meeting because the Defense Department had published pictures of launching sites of the Nike guided missile. Yet any kid with a Brownie camera can go out to Arlington and take the same pictures.

Again, the President has told the able Assistant Secretary of Air, Trevor Gardner, to go and stand in a corner because of a speech about the Air Force's Falcon missile. Yet the speech contained no fact that had not been previously published, and it had even been given the most elaborate clearance by the new American chief censor, Secretary of Defense Charles E. Wilson.

Or again, the Civil Defense Agency was shockingly obstructed and the American people were kept in dangerous ignorance for more than a year by Adm. Lewis E. Strauss' suppression of the facts concerning radioactive fall-out from the H-bomb. Yet all these facts were fully known to the Soviets even before they were learned by Adm. Strauss.

In a remarkable piece for the "New York Herald Tribune," Walter Kerr has tried hard to explain this seemingly inexplicable urge to keep from the American people even those facts that the enemy quite surely knows.

Explanations were sought from Defense Department information chief Herschel Schooley; from United States Information Service chief Theodore Streibert, and from R. C. Honaman, the new Assistant Secretary of Defense, who has the special task of hiding the life-and-death facts of their national situation from the American people. The official rationalization of the President's desire to keep the people in the dark was summarized as follows by Kerr:

"The President recognizes (that) many items of military information . . . become known to the military tacticians of other countries—of Russia, for example. He believes, however, that these technicians are unable to influence their country's top officials. (Their information) is buried in a report and forgotten. . . .

"Then, the reasoning goes, this same information . . . is released to the American press. It is widely published. It is commented on at length . . . Soon the item which was originally technical is no longer technical. It has political significance. It comes to the attention of political leaders. Then, and perhaps only then, the Soviet leader . . . translates into action a technical proposal that had been safely buried."

According to those who have worked intimately with the President on the censorship problem, these interesting statements genuinely represent the Eisenhower viewpoint. As a description of Soviet planning methods, they are of course inaccurate to the point of being downright alarming. They are directly refuted, in fact, by the whole history of Soviet military technology from the T-34 tank to the new heavy bomber.

In the last twenty years all-out development of all the brilliantly successful new Soviet weapons produced in this period was quite certainly started before the readers of the American press, or any other press, had heard about such weapons. The fact is proved by the speed of development, unless you prefer to assume that Soviet engineers are ten times quicker than American engineers.

On the other hand, the President's theory of Soviet behavior is highly applicable to the behavior of his own Administration. As so often happens when syndromes are serious, there has been a transference of symptoms. The Eisenhower administration, not the Soviet government, has the habit of ignoring technicians' warnings until they cease to be technical, and become political, because of publicity.

That was most recently proven by the true story of the Moscow overflights, previously told in this space. Long before the overflights, the technicians had been warning that we were lagging behind the Soviets in air development. But the warnings were ignored until the overflights occurred, the attempted censorship failed, and the facts became known. After that, our lag in air development was a political issue, and corrective action was taken.

Such incidents in turn reveal the roots of the censorship syndrome. It is rooted, obviously, in the Administration's eagerness to cut taxes, balance the budget, and do other popular things.

The people are not to be told the life-and-death facts because the facts would stir up the people to demand necessary Defense Department spending, which would in turn make the Treasury Department program harder to carry out.

Unfortunately, however, the diagnosis of the disease does not make the symptoms more attractive or the disease less dangerous.—June 12, 1955 (JA & SA).

While the Far Eastern crisis was dying down, the Kremlin began making novel gestures and novel noises. The Austrian peace treaty and the renewal of relations with Yugoslavia were the two most important gestures. The noise that attracted the most attention at the time was the friendly letter that Marshal Zhukov suddenly sent, out of the blue, as it were, to his old comrade in arms in the White House. In addition, Georgyi Malenkov was abruptly demoted, that winter, from the Soviet premiership where we had wrongly imagined that he was firmly fixed. The new partnership of Khrushchev and Bulganin, the world famous vaudeville team of Khrush and Bulge, moved into the lead in Moscow.

In these circumstances, the younger member of our partnership who had been trying for years to get a Soviet visa, took the unconventional step of writing a personal letter to Nikita Khrushchev. The visa that had been previously refused was now granted at once. The following columns bear publication dates long after the dates when they were written, since the famous summit meeting at Geneva disrupted our schedule. But they seemed worthy of delayed publication then, and they seem worthy of re-publication now.

DNIEPROPETROVSK

The feeling that you don't really understand, and never could understand in a million years, is one reason why a visit to the Soviet Union is such an oddly oppressive experience for an American.

Nowhere is the feeling so strong as on a kholkoz, or collective farm. Take, for example, the pig pen on the Stalin kholkoz near here, which this reporter has just visited. Comrade Lepscha, the shy, eager, thin-faced vice-chairman of the collective, could hardly wait to show off his new pig pen.

And indeed, it turned out to be a regular Ritz of pigland, a porkers' paradise, every spotless sow in her own spotless pen. There were several peasant girls about, acting as solicitous pig valets, scrubbing the pens, or washing and brushing the sows and the little piglets.

But why? Why this heavy investment in effort and woman-hours to keep pigs in such a state of unnatural cleanliness? Why was it worth it?

One possible answer of course immediately suggested itself—that the pig pen was a sort of porcine Potemkin village, erected to impress the gullible foreign visitor. But this theory could not hold water. The decision to visit the collective farm had been taken at the last minute, when it turned out to be impossible, for the usual mysterious reasons, to visit the famous Dniepropetrovsk Dam.

Besides, Dniepropetrovsk is well off the usual route for foreigners—there is not even an Intourist hotel—and it just does not seem likely that the Russians would build a beautiful pig pen and stock it with beautiful pigs just in case a stray foreigner happened along.

Part of the real answer was visible, instead, in the almost fanatic pride in Comrade Lepscha's eyes, as he surveyed his gleaming pig house and his gleaming pigs. The porcine Ritz was clearly a sort of private hobby, a personal hobby of Comrade Lepscha's, built without any of the usual dreary prior calculations of the corn-hog ratio which American farmers are forced to make.

And another part of the answer was found in Comrade Lepscha's carefully rehearsed lecture about the kholkoz, which he gave in his tiny office under the inevitable picture of Stalin in an agricultural moment. According to Comrade Lepscha, there are 14,000 acres on the Stalin kholkoz, and 1,400 people.

This works out, of course, to one person per ten acres. The comparable ratio on American farming, in a good district, is one family to 160 acres, with father doing almost all the work. It was obvious to the naked eye that there were plenty of people about on the Stalin kholkoz. And with plenty of people, it is not difficult to keep large numbers of pigs unnaturally immaculate, if the local powers that be, like Comrade Lepscha, decide that keeping pigs immaculate is a good thing.

This may explain the mystery of the immaculate pigs. But in Russia the explanation of one mystery only leads on to another mystery. For how does this incredible system, in which there are no normal economic incentives or economic sanctions, manage to work at all? You can see that it works, after a fashion, with your own eyes.

To be sure, the corn looks thin, the brown cows seedy, and the pasturage terrible. But the wheat looks fine, the fruit is abundant and delicious, and the people of the kholkoz are certainly healthy and vigorous.

Some of the people even seem happy. Take Ivan, the tractor driver. Comrade Lepscha says that Ivan has piled up a record number of "norms," the norm being the unit of measurement in the speed-up system which is universal in the Soviet Union. (Another mystery: how can you measure with any real accuracy the normal output of a tractor driver or a pig-tender?)

At any rate, Ivan the tractor driver is one of the two or three top earners on the farm. Ivan is a big, brawny man with an enormous grin and stainless steel teeth. He proudly invites the foreigner to visit his house. From the outside, it looks precisely like every other house on the dusty, rutted kholkoz street, and like every other house, it is surrounded by a couple of acres of carefully tended private land.

(From the air, you can see the pattern of the Russian land endlessly repeated—lush, heavily cultivated, private plots around the little houses, giving way to huge, scraggy-looking collective fields).

Ivan's wife, a big cheerful woman who has lost one eye to trachoma, is touchingly proud of her house. It has three tiny rooms, with a front parlor which looks amazingly like a miniature of a front parlor in an old-fashioned American farmhouse. There are prim wedding pictures on the walls, and hand-crocheted antimacassars, and, as befits such a successful man as Ivan, a new radio.

As he says goodby after showing his house, Ivan smiles his broadest smile, and repeats a phrase you have been hearing all over the kholkoz: "Our greetings to the simple peasants of America." Better than anything else, the phrase suggests the vast gulf which separates the Soviet and the American systems.

Yet somehow, mysteriously, messily, uneconomically, with little comfort and no private values at all, this system works. The food comes out of the ground, and unless all Russians are consummate actors and this reporter a complete fool, there are even Russians, like Comrade Lepscha and Ivan, the tractor driver, who take real pride and pleasure in this incomprehensible way of life.—July 31, 1955 (SA).

ON THE DNIEPER RIVER

For the visiting American, there is no sense of fear in this country at all. You soon learn that the knock on the door is far more likely to be the waiter than the secret police and even if you do naughty things, like taking pictures of factories and bridges, you are very politely, if firmly, disciplined.

Yet once in a while, you may feel a small shiver of fear. I felt such a shiver this morning. It was caused by a remark by a pleasant-faced, intense young man, during a talk in the lounge of this agreeable river boat on the Dnieper River.

Any one who wants a couple of days to rest and reflect can hardly do better than take this steamer which plies the Dnieper between Kiev and Dnepropetrovsk. The boat is comfortable, at least for first-class passengers. (The peasant girls sprawled among their strawberry baskets on the lower deck are perhaps not quite as comfortable.)

The boat is also a side-wheeler and there is something wonderfully peaceful and pre-atomic about traveling down a river in a side-wheeler, in Mark Twain manner. Most of the men on board wear pyjamas all day—a peculiar Russian symbol of escape from care—and the river itself is calming in its very sameness, as it flows gently past the endless, rolling, empty-seeming plains.

Even so, there were a couple of times this morning when I felt my blood pressure rising. In the tiny lounge, my interpreter and I had got into casual conversation with a nice Russian engineer, and soon there were three more Russians, and then ten, and then I found myself holding a sort of impromptu press conference.

Talking politics with Russians is an experience to try the soul of the calmest man. (My partner, known for his low boiling point, would certainly have exploded this morning into pieces small enough to feed the Dnieper's pickerel.) It is not that Russians are intentionally rude. On the contrary they are very polite, and genuinely interested. When my voice betrayed my rising blood pressure this morning, the nice young engineer pleaded anxiously with me: "Do not become angry. This is a rare experience for us and if we seem rough and uncultured it is because we are simple people."

But they are not rough or uncultured or simple. They are just infuriatingly smug. Here is a brief sampling of our conversation.

I asked who was the No. 1 man in their country these days. They all ducked this question and then a young man with very white teeth smiled and said: "And the No. 1 in your country is not Eisenhower, but Morgan or Ford, no?"

This sally was greeted with appreciative laughter. When I said that the United Auto Workers, for example, carried a good deal more political weight than the Ford company, they all chuckled in a knowing manner and winked at each other. They knew better. They always know better. Every time I said something about America which did not fit their preconceptions, they chuckled and winked at each other.

An older man, sensing my frustrated irritation, sought to introduce a mollifying note. "For your simple workers and peasants," he said, "we have nothing but comradely love. We distrust only your ruling clique that profits from war."

I replied that we also had plenty of comradely love for the Russian people but in view of the betrayal of the Yalta agreements, the blockade of Berlin and the Korean aggression, we had reason to distrust the ruling clique of Russia. "Amazing," said the older man. "Amazing, I have never heard anything like it before"—which was no doubt true enough.

But when I chose Korea for my text, I was quickly defeated. Mischa, the intense young man, cited "documents" to prove that the Korean war had been started by the "international adventurer," John Foster Dulles. "Facts," said Mischa, "are, after all, facts." And everybody nodded solemnly in agreement.

At length I tried a different tack. "In America," I said, "if there were a dozen Americans talking politics in one place, they would soon be arguing loudly with each other. Don't you ever argue with each other about anything?"

Mischa had the answer to that one too. "There is an old saying," he said, "that argument is the birthplace of truth. But we already know the truth. Therefore we have no need to argue with each other." Again, all the others nodded solemnly in agreement.

It was then that I felt my small shiver of fear. For it seems to me that this impenetrable, self-righteous blindness is far more dangerous than the caterwaulings of politicians. Indeed it is the stuff of which wars are made.

Meanwhile, it is a lovely day as the side-wheeler chugs calmly down the river and the cliff swallows fly gracefully all about. A small Russian boy peers at me stolidly as I write, as though I were a queer but interesting animal.—August 3, 1955 (SA).

No one in the West as far as we know, and certainly none of the leaders of the British or French or American governments, foresaw the real results of the famous summit meeting at Geneva. Yet by the light of hindsight, one can argue that these results ought to have been foreseen. The first contacts that led to the Soviet-Egyptian arms deal occurred in Washington in April. President Eisenhower and Secretary Dulles also went to the summit with knowledge that an arms deal had just been tentatively discussed in Cairo, by Nasser and the Soviet ambassador there.

By hindsight, in other words, it is clear that Khrushchev, the new man at the Kremlin helm, was already thinking about breaking Stalin's cautious rule, "Hands off the Middle East." From the withdrawal from Azerbaijan until the summit, this rule was always followed, no doubt because Stalin and his first heirs thought the Middle East was too close to the bone of Western vital interest, and therefore too dangerous to probe into. By hindsight, it is also clear that the summit tipped the balance, persuading Khrushchev that Middle Eastern probing would be entirely safe. The President's and Sir Anthony Eden's loud, competitive protestations of total dedication to peace-at-any-price were only too disastrously convincing. Immediately after the summit, Khrushchev sent Dmitri Shepilov to Cairo to sign the arms contract with Gamal Abdel Nasser. So Stalin's rule was broken, and so began the Middle Eastern catastrophe that is now in its last stages.

We knew nothing of all this then, although we were a bit leery about those protestations of dedication to peace-at-any-price. Yet the opposite opinion was held by men in the government whom we thought wiser than ourselves, and who have been much wiser than we have been on almost all other occasions; so we did not voice our doubts.

The following column about the summit does not represent what we think now. But the column is still interesting, as representing the view that was then held by almost all informed persons, and is still held today by some people we respect, such as Walter Lippmann.

GENEVA

The Big Four conference here has now reached its first, and very probably its only, important agreement. The agreement is unwritten and even unspoken. Yet it is implicit in everything that has been done and said since the conference began. The four powers, and above all the United States and the Soviet Union, have agreed not to have a war if they can possibly avoid it.

That is about all there is to this meeting. It is the real meaning of the mild and even cordial tone in which the spokesmen of the two sides expressed their totally irreconcilable views. It is even the real meaning of the toothy, gold-plated smiles which Soviet Communist party boss Nikita Khrushchev bestows on President Eisenhower at every possible opportunity; and of the inscribed desk set which President Eisenhower gave to his old friend Marshal Zhukov to pass on to his newly-married daughter.

At the moment, it looks as though the conferees are going to be satisfied with this tacit agreement to avoid mutual destruction, if at all possible. This report is written in mid-conference, and international conferences have a tricky habit of producing some sort of seemingly important decision at the very last moment. But it is hard to see what kind of miracle is going to produce any really significant, substantive agreement here.

During the debate on the problem of German re-unification, Prime Minister Bulganin remarked mildly that the German problem "should be decided by time." The meaning of this remark is obvious. The Soviets did not come here seriously expecting the West to accept the Soviet plan for Germany, which would require the dismantling of the Western defenses in return for vague promises. For that matter, the Western powers did not seriously expect the Soviets suddenly to accept a plan which would tie all Germany into the Western alliance.

Without an agreement, or at least the beginnings of an agreement, on Germany, there is not much use talking about European collective security arrangements, and there can be only the most tentative sort of feeling-out process on arms reduction. Perhaps some sort of progress can be made on such secondary matters as East-West contacts, the fourth item on the agenda. But that, as it looks now, is about all that can be expected.

Yet the importance of the silent, unspoken decision not to have a war if it can possibly be avoided should not be under-estimated. In the euphoria generated at first by the rather phony good-fellowship which has been the hallmark of this conference, some silly people actually began to expect peace to break out all over as a result of a few days' chat. In fact, the purpose of this conference never was to reach substantive, meaningful agreement.

The real purpose was quite different. Both sides came to this conference with the same question in the backs of their minds: "Can we somehow manage to live with these terrible people or must we really have a war with them?" The purpose of the conference was to find the answer to this question. Both sides seem already to have arrived at what is at least a tentative answer—that we can rock along for a long time without a war.

President Eisenhower has assured the Russians, in so many words, that, much as we detest their treatment of the satellites, we do not intend to go to war about it. The Russians have made it equally clear that, much as they detest the rearmament of West Germany, they do not intend to fight to prevent it.

Asia, where by far the greatest danger of war lies, has, to be sure, only been discussed obliquely, in informal conversations. But while neither side has budged an inch from its official position, there have been well-received hints from both sides that it would be better to settle such issues as Formosa without shooting.

For the short run, at least, this silent, unspoken decision to avoid war if at all possible promises a breathing spell, or rather a talking spell, for the world. But in the long run, a tacit agreement to talk rather than fight is no substitute for a real settlement. For in the long run, the pattern of the present situation, on which the tacit agreement is based, is sure to be broken. It could even be broken in a few weeks, since shrewd observers here are beginning to suspect that the Soviets are getting ready to offer German Chancellor Adenauer the kind of deal he could hardly refuse. On the other hand, the present situation could last much longer than now seems at all likely.

In the meantime, both sides are now convinced that the other side quite genuinely wants to avoid war. And, just possibly, this simple conviction may provide the time to "build the bridge" that President Eisenhower wants to build, across the chasm that divides the world. —July 22, 1955 (SA).

After the summit meeting, as already noted, the Kremlin swiftly and decisively switched its pressure-hose away from the Far East to the new task of washing out the vital Western positions in the Arab lands of the Middle East. When the Soviet-Egyptian arms agreement was announced, Secretary Dulles sent assistant Secretary of State George Allen on a plane to Cairo, with what must surely stand as the silliest mission ever given an American diplomat. Allen was in fact told to order Nasser not to carry through with his agreement, but he was given nothing to back up the order.

As might have been expected, Allen was publicly humiliated in Cairo. He came back from his trip with solemn warnings of an impending Israeli attack on Egypt—premature but not unfounded, as events later showed—and these warnings produced a war scare. The next stage in the somber drama was the Dulles offer to build the Aswan dam for Nasser. We broke that story. And after the dam offer, which the Egyptians received with marked haughtiness, Dulles set himself fruitlessly to work for an Arab-Israeli understanding, which he thought he could achieve by tossing the Arabs little bits of Israel.

Meanwhile, the French defeat in Indo-China was producing the inevitable repercussions throughout the French-held Arab lands of the North African Maghreb. The process that now centers in Algeria was in full swing, that summer, in Morocco and Tunisia. The younger member of our partnership therefore ended his overseas journey with a series of reports from Morocco. The following describes the most deeply depressing experience either of us has ever had abroad:

CASABLANCA

The story of the sack of Oued Zem has already been told—how several thousand Moroccan tribesmen descended on the small town and slaughtered fifty-one Frenchmen and many more of their fellow Arabs. But because it suggests how terrible is the hatred which tortures this country, the story may be worth telling again, as it unfolded before this reporter's eyes.

Last Saturday evening "The New York Herald Tribune's" able correspondent Barrett McGurn, who had made an expedition into the countryside, brought back reports of very bad trouble in the area of the town Oued Zem. So this reporter and a friend, Blair Clark, of the Columbia Broadcasting System, set off in a taxi shortly before dawn on Sunday for a look at Oued Zem.

Oued Zem is about ninety miles from Casablanca. McGurn had been ambushed by Moroccans on the same road the day before, and had been very lucky to escape. So at first we had a certain tendency to peer anxiously ahead. But as day broke over the low, rolling hills, such anxieties began to seem silly, and the drive was like a pleasant country excursion.

The countryside in Morocco—the Bled—looks ridiculously like a picture postcard depicting the Moroccan countryside. The camels strike appropriate poses against the skyline, and people wander about, among spidery black tents, in more or less biblical costumes. Clark remarked that it resembled a combination of the Bible, the deep South, and the far West, which it did. Then the conversation shifted to such subjects as the difficulties of foreign reporting and the frightful expense of educating children, and before we knew it we were in Oued Zem. As the Arab driver picked his way carefully through the rubble, we fell silent. There was an odd smell in the air, half sweet, half bitter. The small houses on both sides of the street were burnt-out shells, with a wisp of smoke still rising here and there.

On the left was a gas station, built on the American model, with a familiar sign Mobiloil—Mobilgas, and with the familiar red flying horse trademark. But the flying horse had been burned till the paint cracked, and through the open doorway of the burnt-out gas station four or five corpses were visible in a tangled mass.

A little further down the road, there was another corpse, curled up in a sort of ball, so badly scorched that it was impossible to tell to what race it had once belonged. We passed a company of Foreign Legion troops, and got out of the car. A middle-aged French woman with a huge bruise on her arm came trotting round the corner, carrying a squirrel rifle, and sobbing, her face contorted like a baby's.

"Oh, it was terrible," she said, although we had said nothing to her. "It was terrible to hear the children crying, I do not want to die, I do not want to die." A white-haired Frenchman came after her, carrying a shotgun, and muttering half to himself. "Oh, this day I am ashamed to be a Frenchman. That they could not give us arms and the troops to come so late. And now! Grandval, come see what you have done!"

There were a few scattered shots from somewhere, and a furious young lieutenant ordered us out of Oued Zem on pain of death. We grumbled a little, but we were not really sorry to go. We had seen what there was to be seen, and it was enough.

From a French reporter just outside of Oued Zem, and a railway worker, and a doctor, and others, we learned what had happened— how the surrounding country people had descended on the town in the morning, to burn and kill.

We learned details which scarcely bear repeating—how the Moroccans had cut the throats of all fifteen children they caught, and of the seven patients in the hospital, French and Arab alike. We learned also how they had cut off the noses and tongues of several men they captured. This sounds unlikely, but it is true.

Later, we stopped at a hospital on the way to Casablanca, to inquire after two wounded French newspaper men. One of the men of Oued Zem was there, his face all swathed in bandages, and no bump where the nose should have been.

We learned other details which do not bear repeating at all. But the above sufficiently suggest how hot and horrible the hatred of the Moroccans for the French must be. There was clearly an element of pure primitive savagery in what happened—the bellies of the rabbits which were kept in the hospital garden were slit, and the pigeons in the pigeon coop were decapitated. But primitive savagery cannot be the whole explanation. There must also be a wolfish hatred unimaginable and inexplicable to the Western mind.

At any rate, as we rode back to Casablanca through the rolling, sunny countryside, we agreed that it seemed somehow to have lost its peaceful, picture postcard look. We also agreed that what we had seen might have the most terrible consequences.

It was impossible even for an outsider to walk through the streets of ravaged Oued Zem without feeling an instinctive desire for revenge. It would be natural for the French to respond to this instinct, and it may even be inevitable. But, alas, revenge begets revenge begets revenge, in an unending cycle.—August 24, 1955 (SA).

This was our attempt to sum up the character, position and influence of the man who was much more truly President of the United States than Dwight D. Eisenhower during all of the first Eisenhower years. The reasons for publishing such a column at this particular moment will become apparent in the column that follows on its heels.

WASHINGTON

This city is going through one of its invisible but vitally significant annual proofs of who's boss. Except in periods of crisis, President Eisenhower reigns but does not rule a good deal of the time. But his true vizier, George Magoffin Humphrey, never stops ruling any of the time.

There is a simple reason why this is the season for the annual proof that the Secretary of the Treasury is immeasurably the most powerful man in the Eisenhower administration after the President himself. This is the grim season of budget-making, when the departments and agencies are struggling to decide who shall get what share of the financial pie next year.

Through the budget-making process, George Humphrey, assisted by his sub-vizier, Budget Director Rowland Hughes, exercises a predominant influence in the American government. His unseen hand, always holding the purse strings, effectively shapes American policy in fields theoretically far beyond his competence. In foreign policy-making, when the chips are down, he often plays a larger part than the Secretary of State; in defense policy-making, an infinitely larger part than the Secretary of Defense.

This year, moreover, Secretary of the Treasury Humphrey is trying to do something extra. He is not merely seeking to balance the budget for the next fiscal year that will be presented to Congress next January. He is seeking to balance the budget for the current fiscal year. His revenue estimates have been raised. If he can make the departments cut a little more here and hack a little more there, this year's outgo can be held within the probable limits of this year's income.

The sum to be saved is no more than 3 per cent of total spending, which looks trifling enough. But, as usual, the big domestic spenders like the Veterans Administration and the Agriculture Department are protected by domestic political pressures. So, as usual, the real cuts are likely to be made in this country's survival insurance.

It seems to be the rule that we must always imitate the kind of family that lets the insurance policy lapse and allows the mortgage payments to fall behind long before the payments on the television set are suspended. This being our habit, it is a fair bet that $200,000,-000 to $300,000,000 of already appropriated funds will be cut out of the foreign aid programs, although the desperate situation in the Far East demands a bold additional program there. And, by the same token, the funds that Congress provided for defense are likely to be cut back $1 billion or so; and, as usual, $9 in every $10 of this "economy" will come out of muscle rather than fat.

The first question raised by this process that is now going on behind the closed doors of the Administration is the simple question, "How does George do it?" The first part of the answer lies in the fact that in Charles E. Wilson, George Humphrey has a faithful crony who has more the outlook of an assistant Secretary of the Treasury than of a Secretary of Defense.

The second and vastly more important part of the answer lies, however, in an equation of personalities. Humphrey has become the strongest man in the Eisenhower administration for the excellent reason that he *is* the strongest man.

He is intelligent, charming and vital. He is sure-footed but determined, cautious but singularly courageous in fighting for his position once he has taken it. He does not suffer from self-doubt. And with good reason. His management of the domestic economy probably constitutes the greatest single success of the Eisenhower administration.

In the crucial fields of foreign and defense policy, moreover, the natural competition suffers from certain handicaps. President Eisenhower deeply respects the intellect of his Secretary of State, but there is a wide temperamental difference between the pessimistic John Foster Dulles and his always sanguine chief, whose good luck has encouraged him to believe one may often trust to luck. In the pre-Geneva period, for instance, the difference in temperament between the two men produced rather sharp policy differences; and on one occasion the President is known to have rebuked the Secretary for his excessive caution at a large White House meeting.

As for Defense Secretary Wilson, as noted above, he is never much inclined to oppose Treasury views, and even if he were inclined to fight, Wilson's influence with Eisenhower is not great. For Eisenhower's remaining interest in defense is wholly directed to the great theoretical and stragetic problems, whereas Wilson's whole theme and interest center on the administrative problems for which he has been equipped by experience.

No wonder, then, that Secretary Humphrey, with all his immense advantages, weighs more in the councils of the Eisenhower administration than almost all the rest of the Cabinet combined. No wonder, then, since the budget problem embraces all other problems, that Humphrey has become the predominant policy-maker.

The final question still remains, however, whether even a man who would make a great Secretary of Defense if he had to deal directly with defense problems, and should make a fine Secretary of State too, if he had to deal directly with the problems of foreign affairs, is really able to make final judgments on foreign and defense policy with no problems directly in mind except the problems of the Treasury.— September 4, 1955 (JA).

Even after the final wrong turning represented by the so-called "new look" at American defense, the Eisenhower administration continued to have twinges of conscience. The only result of these twinges was always the appointment of a high-powered committee to study the defense picture once again. The reports of these committees were always filed away in an NSC safe, without much further action, for precisely the reasons noted in the Humphrey portrait. Yet when one learned that another such report was in preparation, one always succumbed to a new twinge of hope that the administration's latest twinge of conscience might at last lead to real corrective action. Before the Gaither committee, the most important single report of this character was prepared by the Killian committee. We broke the story. As it was

a big news story, we wrote fully. The details which have now lost
their interest have been cut out of the following piece.

WASHINGTON

According to an official report that has been presented to the National Security Council, the Soviet Union is now overtaking the United
States in the air-atomic weapons race.

As of now, by this report's estimate, the frequently mentioned
"American lead" may be expected to become a Soviet lead in the
period 1960-1965. The basis of this estimate is the expectation that
in 1960-1965, the Soviets will enjoy a decided superiority in intercontinental ballistic missiles. They are the multiple-staged rockets that
will be able to carry A- or H-bomb warheads at speeds of many thousands of miles an hour through the upper air from Russian launching
sites to American targets.

The report that the National Security Council now has before it also
includes recommendations for reversing this unfavorable trend in the
Soviet-American balance of power. But these recommendations will
be difficult, if not impossible, to implement without upsetting the Administration's present budgetary and fiscal plans.

Such, it can now be revealed, are the essential results of the most
important and intensive high-level study of the relative curves of Soviet
and American armed strength that has yet been attempted. The study
was made by the Killian Committee, so called from its chairman, the
president of the Massachusetts Institute of Technology, Dr. James R.
Killian Jr.

The committee, which included both leaders of science and leaders
of industry, was set up by the National Security Council by direction
of President Eisenhower, in the troubled aftermath of the second
American H-bomb explosion at Eniwetok in the spring of 1954. . . .

The committee was given complete access to all the huge mass of
information available to the American government. It labored for
many months, twice requesting and twice receiving extensions of the
deadline that the National Security Council had originally set for its
report.

In the end, rather more than two months ago, the committee laid
before the President a unanimous report, with no significant dissents
on any point. . . .

Such is the background and history of this disturbing document.

Three main factors are known to have led the Killian committee to the somewhat bleak conclusions set forth above.

The first factor, which is almost old hat by now, was the continuous build-up of the Soviet A- and H-bomb stockpile. . . .

The second factor, which was long suspected and finally positively confirmed by the so-called Moscow overflights last spring, was the massive Soviet production of high quality long and medium range jet bombers and night and day jet fighters. . . .

Finally, the third and most important factor that influenced the Killian Report was the presumed Soviet progress in guided missile development. As has been pointed out before, the Soviet guided missile effort has been organized on a Manhattan District pattern, with a comparable priority, ever since the end of the last world war.

In America, the Eisenhower administration has stepped up outlays on missile development and very important successes have already been achieved with the shorter range missiles. Yet even today, the American guided missile effort is essentially organized on a business-as-usual basis. . . .

After reviewing all the evidence concerning present development curves, the members of the Killian committee concluded that we should expect the Soviets to enjoy an important predominance in intercontinental guided missiles from 1960 to 1965. The committee's judgment, in short, is a judgment of relative strength and not a judgment of absolute strength. But it is none the less significant for all that, as is shown by the committee's reported analysis of what may be called the phases of the Soviet-American power balance.

The first phase, which is definitely stated to be past, was the phase of unchallenged American superiority in strategic air power and atomic bombs. In this phase, the American bargaining position was greatly superior to the Soviet bargaining position in all international dealings.

The second phase, in which we now find ourselves, is a transitional phase. For the present, although the United States has long ago lost anything like unchallenged superiority, this country still has the edge in strength. Therefore this country still possesses some remaining bargaining advantage.

On the other hand, this American edge is constantly being narrowed by the improvements in the Soviet Strategic Air Force and Air Defense Command above noted. Perhaps in two years' time, the

American edge will cease to exist altogether, if the edge does not then actually pass to the Soviets. The bargaining position, therefore, is changing and will continue to change for the worse in the present phase.

As for the third phase, it is of course the final period when the Soviets will attain predominance in intercontinental guided missiles. There will be a Soviet lead comparable to the American lead that existed in the first phase of the power balance. In this phase of the Soviet lead, the international bargaining position of the United States, and indeed of the whole free world, will be markedly inferior to the bargaining position of the Soviet Union and its Communist empire.

The emphasis on the relative bargaining positions of the contestants in the world power struggle is noteworthy. If authoritative reports are to be believed, the Killian committee made no highly colored forecasts that the Kremlin would launch a general war during the predicted period of the Soviet lead. Whichever side has the lead, general war will no doubt remain a fearful risk for both sides.

What is clearly expected, rather, is bold and determined Soviet exploitation of a superior bargaining position, whose very superiority, in turn, will cause a relatively feeble and uncertain American and free world response to the Kremlin's moves.

The Killian committee, of course, had no opportunity to relate its projection of Soviet and American strength curves to the events of the summit meeting at Geneva. But a good many of the policy makers who are studying the committee's report have pointed out that if the analysis of phases is correct, it suggests a special Soviet motive at Geneva. Obviously, it is only prudent for the Soviets to promote a general relaxation of Western effort and alertness, pending the moment when the international bargaining positions will finally be changed in the Kremlin's favor.

The Killian committee's recommendations for altering the projection of Soviet and American curves of strength are not known in detail. They take the form, apparently, of proposals for revision of the first N.S.C. directive of 1955—the first N.S.C. paper of each year, according to custom, being a broad blueprint for the year's defense program.

It is quite clear, however, that implementation of the Killian committee's recommendations will necessitate a pretty sharp reversal of present fiscal and budgetary trends. A major intensification of the long-range guided missile effort, for instance, would show up primarily in the form of increases in the Air Force's Research and Development expenditures. . . . At present, instead of granting this increase, Secretary of Defense Charles E. Wilson is pressing for a decrease of $200,000,000 in these same expenditures.

Any real, all-out, Manhattan District-style effort to build intercontinental missiles would certainly require authority to let contracts well above an additional $200,000,000 in the current fiscal year. And it would equally certainly have far more volcanic effects on next year's important budget.

Then again, there is a theoretical possibility of an anti-air missile with the range and speed to intercept and destroy intercontinental ballistic missiles before they re-enter the earth's atmosphere. An all-out, Manhattan District-style effort to produce such defensive missiles must begin in a small way, of course. But from the start, such an effort will constitute a commitment to an immense double burden in the future. Both offensive and defensive long-range missiles will have to be produced in quantity, and launching sites and expensive manpower to stand ready to fire both kinds of birds will be needed too.

In short, if the projections of the Killian Report are correct, the report demands a series of distinctly painful choices. Furthermore, the time scale covered by the Killian Report's projections is very short, in terms of the slow process of weapons development and weapons production.

Hence, the choices cannot easily be delayed until next year or the year after. Putting off implementing the Killian Report's recommendations will be another way, in fact, of rejecting those recommendations. For the loss of time will mean the loss of opportunity to change the present Soviet and American strength curves.—September 19, 1955 (JA).

1956 was the last year of the euphoria, and the strongest mark of this euphoria was certainly the President's decision to run again, after the severe heart attack he had suffered in Denver the previous summer. It was hard for us to believe that the President would seek re-election to the most taxing post in the whole world, after this basic impairment of his health and strength. But he not only ignored the heart attack. Endlessly persuaded and cajoled by those around him, the President further ignored the operation for ileitis, which weakened him even more than the heart attack. The theory seemed to be that being President during the next four years would not be terribly difficult, and might even be a sort of health-cure.

In this peculiar national atmosphere, as the year began, we complained of having a "very peculiar feeling—the feeling of being suddenly transformed into one of those super-super bores who insist on reciting last night's bad dream at this morning's sunny breakfast table." The quotation is from a column pointing out rather bitterly that our alleged wails of "gloom and doom" about the tilt in the world power balance were no different from the national intelligence estimates locked up in the NSC safes. Unfortunately the sunny breakfast table was the real dream, so we went on wailing.

At this time we learned that the U.S. had actually been radar-tracking Soviet ballistic missile tests—the whole story is told elsewhere in this book. The result was the following piece. The point concerning our overseas bases is still of great interest, since the administration is currently claiming that our manned-bomber force will be a sufficient defense against the overwhelming power in intercontinental and intermediate range missiles which the Soviets are now building up. The doubts about the accuracy of Soviet missile guidance represent a lemon sold to us by men in the Air Force. We now know, and the men who sold us this lemon then knew, that our radars showed the Soviet missiles regularly falling in the same impact area—which meant accurate guidance.

A little later, it may be added, we published the alarming news that Secretary of Defense Wilson had just cut the Air Force's "minimum budget" of twenty billion dollars by nearly one-fifth, to sixteen and one-half billion.

WASHINGTON

The American government now has in its possession convincing evidence that the Soviet Union has successfully built a guided rocket with a striking range of approximately 1,500 miles.

This is the so-called intermediate range ballistic missile, or IRBM in common Pentagon jargon. Building an American IRBM is the purpose of newly authorized, highest priority weapons development programs of the United States Army and United States Air Force.

There have been earlier rumors and reports that the Soviets might probably have this weapon which the American services have just begun scrambling to get. These have come from several sources, notably

Sen. Henry Jackson, of Washington. This is the first time, however, that it has been possible to state on undoubted authority that the Pentagon has in its hands virtually conclusive evidence of the existence of a Soviet IRBM.

There is a good deal more than this, in fact. One new weapon may be the result of a brilliant accidental breakthrough. Producing a family of new weapons requires a general forward movement on all technical fronts, and the evidence indicates that the Soviets have such a family of intermediate ballistic missiles with ranges varying from 800 miles to 1500.

This in turn confirms the long-prevalent suspicion that the Soviets have achieved massive advances in the missile art. To be sure, the data are lacking to show positively whether the Soviet test missiles have yet attained satisfactory accuracy in guidance. It is not positively known, either, whether these test missiles have been capable of being fitted with a nuclear warhead.

Yet these two unknowns in the equation are not so impressive as they may seem at first glance. The problem of fitting a nuclear warhead is relatively minor, compared to the really basic problems of ballistic missile design. Even the design of efficient guidance mechanisms is no more difficult than engine design, metallurgy and all the other problems which the Soviets must certainly have solved in order to make their birds fly at all. And the birds have flown; there is no question about that.

For these reasons, it must now be assumed that the time is fairly near at hand, if indeed it has not been reached already, when the Soviets will pass from the testing phase into the vital phase of producing intermediate range ballistic missiles in militarily significant quantities. By the same token, it is also reasonable to suppose that the Soviets are well on their way to building the even more important intercontinental ballistic missile, or ICBM—the ultimate weapon which will carry nuclear warheads from continent to continent. Marshal Bulganin recently made a public boast on this point.

The Soviet IRBM tests are also rather final and decisive proof that this country has lagged far behind in missile development. Until a few months ago, the American missile program altogether neglected the intermediate ranges, which had been the subject of an interservice quarrel of classical venom and dimensions.

There were short-range, tactical missile projects, such as those which have centered at the Army's Redstone laboratory. There were also long-range projects sponsored by the Air Force—"Atlas," for an intercontinental ballistic missile; "Navajo," for an intercontinental ramjet, and the highly dubious "Snark," for a long-range pilotless aircraft.

But the projects for intermediate-range ballistic missiles only came to life some months ago. At that time the National Security Council, no doubt partly moved by the news of the Soviet IRBM, gave an overriding priority to guided missile development. Final approval of the Army's paper plans for producing an IRBM at the Redstone laboratory was granted only last week by the Pentagon's Ballistic Missile Science Advisory Committee headed by Dr. John von Neumann.

Besides the Army project, there is one more American IRBM project, controlled by the Air Force. Both these IRBM projects are going forward concurrently with a crash effort to get the earliest possible results from the intercontinental missile projects. There is even some Air Force criticism that the extremely belated attempt to get IRBMs will interfere seriously with the more important attempt to get ICBMs.

Thus the Soviets now have an intermediate range missile, which we have not got and can hardly get for a considerable time to come. In the form of this IRBM, the Soviets also have a solid leg in the race for the intercontinental missile, which we are now trying to win by a crash effort. By any reasonable test, therefore, the Soviets are importantly ahead of this country, at least for the present, in the vital field of guided missile development.

Curiously enough, however, the most important short-run effect of the Soviet success with the IRBM may well prove to be its effect on the American Strategic Air Command. Very few Americans realize that the great SAC force, which is the mainspring of American and free world strategy, is not really a long-range air force. Yet about 80 per cent of SAC's fighting aircraft are medium range B-47s.

To reach Soviet targets, the B-47s must either take off from overseas air bases or else be twice refueled in the air. SAC's tanker fleet is insufficient to provide double air-refueling for more than about onefifth of SAC's 1,500 B-47s. Hence SAC today is almost wholly dependent on its overseas air bases. And it is precisely SAC's overseas air bases that the new Soviet IRBMs will threaten most directly.

Protecting the overseas air bases against destruction by ballistic missiles is utterly impossible in the present stage of the missile art. The difference in time factors for missiles and aircraft is so enormously great that the overseas bases might be utterly destroyed by IRBMs before "massive retaliation" could even be ordered.

With the overseas bases out of commission, in turn, there is every reason to think that our "massive retaliation" would not be nearly massive enough. The SAC commander, Gen. Curtis LeMay, would then be able to mount an attack on the scale of only a little more than 600 aircraft, rather than the attack on the scale of 1,900 aircraft—which is the size of his total force.

This explains, no doubt, why Gen. LeMay asked this year to have his B-47s replaced by urgent and greatly stepped-up production of B-52s. His request was rejected for reasons of budgetary economy, but here again, the news of the Soviet IRBM would seem to change the picture.—January 13, 1956 (JA & SA).

Nine months ahead was the new dawn of hope in Poland (which is now, alas, too likely to prove a false dawn) and the hideous blood-bath in Hungary, where the Soviets "made a solitude and called it peace." Looking back over the columns we wrote about these enormous events, we are not very proud of them. What we wrote, like much else then written by others, only proved again that going there yourself is essential for a reporter; so we shall reproduce none of it. But there are times when an eccentric preference for history instead of television can be genuinely helpful. History suggested to us that one ought to be a bit suspicious of the great change in the Soviet Union that seemed to be inaugurated by Nikita Khrushchev's famous attack on Stalin at the Twentieth Party Congress. The following analysis still sheds light today.

WASHINGTON

In the Soviet Union the truth about Stalin is now being told with a vengeance, and even rather vengefully.

It is difficult to imagine a more macabre scene than the special session of the Communist Party Congress at which Nikita Khrushchev made the astonishing speech that has now leaked out. Here were the heirs of Stalin, and all the higher managers of the iron system that he formed. Here, on the platform itself, were not a few whose hands were deeply stained with the blood Stalin shed.

Here, at the speaker's stand, was the stocky, outwardly jolly little man whom Stalin personally chose to preside over the ruthless massacres that reduced the restive Ukraine to final subjection after the war. And this little man was saying the unsayable, mentioning the unmentionable, speaking about the unspeakable—pouring out all the long tale of Stalin's purges in the army and purges in the party, of Stalin's secret assassinations and encouraged suicides, of Stalin's plots and counterplots, of Stalin's sadism and megalomania.

And he was saying furthermore, that almost all of Stalin's victims, who were also the victims, remember, of the same iron system Nikita Khrushchev now directs, had after all been innocent of any crimes. And so the memories were honored of those same "criminal beasts" whom Nikita Khrushchev and every other man on the platform and in the hall had so loudly reviled, when they fell under the displeasure of the old dictator and were thus condemned to die.

If the reports of Khrushchev's speech are correct, in truth, this scene at the party congress must have reached the heights of sordid drama of those scenes in the Roman Senate, after the death of one of the tyrant emperors, for which the great Tacitus always dipped his historian's pen in acid of double strength.

The magnates of the empire, living in fear no longer, would hurry to celebrate the tyrant's passing. Days or even hours before, they had prostrated themselves before the dead man to lick the dust from his shoes, and they had hastened to obey his most sanguinary whims. But now they would draw their purple-bordered togas close about them in a brave show of righteous indignation. And one by one, they would bitterly denounce the crimes they had formerly applauded, and boldly heap blame on the dead for the crimes they had themselves committed.

Thus far back in history one must go to find an adequate parallel for the scene at the party congress. But the question remains, just what does this scene mean to us?

A simple answer is given by George F. Kennan, the student of the Soviet Union whose judgment has most often been sustained by events. It means, he says, "that a morbid monster has now been replaced by jolly gangsters." In Kennan's opinion, Stalin was one of those whom the corruption of absolute power deprived of common humanity, without, alas, depriving him of uncommon ability. His successors are products of the Stalin system, but they are not inhuman; they are embittered by all the humiliations that Stalin made them suffer; and in a sense they mean what they are saying about him.

For the people of the Soviet Union, this new tincture of humanity among their rulers no doubt promises somewhat better days. The terror is over. It is not likely to be reinaugurated either, although the instruments of terror still persist, because the great post-war rise of Soviet national income has now given the Soviet peoples a standard of living high enough so that terror is needless.

At the same time, the true priorities in the Soviet state were strongly re-emphasized at this same party congress by none other than Georgi Malenkov, whose complicity in Stalin's plots is now a source of great personal danger. As premier, Malenkov had advocated more consumer's goods to gain support for his failing power. As a beaten man in the power race, Malenkov confessed his former error. Under orders, he promulgated the still-standing rule of the Soviet Presidium, that the needs of the Russian people must be wholly subordinated to the needs of the state's heavy and military industry.

The Malenkov speech, in turn, is the real key to the riddle; it is the ugly answer to the complacency-mongers who say the Soviet Union has changed, and so the West may now disarm, and go to sleep. It shows that the new Soviet rulers have abandoned Stalin's ways, but they have not altered Stalin's priorities or forgotten his goals.

Of course the Soviet Union has changed. So did Rome change when Claudius replaced the mad Caligula, and Vespasian won Nero's purple. The good emperors were certainly better than the bad emperors. But alas they were not better for Rome's neighbors. A considerable part of the "Meditations" of Marcus Aurelius was written in the field, in a general's tent by night, in the camps of the legions. And the Romanians of our own day owe the language they still speak to the philosopher-emperor's career as a stern conqueror. Khrushchev is no philosopher-ruler, but once again the parallel fits.—March 19, 1956 (JA & SA).

What may be called the ante-penultimate stage of the Middle Eastern catastrophe was reached when King Hussein of Jordan abruptly dismissed the old British soldier, General Sir John Bagot Glubb, who had organized and long commanded Jordan's Arab Legion. This aroused London to the extreme insecurity of the surviving neo-imperial positions that guarded Britain's oil sources. In January, the new British Prime Minister, Sir Anthony Eden, flew to Washington to try to hammer out a common Middle Eastern policy with the President, but he got exactly nowhere.

Accordingly, the older member of our partnership left for a long Middle Eastern journey, with a first stop in London. Thence he wrote:

"A bright spring sun has shone on London all this past week, bringing out the young green in the parks and squares, and gilding the whole beautiful, luxurious London scene with an extra sheen of gaiety and hope. But beneath the smiling surface, at least in the small circle of those who know the inwardness of Britain's world position, Middle Eastern developments are causing gloom so deep that it all but approaches despair.

" 'It feels now like 1936 or even 1937.' Again: 'This is the worst moment in the last ten years; I've not felt like this since just before Munich.' And once again: 'Finding a way out in the Middle East is so urgent that it may not be just a matter of days, but even a matter of hours.'

"Those are not the remarks of shallow and hysterical men. They are statements that have been made to this reporter in the past few days by responsible and experienced leaders of the British government— brave men who have played great parts and have not flinched or quailed through all the perils Britain has experienced since the rise of Adolf Hitler.

"The third of the foregoing quotations, moreover, is a paraphrase of the summation in a personal message sent by Prime Minister Sir Anthony Eden to President Eisenhower some days ago through an American official with whom the Prime Minister discussed the present Middle Eastern situation."

The revelation of this despairing message from Eden to Eisenhower caused a considerable flap. What made the flap worse was the simple fact that the President had never seen the message—a fact which the younger member of our partnership brought out after the President was asked about the Eden message at his press conference. Our affairs had reached the stage where the President was "spared the bother" of being shown a personal communication from the Prime Minister of Britain. In that election year, in any case, no amount of personal messages could have stirred the administration into controversial action. From London, therefore, the reporter summed up as follows:

"In brief, this country, the second partner in the Atlantic Alliance, is utterly dependent on Middle Eastern oil. Once deprived of the oil from the Middle East, Britain will be irremediably bankrupt. Being bankrupt, Britain will perforce lay down the heavy burden of Western defense in NATO and elsewhere. And in these circumstances, Britain

may perhaps take the kind of political turning that now seems unthinkable.

"The surge of Arab nationalism is . . . immediately directed . . .
against what remains of the old British imperial position in the Middle
East. London's first reaction has been to try to prop up the old familiar
order by any means available and at all costs. . . . The policy towards which London is tending means, in effect, fighting Arab nationalism all-out and without quarter, with the Soviet Union on the
other side.

"Even from this angle of vision, the policy of trying to crush the
new Arab nationalism does not look practical. There are alternative
policies, all of them variants of the main theme of trying to come to
terms with Arab nationalism. But these alternatives are not practical
either, unless the United States boldly and constructively takes the
leadership. Above all Washington must promise in plain terms to
reinsure London against the risks that may be involved in a new way
of doing business in the Middle East.

"Washingon is plainly trying to dodge this alarming responsibility,
taking refuge in empty optimism and bland generality. . . . The drift
in Washington is extremely likely to cause the British to drift, in their
turn, into the policy that already tempts them.

"(Yet) the British have nowhere near the resources now needed to
carry through such a policy successfully. Britain is just as important
to the United States, in a strategic sense, as Middle Eastern oil is to
Britain in an economic sense. And if the British go in over their
depth, we shall have the unpleasant choice between going in ourselves
to bail Britain out, or letting Britain founder, and so permitting the
Atlantic Alliance to founder."

Thus Suez could then be seen, looming ahead, in London in early
April. In Cairo, the reporter twice saw Nasser, and found him "not an
easy man to read." But as he travelled onwards through the Arab
lands, he came to realize that vicious anti-Westernism was Nasser's
chief political stock in trade. It had to be, for Nasser feared going
too far on the anti-Israeli line, for the very practical reasons that the
Israeli army showed were sound in the Sinai desert later on.

Even in Cairo, however, the reporter could discern the main design of Soviet Middle Eastern policy, as follows:

"Toward the Arab nationalists, in fact, the masters of the Kremlin
are now using the phrases of an old-fashioned European hotel con-

cierge—'At your service, gentlemen, you have only to command, it will be done.'

"Altogether, it will be just as idiotic for the Washington and London policy makers to ignore the present Soviet diplomatic and propaganda offensive in this area as it was idiotic for them to ignore the many advance warnings that the Soviets were about to sell arms to Egypt. Above all it must be understood that the Soviets enjoy great advantages here in the Middle East.

"In their dealings with the excitable Arab nationalists, the Soviets do not have to make the bothersome conditions that the West must make. They do not have to say 'we cannot allow you to attack Israel.' They do not have to say, 'leave the oil alone, it is our lifeblood'; they can say instead, 'take the oil, it has been stolen from you.' And with all this they can play the anti-colonial trumpet in a way that sounds extremely convincing to Arab ears.

"The real Soviet aim, of course, is to use Arab nationalism as a weapon to cut the oil jugular of Western Europe. Thus Britain is to be bankrupt, NATO is to be brought down in ruin, and the Western alliance is to be crippled or destroyed."

That summary of Soviet Middle Eastern tactics and purposes is as valid today as it was when written, in April, 1956. At this time, however, Gamal Abdel Nasser's powerful propaganda apparatus and costly, wideflung net of agents, conspirators and hired assassins were not being paid for by the Kremlin. That began later, post-Suez, when the United States persuaded King Saud of Saudi Arabia to cease financing Nasser and break with him.

The following piece is a portrait of King Saud at the period when he was Nasser's chief ally and source of funds. In another column from Saudi Arabia, the reporter noted that "this ancient tribal society . . . in full decay" because of the inflow of oil money, was too weak to withstand an all-out, propaganda-and-conspiracy attack from Cairo. That proved true this year. But in the spring of 1956, the surface of Saud's air-conditioned Oriental despotism was very prosperous, and sufficiently bizarre to be worth commemorating. The column is also interesting because it hints at the King's mood, which caused his later turn against Nasser. On the same evening, the reporter was also received by the Crown Prince, Faisal, and found him viciously anti-Western and strongly pro-Nasser. Faisal has now played a leading role in his brother's defeat by the Egyptian dictator.

JEDDAH, SAUDI ARABIA

The cloister of King Saud's new palace at Jeddah, where his guests assemble for state dinners, is about 100 yards long by 80 wide—a gigantic rendering of an Alhambra courtyard by the latest French-trained Cairo architect, with a swimming pool complete with copper exit ladder where, in the Alhambra, you would find a small, lightly splashing fountain. Yet the swimming pool beautifully reflects the star-studded brilliance of the night sky above.

The Arab dignitaries—no lean men of the desert these—are plump, prosperous and dignified in their flowing robes and corded head dresses. Wisely, they sit quietly, gossiping with their next-door neighbors, in long rows of chairs. But in their nervous way, the foreigners, the diplomats, mill about exchanging greetings in a rapid fire of "excellences."

Instead of cocktails, glasses of orange pop are offered with paper napkins, which blow about in the night wind off the desert and send the white-robed servants on an anxious chase. Suddenly, through the long windows that open on the vast Arabo-Louis XIV reception room, some one glimpses the procession of the Negro guards. The King inherited them from his father, the great Ibn Saud. So the guards are rather fat and elderly and unintimidating now, despite the gilded scimitars they wear beneath their black and gold embroidered jackets.

The guests spring to attention and watch the rest of the procession through the windows—a troop of the Saudi Arabian Army M.P.s in helmets brightly painted in the American style to strike a modern note; then a large troop of soldiers from the Yemen, scrawny little men, turbanned, tunicked, exotically scarved and heavily be-scimitared, but wearing cheap Czechoslovakian shoes; and then a troop of Saudi princes led by the tall, impressive heir to the throne, Faisal, prince of the Hejaz.

Finally comes the King himself, tall like his brother Faisal and with a superb natural dignity. The short, stout, little Imam Ahmed of Yemen, the evening's guest of honor, trots alongside with his hand in King Saud's reassuring hand.

The poor Imam needs reassurance, for he is old and ill and this is his first trip beyond the borders of the least known country in the modern world. Besides the politics of Yemen have been sadly troubled and intermittently sanguinary since the death of the Imam Yaya. It is even rumored that the Imam Ahmed has had to bring his crown prince along to insure against trouble in his absence; and the young crown prince is certainly frowning rather somberly, as though at a missed opportunity.

But these are dark thoughts, inappropriate to the occasion. The guests file, bowing, past the benevolently smiling King and the little Imam who waggles his big, richly turbanned head like a teetotum in a sort of passion of politeness. Then comes the second march, into the enormous state dining room where the tables could accommodate the 400 guests at least twice over.

Once again soda pop replaces wine, so the conversation is perhaps even more pallid than is usual on such occasions. One of the foreigners whispers that "this is the house Aramco built," and it is indisputable that oil money paid for the new palace. Another says, a little peevishly, that he has learned to be "pro-American in everything, even pop, but why does the King have to have an American chef"; and again it is true that King Saud's foreign cook, who has come out to survey the feast, looks suspiciously like a mess sergeant of the old U.S. Army.

Course succeeds course. A military band plays Arabic music, high and haunting in a curtained alcove. A court bard, descended straight from the poetic line that sang before Agamemnon at Mycenae and in Harald Fairhair's hall in Norway, recites a long poem in praise of the King and Imam into a deafening loudspeaker system. And then the dinner is over; the servants perfume the guests with the smoke of burning sandalwood; and the King strides off to his private room, eagerly followed by half a dozen of his youngest sons, bright-eyed, irrepressible children in white garments and gold skull caps, who chatter delightedly among themselves.

In King Saud's anteroom there is the inner circle of the court—the master of ceremonies who controls access to his majesty; the tall, coal-dark, brilliantly intelligent Finance Minister, grandson of a slave, briskly giving orders into a telephone; and one of the King's three refugee advisors, Jamal Bey Husseini, nephew of the Grand Mufti of Jerusalem, who distills venom against Palestine's invaders and all the West in a beautifully educated English voice.

There is no smoking in the King's palace—there has been no smoking for more than three hours—so the foreign visitor is a little nervous for want of a cigarette when the call comes to the audience. But King Saud is graciously welcoming, and so the audience begins.

As is customary on these occasions, nothing very startling is said, the King shows a generous forbearance toward the British over the Buraimi dispute, which arouses violent feelings here. One remembers that this meeting with the Imam and Egypt's Col. Nasser is likely to mean bad future trouble for the British in their Aden protectorate. Yet the King's words of friendship for America are obviously sincere.

The conversation does not make one quite forget the scene itself— the King, somehow a grand figure, sitting impassive at his desk and gently smiling when he is not speaking, and then, between the King and his visitor, the young interpreter, last seen in Washington in a fairly sensational convertible, but now a figure out of the Arabian Nights as he kneels on the floor by his master's chair, translating his master's words with downcast eyes.

Then, as the talk continues, one gets a sense of the King's character and of his predicament, a sense of a good man, born into old ways, attached to all that is customary and familiar, yet required by fate to carry his country through the baffling transition from the past into the present. But the little princes are already hammering at the door, for their after-dinner hour with their father. No more can be ventured except a compliment on the discovery of plentiful fresh water at the King's second capital of Riyadh, which causes the King's whole face to light up as he remarks that this was better news than the new oil field Aramco told him about the other day.

And so the audience ends, with the interpreter kneeling again to kiss the King's hand, and the little princes pouring into the room in a desperate hurry to be first at the King's knee. Somehow, although social notes do not generally appear in this space, the contrasts of the evening seemed to tell a great deal about this remarkably interesting and increasingly critical country.—April 27, 1956 (JA).

As these words are written, the British and American governments are arguing about whether Britain should try to save something from the Middle Eastern wreck by taking the steps indicated in the following column. The outcome of the argument is not yet clear.

KUWAIT, PERSIAN GULF

Here in Kuwait, the West's extreme vulnerability to the new Soviet flank attack in the Middle East is brought home with extreme vividness.

This tiny desert Sheikdom at the head of the Persian Gulf is now little more than a vast oil well with a small town on top of it. Kuwait's oil output now substantially exceeds the combined output of Iran and Iraq. The famous "sweet crude" of the Kuwait wells now provides two-thirds of the oil fuel of the British Isles.

The 50 per cent of profits paid to the Sheik of Kuwait by the half British, half American Kuwait Oil Company currently amounts to about $260,000,000 a year, or rather more than $1,000 a year per head of the whole population of the Sheikdom. And the people here are getting good pay, too, from the oil company and on all the construction and other projects that have been started by the influx of oil money.

In these circumstances, it is hardly surprising that Kuwait is a boom town. By Saudi Arabian standards, the ruling clan of Kuwait, the house of al-Subah, is distinctly restrained, yet the desert is dotted with their palaces, which they like to illuminate by night in a way that puts Broadway to shame. With a lavish hand, the Sheik is also building schools, hospitals, new roads, water distillation plants and great numbers of houses for his people.

Even after all these expenditures, so much is left over that the British government thought it worth while to send the British Ambassador in Washington, Sir Roger Makins, on a special mission here when he was one of the top officials in the Foreign Office. Sir Roger's task was to persuade the Sheik of Kuwait to invest his reserve funds in London. The Sheik complied. Today his money is probably the biggest single sum of new capital annually available for investment in the sterling area.

In these circumstances, it is not surprising that the British regard the Persian Gulf Sheikdoms, and especially Kuwait, as their hole card.

The entire population of the three oil-producing Sheikdoms, Kuwait, Bahrein and Qatar, hardly amounts to more than 400,000 persons. But even if all the other Western positions in the Middle East crumble in the end under the pressure of the new Arab nationalism, spurred on and supported by the Soviets, the oil wells of these little Sheikdoms can be made to meet Britain's and Western Europe's requirement for fuel-lifeblood for a long time to come.

If these grim circumstances ever arise, Britain will have to choose between holding the Sheikdoms and surviving and risking the loss of the Sheikdoms and ending her career as a serious world power. The choice has already been made in London. The Sheikdoms will be held, by naked force if necessary. The ugly war in Cyprus is being fought to make sure of a transit base for troops bound to this region. The question is whether this British strategy of the hole card will really work. Certainly it will be difficult to execute. To be sure, there is little of the popular unrest in Kuwait that is creating such a problem in Bahrein. The house of al-Subah really rules its Sheikdom, and with an iron hand. Most Kuwaitis are contented by the new prosperity, and for any who are known to be subversive there is harsh and summary punishment.

But even the house of al-Subah will be anything but pleased by military occupation, if this becomes necessary to protect the Kuwait oil source from the drive of nationalism in the rest of the Arab world. The trouble in Bahrein, in this event, would of course be even worse. Furthermore, if the Arab nationalist drive finally forces Britain to play her hole card, one can foresee all sorts of other very grave troubles, perhaps on the borders here, certainly at Suez, and quite probably at Aden.

The Soviet object in the Middle East is simply to use Arab nationalism to bring down the Western Alliance, by encouraging the Arab states to deny to the West the vital oil on which Britain and Western Europe so absolutely depend. Since this is quite certainly the Soviet purpose, it is a little difficult to see what good results can be expected by trying to negotiate a Middle Eastern settlement with the Soviets. This increasingly popular expedient will be like sitting down with your own murderer to argue about whether he will stab you in the heart or only cut your jugular vein.

By the same token, however, the present British plan for dealing with the Middle Eastern danger if worst comes to worst does not look very practical or very attractive when one examines it on the spot, here in the gulf-coast Sheikdoms where the last-ditch defense is to center.

The problem in the Middle East, therefore, is not just to prevent a new outbreak of Arab-Israeli fighting. The problem is to find a firm, united, imaginative and generous Anglo-American policy toward Arab nationalism which will frustrate the Soviet strategy and protect the oil source without recourse to desperate measures.—May 11, 1956 (JA).

The following column foresees and explains the tragedy in Iraq that has produced the Middle Eastern catastrophe.

BAGHDAD

When this reporter called on the famous Nuri Pasha, the strong man and perennial Prime Minister of Iraq, it was rather alarmingly like disturbing an owl in the daylight hours. Forty-odd years have passed since this remarkable man became one of the founders of the Arab independence movement as a young officer in the Turkish Imperial Army. He has lived hard through all the subsequent decades. He is sixty-seven. That morning, moreover, his blood pressure was troubling him. He was waiting impatiently for his doctor. And meanwhile he sat huddled in his dressing gown, his piercing eyes hooded as though against the light, and really looking remarkably owlish.

One sensed at once, too, that Nuri Pasha was quite justifiably embittered by the fantastic choppings and changings of American policy towards the Baghdad Pact, on which he has gambled Iraq's future. Hence he was cynical about the usefulness of any message he might address to the United States. So he came to life only once, when he was asked about the venomous propaganda aimed at him and his government by Egypt's Gamal Abdel Nasser, who is Nuri's presently successful rival for leadership of the Arab world.

Then the deep eyes flashed, and Nuri Pasha declared firmly that he had been risking his life for the cause of Arab independence before Gamal Abdel Nasser was out of swaddling clothes. For the rest: no, he was not troubled by the weakening link between Iraq and Jordan; no, he was not disturbed by Syria's closeness to Egypt; no, he was not disturbed either because Iraq was the only Arab state in the Baghdad Pact.

In a way, the situation here in Iraq rather resembles this curious meeting, so reassuring on the surface, yet not without its disquieting side if you think about it a little. On the surface all is well in Iraq. Nuri Pasha's government is strong, and Communist and Egyptian agitators are sternly controlled by an efficient police. The magnificently conceived Iraqi development program is already bringing a bustling new prosperity. Later, it should make Iraq the economic showplace of the Arab world.

Even today, moreover, the dictatorship here is far less severe than in Egypt. From the social welfare standpoint, this is Utopia compared to Egypt's strange ally, Saudi Arabia, whose oil dollars finance Egypt's policy. Outwardly, therefore, it seems perfectly reasonable to hope that pro-Western Iraq will serve as an example and a magnet, to attract the other Arab states towards a policy less hostile to the West.

This theory of Iraq's magnetism is important, because it is held in many quarters in Washington and is the declared basis of British Middle Eastern policy. But as of today, the theory is not working out in practice. Iraq's isolation from the rest of the Arab world is in truth increasing, at this moment, with every passing week.

Furthermore, the failure of the theory is having serious effects within Iraq. Nuri Pasha may tell a casual interviewer that he does not mind being isolated from his Arab brothers, so long as he is doing the right thing. But in fact he told the British government that it was absolutely essential for his government to have at least one other Arab state in the Baghdad Pact. The British attempt to meet this plea from Nuri in turn led to the disastrous mission to Jordan of Gen. Sir Gerald Templer, which ended by making matters a great deal worse.

The truth is that all the nationalist emotions that have gripped the rest of the Arab world are powerfully surging beneath the surface here in Iraq. The impulse towards Arab unity is only one of these emotions, but it is particularly strong here because so many Iraqis blame the Western-sponsored Baghdad Pact for Iraq's isolation. The truth is, further, that in these nations which are making the enormous transition from an ancient form to a modern form of society the normal tests of reason and self-interest often do not work very well in shaping events. Pure emotion is often more decisive.

In this circumstance, if present trends continue, one can predict rather positively that the theory of Iraq's magnetism will never become valid. If present trends continue, in truth, one can predict eventual bad internal trouble here in Iraq—and if Iraq abandons her present pro-Western orientation, nothing but naked force will cure the situation in the Middle East.

The point is, however, that present trends do not need to continue unless the American government is permanently wedded to its present line of blandly hoping for the best and blindly refusing to prepare for the worst. In the Middle East as in the Far East, strength is respected and nothing succeeds like success. What is needed to reverse present trends is simply a firm, clear and united Anglo-American policy, better adjusted to Middle Eastern realities than the present British policy, and immeasurably more positive and determined than the curious mixture of aimless drift and adman's slogans that now passes for a Middle Eastern policy in Washington.—March 21, 1956 (JA).

The fascination—and the horror—of the Middle Eastern journey built up a considerable head of emotion in the reporter. The climax came with a visit to one of the horrifying Arab refugee camps. The bitterest pieces each of us has ever written concerned these camps. If you see them once, you can never forget your indignation against the Israelis for their callousness about the refugee problem; against the Arab leaders, who have made political capital of the refugees' misery; against the Western nations and the UN, because the provision for the refugees is so pitifully inadequate; and against the very world we live in, for producing such horrors. No one even remotely involved in this matter has come out well except Henry Labouisse, the American UN administrator of the camps, who did marvels with the miserable resources made available to him. But all informed persons should know by now of the horrors of the refugee camps. Very few people know about the other, almost equally unfortunate Palestinian Arabs, who are not refugees because they still have their homes, but are destitute because their fields have been taken from them. They get no UN dole. They sit all day, longing for the land that is across the closely guarded Arab-Israeli truce-line. And they are near to starvation. The following column concerns their plight:

EMMAUS, JORDAN

The little village of Emaos, or Emmaus in the more familiar spelling of the Bible, is no more than a cluster of mud-built Arab houses nestling among sparse olive groves on the crown of a rocky hill.

Just down the sunlit slope there is the immemorial village threshing floor, bright now with the golden harvest. A swarm of tragically thin children are cheering the work on. Two old men guide the scrawny ox and bony donkey which are trampling the wheat stalks in the ancient way. And half a dozen women are briskly sifting the grain from the chaff in big basket-work sieves.

The ribbon of road winds up from the vale of Ajalon, past the threshing floor. It is the road we have been brought to inspect by Brother James Nolan, an aged, merry, lavishly bearded English Cockney monk who lives in the abandoned convent of Emmaus and works for the Trappist Fathers in their great nearby monastery of Notre Dame de Latroun. Brother James overflows with little jokes—

for instance, he says his Trappist friends drink only "baptized wine," by which he means wine heavily diluted with water. But now his eyes' customary twinkle has been replaced by a different light.

Partly it is the light of combat. It angers Brother James that Biblical commentators are not sure that his Emmaus is the real Emmaus of the Bible. As for Brother James, he has no doubt about it. Pointing to the road, with the tears of simple faith suddenly welling forth, he tells us solemnly, "There is the road where our blessed Lord, crucified for our sins, risen again from the dark tomb, met the disciples on Resurrection Morn."

Moreover, even if Brother James cannot quite prove his identification of Emmaus, this is a place that has known more history than most. Here, we are told the moon stood still, for did not Joshua give the command, "Sun stand thou still upon Gibeon, and thou, moon, in the valley of Ajalon"? Here too the mighty Judas Maccabeus fought one of the first and bitterest battles in the Jews' long war of independence against the Seleucid heirs of Alexander the Great.

Here came the Romans when the Maccabees weakened—in the Trappist Fathers' garden, in the walks deeply shaded by clipped orange trees, white marble fragments of a Roman temple show palely in the cool gloom. Here too came the wild desert-riders of the Caliph Omar, second successor to the Prophet, who started the transformation of the Aramaic Christian peasantry into the Muslim Arabs that they still are.

Here came also the Crusaders—Richard the Lion Hearted once took his Christmas dinner in the grim keep of the Knights Templar on the high crag of Latroun. Then Saladin drove the Templars from their castle, and after that there were the Turks, and after that the British, and finally the Jews returned again. And here the Arab Legion, dug in among the ruins of the Templars' castle, held the Israeli advance down the Emmaus road in a long and bloody fight.

But skirt the barbed wire that marks the beginning of no man's land between Jordan and Israel. Go to the fine gate of the handsome Trappist monastery, where it looks out across its vineyards to the untilled fields of the wide neutral zone in the valley. See the heirs of all this history, the many scores of half starved poor people of Emmaus who come to share in the monastery's daily distribution of soup and bread. Then you think men can have too much of history.

Seek out the Trappists' tall, slender, wise-eyed Father Abbot, who was a Belgian parachutist in the war against Adolf Hitler. He tells of the fighting at Latroun between Arabs and Israelis. He explains that under the armistice agreement, all the rich valley lands in the neutral zone are forbidden to be tilled. He describes how the people of Emmaus tried to work their forbidden fields back in 1953; how they managed well enough until the harvest; and how they were caught in the fields at harvest time by the Israeli border guards. "Three were killed among the grain," he says drily. "They had broken the armistice agreement." Once again you think that it is better for poor people to keep out of history's path.

Or go again among the dusty melancholy streets of Emmaus, to the once prosperous, now shabby house of the Mukhtar who leads the village. Tonelessly, as though telling a story already told too often, this shrewd old farmer describes what has happened to his people. They held no less than 7,500 acres of land "in the times before the war when we were rich." Now, "those people over there"—the Mukhtar means the Israelis—hold 4,000 acres of the lands of Emmaus. Another 3,000 acres lie in the neutralized zone, "where we learned our lesson three years ago." And all the lands that Emmaus can till are now the few patches among the rocks on the hill where the village stands.

"We are 2,000 people, we of Emmaus," said the Mukhtar. "With our lands we lived well. Now we beg from the monastery. Our men go to other places to earn support for their families, but they know only the farmer's trade so they earn little. We are not refugees so your United Nations gives us no relief. Many among us starve. Where can we turn, and what have we done to deserve this?"

At the last question, the old man's voice grows harsh and he looks out across the valley, gesturing toward the Israeli side. "Ah, it is bitter to see our good acres that have been taken from us"—and here there is another gesture down toward the untilled valley—"but it is almost worse to see those fields grown up in weeds, used by no man in no man's land when even this part of our lands might keep Emmaus from hunger." Then indeed you wish to cry out in warning to all simple people everywhere, to flee those places where history may tread with heavy foot.—June 8, 1956 (JA).

The Middle Eastern journey ended in Israel, the most physically uncomfortable modern nation in the world, but the best for what one can only describe as moral sight-seeing. The following column is still important, because the spirit it describes, whose power was to be proven in the Sinai desert, is still undimmed and undiminished; and this spirit of Israel is a factor in the Middle Eastern situation that no one should ever forget, even today when Gamal Abdel Nasser's final triumph seems so near.

JERUSALEM

The face is strong featured and almost square, bright crimson from hard work under the Negev sun, and oddly framed by two high-standing wings of silver hair. The massive head is far too big for the short, sturdy body. The arms are also very short and muscular and they are often waved like flippers to emphasize a point.

From these details of the outward appearance of David Ben-Gurion, you might suppose that the Prime Minister of Israel cuts a ridiculous figure. But you would be wrong. Even although he so strongly resembles a large, elderly baby, Sir Winston Churchill somehow conveys an overwhelming impression of personal grandeur. And this mysterious trait of the old Englishman who saved his nation is rather conspicuously shared by the old Jew who made his nation.

As Ben-Gurion talks, now philosophically, now with harsh practicality, now with nostalgic recollection of his past struggles, you keep thinking of Israel's judges (particularly the more belligerent judges) and Israel's prophets (particularly the tougher sort of prophets) in the old Bible times.

Ben-Gurion, the sharp, sometimes unscrupulous politician, is there too. So is Ben-Gurion, the leader of such ruthless single-mindedness that he was wholly ready to sacrifice the simple Arab peasantry of Palestine in order to create the Israeli state. But Nehemiah, for example, was also something of a politician. And Nehemiah was certainly fierce enough toward the "Arabians and the Ammonites and the Ashdodites" when they tried to stop him rebuilding the walls of Jerusalem after the Babylonian captivity.

In these days, the Old Testament is hardly news. Yet every Western policymaker and every Arab leader ought to study it prayerfully, for there is no other way to understand the spirit of David Ben-Gurion, which is also in large measure the spirit of his people. That spirit is a cardinal political fact in the Middle East; and if you do not take it as a fact, you are bound to make the wildest misjudgments and nourish the most idiotic false hopes.

It explains, in the first place, why Ben-Gurion and most of the other Israeli leaders are not at all averse to living in a state of siege almost indefinitely. The Arab boycott of Israeli trade, the ever present tension on the borders, the constant menace of attack, would cause most Western statesmen to suffer a nervous collapse within a month. But Ben-Gurion plainly finds danger invigorating, and considers that a state of siege has positive advantages.

"We have gathered in our tribes from all over the earth," he says. "From them we must make our nation. Those who never held a plough must learn to till the soil. Those who were always humble must learn to be proud. It does not hurt for all our people to know that now they must rely on themselves and only on themselves. So the new nation comes to birth. We want peace, but not at any price. And if we cannot get real peace for ten years or twenty years, why we can stand it, and there will be some blessing in it, too."

It seems a fantastic statement, in this self indulgent age. It is made with a slight smile, a quick shrug, and the flipper-gesture. But every word of it is plainly meant in deadly earnest. Ben-Gurion is just as serious too, although again he smiles, when he describes how the British Prime Minister tried to persuade him to seek peace, some months ago, by offering important territorial concessions to the Arabs.

"I told Sir Anthony Eden's representative," he says with a happy grin, "that if he really wanted to take this land from Israel, he had better mobilize the British Army."

The spirit that breathes through these remarks is the same spirit that animates Ben-Gurion's approach to two problems of the most vivid current interest. One is the problem of border incidents, which was supposed to have been settled, only a few weeks ago, by U.N. Secretary General Dag Hammarskjold. If anyone imagines Israeli policy has been changed by the Hammarskjold mission, he is altogether wrong.

Since the victory over the Arabs in 1948, Israel has always been troubled, and is being troubled today, by constant pinpricks along her borders. With or without the toleration of the Arab governments, border crossers steal the harvest here, make off with the irrigating pipe or animals or other valuables there, or open fire on an exposed road or even commit a murder somewhere else. The Israeli policy always has been to wait just so long, and then to order one of those major retaliatory operations which have caused so many flare-ups of tension in the last eight years. That is still the Israeli policy.

Ben-Gurion argues that if all the little border incidents went unpunished, their numbers would increase and they would grow progressively more serious "until our people would have no security." Therefore, he declares grimly, "Israel cannot tolerate these terrorist acts."

By the same token, although the Syrian government has publicly stated that the project would be a *casus belli,* Ben-Gurion also declared grimly that Israel must proceed this year with the Jordan water diversion scheme. Water is Israel's lifeblood. The proper sharing of the Jordan waters has already been planned. Israel will "explore all avenues to avoid a quarrel." But, says Ben-Gurion, "if the Arabs decide to start a fight over this problem, let them do so; if we cannot get peaceful agreement, we shall go to work and damn the consequences."

What then, you ask the old man, if the consequence to Israel is a war between this tiny nation and all the millions of Arabs? And to this he answers that he will never make a preventive war "because even a bad peace is better than victory in war"; but he will not be frightened or blackmailed, either, by his neighbors' power and his neighbors' threats.

"Time," he remarks, "is supposed to be on our enemies' side. But in these last eight years, we have doubled in material strength and we have much more than doubled in moral strength, which is the most important strength of all. With all their MiG 15s, I do not think that Arab strength has doubled. You say I am not logical. I answer that only fools look for logic in history. And I tell you, whatever power they may bring against us, Israel will not falter or submit."

On this note ended both the long conversations that I had with this remarkable man. And both times, as I went out of his simple office, I found myself recalling the passage in which Nehemiah describes how he refortified Jerusalem—a passage often proudly quoted in Israel today.

"(In) that time," says the prophet, "half of my servants wrought in the work, and the other half of them held both the spears, the shields and the bows, and the habergeons. . . . They which builded on the wall, and they that bare burdens, and those that laded, every one with one of his hands wrought in the work, and with the other held a weapon. For the builders, every one had his sword girded by his side, and so builded."—June 13, 1956 (JA).

Just before the political conventions, John Foster Dulles precipitated the Suez crisis by withdrawing the Aswan dam offer at the precise moment when the Egyptians were getting ready to accept it. His aim was to appease the Senate's Republican right-wingers, and although the attempt to purchase Nasser's goodwill with the big dam was always dubious, Dulles might at least have avoided public rudeness when he abandoned the attempt. We described the episode at the time as "one of the strangest exercises in diplomacy since Secretary of State Dulles took office, which is saying a good deal." A couple of weeks later we wrote that "the further you look into the constantly developing Middle Eastern crisis, the more likely it seems that there may be shooting in the Middle East this summer," with the British, French and/or Israelis named as the ones who were likely to start the shooting.

In these circumstances, it was not easy to concentrate on one of the dullest and most unreal Presidential campaigns the American people have ever been exposed to. The preliminaries had their comic aspects—Harold Stassen's boobish "dump-Nixon" movement was the funniest. Because of Harry Truman's intervention in support of W. Averell Harriman's Presidential candidacy, the Democratic convention was not absolutely devoid of drama, either. But even the charm of San Francisco could not make the cut and dried rituals of the Republican convention either interesting or enjoyable. The only politically interesting feature of the situation, in fact, was an empty space where the issues ought to have been. Concerning this empty space, we had the following to say in a post-San Francisco column:

"Many people have pointed out that their long experience of opposition left the Republicans, particularly the Congressional Republicans, sadly unprepared to act as a party in power, but it is also true that this long experience of power and responsibility left the Democrats sadly unprepared to act as an opposition.

"Specifically, they forgot that political issues do not lead an independent, God-given existence of their own. They did not realize, any longer, that issues have to be made, and made in particular by the opposition. And they neglected to make several of the most important issues, for which there was ample raw material lying about, because the task of making issues is almost always unpleasant and controversial at the outset.

"The classic example in our own time was Winston Churchill's handling of the issue presented by the rising menace of Nazi power. Churchill had to undergo years of ostracism and abuse because he insisted on the vital importance of that issue. But in the end, because he stood the racket when the going was rough, he was the sole, inevitable Prime Minister in England's darkest hour.

"The Democrats did not have to be Churchills to make very great and stirring issues in the areas of defense and foreign policy, for instance. They only had to have some knowledge of the problems, to show some guts in discussing them and to hammer away until the country turned its attention to the problems. But they did not do any of this because it would have been initially uncomfortable.

"And so today, while Adlai Stevenson frankly regards the defense and foreign issues as far and away the most important of all, he has said with rueful frankness that he does not think "there is much mileage in them." And Stevenson is right, no doubt, because issues cannot be made at the last minute either."

The campaign was as dull as the conventions, but it was the first in which we experimented with the solution, invented by the younger member of our partnership, of the always trying problem of election coverage—the system of imitating and sometimes going along with the professional pollsters. This system does not predict election results with any certainty. (We do not think the nationwide polls are really reliable either.) But at least when the reporter comes in from his doorbell ringing and sits down at his typewriter, he feels he has done real work, has collected some real experience to chew on; and this feeling is always a consolation.

Sometimes the experience may have such impact that it drives the election itself from one's mind. Just this happened before the reporter wrote the second of these pieces—for you do not soon forget it, when you see with your own eyes, for the first time, that a minority of Americans live worse than the poor people of Moscow.

Our polling all over the country finally led us to the conclusion that the voters would re-elect the President by a "fairly handsome majority." We did not foresee the majority's size. The real key to the Eisenhower landslide is suggested by the first of these pieces, the first experiment in our new system, written before the conventions, and the third, a non-polling column describing "the Eisenhower aura." The key was simple liking for Eisenhower as a human being. But many voted for all the Democratic candidates except Adlai Stevenson, whose almost total failure to get through to the electorate was another major factor. And so you got the election pattern everyone must still remember—Eisenhower triumphant, but his party, as a party, very far from triumphant.

CHICAGO

The rather exhausting experience of interviewing at some length seventy-five American voters of all shapes, sizes and shades of political opinions leaves you with a curious jumble of recollections. You remember how friendly people are, even when their privacy is invaded by total strangers. You remember how uninformed many are ("Harriman? Well, I can't rightly say who that is") and how inarticulate ("Why do I like Ike? Well, he just seems like an awful nice sort of person"). You remember the shameful squalor of the Negro slums here in Chicago (worse than anything in Moscow), and the sense of modest prosperity elsewhere, with an under-layer of nervousness about the future ("Why, there isn't a house or a car on this street that's paid for").

You remember also certain totally unscientific, purely personal, but nevertheless very vivid political impressions. This reporter has brought away with him two such impressions.

One is that President Eisenhower is stronger with the voters—at least outside the farm areas—than in 1952. The other is that something sad and mysterious has happened to tarnish the public image of Adlai E. Stevenson.

This reporter embarked on the pulse-feeling expedition suspecting that President Eisenhower's popularity might be thin and brittle, an artificial product of political propaganda. The suspicion was totally unfounded. The President's popularity is genuine and deep-rooted, and it will be extraordinarily difficult for the Democrats to counteract it.

Of the seventy-five persons this reporter and the expert professional pollster, Louis Harris, have interviewed in this area, only one previous Eisenhower voter showed any signs of defecting. Eight previous Stevenson voters had gone over to Eisenhower, or moved into the "don't know" category. But these meager statistics are unimpressive. What was impressive was the way people talked.

"President Eisenhower is a man of peace." We heard that phrase, or something like it, again and again. Moreover, distasteful as it is for this reporter to admit, there was virtually no feeling that the Eisenhower peace was insecurely defended. One big, jovial woman on a middle-class street said she had her doubts about the Administration's defense policies, as a result of listening to Arthur Godfrey. But that was all. "Why, that's the first thing Ike would think of," another lady said, and she spoke for the vast majority.

Prosperity, unlike peace, is a negative Eisenhower asset. Not many people feel better off than they did in 1952. But they do not feel worse off, and it is clear when you talk to them that many expected to, under a Republican administration.

The President has a third, and rather astonishing, political asset—his heart attack. A good many people apparently intended to vote for the President rather as one might send flowers to a sick friend, to cheer him up. We were unable to find a single person who had decided to vote against the President because of his health. And the heart attack has clearly made a real human being of the President, in a way that no other political personality is real and human.

That is what the Stevenson candidacy seems to lack—a sense of the reality and humanness of the man. Stevenson was quite right when he complained, after the Minnesota primaries, of a "failure to communicate." As one Democrat put it, "Stevenson just doesn't stand for anything any more. He talks with that big vocabulary but it doesn't make any sense any more."

Of course there are plenty of Stevenson supporters and even enthusiasts—particularly among the Negro voters, among whom Stevenson is miles out in front of both President Eisenhower and Sen. Estes Kefauver. ("Are you against Kefauver because he's a Southerner?" we asked one big, genial Negro lady. "Amen," she replied fervently.) But outside the Negro areas, even in the heavily Democratic precincts, we repeatedly ran across a curious and inexplicable hostility toward Stevenson. "I just don't go for that Adlai," people would say.

There was some spotty enthusiasm for Kefauver ("he's the only honest one, all the rest are crooks"). But it seemed clear that no Democratic candidate has even begun to light a fire in the land. If one may be permitted to draw a large conclusion from a tiny sampling of the way the voters talk, it is this: Something big and important and dramatic, either here or abroad, is going to have to happen to change the situation, if the Democrats are to have a ghost of a chance of recapturing the White House in November.—May 4, 1956 (SA).

HARLEM

The big, asthmatic Negro woman leaned heavily against the door of her cell-like room on the second floor of a rickety nineteenth century slum building. Through thin walls came the sound of furious argument, followed by the thud of something thrown, and silence. A forty-watt bulb glowed eerily down the long hall, barely illuminating the scratched and scabrous walls. A black cat arched against the woman's leg, looking up with blank, suspicious eyes at the unfamiliar white faces.

"We live in these rat traps," the woman said dispassionately, without rancor, gasping a little for breath, "and nobody cares, and there's no hope for us, at least as far as I can see."

The big woman with the cat represents one aspect of Harlem—and no doubt of the Negro sections of other big cities—to which sufferers from excessive complacency ought to be exposed. The Harlem slums make you wonder whether the North's smug assumption that only the backward South has failed to solve the problem of the Negro minority is soundly based. They even make you wonder if all our boasts about the American standard of living are entirely justified.

The big woman's cat was not a pet. It was a necessity. In the slum apartments in Harlem, you always find a cat or two, for protection against the swarming rats and mice, and usually a dog, for protection against two-legged enemies. This is one of the small discoveries made by this reporter and Louis Harris, the public opinion expert, in an expedition of political inquiry in Harlem.

There are other discoveries to be made. Most Americans go through life without ever meeting an adult fellow American who cannot read or write. But in the Harlem slums, illiteracy is not uncommon. One grizzled old man, a recent arrival from the South, said earnestly that he wanted to vote before he died, because "voting makes a man a real citizen." He had tried, but had been turned down because he couldn't write his name, but now, he said, "I've learned to print my name pretty good, and do you think they'd take just printing?"

As you talk to people in the old buildings, in the dark and littered hallways, you sometimes hear a chance remark which sheds a grim light on Harlem slum life. There was the high-strung well-dressed man on the fourth floor of a condemned house. He said he had to get out of there—he just couldn't stand it any more. He paid $50 a month for his miserable rooms, but that wasn't the main reason. "All night long they're running up and down the stairs and fighting and jumping from one roof to another."

Occasionally you come upon grotesque, Hogarthian scenes. There was the young girl lying on a couch, her face to the wall, her body oddly crumpled, whose only response when we tried to quest... her was to curse and throw a pillow at a whimpering child. More often, we were asked hospitably to come in and have a seat, and we saw around us a pathetic attempt to live decently under impossible conditions, to rise above the grimness of the surrounding poverty.

Fortunately, the Harlem slums are only part of the Harlem story. It is an extraordinary experience to cross a street from a slum area, and go into one of the low income housing projects—precisely like moving out of the dark into the light.

In the projects you find hard-working and often intelligent people living decently, in a kind of colorful and noisy austerity, in small, clean apartments. The difference is not in incomes—the project apartments are often cheaper than the slum rooms. A sailor in a project explained: "Housing changes people. In a good place, everybody tries to do a little better. Like I tell my son, even if you are a Negro, if you want to do something, like say you want to be a doctor, you can do it."

Or go to a good private apartment house, like the Metropolitan Life Insurance Company's Riverton Apartments, and you find people living in considerable elegance. You also find that they are often far better informed politically than their economic equivalents in a white community, and remarkably articulate.

There are political similarities between the three categories of Harlemites, the slum livers, the project livers and the small upper class of Negro intellectuals and opinion formers. Above all, in all three categories there is an amazingly large and solid bloc of convinced Democratic voters. But there are marked political differences, too, which will be described in a second report on Harlem, and which could have real political meaning for the future.—September 17, 1956 (SA).

DES MOINES

Those Democrats who are already beginning to count unhatched chickens—and there are a lot of them—ought to have followed Dwight

D. Eisenhower around during the hours he spent here, the day before Adlai Stevenson's appearance. The experience might have proved a rude shock to their complacency.

In a brief speech at the airport, Eisenhower remarked that the crowds that lined the streets to see him and Mrs. Eisenhower were "a turn-out such as we've never seen before." Veteran reporters agreed with him. But the vast, good-humored crowds which lined the streets weiᴄ ᴜnly part of the story.

A more important part was the Eisenhower aura, the effect he has on people. It is a very special sort of aura, exclusively his own. Unlike Franklin Roosevelt or other great politicians, he inspires no fanatical admiration, no deeply emotional hero-worship. He inspires, instead, genuine personal affection. Above all, he cheers people up.

You only had to look at people's faces after he had passed by to see that this is so. They looked as though they had had a good tonic. They looked cheerful, amused, and happy. They were almost all smiling.

It is interesting to watch Eisenhower closely, as he passes through a crowd, and try to analyze the special quality of the aura. The smile is part of it, of course. But a kind of shy-seeming earnestness is another part. And still another is a sort of "aw shucks" manner, as though to say, "I don't know what you people are making such a fuss about me for."

At the national plowing match which was the President's most important port of call, a row of children had been lined up to meet him. They were nervous, standing awkwardly at attention in the way that children have on such occasions. But the President talked to them seriously, without condescension, in the manner of a man who really likes children, and they were immediately smiling and at their ease.

At the livestock show, when he asked about such matters as the average number of piglets per litter, he sounded genuinely interested in the answer—which, like any other amateur farmer, he no doubt was. And in the two brief speeches he made—one at the plowing match and the other at the airport—he displayed conspicuously his great asset as a public speaker, the ability to seem to mean what he says.

What he said was certainly not very original, and not even very interesting. Another politician who talked, as the President did at the plowing match, of "the plow as the symbol of peace," might well have sounded like a vote-grubbing hypocrite. But the President sounded as though he were deeply dedicated both to peace and to the plow. Another politician who talked, as the President did at the airport, about how he always "thought first about the interests of all 168 million Americans," might have aroused cynical snickers. But the President aroused, instead, to judge from the reaction of the enormous crowd, sympathy and belief.

No one who saw him in action here, in short, could doubt for a moment that the Eisenhower aura is far and away the Republicans' greatest asset. It remains to be seen, of course, to what extent that almost universal liking for the man will be translated into votes. This reporter had a chat with a master-plowman who had just been congratulated by the President for his prowess.

"He's a fine man, a great man," said the master-plowman, still a bit starry-eyed. "Then you're going to vote for him?" he was asked. "Well, uh, no, I guess not," the master-plowman replied.

No doubt there are others like the master-plowman. But surely there are many more whose "I like Ike" is translated in their minds into "I'll vote for Ike." That raises the question of how the Eisenhower aura, as the central Republican asset, is to be exploited. The question is particularly important since the President's two illnesses. Many in the huge crowds that turned out here must have come to see for themselves how the President looks. He looks well. Indeed, part of the Eisenhower aura is a certain ruddy vigor, far more apparent in person than on the television screen.

Thus there will surely be heavy pressure on the President to repeat his triumph here in Iowa—for his day here was indeed a personal triumph. The pressure will come, of course, from Republican politicians who want to benefit from the aura, but it may come also from within the President himself. For he very much wants to win. And the pressure will mount if the indications increase—as they have been here, where polls show Adlai Stevenson steadily closing the gap—that his winning is no sure thing.—September 24, 1956 (SA).

While the campaign was going on, John Foster Dulles tirelessly struggled to shove the hideous Suez crisis under the nearest rug, by a series of complex and devious maneuvers. These maneuvers were feasible because our allies, and especially the British, greatly hankered to avoid violent action; and if violent action proved unavoidable, our allies desperately wanted American support. The basic pattern of each Dulles maneuver—there were three in all—was to say to our allies:

"Don't do anything just yet, and if you're a little patient, then you'll have our strongest support." The promises of American support turned out, in each case, to be transparent frauds. In this period, in short, our diplomacy was marked by shameful duplicity.

Our duplicity in turn begot the duplicity of the British and French. It became a case of "I sold you, and you sold me, underneath the greenwood tree"—to quote George Orwell. Sir Anthony Eden's illness and several other almost accidental factors further caused the Suez operation to be one of the worst planned and prepared in modern history. Our own view was, and is, that once the operation was launched, simple self-interest forbade recrimination among the Western allies. All that mattered any longer, we thought, was a victorious outcome, since the vital interests of the whole Western alliance were automatically involved. This was not a fashionable view at the time, for the Eisenhower administration took Suez almost as an ugly British plot to destroy the President's precious "peace issue" at the climax of the campaign. In consequence, the government indulged in a positive orgy of smarmy self-righteousness. In addition, the President himself, for once galvanized into strong personal action, did everything he could to make the Suez operation fail. His efforts turned the balance in London, despite Gamal Abdel Nasser's shattering defeat by the Israelis—surely the most shameful defeat experienced by any national army in modern times.

Every major Western leader was to blame, in one way or another, for the appalling outcome of Suez. But we have always believed that if your own government can prevent a great blow to the national interest, you must blame your own government first and foremost. In fact, we think it a mark of national decadence to wail that "we have suffered this or that misfortune because of these wicked or foolish foreigners," when and if the misfortune was preventable by American effort. The following piece was our post-Suez attempt to cast up the balance sheet, which has now been proved painfully accurate. Before this piece was written, the older member of our partnership had already decided to transfer his base abroad. He felt he must become a permanent foreign correspondent in order to provide uninterrupted coverage of the chain reaction of disasters that we foresaw must follow in the wake of Suez. If the following column sounds venomous, the reader should remember it is not easy to write amiably when, as it were, you have the ugly future burning in your belly.

One footnote may perhaps be added. Unluckily, in our opinion, John Foster Dulles was not on deck during the crucial period of the Suez crisis. When he returned to his office, he addressed the following question to the first important British official he saw: "I thought you did the wrong thing at Suez; but once you had done it, why on earth didn't you finish the job?" The Britisher nearly struck him.

WASHINGTON

It will take a long time to add up the full cost of the disaster in the Middle East, but its chief effect is already pretty clear. The most strategically vital region of the modern world has been handed to the Kremlin on a silver platter—with the American government as a rather conspicuous platter-bearer.

Or putting it another way, the American government has energetically assisted in installing Egypt's President Gamal Abdel Nasser as the Soviet viceroy of the Arab lands. That is almost sure to be the practical result of recent events.

There is no use complaining, any longer, about the unwisdom of the Anglo-Franco-Israeli intervention in Egypt. The important thing, now, is to realize the effects of the Anglo-Franco-Israeli failure to attain their aim. Their true aim was to topple Nasser from his position of vast influence and power throughout Pan-Arabia. Nasser was in fact toppled—for he could never have survived his humiliating military defeat by the Israelis without active American and Soviet help.

But the Egyptian Humpty-Dumpty was put back on the wall again, partly by parallel Soviet and American action in the United Nations, partly by intense American pressure on our allies, and partly by the apparent Western surrender to loud Soviet threats. The last factor is the most significant, since all Arabs are now convinced that the Egyptian cease-fire was granted in response to the Bulganin ultimatum to Britain and France.

The State Department, which used to call Nasser a Soviet stooge, now portrays him as full of gratitude to us. He has, it appears, been very nice to our new ambassador in Cairo, Raymond Hare. But in fact every one with first hand knowledge of the Middle East is convinced that the Department's former view of Nasser is now more correct than ever.

Nasser's psychology is such that he will surely consider recent American actions were largely motivated by fear of the Soviets. He will feel that this country and the other leading Western powers turned and ran as soon as the Soviets began fingering a gun. Far more than in the past, he will look to the Soviet Union as his guide and protector.

Nor is this any more than the beginning of the story. Nasser both symbolizes and leads the predominant nationalist movement throughout all the Arab lands. There is very little of the Spirit of '76 in this Nasser brand of Arab nationalism. It is neurotically hate-ridden and viciously anti-Western. It is marked, above all, by the conviction that old grudges can now be vented on the Western powers with perfect safety, because the West is now too weak-willed and impotent to respond to any provocation.

If Nasser had been toppled, it would have been like the slap on the face that doctors recommend as a cure for hysteria. The Arab nationalists would have stopped screaming and drumming their heels on the floor, and would have started dealing with hard realities. They might then have begun to act as serious nationalists, offering constructive programs for their own countries, and forthrightly seeking a constructive accommodation with the Western nations.

But since Humpty-Dumpty has been put back on the wall again, the opposite effects can be anticipated. Nasser's followers in other Arab lands will of course take notice of the Israeli's brilliant victory. They will be chilled by this demonstration that Nasser's vaunted military power is a busted flush. But this setback for Nasser will be more than balanced by the enhanced prestige of the Soviet Union, and the reflected glory of Nasser as the Kremlin's special Middle Eastern favorite.

What must now be expected, therefore, is the progressive collapse of every remaining Western position in the Middle East, under the assault of the Nasser-led Arab nationalist movement. Arab nationalism will now be more inflamed than ever before, because of the fruitless attempt to topple its leader. It will be more confident than ever because of the apparent Western surrender to the recent Soviet threats. It will be more Soviet-influenced than ever because not only Nasser, but the Arab nationalists everywhere will now tend to accept the Soviets as their guides and protectors. And the Soviets will use the Arab nationalists, coolly and ruthlessly, as instruments to cut the Western Alliance's oil jugular in the Middle East.

There are other probable consequences of the Middle Eastern disaster, such as the replacement of the present British government by a strongly anti-American Labor Cabinet, the onset of political chaos in France, and so on. But this storm which is shaking the whole Western Alliance to its foundation still chiefly centers in the Middle East.

Maybe the British, French and Israelis were wrong to try to topple Nasser at all, and certainly the British and French played their part in the operation as badly as possible. But once the attempt had been started for good or ill, the fate of the Western Alliance automatically hung upon its success. That is the point the American government has refused to recognize. Maybe it is not too late, even now, to recognize this central point and thus salvage something from the ruins.—November 16, 1956 (JA & SA).

X

The Chickens Start Home
to Roost

*1957 can best be described as the year when the chickens began
coming home to roost. By now, they have arrived in flocks, and they
look like vultures.*

After the orgy of self-righteousness at the time of Suez, the administration had to face up to the consequences. Old Nuri Pasha in
Iraq and all the other remaining friends of the West in the Middle
East were sending desperate messages, warning that they could not
long withstand the pressure of the now-triumphant Nasser, unless
urgent measures were taken to strengthen their positions. The destruction of all the vital Western positions in the Middle East was in
turn certain to impose the severest strains on the Western alliance
itself, because of Western Europe's dependence on Middle Eastern oil,
and above all because of Britain's very special dependence on the
revenues from the oil sources.

With these ugly prospects opening before them, the administration's
policy-makers responded in two different ways. Generally speaking,

Secretary of State Dulles now took over, *en bloc,* the former Middle Eastern policy of Sir Anthony Eden—the policy of "the good Arabs," as Eden used to call it. This was simply a policy of building up a grouping of pro-Western Arab leaders to serve as a counterweight and an opposition to Nasser. Dulles brought nothing new to the British "good Arabs" policy except America's greater resources and power, plus two additional Arabs. Chamoun of Lebanon had always been more closely linked to the United States than to Britain. King Saud of Saudi Arabia was violently at odds with Britain, because of the Buraimi dispute; but he was a warm friend of the United States; and King Saud was persuaded to cease financing Nasser's conspiracies and propaganda, to break his former close link with the Egyptian dictator, and to take his stand with the West.

The new Dulles policy of the "good Arabs" in fact meant the most active struggle to contain and cut down Gamal Abdel Nasser. But the United States had just intervened to save Nasser from destruction. Hence it was necessary to give this new policy some tangible expression, in order to convince the West's Arab friends that our new policy had any meaning. Nuri Pasha, particularly, had been clamoring for American adherence to the Baghdad pact (originally invented by Foster Dulles, and then backed away from by him after he had played a considerable role in persuading Iraq to join the pact). As a substitute, which would permit the U. S. to help Iraq just as much as adherence to the pact, the administration offered the Eisenhower doctrine, with all its curious marks of Foster Dulles' legal mind. The doctrine was presented with the usual huckstering fanfare, and evoked the following column.

WASHINGTON

There is an old military maxim: "If you don't know what to do, do something." It is a good rule, because in a time of danger, doing something is almost always better than doing nothing. By the same token, the administration's double-barrelled plan for dealing with the Middle Eastern crisis is a great deal better than nothing. But the plan has been widely hailed both as a potential solution for the crisis, and as a bold new departure like the "Truman doctrine" or the Marshall plan. In fact, it is nothing of the sort.

The plan has two parts. Congress will be asked to authorize the President in advance to oppose with force a Soviet aggression in the Middle East. At the same time, the Middle Eastern countries are to get "special attention" within the framework of a foreign aid bill somewhat smaller than the administration requested last year.

The request for stand-by authority is really hardly more than a restatement of the obvious. The United States is already legally committed to defend Greece and Turkey against Soviet aggression, and morally committed to defend Iran and Pakistan. Soviet forces would have to pass through or over these countries to attack other Middle Eastern countries.

No one seriously believes that the Soviets intend to launch a parachute attack on, say, Iraq, or that the United States would look the other way if they did. In fact, it has been clear ever since the Azerbaijan crisis in 1946 that overt aggression by the Soviets in the Middle East would invite American intervention and a third World War.

It is equally clear that there is nothing really new about the second part of the plan. Under the current foreign aid program, the administration asked for more than $300,000,000 for the Middle Eastern countries. The administration may ask for $50,000,000 or even $100,-000,000 more this year. But this is not a bold new program. It is a change of emphasis in an existing program—no doubt a desirable change of emphasis, but no more than that.

In fact, the real danger in the Middle East springs neither from lack of dollar aid nor from the threat of overt Soviet aggression. The oil producing countries, Iraq and Saudi Arabia notably, have dollars coming out of their ears. Syria has refused dollar aid already, on political grounds. Egypt's Col. Nasser is regarded with good reason by the British and French as their mortal enemy. If he is now rewarded with generous helpings of American dollars, without any firm commitments in return, the strained western alliance will endure another heavy blow.

As for the military threat, it is indirect rather than overt. On Monday, Frank Kelley, able foreign correspondent for the "New York Herald Tribune," reported that the Soviet and Syrian governments have reached a firm agreement. The agreement provides not only for the continuing supply of Soviet arms to Syria, but for placing Soviet technicians actually in command of key Syrian units.

If there is any provision in the new plan for dealing with this kind of indirect threat, it is not visible to the naked eye. The fact is that the Soviets have no reason to resort to overt aggression in the Middle East. Nasser and his Syrian imitator, Col. Serraj, are not Communists. But they share the same objectives as the Soviets—to eliminate all western interests and influence, ultimately including American interests and influence, in the Middle East. Thus, the Soviets need only to arm and otherwise encourage Nasser-type Arab nationalism in order to serve Soviet ends.

All this is not to suggest that the proposal to give the President stand-by authority to resist Soviet aggression in the Middle East is not a useful proposal. A restatement of the obvious can often be very useful. It may be particularly useful now, since (as Ambassador to France Douglas Dillon undiplomatically but accurately pointed out) Soviet threats of aggression were a key factor causing the collapse of the Anglo-French Suez adventure. Moreover, foreign aid dollars, though they will not miraculously transform the situation, can be usefully used to deal with the cancerous Arab refugee problem, to bolster collapsing Jordan, and to give the West some sort of bargaining power with Nasser in negotiations for a canal agreement.

But it is dangerously misleading to elevate a restatement of the obvious to the status of a new, historic "doctrine," or to represent as a bold, new departure what is really a rather cautious change in emphasis.—January 2, 1957 (SA).

Meanwhile, the older member of our partnership had departed for his tour of duty as a foreign correspondent permanently stationed overseas. His first major stop was in Moscow. His most important first impressions, which proved to be enduring, were as follows:

"The central surprise is that, although the problems of this powerful Soviet society are wildly different from the problems of our Western society, they are very real problems for all that.

"It sounds banal when put like that. It may also sound too reassuring; and it is well to remember that the Soviet leaders do not appear to have any current problem so urgent, so hard to solve and so likely to produce a weakening result as the crisis that now confronts the Western leaders in the Middle East. The central Soviet problem, which the wisest foreign observers regard as having a deeper importance than the unrest in Eastern Europe, is in fact a long-term problem.

"The problem actually arises from the greatest single Soviet achievement. By great sacrifices, at fearful cost, the Soviet Union has now been raised to the level of a high technical society, with an industrial production surpassing the combined production of the two originators of the industrial revolution, Britain and Germany. As a high technical society, the Soviet Union may seem malformed and misshapen to our Western eyes. Consumer goods have been persistently slighted, and are being slighted today, in favor of the kinds of industrial investments that increase the strength of the state rather than the comfort of the citizens. But this is now a high technical society all the same.

"In political terms, that means two things. On the one hand, education on a wide scale has been essential. So the Russian people are no longer the dumb, compliant mass of illiterate peasants that the Soviet leaders inherited forty years ago. The people now include a very large educated element who know about and hanker for broader horizons.

"On the other hand, precisely because the status of a high technical society has now been achieved here, the methods that were used to achieve this great result are no longer really workable. In the building phase, to put it crudely, it was possible to use the knout, as Stalin may be said to have done. But once it has been successfully built, this kind of society is too complex, too massive, too delicate in its inter-relationships, too full of ramifying chains of consequence, to be successfully managed with the knout alone. Thus while the education necessarily given to the people has created a longing for broader horizons, the progress in the society itself has created a positive need of an even more important character. This is the need for more independence of judgment, more freedom of decision, more flexibility and more open communication at all levels of the Soviet managerial apparatus.

"The Soviet leaders unquestionably launched the famous de-Stalinization campaign because they recognized the demand and the need too briefly and crudely set forth above. Almost equally unquestionably, they were as surprised as everyone else by the uncomfortably dramatic response which followed, in the form of loud demands for much greater freedom. Hence the statue of Stalin is now being regilded in patches, and the patches are likely to get considerably bigger in the near future. Yet that will only obscure, and cannot permanently solve, the problem created for the Soviet leaders by their own success."

The foregoing was written in Moscow on the eve of departure for a long trip in mid-winter Siberia, from Kuybyshev to the center of the Kuzbas mining area, Kemerovo. This was the truly unusual feature of the visit to the Soviet Union. This kind of trip, entirely off the beaten path marked out by Intourist, has almost never been authorized for any Western newspaperman. Precisely because the trip was off the beaten path, it had its penalties—there was no running water nor any indoor plumbing from Kuybyshev all the way to Barna Ul, a five-day journey. But the great reward was a close look at the actual working of the strange Soviet society.

One of the prime discoveries was the power and impressiveness of the wholly new Soviet class of industrial managers—a class created out of almost nothing in the period of the five-year plans, but a singularly uniform and cohesive class all the same. The following column describes a particularly important member of this intensely significant new group in the Soviet Union, and offers the first look vouchsafed to any Westerner at the largest single mining enterprise in modern Russia.

KOUSTENAY, SIBERIA

Over the flat, featureless, illimitable, snow-clad plain of this strange land of western Siberia, a young pilot was flying about six years ago towards this place, which was then a lonely railroad town of about 30,000 people.

Some seventy kilometers from here, the pilot's compass failed him utterly, in a way that indicated a strong magnetic disturbance. That was how the vast twin bodies of magnetic iron ore of Sarbi and Sokolovsky were first discovered. And that was the beginning of one of the most astonishing enterprises this reporter has ever seen.

Since then the immense government-directed plough-up of the virgin plain has transformed little Koustenay into a roaring frontier city of more than 80,000 people. But the transformation of Koustenay seemed to me a mere nothing, when compared to the transformation wrought by the discovery of those two ore bodies. I learned the story in half a day's talk with Nikolai Fadyevich Sandrigailo, one of the three or four top men in Soviet iron mining and now the director of the Sokolovsky mines.

As he told the story, the Soviet Geological Survey moved swiftly to map the ore bodies the young pilot had discovered. The Sarbi ore deposit was estimated at above one billion tons of magnetic ore with 48 per cent of iron content. The Sokolovsky deposit was found to be almost equally large.

The report was then transmitted to the Ministry of Black Industry, which controls all iron and steel production in the Soviet Union. The ministry decided that the discovery should be exploited, and ordered a project drawn up by its hive of experts at "Lengyproruda"—the Leningrad Institute of Ore Projects. The project officer at Lengyproruda in turn called for help from fourteen other project planning agencies, ranging from the Leningrad City Planning Institute to the Leningrad Industrial Projects Institute.

The result was a massive combined plan for two enormous open cast iron mines at the Sarbi and Sokolovsky deposits; an ore-enriching plant using a magnetic separation process situated half way between the mines; a small city and a lesser town to house the miners and enriching-plant workers; two new railroad lines to carry the ore to the outer world; a local narrow gauge rail system large enough to require 120 electric locomotives; plus power stations, shops, water reservoir, recreation facilities and everything else needed for a new mining development almost comparable in scale, cost, difficulty and remoteness to the famous Labrador mining project originally sponsored by Secretary of the Treasury George Humphrey.

Sandrigailo is a big, calm, solidly self-possessed man, who is not much given to humor about his mines. But even he smiled a bit ruefully when he recalled how the ministry uprooted him from his previous job as boss of all the iron mines in the Urals. Without warning, he was confronted with the thirty-five stout volumes in which Lengyproruda and its assisting project institutes had set forth the completed Sokolovsky project in full detail.

"This," said the Ministry, "is your new job."

That was in 1954. The seemingly ponderous machinery of the Soviet state must have moved rather swiftly to meet Sandrigailo's needs for everything from a mobile power station on flat cars to an initial cadre of skilled workers. At any rate, half his new city is built now. Six thousand five hundred people (out of a planned labor force of 12,000) are already at work. The ore-enriching plant is on the way up. And at the Sokolovsky deposit, the gigantic Soviet-built excavating machines have already dug a hole in the ground that is two kilometers long, more than a kilometer across, and about forty meters deep.

"By the beginning of 1961," said Sandrigailo with visible assurance, "our mines will be in full operation and each year we shall be shipping out 12,000,000 tons of enriched ore with 59 per cent of iron content. Not long ago big coal deposits were found about one hundred kilometers from here. When they are producing, too, it will be time to think about marrying our coal and our ore to make iron and steel right here."

It is tempting to try to record more of the pictures and impressions left by this day with Sandrigailo and his staff—pictures such as the dark-clad workmen still swarming in the freezing dusk to complete assembly of a fourteen-cubic-meter excavator as big as six houses; and impressions such as the sharp, yet dreary, impression of a company town's atmosphere that one got at the movie offered by the "Palace of Culture." But one impression left by this great enterprise springing up in a wilderness really overwhelmed all the others. It was an impression of the great and ruthless power this strange Soviet economy is able to mobilize.—February 11, 1957 (JA).

The reporter was allowed to see and talk for hours with almost anyone he liked—industrial managers, bankers, educators, doctors, newspaper editors, and so on and on. The only two groups under an interdict were military officers and members of the party apparatus.

The interdiction of the latter group was especially regretted because the reporter soon began to wonder just what the members of the party apparatus really did. In the earlier period, before the Soviet Union had trained literally millions of technicians and specialists for every imaginable purpose, the main job of the *apparatchiki* was easy enough to identify. They ran things. A mine like Sandrigailo's, for instance, would have had two or three trained staff engineers at most—there were no more available in the early days, and those who were available were not politically trusted—and Sandrigailo's job and most of the other managerial jobs would have been assigned to activists chosen for this duty from the party apparatus.

It was also easy enough to see how this kind of broad training produced men like Nikita Khrushchev, to name just one. But in the interval since Khrushchev's youth, the need for the activists outside the apparatus had ceased to exist. Technicians had been trained to do the jobs the *apparatchiki* formerly did. Furthermore, the emphasis on technical training was very great. It was "unthinkable," as several industrialists and the like told the reporter, for anyone who was not a technician to receive an appointment in industry or any of the other new Soviet careers. The members of the party apparatus were not and are not technicians in this sense of the word. One began to suspect, therefore, that the so-called "party career" must have become pretty arid, at shouting do not add up to an attractive career, after all.
least below the topmost levels. Obedience, espionage and slogan-

Finally in the small town of Koustenay, at a very drunken dinner given by the amiable mayor, the reporter succeeded in cornering three genuine *apparatchiki*. Because the subsequent despatch had to pass through censorship, the most amazing ensuing exchange was not included. This occurred when the reporter asked whether it was not a bit of a gamble to plough up 90,000,000 acres of semi-arid steppe under the "virgin lands" program. The answer was, in effect, that the weather would just have to follow the party line, like everybody else. But even with this omission, the following column gives the flavor of these men; and their flavor in itself quite certainly constitutes a primary Soviet problem.

KOUSTENAY, SIBERIA

In this metropolis of the new Soviet frontier in western Siberia, the presumed sanctum sanctorum is the office of the First Secretary of the Communist Party Committee, Comrade Lazar Ivanovich Popov.

It looks, too, as a sanctum sanctorum ought to look. By Koustenay standards, which are appropriately the standards of Tombstone, Ariz., circa 1880, it is a large and handsome room. The ikons of the holy men of communism are also large and handsome. And so is the desk at which Comrade Popov receives his callers with an expression of stern, unbending purpose.

I went to call on Comrade Popov in order to ask a question that seemed to me centrally important. But it is perhaps better to begin by introducing Comrade Popov and his two colleagues, Second Party Secretary Yefim Andreievich Marosov and Third Party Secretary Aleksandr Vassilievich Shilov.

They are all middle-aged men. They all started their careers in rather humble ways—Comrade Popov was a primary school teacher, for instance. But all three "took up full-time party work a long time ago," as they put it. All have followed this specialized career since at least 1940, and none has had any higher technical training beyond that offered in the party schools.

These, then, were the trio to whom I put my question. I had been greatly impressed by the boldness, size and apparent success of the huge Soviet industrial and agricultural enterprises which have been shown me in the course of this Siberian journey. I had been equally impressed by the caliber of the leaders of these enterprises. Such men are, of course, members of the Communist party. But equally, of course, having huge jobs of their own to do, they do not function primarily as Communists any more than the chairman of U. S. Steel functions primarily as a Republican or Walter Reuther functions primarily as a Democrat.

What then was the role of the party itself in these enormous and technically complex enterprises? Where exactly did Comrades Popov, Marosov and Shilov fit into the grandiose and dramatic pattern of western Siberia's agricultural and industrial development?

"There the role of the party," replied Comrade Popov, with a powerful didactic scowl, "is the role of leadership. For example, the colossal spaces of our steppes lay waste for centuries, but now they are being plowed. For this purpose, it is necessary among other things to win the struggle to keep moisture in the soil. This is the successful offensive against nature, in which the party leads."

In the beginning was the party, Comrade Popov and his colleagues jointly explained. The party and its junior branch, the Comsomols, had the opening task of organizing the movement of people to work on the new lands and in the new industries. "Once again," said Comrade Shilov, pride shining through his spectacles, "the role of the party and its members was the role of leadership in accomplishing this great task. The leading role was immense."

"Initially it is not easy," added Comrade Popov, "because we must create from nothing everything, from housing for the people who come, to needed cultural facilities. Yet it can be easily understood why our people go to such distant places. It is because of the care of the Communist party for the people."

But more specifically, I asked, in a tone somewhat subdued by the flow of eloquence around me, what was the party's role in the actual management of the largest single local enterprise, the great new Sokolovsky mines? Do party officials like my kind hosts debate the complex questions of open-cast mining on a titanic scale with the formidably capable mine manager, who is one of the two or three leading Soviet technicians in this field?

"The mine manager," replied Comrade Popov, "is a member of the collective. In this respect, our strength lies in working as one collective body. The collective effort of our people, in which the leading role is played by the Communist party, is the real force that permits us to cope with our great tasks. People can solve any problems if they are well led.

"Therefore the Communist party never loses its close connection

with the masses. Party members equally work together in such industrial enterprises as you have mentioned. So they help all people to solve
problems, and so the rule is followed that the decisions taken by the
collective body of the people must be fulfilled by all means."

On these lines, with the waves of eloquence rising and falling in
majestic tides, the conversation continued for nearly two hours. But
such, in general, were the answers I received to one of the fundamental
questions of Soviet society in its present stage of development.—February 13, 1957 (JA).

Contact with working men, 'though permitted, was not easy. None
the less, by the end of the Siberian journey, one had an overwhelming
impression of the new Soviet industrial proletariat—a class just as
recently created as the new managerial class. The following column
tries to convey that impression. It tries to convey, too, the impression
left by the new Soviet industrial cities that the Intourist travellers seldom visit.

KEMEROVO, U.S.S.R.

The plump, fussy restaurant manager is greatly upset by the party of
miners demanding a table. They are too cheerfully tight for his taste.
But they grow angry and shout:

"The reason you don't want us in your damned place is that we're
members of the working class. You only want those others in business
suits."

So, fearing a scene, he lets them in. It is lucky for the miners that
he did not call instead on the militiamen always stationed in the vestibule. For this large, bleakly ornate room, with its depressed and inter-
mittent orchestra, is literally Kemerovo's sole restaurant in the Russian
usage of the word. Nowhere else in this great and growing mining center of a quarter of a million people, can you sit at a table and have both
a meal and a glass of vodka.

In these circumstances, the restaurant atmosphere tends to be a bit
rowdy. But at the big, pompously pseudo-classical "House of Culture,"
which the Kemerovo Coal Trust has just built in the miners' district,
the atmosphere is prim enough to please the strictest nursery governess.

In the wide lobby, during the halfway interval of the new movie
(about the loves of a boy and girl for their dear tractors and one another) the young people are dancing, mostly boys with boys and girls
with girls. Boys who have actually captured members of the other sex

are proudly buying their girls grayish cakes and soda pop in the buffet. Upstairs, a children's song group is letting go with "Thank you, Party, thank you, great Party."

In the big lecture hall, a rather small crowd is glumly watching a propaganda film on war. And in the House of Culture's vestibule, two irreverent miners are making a joke about the Comsomol's display of villains of the month—a set of photographs of drunks, idlers and other uncultured persons. The director of the House of Culture, a demobilized political officer from the army, explains proudly:

"Our main task is to organize the recreation of the people."

At the miners' club (each mine and every factory has a club) the menu of activities is much the same as at the House of Culture. But the building is smaller, shabbier and looks more lived in. Here there is an almost bar-like buffet, where bread and sausages and wine and weak beer are sold. And here an obvious candidate for the Comsomol villain display is having a loud argument with one of the omnipresent militiamen.

These sketches of trifles seen in Kemerovo may help to suggest why places like this affect the Western traveler as though they were cities on the other side of the moon. For the traveler himself, the sensation is not exactly disagreeable. In truth, I have enjoyed almost every moment of this Siberian journey, mostly because the innumerable people I have met have generally been very pleasant and often very impressive human beings.

Furthermore, although the Soviet Union is certainly no Lotus-land, the average man's lot has certainly been greatly improved in recent years. The people still have the grayish look that comes from eating a great deal of starch and too little protein and fat. Although warm and serviceable, the clothes they wear are inexpressibly dreary. Their housing is shockingly overcrowded. But there is no doubt about it, the time of real misery and real fear has altogether receded into the past.

The strangeness that one feels really lies, I think, in the fact that these Soviet cities rather resemble carefully organized company towns of the earlier period of American industry. There is much literal truth in the comparison. The mine or factory not only provides the club, the clinic, the dining hall and the vacation camp for its workers. It also builds and owns most of their housing—a strong link, that one.

But this is by no means the whole story. As the foregoing short sketches may perhaps suggest, very great efforts are also made to keep the working masses on the path of virtue. Governess-management, governess-municipality and governess-state all join hands to diminish the temptations to be "uncultured" and to encourage right thinking, general good behavior and, above all, unremitting hard work.

Thus far the system has produced the desired result. With carrot and with stick, this country has not only trained up a remarkable new executive class. It has also trained a wholly new industrial working class with a constantly increasing level of technical skill.

Two things have struck me about these Russian industrial workers. One is their sturdy pride in "moya professy—my speciality." The other is their unvarying habit of pointing out that "We are members of the working class." Judging by my own experiences, at least, those miners in the restaurant were wholly characteristic in their interesting consciousness of the wide difference between "us of the working class" and "those others in business suits."—February 20, 1957 (JA).

No seven weeks in the reporter's life were ever so crammed with new experience as those seven weeks in the Soviet Union. For the long run, the most important experiences were those like the ones in Siberia. They led to the following formulation, in which the reporter still strongly believes:

A. The Kremlin is a pre-industrial government, which has made its own industrial revolution.

B. An industrial revolution is a genuinely revolutionary event, which changes everything, including, in the long run, the character of the government. The changes, however, come slowly.

C. Therefore great changes are inevitable in Soviet society. But change is bound to be very difficult, because the society is a total tyranny. Furthermore, the outcome is wholly unforeseeable, because just this kind of change has never before taken place in just this kind of society. In sum, we of the outer world, watching this strange Soviet society, are in the position of biologists who are watching their first tadpole, and have never heard of a frog. Biologists in this position could note the diminution of the tail, the shrivelling of the gills, and other features of tadpole-an metamorphosis. But they would never be able to predict the frog at the end of the process, until the process was virtually at an end.

Among all these Soviet experiences, again, the most important for the short run was a two-hour interview with Nikita Khrushchev. He had much to say about Soviet-American relations; and he gave the reporter the first full picture ever given to a Westerner of his vast and radical program of industrial reorganization. As a man, he seemed "powerful, resilient, gutta-percha-like . . . astute, (with) a talent for survival . . . singularly practical and hard-headed . . . possessed of an incomparable energy, an astonishing verve and gusto . . . (and) a cool but immensely bold gambler." The quotations are from a written portrait of him. The published interview with Khrushchev was a considerable feather in our journalistic cap, but it was perishable, like most straight news stories. The following analysis of Soviet-Western relations, quite largely based on what Khrushchev said, has a more enduring interest. It was written in Paris, just after the departure from Moscow, and therefore did not have to pass censorship.

PARIS

For the Soviet citizen, the gradual evolution of the iron society in which he lives and has his being must be a matter of really passionate concern. And this same evolution should also be a matter of deep interest for Americans.

All the same, the evolution of Soviet society that began with the death of Stalin has neither softened nor deflected Soviet foreign policy. On the contrary, while considerably more supple than their late master, Stalin's heirs have actually proven somewhat more adventurous. And on the basis of a rather intense experience in the Soviet Union, this reporter is convinced that a wholly new generation of Soviet leaders will probably have to come to power before there is any real change in the meaning of "peaceful coexistence."

Thus the fundamental Western problem remains unaltered except in detail. In the satellite area of Central Europe, to be sure, the Soviets have recently suffered a severe setback. But by the ruthless use of their great military power, they have recovered a large part of their losses, at least for the time being. Meanwhile, the West has also suffered severe setbacks, especially in the troubled Middle East. And the Western losses have most conspicuously not been recovered.

At the present juncture, moreover, the West has found no effective way to exploit the Soviet setbacks. Yet the Soviets are exploiting the Western setbacks with great daring and astuteness. Thus Soviet world strategy has actually gone forward. What then is the nature of this Soviet strategy which the Western allies must somehow find means to parry?

It comes in three parts. Toward the United States, first of all, the Soviets present a firm military front. At the same time, they seek bilateral negotiations between the two giant powers, but always and only on strictly Soviet terms.

Second, in all the vulnerable ex- and semi-colonial areas in which the Western powers have vital interests, the Soviets are doing everything possible to transform the inflamed native nationalism into a weapon against the West. In Stalin's time, the center of this effort was the Far East. But the great innovation of the Khrushchev era has been Soviet intervention in the Middle East, where Stalin hardly raised a finger after his retreat from Azerbaijan.

In his talk with me, for instance, Nikita Khrushchev openly indicated active Soviet support for nationalization of the Middle Eastern oil sources, whence flows the economic lifeblood of Britain and Western Europe. Thus he revealed the Soviet aim. The masters of the Kremlin do not want Communist satellites in the Middle East. They want Soviet-backed, vengefully anti-Western Arab governments which will nationalize the oil sources and take other steps of a similar nature.

Thus Britain, particularly, is to be ruined. France and the other Western European powers are to be weakened. And by this economic flank attack, the chief trans-Atlantic partners of the Western alliance are to be knocked out of the great power game.

Third, however, while they are thus encouraging their Arab friends to strike at the vitals of Britain, France and the other European nations, the Soviet leaders are shrewdly seeking quite another sort of success in Britain and France. In both these countries, the men of the political right place the whole blame for the setbacks in the Middle East on the follies of American policy, conveniently forgetting their own follies. And on the political left, the American alliance has always been a source of profound disquiet.

In this confused state of British and European public opinion, the Soviet leaders hope to make great gains with still another weapon—the cold fear which always inspires wishfulness and bad judgment. With virulent anti-Americanism already rampant, they are going to brandish their new arms. It is a fair bet that they will shortly make some sort of public showing of an intermediate-range ballistic missile with an atomic or hydrogen warhead, which will inspire very cold fear indeed. And they are going to say to our partners in the Western alliance:

"These Americans are terrible people, anyway. If you only were not linked with them, we should be nice as pie to you. So why do you run the risk of being devastated by these dangerous toys of ours in a quarrel between us and the Americans, just because you obstinately continue to grant the Americans bases in your countries?"

Once again, in the interview he granted me, Nikita Khrushchev quite discernibly hinted at this Soviet approach. He also quite confidently predicted that the American overseas bases would eventually be liquidated.

By these means, in sum, the masters of the Kremlin hope to organize a gigantic upset of the world balance of power, only comparable to the upset in the European balance of power that occurred in the thirties.

If you look at this Soviet foreign policy coldbloodedly, without the cheap self-indulgence of easy indignation, you have to admit that the Kremlin's masters are very far from stupid or weak. Their strategy, alas, is prudently bold, well adjusted to the means at their disposal, and on the whole well calculated to attain the aims they have set for themselves.

In truth, the Soviet strategy leaves only one key question unanswered. If the world balance of power is successfully upset as planned, how will the suddenly aroused United States then react? —March 8, 1957 (JA).

The most astonishing single episode in the whole history of the Eisenhower administration, and one of the most meaningful too, was the retreat from the 1957 budget. This began when Secretary of the Treasury George M. Humphrey publicly denounced the budget just presented by the administration that he served, as likely to produce a depression that would "curl your hair."

1956 (when the budget was prepared of course) was in fact the last year when the President offered any opposition to the Humphrey priorities, which put fiscal orthodoxy first and national security almost nowhere. When Humphrey openly rebelled against the Presidential decisions embodied in the new budget, the President surrendered to his rebel-subordinate. By the spring of 1957, the decision had been taken to reduce the Strategic Air Command's budgeted complement of B-52 bombers from the former "minimum" of seventeen wings to only eleven wings—and this is still the planned complement, although the B-52 will be just about our only answer to Soviet guided missiles for some years to come. That summer, now completely mesmerized by Humphrey, the President actually issued orders to slash defense spending by a further five billion dollars, in order to facilitate an election-year tax cut. But of this, more later. The first Humphrey triumph in 1957, which prepared the way for the rest, is herein described.

WASHINGTON

Secretary of the Treasury George M. Humphrey seems likely to have his way in the end, as is his custom. In other words, the national program to emerge from the current session of Congress will probably be much more a Humphrey program than an Eisenhower program.

In the struggle within the Eisenhower administration which preceded the President's budget message, Humphrey, of course, fought and bled to hold down and cut back the budget. But his power in the Administration is not quite what it was, and in this preliminary struggle he suffered a partial defeat.

For example, the requested fiscal 1958 defense budget was up somewhat more than $2 billion over the sum requested for the current year. This is a lot less than the $6 billion increase which Gen. Nathan Twining, Air Force Chief of Staff, said last year would be necessary to maintain current Air Force strength. Even so, it is certainly more than Humphrey wanted to spend for defense.

It is too early to make any precise predictions about the defense budget which will eventually emerge from Congress. But the best guess of the best guessers is that defense, which was increased by $900 million by the Senate last year, will be cut back this year by between one and two billion. This is close to what Humphrey wanted in the first place.

Again, it is no secret that Humphrey is less than an enthusiast for foreign aid. He was no doubt disappointed when the Fairless committee, which was largely his creation, failed to propose cutting the liver and lights out of the program. But again, Humphrey seems likely to have his way in the end. Current estimates on Capitol Hill are that foreign aid will be reduced by between $1 billion and $1.5 billion.

Or take the Eisenhower-sponsored program for Federal aid to schools, with a price tag of just under a half billion dollars in the

Eisenhower budget. The school aid bill is probably the most important item in the Eisenhower program of "new Republicanism."

A few weeks ago, it looked as though the school bill would pass rather easily, if the civil rights hurdle could be overcome. Now, there is an increasing tendency in both parties to shy away from the bill. The present prospect is that it will pass only if the President himself is prepared to make a real fight for it.

If the bill does not pass, it is exceedingly unlikely that George Humphrey, who is hardly an evangelical "modern Republican," will shed tears for it. Nor will he weep very bitterly if the costly farm program, another "modern Republican" item, is cut back sharply, as also seems possible.

In short, something rather close to the kind of budget Humphrey wanted in the first place seems likely to emerge. The main reason is the pressure on Congress, the most intense in years, to cut spending. The man chiefly responsible for generating the pressure is, of course, George Humphrey.

Humphrey's famous "curl your hair" press conference, in which he attacked the Administration budget head-on, was the real kick-off for the cut-spending campaign. The campaign, pushed by the Chamber of Commerce and similar organizations, has flooded Congressional offices knee-deep in mail.

While the pressure to cut is much heavier than ever, moreover, the defense of the President's budget is dishwater-weak. Ordinarily, an Administration defends its budget with all the ferocity of a mother protecting a favorite child. But this Administration is acting toward its budget more like a mother who leaves an unwanted child on a strange doorstep.

It is hardly surprising that the defense of the budget is weak, since the President himself, commenting on Humphrey's statement, seemed to agree with him. In the circumstances, the Republicans feel no obligation to defend the Eisenhower budget, and neither, naturally enough, do the Democrats.

Altogether, it is a queer situation, and a tribute to the power and pertinacity of George M. Humphrey, a man accustomed to getting his way. If Humphrey's getting his way means wrecking or watering down the whole Eisenhower program, in the defense, foreign aid, and domestic fields, no one seems to care very much, not even President Eisenhower.—March 24, 1957 (SA).

After the Soviet journey, the older member of our partnership made a brief stop-over in London, whence he reported, alas correctly, that the Eisenhower-MacMillan meeting in Bermuda had not resulted in any detailed, serious Anglo-American agreement on a joint Middle Eastern policy. (However, he did not report the much-repeated, almost certainly authentic London story of Prime Minister MacMillan's reply when he was asked what "it had been like, meeting with the President at Bermuda." MacMillan answered: "What was it like? Why very pleasant, very friendly, very encouraging; but not at all like an experience in the modern world. More like meeting with George III at Brighton, I should say.")

From London, the reporter went on to the Middle East, and there he almost immediately found himself caught up in the immensely dramatic and exciting April crisis in little Jordan, caused by the conspiracy of Nasser's local agents and their Communist allies to dethrone or destroy King Hussein. No crisis has ever been quite so humanly stirring. Nasser's chief agent was the king's closest friend, Ali Abu Nuwar, whom Hussein had promoted from Major to Major General and placed in command of the famous Arab Legion. The climax of the crisis was reached when the Legion's Bedouin troops chose to follow Hussein instead of Ali Abu Nuwar. Their choice manifested itself in open mutiny against Ali Abu Nuwar's subordinate legion commanders and co-conspirators. And the first parting between the two friends, Hussein and Ali, occurred when they were driving to the Legion camp together to put down the mutiny, and encountered a road-block set up by troops loyal to Hussein.

Here Ali showed himself an utter coward, pleading with the King in tears to permit him to return to Amman, the capital, instead of going forward to face the music at the Legion camp. As Hussein quite clearly intimated to the reporter later, it was this incident that bit deep in his young soul. He did not so much mind discovering the treachery of this friend whom he had trusted and favored; for he took treachery as a mere regrettable incident of Arab politics. But he deeply minded the discovery that the friend he had chosen was a coward; for this he took as the worst sort of reflection on his own judgment of character.

The swift movement of the Jordanian crisis temporarily transformed the older member of our partnership from columnist into straight news-reporter; and although the results were useful in our joint enterprise, they had the perishable character, already noted in connection with the Khrushchev interview, of all news stories written in great haste for tomorrow morning's papers. Hence they are not reproduced here. A series of columns written from other countries in the Middle East are more tempting to reproduce in full, but a few extracts will serve to show the picture as it then was. In Syria, for instance, Gamal Abdel Nasser's viceroys were (as they still are) the leader of the Baathist party, the brilliant, tough Akram Hourani, and the then-chief of the G-II section of the Syrian army, Colonel Abdulhamid Seraj. They were already the real masters of Syrian politics. The victory of King Hussein over the Nasserite conspirators in Jordan none the less produced sharp repercussions in Syria—for the atmosphere of every Middle Eastern country is much affected by the atmosphere of all the others. This was how the response of Hourani and Seraj was then summarized:

"Annoyingly, the politicians whom Hourani manipulates, the senior army officers who never make a move without considering Seraj, may be intimidated, but they are not inanimate. For the last year or so, therefore, Syrian politics has rather resembled the surrealist croquet game in 'Alice,' with Hourani and Seraj as the exasperated human players, and most of the other civil and military personalities as the troublesome flamingo-mallets and the unwinding hedgehog-balls. Using the flamingo-mallets to drive the hedgehog-balls through the desired Left-Wing wickets has really been a very trying business. . . .

"Hourani and Seraj are now preparing to make another attempt to freeze the flamingoes and hedgehogs into total docility. . . . The great upset in Jordan has provided the spur to fairly early action."

Again, in that spring of 1957 in Lebanon, which was enjoying good government and high prosperity under President Camille Chamoun and Prime Minister Sami-Es-Solh, Nasser's agents were rather successfully seeking to disrupt the oncoming election by a series of bomb outrages. The government enjoyed an undoubted popular majority. Yet the Lebanese leaders were still quite visibly very much afraid, not of Nasser's agents' bombs, but of Nasser's propaganda-and-conspiracy political pressure. After spending an evening with the Lebanese Foreign Minister, Charles Malik, talking about Middle Eastern problems between bomb-explosions in the nearby streets, the reporter addressed himself to the basic Middle Eastern problem. This was the problem of Nasser's powerful hold on the Arab masses, which gave him strong minority support even in Lebanon, and the full support of the street mobs in every other Arab country. The following analysis of Gamal Abdel Nasser's special brand of Arab nationalism is still valid, in our opinion:

"In the Arab lands, the masses are still tragically ignorant and tragically poor. They cannot conceive of the good things that wise government can do for them in time (which is the real reason for the lack of true popular enthusiasm for the wise Iraqi development program). They do not demand these good things. They are politically conscious, but they do not ask their political leaders to talk practical good sense.

"This situation in turn provides the ideal opening for the Arab leaders of whom Nasser is both the master and the archetype—the Arab leaders who win mass support by venomous but powerful emotional appeals to ancient and justified hatreds.

"The word 'justified' must be emphasized. It is precisely because the hatreds are justified that Chamoun and Solh fear Nasser despite their own strength. But the fact that all these hatreds have a solid base in the countless tragedies of Middle Eastern history does not alter the character of Nasser-style Arab nationalism.

"Like all movements that live by the appeal to hatred, this nationalism which attracts so many young people and idealists is none the less an inwardly ugly movement. It is capable of such dark treachery as the bomb plot against King Saud of Saudi Arabia organized by the Egyptian military attaché. In propaganda and in organization, it employs every device in the Fascist book. . . .

"By hatred, this nationalism wins support. But it is also a betrayal of the masses to whom it beckons. For every practical Arab interest now calls for equal friendship with the West. Yet Nasser is moving more and more rapidly towards the kind of overt cold war with all the Western powers, including his recent rescuer, the United States, which will surely condemn the masses he leads to another generation of squalor and suffering.

"One cannot help sympathizing a little with Arab politicians who are tempted to make the easy appeal to hatred, instead of the very difficult appeal to national self-improvement. But in judging this nationalism, which claims the sympathy reserved for nations struggling to be free, it is important to remember its true character as well as the strong mass support that it commands."

Meanwhile, the Jordan crisis, in which King Saud of Saudi Arabia valuably supported King Hussein, and the Lebanese election, which Chamoun and Sami-Es-Solh won handsomely, were the first fruits of the new Dulles policy of the "good Arabs." For a moment, it appeared as though the policy might work. The following column was written after the Jordan crisis had simmered down to an uneasy calm. It records this near-turning point in the Middle East's troubled affairs. It serves as a memorial to poor Hussein's vainly expended courage. And it forecasts the consequences that can be expected to flow from our recent terrible reverses in the Middle East.

AMMAN, JORDAN

In the hollow calm that has been imposed on this little country by the forces under King Hussein's command, it is possible to begin to think a little about the real meaning of the drama that has been played out here.

The trappings of the drama have been story book stuff—the young King, beleaguered and betrayed but riding out the storm with incomparable dash and courage; the plotters, at first so overwhelmingly confident and then so eagerly ready to flee in all directions; the picturesque Arab Legion, torn by intrigues and divided loyalties but rallying to the young King in the very nick of time. No news story in this reporter's sadly long experience has been quite like this.

But behind these splendid trappings, there is the drama's real meaning. It is an immensely important meaning. Indeed, as a turning point in Middle Eastern politics this wild drama in little Jordan may later be remembered as equal in significance to the Suez crisis itself. And in order to place the grimly practical inner meaning of the Jordan drama in its proper context, one must begin with the Suez crisis. The Suez crisis was touched off—Egypt's President Nasser was moved to nationalize the canal—by the calculated humiliation so incomprehensibly administered by Secretary of State John Foster Dulles in the matter of the Aswan Dam. But the Soviet role was vastly more important than the American role. Nasser gained the courage to nationalize the canal from the actuality of Soviet arms and the promise of Soviet support.

Realistically regarded, the final outcome of the Suez crisis was the highwater mark to date of Soviet political success in the strategically vital Middle East. Soviet policy here, it must be understood, is not to promote communism for communism's sake. Soviet Middle Eastern policy is to use Nasser-style Arab nationalism as a dagger to strike at the oil-jugular of the Western Alliance.

The final outcome of the Suez crisis was the transformation of Nasser's shameful military defeat in Sinai into a political victory of extreme brilliance. The political victory seemed to provide the ideal opportunity for the next move along the road charted by both Nasser and the Kremlin, for their very different reasons. And this next move was to be a coup in Jordan.

Jordan's extreme Arab nationalists, who are controlled from Cairo; Jordan's small but well organized Communist party, controlled by the Kremlin but placed under Nasser's command, and the disloyal elements within King Hussein's government, were all to combine together. In combination, they were to hand over Jordan to Egypt.

The coup very nearly came off too. Nasser was within a hair's breadth of gathering up little Jordan as you might gather up a windfall in an autumn orchard.

If the coup in Jordan had come off, the way would have been ideally prepared for an attempt to subvert the Iraqi government of King Hussein's cousin, King Faisal. Thus the first of the oil-producing Arab lands, where you find the real dagger the Soviets want the Arab nationalists to use against the West, would have come under Egyptian domination.

With Iraq lost, in turn, it would have been time for Nasser to think of the oil-rich Gulf Coast sheikhdoms dominated by the British, and, last but not least, Saudi Arabia allied with the United States. And with Egyptian-dominated governments installed in all these vital regions, the time would have been ripe to drive the dagger straight home into the West's exposed jugular.

That was the delightful prospect until the failure of the coup in Jordan changed every calculation. It failed not only because of King Hussein's energy and verve. It also failed because King Saud of Saudi Arabia had noticed the important role being played by the Communists in Jordan, and had begun to be aware that his own fate was already being prepared.

If a stable, independent government can finally be organized in Jordan, the change of calculations will be radical indeed. Instead of pro-Western Iraq being imperilled, the example of events in Jordan will seriously imperil Egypt's satellite government in Syria, with its heavy load of fellow travellers. Then the tide will have turned in deadly earnest. But it will be many months yet before anyone can say that young King Hussein, with all his verve, can possibly organize a stable, independent regime in this tormented, infiltrated little nation. —March 1, 1957 (JA).

The following piece first gave the general public of the Western world what was probably the worst single piece of news of the post-war years, the news of the Soviet success with intercontinental ballistic missiles. The story behind the column is told elsewhere. It is enough to say that the Pentagon authorities, with flagrant untruth, denied the facts herein published; and no one paid much attention to them at the time. It must also be added that the piece was too optimistic. We were actually much further behind in the ICBM race than the column suggests. The reporter succumbed to the temptation, common enough when reporting desperately bad news, to find some blue in the sky somewhere. Despite our reputation as pessimists, we have far more often gone wrong from succumbing to this temptation than from over-painting a dark picture.

WASHINGTON

The American government now has convincing evidence that the Soviets have successfully tested their first experimental version of a very long-range, multi-stage ballistic missile. The Soviet prototype was tested only a few weeks before "Atlas," the first American version of an intercontinental ballistic missile, was blown up off the Florida coast, on June 11th.

This first Soviet test of an ICBM prototype is, of course, an event of grave international significance. It is comparable, as a technical achievement, to the first Soviet test of an atomic bomb, in 1949, and to the first Soviet hydrogen bomb test, in 1953. Eventually, it may be expected to have the same profound effect on the world balance of power as those two Soviet technical triumphs.

The ICBM has been called the ultimate weapon because there is no known defense against it. A fully operational ICBM is designed to fly half way round the world at several hundred miles altitude, in a matter of minutes, armed with a thermonuclear warhead—character-istics which suggest why any defense against it is for the present wholly theoretical.

The Soviet test version was a multi-stage rocket with an "opera-tional configuration." In other words, it was a first test version of a weapon designed for ultimate military use, rather than a mere research vehicle. This does not mean, of course, that the Soviets will have operational ICBMs in strategically decisive quantities in the very near future. There is a long, difficult road to travel between the first test firing of a prototype multi-stage long-range missile and the achievement of an operational weapons system.

An ICBM consists essentially of three parts—the enormous first-stage rocket which powers the initial flight, the second-stage rocket which carries the warhead over the target area, and the warhead itself. The first stage must be tested again and again to eliminate "bugs." Then the accurate "divorce" of the second stage from the first must also be repeatedly tested—it is no easy task to launch one rocket from the back of another, travelling at many times the speed of sound, so accurately that the second rocket remains on course.

Finally a thermonuclear warhead must also be designed capable of withstanding the terribly high temperatures caused by the friction of the re-entry of the rocket into the earth's atmosphere. And, once all these problems have been solved, it is then necessary to build decisive numbers of these enormously complicated and expensive weapons, construct launching sites for them, and train personnel in the complex business of maintaining and operating them.

For such reasons it is probably—one cannot say surely—safe to assume that several years will elapse before the Soviets have achieved an ICBM system capable of a decisive surprise attack on the United States. But the first Soviet test of a prototype ICBM is clear warning that this time will come. Much will depend on whether the United States has the capacity to respond in kind.

ICBM bases are, compared with bases for long-range aircraft, mobile and easily concealed. If both sides have an operational ICBM base system, neither side can knock out the other's delivery system. But if the Soviets are the first to create an operational ICBM system, they could then, in a surprise attack, destroy the Strategic Air Force bases, and thus destroy the American capacity to retaliate decisively. No one can judge whether they might actually do so. But the opportunities for blackmailing the United States into accepting a super-Munich are obvious, and past history suggests that the Soviets would certainly take advantage of these opportunities.

This is enough to suggest why the Soviets, in the midst of the talk of disarmament and "peaceful co-existence," have made an enormous effort to win the ICBM race. The fact that the Soviets tested their prototype shortly before the first American ICBM test (whose testing this year was first predicted in this space) does not mean that they have won the race. Nor is it too significant that it was necessary to explode the first American ICBM prototype in the air shortly after take off. In the missile business, accidents happen, and they can even be usefully instructive.

Yet though we have not yet lost the ICBM race, we have received clear warning that we may lose the race. And the Soviet ICBM test is only the latest item in an accumulating wealth of evidence, which will be described in a forthcoming report, that the Soviets have made giant strides in missile development. These Soviet triumphs have been achieved at a time when the American missile effort is being sharply cut back in the name of economy and in deference to the budget ceiling. Because this is so, the decision has apparently been taken to play down the danger, and to hush up the evidence of the first Soviet prototype test. Yet the test occurred, and it has gravely shaken the highest official circles as well it might.—July 5, 1957 (SA).

In 1957, the stern processes of history were accelerating in a fairly dizzying manner on both sides of the line that divides the world. In June came the famous plenum of the Central Committee of the Soviet Communist party, at which Khrushchev triumphed over the "anti-party group" headed by Malenkov, Molotov and Kaganovich. The triumph was made possible by the powerful support given to Khrushchev by Marshal Georgi Zhukov.

That was not the end of the story, either. When the older member of our partnership went to Warsaw in October, he found the Polish Communist leaders greatly agitated by a renewed struggle for power which had now broken out between Khrushchev and Zhukov. High Polish sources stated that when Wladyslaw Gomulka visited Belgrade a little earlier, Marshal Tito had confidentially given him very grave news about this struggle. Zhukov, according to Tito, had taken substantive control of the Soviet secret police as one part of his reward for the support given Khrushchev in June. The other part of Zhukov's reward, of course, was the virtual expulsion of the Communist party's political agents from the Red Army. The Poles greatly feared the rising power of Zhukov, because of his famous remark at the time of the previous year's Warsaw crisis, when Poland won semi-independence.

After it was all over, Zhukov said to one of the Western ambassadors, with visible regret: "We could have crushed them like flies."

There is no doubt, now, that the above-noted extensions of Zhukov's power in turn stimulated Nikita Khrushchev to strike down his former ally and supporter. This was done while Zhukov was visiting Jugoslavia. As we noted at the time, Zhukov's power was greater than Khrushchev's, but it was illegitimate power in Soviet terms. In other words, it consisted only of Zhukov's control of the army and growing influence in the secret police; it had no sanction from the Communist party; and it lapsed when Zhukov's hands were not on the immediate levers of power. As head of the party and leader of the presidium, in contrast, Khrushchev possessed legitimate power. In the name of legitimacy, Khrushchev used his lesser power to destroy Zhukov's greater power, simply by getting a vote depriving Zhukov of the Defense Ministry while Zhukov was absent from the country, and then confronting the returning Marshal with this brutal *fait accompli*.

As we then pointed out, the most remarkable feature of this ruthless operation was the use made by Khrushchev of Zhukov's rival, Marshal Rodion Malinovsky. In June, as we had also learned in Warsaw, Molotov, Malenkov and other members of the "anti-party group" had looked to this same Marshal Malinovsky to provide them with army support against the Khrushchev-Zhukov partnership. Now, in order to strike down his own savior of the June crisis, Khrushchev turned to the man who had been the ally of his enemies in June. Malinovsky therefore replaced Zhukov as Defense Minister, with consequences which are not yet completely calculable by any means.

The Khrushchev-Zhukov phase of the struggle for survival in the Kremlin of course began after publication of the following column about the defeat of the "anti-party group" in June. We choose it as our comment on the 1957 convulsions in the Kremlin, however, because it describes some of the large, impersonal forces that were, and are, at work in the Soviet Union behind the interplay of venomous personal power contests. If it had been written a little later, it would have included the most radical of all Khrushchev's new departures, the abolition of the so-called machine tractor stations, and the semi-liberation of the collective farms. This was, and is, another gigantic contribution to the Soviet ferment.

LONDON

Now that more is known about the circumstances of Nikita S. Khrushchev's triumph in the Kremlin, at least one fairly firm and highly important conclusion can be drawn from it. The collapse of the famous system of "collective rule" is almost certainly a mere intermediate convulsion in the strange, convulsive process of Soviet evolution.

The reasons for this conclusion have little to do with personalities. It may well be true that Premier Bulganin will later be replaced; it may also be true that Marshal Zhukov will be the chosen replacement.

But such changes of personalities, if they occur, will still be less significant than the changes of a quite different sort that have already been revealed by the recent events in Moscow. These are broad and basic changes in the inner relationships of Soviet society.

One of these great changes may be inferred from facts rather widely discussed. In brief, it now seems clear that Molotov, Malenkov and their allies originally commanded an actual majority, and perhaps a very heavy majority, including Bulganin himself, in the crucial vote against Khrushchev in the Soviet Presidium.

With a majority against him, Khrushchev had only one way to appeal from the hostile Presidium to the friendly Central Committee. Marshal Zhukov, speaking for the armed forces, had to insist upon "Soviet legality." There are credible reports from Moscow that the call to the Central Committee was indeed issued in this manner, under threat of force.

These reports are in turn confirmed by other evidence. For example, the call to the committee must have been both hurried and imperative, since the Soviet Ambassador to France, Vinogradov, actually left Paris toward midnight and drove hell for leather all the way to Berlin in order to catch a plane that would take him to the committee's opening meeting.

Because Marshal Zhukov almost certainly intervened to help Khrushchev, many persons now predict that Zhukov will succeed Bulganin as Premier. If it occurs, this promotion to the Premiership of the one Soviet leader who is a true popular hero, with hands unquestionably clean of the blood of the Stalin years, will be an event of vast meaning.

But it will still be less meaningful than the simple fact of Marshal Zhukov's intervention. Here was the first display of political power by the Soviet military class. As wise a judge as former Ambassador to Moscow Charles Bohlen used to maintain that "the political influence of the Red Army in the Soviet Union was about equal to the political influence of the Salvation Army in the United States." And that used to be the case.

But that is no longer the case, as Bohlen himself was the first to recognize. Furthermore, the officer corps of the Soviet armed services is not only a social group with considerable inner coherence. It is also being transformed into an hereditary caste by the device of the special schools for officers' children, which strongly resemble the special cadet schools that trained the officer caste in Hohenzollern Germany.

In sum, this officer caste now in formation in the Soviet Union has for the first time staked a claim in politics. Thus the question of the political role of the Soviet armed services has been decisively posed. And this is the kind of question that, once posed, remorselessly demands an eventual answer.

One such vast question touching the whole future would be enough for most societies. But still another question about the Soviet future, equally huge in scope and import, was also posed by the great events in Moscow.

In brief, there is very little doubt any longer that the high officials, administrators and technicians in the great Soviet industrial ministries composed the rank and file of the defeated army of Molotov and Malenkov. Khrushchev himself scornfully crowed over them in Prague just the other day, boasting that "they would no longer be able to spin out their red tape or send orders by telegram to the factories in the provinces."

These men obviously joined Molotov and Malenkov because the great industrial ministries which were their strongholds were being dissolved under Khrushchev's industrial reorganization plan. And who were these men? They were in fact the leaders of the huge and critically important new Soviet class of higher industrial managers and technicians.

Furthermore, what is to replace the dissolved industrial ministries? The ministries are to be replaced by "territorial economic councils." And these territorial economic councils, if Khrushchev has his way, will not be dominated by members of the industrial managerial class. They will be dominated instead by Communist party bureaucrats—

non-specialist members of the party priesthood of which Khrushchev is the archbishop.

Thus the industrial reorganization plan, which helped to spark the Kremlin crisis, is not merely a scheme of decentralization. It is also a scheme to restore the power of the Communist party bureaucracy over the day-to-day management of Soviet industry. It therefore downgrades the great new industrial-managerial class. But this downgrading of the most important new class in Soviet society can hardly be a closed incident. It must be the beginning of still another long and probably painful and risky process of readjustment of inner social-political relationships.

With two such gigantic processes of change simultaneously at work in Soviet society, future convulsions can hardly be avoided. But not even Nikita Khrushchev can foretell when or how they will occur. —July 21, 1957 (JA).

That summer, the older member of our partnership made his first and longest visit to Poland. He found it "intensely exciting and even inspiring because the people are brave and newly free, because there is a new ferment of ideas, and because a wholly new thing is being attempted." He added that this new thing—the combination of personal freedom, religious freedom and freedom for the farmers with continuing rule by the Communist party—was at best a gamble for Wladyslaw Gomulka and all others concerned.

As he further wrote from Warsaw, the practical significance of the Polish gamble lay in the fact that the "experiment is being watched with desperate interest and widespread envy for the freedom that exists here" all over the vast "part of the world that is still unfree."

"In all this same vast region," he continued, "the forms of society and the structures of government are now slowly, unpredictably changing and evolving. In the Soviet Union, particularly, the pressure to change and evolve is very great indeed. For the Soviet Union has now experienced a successful industrial revolution, which always changes everything in the end.

"The question, therefore, is not whether changes will come in the unfree part of the world. The question is what kind of changes will come. One can imagine a new Stalinist terror, which will doom the world to war and the new Poland to destruction. One can imagine a gradual, stop-again-start-again progress in the direction Poland has taken. One can imagine all sorts of in-between results."

As of today, alas, the first alternative seems more likely than the second, although even now the final direction of the change is wholly unforeseeable. In any case, the sight, the smell, the sounds of liberty replacing terror induced an intense exaltation. That summer visit to Poland was a period of high emotion and brief hope. The following column showed the marks of this state of mind. The monastery of Jasna Gora, which the column describes, is now the storm center of the quarrel that has again broken out between church and state in Poland.

CZESTOCHOWA, POLAND

Properly speaking, the miracle of Jasna Gora, the great fortified monastery of "The Bright Mountain" took place 301 years ago.

On that occasion, the monks and a few score of Polish men-at-arms held and hurled back 10,000 Swedish troops who besieged the monastery's bastioned walls through a long, bitter winter month. The victory was credited to Jasna Gora's precious Virgin image, long ago chance-brought out of late Byzantium into these wild Polish marches.

I do not think there was any higher intervention; but I, too, witnessed a miracle at Jasna Gora just the other day. It was not easy to define, being the peculiar combination of a theme, a ceremony, a crowd and a man. Yet it seemed to me decidedly miraculous.

Imagine, then, a high hill swelling upward from the suburbs of a dreary little industrial town. A broad way leads through trees to the hill's summit. And here there is the beginning of the miracle.

The summit has been leveled, to make a gigantic plaza three times larger than the great plaza of St. Peter's. Only a single column, bearing Christ with his thorny crown, interrupts this vast, flat expanse. And the whole expanse is filled, as though by a fantastic human inundation, by a single continuous sea of people. There they stand in silent patience, men and women, young people and children, literally hundreds of thousands of them. And all gaze toward the towering church, rising in a surge of baroque pinnacles from the same tall bastions that the monks held against the Swedes.

Suddenly, along the battlements, the long procession of the Eucharist winds its way, banner after banner, choir after choir. A monk stationed by the high temporary altar erected on the church front gives a signal through a loud speaker. The crowd bursts, full-throated, into the hymn recounting Jasna Gora's miracle, "On the Heights of Czestochowa."

For a long hour the people stand, singing hymn after hymn and watching the platform around the altar gradually fill with the churchmen of the procession. Last come the Bishops of Poland, splendid in their vestments and mitres. Alas, a closer view reveals chasubles sadly confected of old lace curtains and capes made of the shoddy silk of Communist Peiping. The Church in Poland today is not rich in this world's goods.

Suddenly there is a hush. Stefan Cardinal Wyszynski quietly takes his place under the scarlet canopy that stands by the altar's sides. The wise eyes in the pale, ascetic face briefly survey the scene. Music breaks the silence and Baranjak, Archbishop of Poznan—that place name heavy with memories—begins the celebration of the mass. The crowd joins the responses as though this were a single parish church holding hundreds instead of hundreds of thousands; and after the consecration of the Host the whole multitude sinks to its knees.

When the mass is ended the Cardinal enters the pulpit, and again there is a moment of silence while he stands, vividly outlined against white draperies, a commanding figure in brilliant scarlet. Then he speaks, telling the story of Poland's dedication to the Virgin Mary by King Jan Kazimierz, and saying that this is a time to renew the dedication with an oath. And slowly, in a strong masculine voice, he repeats the oath.

It is a curious oath, resembling a set of New Year's resolutions on a national scale. One catches echoes of certain exhortations to the people by Poland's Communist government in Warsaw—exhortations against the absenteeism that afflicts industry, the alcoholism that is a curse in this country, the disorderliness and lack of discipline that have appeared here since freedom returned. But whether or not the crowd also catches these echoes, all follow the Cardinal when he asks them to repeat after him: "We swear to thee, Mary, Queen of Poland, we swear to thee!"

Then the slender hand is raised in blessing. At a signal, with a passion that fills the hilltop air, the whole multitude breaks into Poland's battle hymn, "Great God Through Ages Protector of This Polish Land." And so the morning comes to an end; and the sea of people flows away again, to picnic in the sunshine and queue up by thousands to say their prayers before Jasna Gora's Virgin image.

But in the dusk, when the enormous bulk of the fortress monastery shows black against the evening sky, the sea of people flows back into the plaza, more numerous than ever. Here and there candles shielded by workworn hands make points of winking light. Once again the old hymns sound out while the procession winds along the battlements. Once again, when the service begins, all these hundreds of thousands join together in chanting the litany to the Virgin. And this time, the Cardinal himself preaches to his people. The sermon is not unlike the morning oath, pressing the government a little on such contentious points as the difficult situation of Poland's Catholic press, but above all exhorting the people to be good citizens, even exhorting the miners to bring up more coal.

"You must understand," the Cardinal tells the listening thousands, "that what could not be destroyed by erroneous political doctrine can still be ruined by national demoralization. You are a generation of heroes, and to you God has given a serious duty—not to lose what was saved by the blood of your fathers."

So the sermon ends. Once more, with the same strange, resonant passion, the whole multitude sings Poland's battle hymn. And then all is over and it is time to journey homeward through the night.

Such was this modern miracle of Jasna Gora. If you think about it, it says a good deal about this new Poland whose two leaders, linked in unlikely partnership, are the brave veteran Communist, Wladyslaw Gomulka and the brave Prince of the Church, Stefan Cardinal Wyszynski.—September 6, 1957 (JA).

Poznan was where Poland's liberation began, with a brave strike that led to the brave events of October, 1956. Hence the reporter went to Poznan, to see how it had ended. He even used the technique invented by his partner to cover American elections, playing pollster in the Poznan suburb of Czechoslowacka. The people welcomed him there, told him they were "content for now," and at one moment engulfed him in the frenzy of a Polish wedding party for good measure. The following column was inspired by a visit to the Cegielski works, where the Poznan strike started.

POZNAN, POLAND

Here in this grimy industrial town in June a year ago occurred the great turning point for Poland which may also some day prove a great turning point for many other nations.

If one can fix the exact instant, it was at the beginning of the Poznan strikers' attack on the huge gray secret police headquarters. The first burst of fire struck down a fifteen-year-old boy with a Polish flag in his hand. As he fell six tanks appeared to overawe the crowd. But in that breathless instant another boy seized the flag from the gutter, dipped it in his dead comrade's blood, and with no other weapon charged the tanks alone.

For fifty yards and then a hundred he was still alone. Then five, then ten, then suddenly two hundred others joined him, all charging the tanks together behind the boy with his blood-stained flag. Quite suddenly, with a fearful grinding and cranking, the file of tanks turned backwards and fled before the charge.

No one knows the name of the young standard bearer who so marvelously proved the ultimate invincibility of the human spirit, but at the great Cegielski (formerly Stalin) steelworks they will tell you:

"He was one of ours. He must have been. After all the whole thing started right here when the men in the railroad car shop downed tools that morning. We began it."

With all this in mind it is a curious experience to visit these same Cegielski Works. Outwardly they seem the archetype of all the dark satanic mills in the world, being a huge complex of ancient brick factory buildings belching smoke from half a dozen chimneys and filling the whole neighborhood with the din of their machinery. But there is a vast transformation beneath the surface of this grim industrial scene.

The men who receive you, to begin with, are new men. The old plant director, a hard-nosed Communist with no technical qualifications, has gone. The new director, Witold Bernatovich, would have been disqualified for the top job in the old days because of his wartime service in the famous Polish army of Gen. Wladyslaw Anders. But all that is over now. Bernatovich, a fine looking, intelligent, desperately earnest man with the fullest technical training, is firmly in charge at Cegielski.

The chief engineer, Sbigniew Lukomski, is new, too, and the plant has a new workers council with altogether new powers, close to those of a board of directors. Felix Nowacki, the elderly gray-moustached statistician who heads the workers council, looks like just what he is—an old-time Social Democrat with a good head on his shoulders.

The plant's young Communist party organizer, Josef Biskupski, is there to receive the guest along with the others, but his presence imposes no shadow of constraint on the talk about the Cegielski Works' past, present and future.

In the discussion of the past the Communist Biskupski admits that he was "a bit shocked" by the strange, sudden, spontaneous movement—almost as purely instinctive as the hiving of bees—that took the Cegielski workers into Poznan's streets, but Nowacki and Lukomski frankly glory in the memory.

Biskupski hardly differs from the others, either, in his attitude toward the almost total change of atmosphere and habit reverting from the October triumph of Wladyslaw Gomulka. That was the sequel of the June rising in Poznan. The most poignant post-October recollection comes from old Nowacki. With his eyes sparkling with delight he describes how all the workers were allowed to destroy their own secret police dossiers which were kept in the plant's personnel department.

"Now," chimes in Biskupski approvingly, "We have a normal personnel department that considers only whether our workers are good workmen."

At Cegielski the great change has brought other, more material benefits to the vast majority. While Director Bernatovich receives only one-third of the salary and one-tenth of the perquisites allowed his predecessor in the Stalinist times, the average of the workers' wages has been raised by close to 30 per cent. Certainly the standard of life is still cruelly low, however.

"Life is still very hard, but we know our country has many difficult problems to solve," says Nowacki. "So we are content that the misery of the past is over, and above all we are happy to be free men. It means most of all to be free."

Freedom! Freedom! Freedom! This is the great recurring theme of all the talk as one goes through the plant. To be sure, it becomes clearer and clearer that this new freedom has not solved all the problems of the Cegielski Works. Demand for Cegielski's steam locomotives has been almost killed by the increasing electrification of railways. Huge concrete emplacements are already being prepared for the new machinery soon to be installed for production of heavy Diesel marine engines. The conversion will hardly be easy.

But even this practical aspect of the life of the Cegielski Works has been affected by the great change. Before, there was complete absentee management by the Ministry of Heavy Industry in Warsaw.

"Even the smallest machine tool design had to go to Warsaw for approval," rather bitterly remarked Director Bernatovich, who used to head the machine tool department. Now the plan for the plant's operation is produced by the plant's own management, and changes desired by the Ministry are made by agreement rather than by command.

"We have the responsibility," Bernatovich concludes. "It is up to us here in the Cegielski Works whether we succeed or fail, and I think we shall succeed."—September 9, 1957 (JA).

At home, meanwhile, the Washington-based member of the partnership had had much to write about too. There had been the retreat from the poor modicum of national security represented by the first version of the President's budget. There had been the "fading of the Eisenhower aura," largely owing to the President's "newly acquired habit of staging public debates with himself on such issues as the budget and civil rights . . . (which) gives an impression of wishy-washiness (that) has greatly undermined his personal authority." There had been the conspicuous, compensating growth in the public stature of Vice President Richard Nixon. And above all, there had been the civil rights issue.

This was the winter, of course, when the civil rights bill passed the Senate. As an innovating statute, the administration's bill was no great shakes. President Eisenhower did not believe in a strong civil rights policy in the winter of 1957, any more than he had believed in such a policy when he successfully blocked de-segregation of the U. S. Army during his service as Chief of Staff. The fascination of the civil rights debate in the Senate lay, rather, in the exhibition of legislative technique, and above all in the brilliant feat of Senate Majority leader Lyndon Johnson. Under any other leader, even such a bill as the administration offered could have been counted on to tear the Democratic party in the Senate permanently and bloodily apart. Johnson arranged matters, however, so that the Southern ultras took their stand and made their record; yet in the end the bill was made law with no Senatorial blood staining the aisles, and with no prolonged filibuster either.

Meanwhile, an entirely genuine and very radical innovation had been made, not by the executive or legislative branches, but by the Supreme Court. The school de-segregation that the court had ordered was due to begin that autumn; and at first it seemed that a good and peaceful, 'though very limited beginning would be made. Then the ambitious Governor of Arkansas, Orval Faubus, intervened to halt de-segregation at the Little Rock High School. The crisis caught the President on the golf course at Newport, and there, in effect, he stayed, while the situation in Little Rock went from bad to worse. Judging by what we now know, the worst might have been avoided by more energetic and forehanded Presidential action. At any rate, the stage was finally reached when the worst could not be avoided without open toleration of the most open flouting of the law of the land; and so the President ordered the Army into Little Rock, virtually giving the order from the first tee.

The younger member of our partnership immediately flew to the storm center of this tragic trouble. There he reached certain broad conclusions, which we believe are just as valid today as they were then. As these words are written, indeed, further ugly proofs of their validity seem likely to be offered in the near future; and at this instant, the need for a strong assertion of Presidential leadership is perhaps as urgent as it was in August, 1957. It is unfortunate, but it is always the case in America, that every great burden must finally fall upon the President's shoulders. The reasons why this was and is so, in the case of school de-segregation, were summarized as follows:

"In the South, there are no white integrationists with any political power at all. There are, instead, two kinds of segregationist. The first kind, which has been until now generally dominant, says in effect: 'We oppose integration, and we favor using all means within the law to stop integration, or, failing that, to slow it down. But we must remain within the law, and we must abhor violence.'

"The second kind says: 'We must use any means, including violence, to prevent integration of the schools, let come what may.' The Little Rock tragedy has unquestionably strengthened the hands of this second kind of segregationist, and the result may be, as 'The Montgomery Advertiser' has said, to usher in 'a new era of violence.'

"There is only one man who can act effectively to avert tragedy, and he is the President of the United States. What the President must do is clear, although how he is to do it, in the wake of Little Rock, is another matter. He must find ways and means, short of an ignominious surrender on the integration issue, to reassure and strengthen the moderate and reasonable men in the South. For these men may otherwise soon have their backs to the wall—in Little Rock today, for example, it takes actual physical courage to take a public stand for moderation on the race issue.

"But the President cannot do the job that must be done sporadically, or between golf games. He cannot do it by issuing occasional statements through press secretaries, or staging an occasional meeting with Southerners. He can only do it by devoting all his time, all his energy, and all his heart and soul to healing the wrenching, tearing disunity which threatens the country."

The vivid experiences that led to the foregoing conclusions were described in two columns which are still worth reading, and especially worth reading by any American who may be complacent about this cruel problem that divides America. Parts of the second column are omitted.

LITTLE ROCK, ARKANSAS

Monday morning dawned bright and clear and cool at Little Rock. At first glance, the scene at the Central High School was an oddly cheerful scene.

The school itself is a vast, ornate monstrosity in yellow brick, just like a thousand other high schools in a thousand other American towns. It is surrounded on all sides by small white clapboard houses, with porches and neat lawns. This reporter, walking up a shaded street towards the school, was greeted twice with a soft, smiling "Howdy." And the crowd around the school seemed at first rather like a crowd at a country fair.

The people stood about in thick clusters in the bright sunlight, the men in overalls or brightly patterned open shirts, the younger women and the high school girls in ballet slippers or saddle shoes and wide skirts. The police stood facing the crowd, smoking, chatting, and often exchanging jokes with people they knew.

But it was not, really, like a crowd at a country fair at all. This reporter, perhaps deceived by the friendly "howdys," moved confidently into a small knot of people on the edge of the crowd, and asked a question or two. There was a heavy silence. Then a man in a visored straw hat said, "We Southern people don't like to talk to strangers." Another pointed to a newspaper in the reporter's hand, and said, "If you want to stay healthy, you better throw that away. Now, that's just my advice."

A little later, in another knot of people, a high school girl with straw-blond hair and red-rimmed blue eyes was saying over and over, with a kind of bewildered ferocity: "A damn nigger come into my English class and sat down. Just sat right down there." The people murmured angrily, glancing over at the school. "I just started crying when I heard they'd got in there," another high school girl said, "I started crying and I couldn't stop."

The reporters, mostly from the North, made a small alien group of their own, marked off by their clothes and their accents, feeling like strangers in a strange land. "Nigger lovers," a big red-faced man shouted at a group of reporters. "Go ahead," a high school boy said, snickering. "You can say anything you want. They're chicken."

Indeed, the press was clearly at least a secondary object of the crowd's hatred. "Why don't you ever write the truth?" was a constantly recurring refrain. "We raised a bond issue here of eighty million," one man said, "and fifty went to the colored schools and the rest to the whites. But I bet you won't print that."

"We never had no race troubles down here," a heavily rouged woman said, "not 'til the Northern press stirred them up, them and the N.A.A.C.P. and the Communists. It's just communism, you know that." All the people around her nodded their heads in agreement, for she had spoken, or so it seemed to them, the simple truth.

"Those nigger kids are gonna have to come out some time," a man said, with awful relish, "and you just see what happens then." After the Negro children were spirited out of the school, there was an obvious sense of anti-climax and disappointment in the crowd. For it was a crowd with a thirst for violence—there should be no mistake about that. And its thirst for violence was by no means satisfied by the beating up of a couple of Negro adults.

How representative of the feeling in Little Rock and elsewhere in the South were these angry people, a few hundred out of a city of more than a hundred thousand? A Southern reporter on the scene, asked this question, said: "Hell, look at them. They're just poor white trash, mostly."

Away from the school, talking to taxi-drivers or storekeepers or other people, you do not find the fierce hatred and the thirst for violence that marked the angry crowd. But there is no doubt that the vast majority of the white people here are strongly, even passionately opposed to school integration. And in this situation, the minority who thirst for blood are able to exercise an effective veto power. The withdrawal of the Negro children from the school was a capitulation to the veto power of violence.

That is why the sunny scene at Little Rock Central High School on Monday was a tragic scene. For its meaning was plain. If the American government chooses to use its great powers to force through school integration in the South, it will pay the price of years of bitterness and violence. Yet if the American government does not use its powers to that end, it will be bowing to the blackmail power of violence, and permitting the law of the land to be flouted. Then the price may ultimately be even higher. Thus either course may have disastrous consequences. The country, in short, is faced with a problem to which there is no easy, good, or wholly moral solution, and perhaps no solution at all. That is the tragic meaning of Little Rock.—September 25, 1957 (SA).

LITTLE ROCK, ARKANSAS
One native of this unhappy city used an odd phrase to describe the situation here. "It's kind of like you put a dragon in a wooden hogbox," he said. "That dragon is sure as hell gonna escape."

In the last few days here, the dragon has all too visibly escaped from the box. For what has happened here has revealed, with awful clarity, the bitter tensions that underly the placid surface of American life.

Little Rock is, after all, a rather typical American town—throughout the crisis, life has gone on here much as elsewhere, with fall bargain sales and bridge teas and meetings of the Optimists Club. Little Rock is not a real Deep South town—the proportion of Negroes here is not much more than half that in Washington, D.C., and there is nothing here like the solid Negro city-within-the-city you find in Philadelphia or New York or Chicago.

Little Rock's race relations have been uneventful in recent years, and the racial extremists have found no support in the press, which is not true in some other Southern towns. The Negroes vote here in important numbers, and the Little Rock integration plan is more symbolic than real.

For such reasons, knowledgeable people here advertised Little Rock's integration in advance as a model of what peaceful integration ought to be. Instead, the dragon of racial violence has escaped, leading to the greatest constitutional crisis since the Civil War. And the end, almost certainly, is not yet.

To be sure, Orval Faubus, Arkansas' devious and ambitious Governor, let the dragon out of the box. The point not to overlook is that the dragon was there all the time, lurking beneath the calm exterior of this seemingly typical American city.

The unreasoning fears and frustrations and ugly hates which surround the race issue—and not only in the South—have boiled horribly to the surface. You could read them on the contorted faces of the housewives screaming outside the high school on Monday morning, or in the sheepish-secret-sullen faces of the crowds retreating before Federal bayonets on Wednesday.

In the streets around the school house on Wednesday morning, you could hear muttered phrases in the sullen crowds: "They're gonna have to pull out those soldiers some time," or "If they want a fight, by God they'll get a fight."

Even the optimists admit that the ugliest sort of racial violence is still possible here, whether in the city itself beyond the reach of the troops at the school house, or at the school after the troops have been withdrawn. But even if the optimists are right, and the dragon is safely nailed in the hog-box here in Little Rock, what has started here is unlikely to end here.

For it is grimly significant that even his bitterest enemies agree that, as of today, Orval Faubus is a hero in Arkansas. If an election were held tomorrow, he would win hands down against all comers. The Faubus formula for political success might read as follows: Defy the Federal government, and thus create a situation in which mob violence and Federal intervention are inevitable, and bask thereafter in the warm glow of popular approval. The meaning of the Faubus formula is not lost, surely, on other politicians of the Faubus stripe.—September 27, 1957 (SA).

As may be remembered, the older member of our partnership, on leaving Moscow, had predicted that the Soviets would shortly stage a dramatic public exhibition of their increasing military power, especially in the field of missiles. The purpose, he then remarked, would be to impress, terrify and divide the members of the Western alliance. This gloomy forecast was only too completely confirmed by the launching of the Soviet sputniks; and the sputniks had all the foreseen effects upon the Western allies.

The effect at home was far more curious. So far as we can judge, all but a few leaders in the American government had actually come to believe in their own public soothing syrup, instead of believing the intelligence reports that were daily placed before them. The sputnik launchings occurred long after the decision to cut the defense budget by a further five billion dollars had been made by the President. All that summer, merely to hold current spending under the artificial debt ceiling, Secretary of Defense Charles E. Wilson had been stopping or slowing down the output and development of every sort of military hardware, conspicuously including missiles. Besides the short-range stoppages ordered by Wilson to stay within the debt ceiling, appalling long-range slowdowns had been ordered for all the most important programs, once again notably including missile programs. The purpose was to facilitate a 1958 tax cut.

Not all these shocking facts were fully known to us when the first sputnik joined the solar system. Otherwise we should have written even more furiously than we did at the time. As it was, the younger member of our partnership directly and accurately accused the government of past untruth about the relative stages of the missile art in the U. S. and the U.S.S.R. Now, moreover, other voices were added to ours. With inconceivable fatuity, Sherman Adams, speaking for the White House, and Secretary of Defense Charles E. Wilson tried to turn the Soviet achievement into a joke. But they were shouted down by the whole country; and the administration was only rescued from the worst sort of trouble by the Vice President, who spoke out about the sputnik on his own initiative, with a bold sobriety and honesty. In the NSC, the Vice President also led the successful fight to junk the plan for the five billion tax cut and further great defense cuts. Nixon failed, however, in his other fight, for a massive intensification of the defense effort. As we now know, the greater effort that the administration promised after the sputniks was in no real sense a greater effort. It was merely greater than the reduced effort the administration had previously planned.

The following column, written immediately after the sputnik launching, is interesting for two reasons. At this early date, Wilson, Adams, *et al.* were still making light of the sputnik in public. The orders given to SAC show that Wilson, at least, cannot have made light of it in private. The story that was broken herein also remains interesting to this day—indeed one might say painfully interesting— because the one-third of SAC planes on permanent alert are still and will for some years remain our main defense against the growing missile power of the Soviets.

WASHINGTON

A rather desperate expedient is being considered at the highest levels in the wake of the mounting evidence that the Soviets have, or soon will have, operational long-range missiles. It is proposed to keep more than a third, and perhaps as much as a half, of the planes in the Strategic Air Command in the air at all times.

The planes would be loaded with thermonuclear weapons, would be fully fuelled, and the crews would have standby orders for a counter-attack on Soviet targets. The fact that this expedient is being seriously considered is a measure of the real meaning of the missile race.

For the real target of the Soviet missiles is, of course, SAC. The Soviets themselves have virtually said as much, as for example when Nikita Khrushchev, boasting that the Soviets already had an operational intercontinental missile, said that henceforth manned bombers are "obsolete."

President Eisenhower has said that a long range missile is a "means of delivering an explosive charge, and that is all that it is for." This is true, of course, as far as it goes. Yet there is one obvious difference between a ballistic missile and a manned plane. Even a supersonic plane takes several hours from take-off to target in an intercontinental flight. A ballistic missile takes only a few minutes.

The Soviets could unquestionably hit our bases and our great cities today with their powerful strategic air force. But they could not possibly hope to catch SAC on the ground in an attack with their comparatively slow manned aircraft. Thus they could only attack with conventional aircraft in the certain knowledge that they would pay the price of enormous retaliatory devastation. But with operational medium missiles zeroed in on the SAC bases abroad, and an ICBM missile system zeroed in on the few SAC bases in this hemisphere, they could logically hope to knock out our ability to retaliate decisively—if they could catch the bulk of SAC on the ground.

The threat to SAC may not be as distant as is commonly supposed. Already, as has been officially acknowledged, it is assumed by the intelligence experts that the Soviets have operational 1,500-mile missiles with which to threaten the forward SAC bases.

And Khrushchev's boasts about the ICBM are taken more seriously than the blandly complacent official attitude would suggest. There is no doubt at all, for reasons already reported in this space, that the Soviets have missiles of intercontinental range. Most experts hope and believe that it will be at least a couple of years before the Soviets have enough operational, accurately guided ICBMs seriously to threaten the SAC bases in this country.

But others are not so sure. The fact that the Soviets have cut back sharply on production of their long-range Bison bombers has been absolutely confirmed by the intelligence. And logic suggests that they would not do so unless they were already producing operational intercontinental missiles to replace the bombers.

The proposal for keeping as much as half the SAC planes in the air at all times indicates how seriously the threat to SAC is taken. But this expedient is only a makeshift. The only real answer to Soviet missiles is American missiles.

Back in 1955, a distinguished scientific committee, headed by Dr. James Killian, of M.I.T., recommended to President Eisenhower an absolute priority for two kinds of American missiles—the ICBM and the submarine-launched medium missile. The reason for the ICBM recommendation is obvious—with a sufficient number of ICBM bases in this country, the Soviets could not hope to knock out our retaliatory capacity.

But even in 1955, there was plenty of evidence that the Soviets might beat us to the ICBM punch. The submarine-based missile was therefore proposed as interim insurance. Land-based medium-range missiles do not provide such insurance, for the simple reason that the foreign countries in which almost all our forward bases are located would exercise a veto power over the use of such missiles.

No foreign country can veto the launching of a missile from an American submarine. Nuclear subs like the Nautilus and the Sea Wolf have unlimited range, can stay submerged indefinitely, and can carry up to sixteen missiles like the "Polaris," which is designed to be fired under water. Thus, with such missile-carrying submarines in service, the Soviets could not hope to knock out our capacity to retaliate decisively.

The Killian report was approved "in principle." But the Army-Air Force battle over the medium land-based missile shoved the Navy's "Polaris" into the background, and it will not be operational for two years at best. Meanwhile, the whole missile effort has been slowed down by the budget-first policy. And the essentially desperate expedient of keeping a huge proportion of SAC's planes in the air at all times is the best measure of the real danger in which this nation finds itself, a danger which has been consistently concealed from the American people by the American government.—October 11, 1957 (SA).

As one looks back, the final critical turning point in the long, cruel, critical story of Western defeat in the Middle East was the left wing coup d'etat in Syria in August, 1957. It occurred quite suddenly, when the older member of our partnership was waiting to see Chancellor Adenauer in Bonn. He wrote from there what proved to be correct, that the result of the coup d'etat must be a decrease of Gamal Abdel Nasser's influence, and a very considerable increase of direct Communist influence, within the government of Syria.

The Syrian coup d'etat was so important for an extremely simple reason. A mass-leader of the type of Gamal Abdel Nasser is like a surf-board rider. He must keep going forward, and if he loses his wave-crest, he quickly goes under. In justice to the Dulles version of the "good Arabs" policy, it must be said that Nasser very nearly lost his wave-crest and went under after his severe setbacks in the Jordan crisis and the Lebanese elections. He was a very desperate man for a while, and rightly so; for the power of the Nasser-brand of Arab nationalism would surely have continued to wane if it had not been for the Syrian coup d'etat in August. This event gave Nasser's movement a strong new forward impetus. And if Nasser paid for this by a temporary surrender to the Soviets of some of his authority in Syria, it was well worth it to him.

We have since learned, on undoubted authority, that Secretary Dulles and British Foreign Secretary Lloyd actually made an agreement, that summer, to support an invasion of Syria by the Iraqis and Turks. The purpose, of course, was to defeat the pro-Soviet and pro-Nasser forces. When the Secretary of State and the Foreign Secretary revealed this agreement to their respective governments, however, the bitterest opposition was aroused, rightly or wrongly, in many different quarters. In London, Lloyd's own Foreign Office staff were particularly pale with horror. In Washington, the State Department staff were utterly inanimate, as always under Dulles; but the Pentagon viewed the project with considerable alarm. When Lloyd and Dulles made their agreement, moreover, both the Turkish premier, Adnan Menderes, and the Iraqi leader, old Nuri Pasha, had been warmly enthusiastic; but when the time came to make the move, Nuri Pasha suddenly hung back and made difficulties. The Turks were willing and even eager to go it alone. Yet an invasion of Syria by the Turks alone, with no Arab army participating, was thought certain to cause the gravest difficulties for all the Arab governments friendly to the West, including Nuri Pasha's own government as well as King Hussein's and King Saud's. Hence the Dulles-Lloyd project came to nothing.

Having got some inkling of the Dulles-Lloyd project, Nikita Khrushchev began bellowing war threats at Turkey. The older member of our partnership hurried to Ankara in November for this new crisis; and then, when the crisis came to nothing, he went on to Damascus, where he obtained the inside story of the crucial change in Syria. The following column was written, remember, when the power of Syria's non-Communist nationalists was rapidly declining, but before they showed any sign of reacting against the rising power of the Syrian Communists.

DAMASCUS

Until this summer, Egypt's Gamal Abdel Nasser called the tune for the left-wing nationalists who have gained such a grip on the Arab world, and the Kremlin supported Nasser without much power to control him. Today, the Kremlin can pretty well call the tune, and even Nasser must dance with the rest.

That is the real meaning of the left-wing coup d'etat which recently convulsed this always lovely, immemorially ancient oasis city. The change in relationship between the Soviets and self-proclaimed Arab nationalists may seem to be only a matter of degree and shading. But it is in fact a change of fundamental historic importance, and it is worth recounting the obscure events that produced this great change.

The story begins last spring, when Nasser and his movement had reached a grave turning point. The governments of Saudi Arabia, Lebanon, Iraq and Jordan had united at last to oppose his interferences in their affairs. His plot against King Hussein of Jordan had ignominiously failed. His attempted intervention in the Lebanese election had also proved a bust. In sum, the band-wagon seemed to be moving against Nasser; and in Arab politics the apparent direction of the band-wagon tends to be decisive.

In this situation, noises began to be heard in Cairo about a blockade of the Gulf of Aqaba to prevent further Israeli use of the Negev port of Elath. A great play was made of the transfer to Egypt of three Soviet submarines useful for blockade purposes. Kisselev, the

Soviet Ambassador in Cairo, meanwhile hurried off to Moscow for prolonged consultations.

It now seems clear that Nasser actually wanted to attempt a blockade of the Aqaba Gulf. This would have automatically forced King Saud and King Hussein, the Lebanese and the Iraqis to rally again to Nasser's standard. But in order to blockade the gulf, Nasser needed an absolute military guarantee from the Soviet Union to protect him from the Israeli army that has proven it can drive to Cairo, if need be, in a matter of days.

It further seems clear that the risk of giving Nasser such a guarantee seemed too great to the masters of the Kremlin. Thus Kisselev was sent back to Cairo with a negative answer. And this explains one of the major speeches at the famous and critical June plenum of the Central Committee in Moscow, which was a bitter attack by Dimitri Shepilov on the alleged timidity of Nikita Khrushchev's Middle Eastern policy.

Having disposed of another squad of his domestic enemies at the June plenum, Khrushchev still had to consider what he was going to do about the unfavorable change of political trend in the Arab lands. Hitherto, even in Syria, the Soviets had always mainly acted through Nasser and in support of Nasser. But now Syria offered an ideal opportunity to reverse the general Arab trend, while reducing Soviet dependence on Nasser and increasing direct Soviet influence on the Arab nationalists, all in one brilliant operation.

The situation was ripe, because the failure of the plot against King Hussein in Jordan had in turn disturbed the uneasy balance in Syria. Both Syria's moderates and Syria's left-wingers were maneuvering towards a coup d'etat. In these circumstances, on June 29, the Kremlin significantly sent a leading economic expert, Nikolai Vassilienko, to Damascus as Counselor of Embassy.

Shortly after Vassilienko's arrival, the astute Soviet Ambassador to Syria, Sergei Nemtchina, was recalled to Moscow for prolonged talks. A little later still, a large Syrian delegation headed by the agile, ambitious and opportunist Defense Minister, Khaled Al Azm, also took the road to Moscow.

The masters of the Kremlin offered Azm and his party a long-term credit for economic development of Syria—reputedly just under $200,000,000, carrying only 2½ per cent interest and with very easy repayment terms. Azm, who had no doubt been prepared in Damascus, swallowed the bait like a delighted trout.

No delight was felt, however, by the leading moderate member of the delegation to Moscow, the Chief of Staff of the Syrian Army, Gen. Nizam Eddine. He protested that Azm was abandoning Syria's policy of strict neutrality by accepting the Soviet credit. He left the Moscow talks before they were completed, and flew back to Damascus to try to rally the support of other Syrian moderates like President Shukry Kuwatly.

But most Syrian moderates have the approximate liveliness of dead fish on a marble slab. Gen. Nizam Eddine got less than nowhere. In fact, the immediate riposte to his protests was the "discovery of a plot" in the army by the younger group of left-wing officers headed by the famous chief of intelligence, Col. Abdel Hamid Serraj.

Serraj now demanded a purge of the officer corps to remove almost all those who still held the views of Gen. Nizam Eddine. The Chief of Staff refused to sign the discharges but could get no support in his stand. Therefore Nizam Eddine himself was forced to resign. A new pro-Communist Chief of Staff, Gen. Afif al Bizri, was at once appointed; and thus the left-wingers at last acquired almost unchallengeable power here in Syria.

This left-wing triumph in Syria automatically reversed the Arab political trend. But it also resulted from a Soviet initiative, not from an initiative of Gamal Abdel Nasser. It was thus a radical innovation, establishing a wholly new system of relationships which was then accepted by Gamal Abdel Nasser, perhaps unhappily but none the less quite meekly, when he sent Gen. Hakim Amer to Moscow to beg for the kind of economic credit that Syria had been spontaneously offered. The Soviets seem to have underlined the great change in relationships by somewhat humiliatingly giving Amer exactly the same deal already given to the Syrians.—December 1, 1957 (JA).

Just prior to the publication of the foregoing Syrian column, the younger member of our partnership had broken a major news story in Washington—the story of the Gaither report. Much earlier in the year, he had been the first to announce the appointment of still another committee, headed by the former president of the Ford Foundation, H. Rowan Gaither Jr., which was to take still another look at the state of America's defenses. By now, the fearful situation forecast in the similar Killian report was beginning to take solid, present shape. Hence William Foster, a member of the Gaither Committee, remarked of his long weeks of work on the report:

"I felt as though I were spending ten hours a day staring straight into hell." The quotation was published in a later column on the report, which also recorded the remarkable fact that the sheer horror of the facts they had to deal with made two members of the Gaither Committee physically ill. Robert A. Lovett was actually hospitalized for a while, with a sharp recurrence of ulcers. It should be added that although the following column contained the first news of the Gaither report, the able Chalmers Roberts of the "Washington Post" later secured a much more detailed story about it. Roberts' story caused a nation-wide furor. But in the end the Gaither report, like all its predecessors, was largely ignored by the administration.

WASHINGTON

The American government has recently been presented with just about the grimmest warning in its history. The warning took the form of a report to the President and the National Security Council by a committee initially headed by H. Rowan Gaither Jr., formerly president of the Ford Foundation.

When the Gaither committee was appointed, its basic assignment, as this reporter noted last August, was to study the means of defense against atomic attack. But, as time went on, it became obvious that it was useless to consider our defense without also considering the Soviet offense.

The committee, moreover, was made up of brilliant men with wide experience in the whole defense field—men like former Secretary of Defense Robert Lovett, his deputy, William Foster, and former Chief Policy Planner Paul Nitze. Such men could not be expected to confine themselves simply to essentially peripheral matters like civil defense.

Instead, the work of the committee broadened until it encompassed almost the whole East-West balance of power in the new weapons. In the process, the brilliant civilians on the committee closely consulted the country's leading scientists; both James Killian, newly appointed Chief Scientific Aid to the President, and Isidor Rabi, chairman of the President's Scientific Advisory Committee, played a major role in preparing the report. Dr. Jerome B. Weisner, of M.I.T., who had the task of marshaling the views of the scientific community, also made a point of bringing in large numbers of the younger generation of scientists for consultation.

Thus the report represents the consensus of just about the best scientific and non-scientific brains in the country. Their judgment was based, moreover, on all the most recent and most reliable intelligence on comparative Soviet and American air-atomic and missile power. The report considers many subjects, including such matters as the shelter program. But the really important conclusions, which amount to a stern warning, may be summarized as follows:

First, the Soviets are so far ahead of this country in the missile race that it will not be possible fully to overtake them before 1960-61, at the earliest. Second, this interval in which the Soviets will be ahead represents an unprecedented danger, not only to the civilian population as a whole, but to the bases of the Strategic Air Force, which has been the shield of freedom. Third, every possible interim measure must therefore be taken, to defend not only our civilian population but our retaliatory power during this period of maximum danger. To overtake the Soviets by 1960-61, and to take the necessary interim measures, will require additional outlays amounting to many billions of dollars.

At another time, these authoritative but somber conclusions might have been filed and forgotten, as has happened before. But this time, thanks in part to the launching of the Sputniks—which may well be the luckiest thing that has ever happened to this lucky nation—the report may have real impact. Indeed, it has already had an impact, in the two weeks or so since it was filed.

Secretary of Defense Neil McElroy has decided, since then, to go ahead with production of the intermediate missiles, well before testing is complete. He has also decided to start work on at least one I.C.B.M. base even before the first stage of the Atlas I.C.B.M. has been successfully test-fired. The report unquestionably played a part in these bold decisions.

There are other reasons for believing that the report will have a continuing influence. McElroy, for example, has already impressed Washington with a decent respect for the facts, and an instinct for dealing with them. His simple statement—"it seems rather obvious that we are behind the Russians"—came like a fresh breeze in a city stale with the smell of soothing syrup. The report should help to silence the previously powerful dispensers of the soothing syrup.

As McElroy's star has risen, moreover, the star of his deputy, Donald Quarles, the Pentagon's chief exponent of the wait-and-see, test-it-first approach to the missile race, is rapidly declining. It is a

good bet that Quarles will have left the Pentagon before many weeks
have passed. Another rising star is that of Dr. Killian. His role is a
difficult one, since he has no operational authority. But the Gaither
report, which he himself played a major part in preparing, will serve
as a backstop and make weight for his views.

All in all, there is beginning to be solid reason to hope that the
American government will at long last get down to business in the
life-and-death race with the Russians. The Gaither committee report,
with its somber warning, should provide a powerful impetus in that
direction. But the race will not be short or easy.—November 25, 1957
(SA).

So 1957 ended, and our collaboration drew towards its close. The
Gaither report announced the approaching reality of one of the two
developments we had always feared the most—the loss to the Soviets
of the former American lead in nuclear striking power. The other development we had equally feared—the loss of a whole series of positions vital to the strength of the West—had already been forecast by
the Syrian coup d'état.

In the end, of course, the Communists were ousted from the position of direct and growing influence that they had established in
Syria in August, 1957. The two non-Communist Arab nationalist
leaders, Akram Hourani and Colonel Abdel Hamid Serraj, moved
suddenly and secretly to unite Syria with Egypt, in order to strengthen
their own hands. The Kremlin's main Syrian stooges, the slimy Defense Minister, Khalid Azm, and the hot-eyed Chief of Staff, General Afif Al-Bizri, were then dismissed from their posts; and Bizri
was later rumored in jail. The leader of the Syrian Communist party,
Khalid Baqdash, actually fled to Moscow with his family. These
drastic moves produced the United Arab Republic, and restored
Gamel Abdel Nasser to comparative independence of the Kremlin.
Yet these new gains in no way diminished Nasser's hostility to the
West, and his determination, for his own reasons, to destroy every
Western position throughout the Middle East.

Even after the formation of the United Arab Republic, no serious
attempt was made to find a workable modus vivendi with Nasser.
This would have necessitated voluntary liquidation of almost all the
remaining British neo-imperial positions throughout the Arab lands;
and this could not be considered, in turn, without special Anglo-
American arrangements to protect Britain from the consequences of

oil nationalization, on the line proposed by George Kennan in 1949. In the absence of this kind of creative policy-making, the outcome was predictable. From Ankara in November, in fact, the assistant Secretary of State had flatly predicted that Nasser would use the renewed impetus gained from the leftwing success in Syria in order to launch a propaganda-and-conspiracy attack on Lebanon within six months' time. He was only too accurate; but even Henderson did not foresee the chain reaction of Western reverses that is now in progress in the Arab lands.

For all these reasons, a frightening upset of the former world balance of power, military, political and strategic, has now begun. Such an upset, so comparable to the upset of the European power balance that produced the last great war, was always our private nightmare of the future. This was why the loss of the American military lead, and the loss of the vital political-strategic positions were the twin developments we always feared most deeply. We think it is not too late to reverse the trend of events by urgent, massive efforts. But outlining the nature of those efforts would take another book, and we are nearing the end of this one. As the last column in our series we have chosen a somewhat off-beat piece that the senior member of our partnership wrote from Turkey, when the subsiding crisis there gave him time for a little sightseeing.

BOGAZ KOY, TURKEY

Even a new earth satellite, complete with dog, even Nikita Khrushchev, complete with all powers of Josef Stalin, cannot alter or diminish the view from the Lion Gate of Khattusas.

The city was mighty in its day, nearly four millennia ago, in our troubled world's first era of great power wars. But this mighty capital of the Hittite power that sacked Babylon and drove Tuthankhamen's feeble viceroys out of northern Syria was still no more than a vast, battlemented fort. Its rough, gigantic walls, girding the highest pinnacle of this high, tawny mountain, enclosed arsenals well stored with weapons, soldiers' dwellings, palaces of kings and generals, but probably little else.

Through this very gate, perhaps, between the crude, brutal yet majestic sculptured lions, came the triumph of the Hittite king after the famous fight at Kadesh, when the young Rameses and all the Pharaoh's chariotry swerved back in sudden terror from the blood-reddened river.

Fiery horses, stronger than the soft breed of the south, iron weapons, the first man ever used in war, and a rough soldier aristocracy, were the sources of the Hittite power. But even the king's horses must have been sadly winded by the long, cruel pull up the steep, enormous slope of mountain-face.

Standing by the Lion Gate, one thinks of those winded horses, and of that crude, tumultuous triumph, and of Rameses also celebrating his still more pompous but more empty triumph for the usual propaganda purposes. Here, from this pinnacle, history seems to stretch out, forward and backward, a dark, illimitable, ever-changing prospect, all mingled iron and ordure, gold and blood.

The real prospect is breathtaking enough, for no empire in all history so magnificently placed its capital city. Khattusas' Lion Gate stands upon the utmost peak of a wild mountain wall, with flanks copper-stained and iron-stained in vast, alternate patches of brilliant green and crimson. And this fantastic mountain wall curves in upon itself, altogether enclosing a wide, rich plain of little fields and little streams so infinitely far below that the autumn-gilded poplar trees lining the stream banks seem less like trees than golden feathers.

But this real prospect, with all its present beauty, is also a worn parchment on which history has written and rubbed out, written and rubbed out, written and rubbed out, a long succession of different human stories. From these heights the plain below shows as from an airplane, with marks of past as well as present. That dimple in the earth there, over by the remotest stream—was it, for example, a village site lived in and loved by men forty or fifty or sixty centuries ago?

It may well have been, for here in Turkey all of history has just been rather drastically revised by a little digging in just such an earthdimple, at Hacilar in south central Anatolia.

The man who did the digging was a young British archeologist, James Mallert. He found pretty red and yellow pottery; and rough images of the Great Mother Goddess; and grains of wheat and barley and a kind of pulse; and a child's toy in the image of an ox; and bones of sheep and goat, pig and cattle. A few drawers in a museum will hold the lot, but Mallert's sherds still tell a stirring story.

In just such villages as these, neolithic man originated what we perhaps too flatteringly describe as civilization, by the simple act of producing more than could be instantly consumed. Of such villages, up to now, there has been Jericho, oldest of all, in Palestine; and the sites in Egypt and Mesopotamia; and Mersin on the edge of Anatolia; and finally Sesklo in Thessaly, the Greek site where civilization's story begins in Europe.

Now, half way between Europe and Mesopotamia, there is also Hacilar. The sherds of Hacilar are the direct link, or so the greatest experts say, between the sherds of Grecian Sesklo and the sherds of Mersin and of Mesopotamian Hassuna. And by this suddenly provided link, the date of Sesklo is moved back a thousand years, to something like five thousand years before our Lord; and thus the history of European civilization has suddenly been lengthened by a full millennium.

To Hacilar and Mersin, Sesklo and Hassuna the same end came. Neighbors or newcomers wiped them out at last. So also ended the story of that earth-dimple in Khattusas plain, if it ever had a story. So also ended the story of this Khattusas of the Hittites, which was the capital of the first true state ever organized by one of the Indo-European peoples, those various tribes with a common tongue out of the misty past, who were the ancestors of Eisenhower and Khrushchev and Nehru, too.

So here, under Khattusas' walls, one thinks of the long succession: the neolithic peoples; the Sumerians trading into Anatolia for copper; and the Hittites pushing in from the Russian-Asian steppes; and all the strange welter of tribes Xenophon found on his road to the sea; and those Celts who were Saint Paul's Galatians; and Phrygians; and Lydians and Greeks; and Medes and Persians and Armenians; and Romans and Byzantines and Turks. All these and many more, this Anatolia has seen grow great and be humbled in the end.

Remembering all this, one remembers, too, the lines of the Polish poet, Antoni Slonimiski, written when freedom made its new start in Poland: "Only the free and fearless thought of man can justify the long survival of this ignoble jungle which we call our world."—November 13, 1957 (JA).

That winter, the "Saturday Evening Post" offered an important editorial-cum-reportorial job to the younger partner. It was a sad wrench for both of us, to break up a collaboration which had gone on so long and had, as we like to think, achieved some useful purposes beyond earning our bread and butter. But where a large family must also be weighed in the balance, considerations of a practical character must always outweigh considerations of sentiment. So that spring we went our separate ways, the younger to the "Post," the older to carry on the

column by himself. As his last contribution, the younger member of
our partnership wrote a parting letter. We think its closing paragraphs
are the best summing up of what we have tried to do that either of us
can offer:

"Our differences have been on matters of detail and interpretation.
On the big things we have always agreed. You remember how often,
when one of us has been abroad, and our letters have crossed, we have
written the same things to each other, almost in the same words. I
suppose that is one advantage of being brothers as well as being partners. On one point especially we have agreed absolutely.

"When we started our partnership on January 1, 1946, the two
great processes which have dominated all the years that followed were
already visible. One was the creation and growth of the vast new
Soviet-Communist empire. The other was the development of new
weapons which will make it possible for man to write finis to the story
of his (and no doubt all the other higher animals') life on earth.

"We have always agreed absolutely that it was our function as
newspaper men to report seriously, and write seriously, about these
two processes. Because we have done so, we have been called pessimists and doom merchants. But I have been leafing back through those
2,500,000 words (that we have written together) and I really think
that we are more open to the charge of excessive optimism.

"We have generally underestimated the capacity of the Communist
half of the world to expand and consolidate its power, to increase its
military-industrial base, to withstand such shocks as Stalin's death,
and the Hungarian revolt. And we have also underestimated the rate
of scientific progress (if that is the correct word) toward the point
where another great war will destroy all forms of life above the level of
the praying mantis.

"In that sense we have been downright Pollyannas. And we have
been Pollyannas, perhaps, in another sense as well. For we have always felt in our hearts that, if the people of the United States and the
West are firmly led and intelligently informed, both freedom and civilization will somehow survive. And so, as we prepare to carry on
separately with the kind of reporting each of us likes best, hail and
farewell, and the best of luck, from one Pollyanna to another."

That is the way we both still feel as we complete this volume.

Fishers Island, New York
Labor Day, 1958

Index

369